THANK YOU, PARTNER

First published in 2009 by
Liberties Press
Guinness Enterprise Centre | Taylor's Lane | Dublin 8
www.LibertiesPress.com | info@libertiespress.com
Editorial: +353 (1) 402 0805 | sean@libertiespress.com
Sales and marketing: +353 (1) 415 1224 | peter@libertiespress.com
Liberties Press is a member of Clé, the Irish Book Publishers' Association

Trade enquiries to CMD BookSource
Tel: +353 (1) 294 2560
Fax: +353 (1) 294 2564

Distributed in the United States by
Dufour Editions
PO Box 7 | Chester Springs | Pennsylvania | 19425

and in Australia by
James Bennett Pty Limited | InBooks
3 Narabang Way | Belrose NSW 2085

ISBN: 978–1–905483–66–2

2 4 6 8 10 9 7 5 3 1

A CIP record for this title is available from the British Library

Cover design by Sin É Design
Internal design by Liberties Press
Printed by ScandBook | Sweden

Thank You, Partner

The History of Bridge in Ireland

Seamus Dowling

How precious the past is, how soon forgotten.
Iris Murdoch

To Maura,
who cajoled me into attending Florence McGillicuddy's bridge classes.
The rest – including this book – is history.

CONTENTS

APPENDICES

ACKNOWLEDGEMENTS

Whatever the merits of this book, it would be the poorer without the individual and collective inputs of those who contributed to the research. My thanks to everybody concerned. (It would require many pages to list all of them).

The Contract Bridge Association of Ireland and the Irish Bridge Union gave me access to their records. Peadar Murnane (Ballybay) and Gerry Murtagh (Dublin) put the results of their own research at my disposal. Eibhlín Counihan searched the Kerry newspapers. John Cunningham, John Fitzgerald, Alan Hill, Barry Hogsett, Katherine Lennon, Sheila Murphy, Ray Norton, Olive Rose and Una Walsh provided valuable documents.

The following supplied relevant publications, correspondence, photographs or information: Pat Barry, Michael Brennan, Tim Bourke (Australia), Fr Enda Burke, PP, Anne Byrne (librarian, Rotunda Hospital), Bishop Derek Byrne (Brazil), Tony Casey (Churchtown), Dermot Cotter, Desmond Deery (Marbella, Spain), Jack Downing, Deirdre Fitzpatrick, Fr Enda Glynn, John Godden, Martin Hayes, Oonagh Hayes, Aidan Hodgers, Per Jannersten (Sweden), Patrick Jourdain (Wales), Frank Kelly, Gordon Lessells, Ian Lindsay, Aoife MacHale, Walter F. Maclachlan, Bridie Mannion, Michael O'Connor, Josephine Purcell, Paul Scannell, Peter Stocken (England) and the late Alan Truscott (USA).

Ruth Giddings' knowledge of people was invaluable. Time spent with her, Michael Lynch, P. C. Kiely and Augusta Shouldice (deceased) was rewarding.

George Ryan read the manuscript, as it was being written, with an expert and ruthless eye, and helped to mould it into a readable product. My sister-in-law, Teresa Dowling and John O'Reilly read the completed manuscript and offered criticism which improved the finished work.

I and the bridge world in general are indebted to Peter O'Connell and Seán O'Keeffe of Liberties Press, who saw some merit in the work, and thought it worth publishing.

FOREWORD

Seamus Dowling's *Thank You, Partner* is essential reading for anyone in Ireland who loves the game of bridge and its intricacies. It is filled not only with stories of the famous players but of the personalities who helped make the game popular in every town in the country. It is an erudite and immensely readable history of how the game grew and spread. It is also a secret history of Ireland in the twentieth century. It tells us more about such things as class systems, women's lives, how Irish society developed and changed, and how people of a certain class actually lived, than any number of books about politics or economics. It is thus a history of leisure, continuity and social ease.

But it paints as well a fascinating picture of Ireland's emergence as an independent state; Dowling's chapters on the developments between north and south in the bridge community in Ireland will have to be taken into account in any future history of cross-border relations. His book sets an example to historians of modern Ireland in its use of detail, its painstaking research, its judicious analysis, but also, perhaps more important, in its way of using sources which have not been looked at before to give a sense of a consolidating social harmony which underlay changes and challenges in twentieth-century Ireland. Its value as social history is considerable, but for those who love the game of bridge there is a sense of deep knowledge and enthusiasm for the cards themselves and how they were played, which gives the book added value and importance. It makes you feel as you read that instead of bridge, with its rules and sense of partnership and decorum, being a metaphor for life, it is perhaps the other way around.

As a novelist, I have used bridge over and over in the way I plan a book, in the way, before I even start writing, I know, or try to know, what

9

will be in each chapter. When I played bridge, I both loved and dreaded that short silent time after the first card was put down and your partner's hand was spread on the table and you were allowed a period to plan, to work out options and (if you knew them) to think about percentages and chances. A time when you could weigh all the knowledge at your disposal from the bidding of the opposition, and then it was your job to put your plan into action and watch the cards fall. Your job was exactly the same as the job of a literary critic as defined by T. S. Eliot – to be as intelligent as possible.

Bridge is probably one of the best ways of training to be as intelligent as possible, but also to be cunning and imaginative, to use your memory, to know when to be daring and when to be cautious. Those who play the game know the difference it has made to lives all over Ireland, how on week-nights in the midwinter in rainy Irish towns it has offered women, for example, or retired people, a way of exercising intelligence and power and flair in the public realm. Or how in bridge clubs all over Ireland it is the cards and how they are played that has mattered, rather than social standing or degrees of wealth.

Bridge is a strange addiction, hard to explain to those who have not come under its spell. *Thank You, Partner* makes you want to pick up a hand of cards again.

COLM TÓIBÍN

1

From the East

In Oscar Wilde's *Lady Windermere's Fan*, Lord Darlington remarks to the Duchess of Berwick: 'it is a curious thing about the game of marriage, the wives hold all the honours and invariably lose the odd trick'.[1] The source of the metaphor[2] is obvious but it is interesting that Wilde's play was first produced in London in 1892,[3] two years before Lord Brougham introduced bridge to the Portland Club. London's most famous card club may have adopted the game and given it a code of laws and ethics, but bridge was already being fostered by English society.

Bridge was popular in the United Kingdom during the last decade of the nineteenth century. Like the gifts of the Magi, it came from the East. A Colonel Studdy played it during the Russo-Turkish war of 1877–78.[4] Archibald Dunn, who wrote a book on the game in 1899, played 'something that resembled the modern game', in Smyrna, Turkey, around 1880.[5] Brougham had played with army officers in India.[6] Military men returning from the East brought the game back with them. By the 1890s, it had become an activity in which the lords and duchesses of the kingdom, and those who aspired to their company, if not their status, indulged.

The game attracted devotees in the professions – legal, medical and banking especially – as well as among newly well-off business people. The poet John Betjeman recalled games at home in north London when he was about four or five – around 1910 or 1911:

> Happy and tense they played at Auction Bridge:
> Two tables in the drawing room for friends . . .
> . . . ladies vaguely designated 'aunts'
> Who came on second Thursdays to At Homes.[7]

John Betjeman's father, Ernest, was a cabinet maker – 'in trade', to use a disparaging description of the time.

11

As a child, Samuel Beckett watched while his father played bridge at home, in Foxrock, Dublin, with friends. Bill Beckett, a quantity surveyor, also played bridge at the Foxrock and Cabinteely Golf Clubs. The future Nobel Prize-winner was described as 'a keen and effective player' while at Portora Royal School in Enniskillen.[8] Bridge was part of such families' efforts to move up in the world in the class-conscious United Kingdom.

A report in the *Irish Golfer* on 20 June 1904 indicates how the game was spreading in Ireland:

> Very soon it may be necessary for golf clubs in Ireland to legislate for bridge players, not only for the gentlemen but also for ladies. Bridge is fast becoming the regular thing of club houses, and even the ladies take a hand for a rubber or two, towards evening.[9]

Ladies, of course, were not admitted to the gentlemen's club or the officers' mess, but they had infiltrated the golf club. Wives, sisters and fiancées were taking to bridge. A widely held view at the turn of the twentieth century was that women did not belong at the card table. The report continues:

> We do not consider that ladies ought to play cards publicly.

Golf clubs became nurseries for the new game. Until the arrival of clubs dedicated exclusively to bridge in the 1920s, golf clubs were among the few places outside the home where men and women could meet and play bridge together.

Although records from the time in general project an image of bridge as the pastime of professional and business people in urban centres, the game was in fact played more widely. Eimer Burke from Nenagh (discussed in more detail later) recalled that her mother, Anna Theresa Murphy, part of a farming family, played bridge at home in Laharden, near Tulla, County Clare. Eimer was born in 1912[10] – a fact which places her mother's family bridge games some time earlier.

The widening appeal of bridge may be gauged by the fact that between 21 October 1906 and 9 March 1907, the *Irish Times*, on Saturdays, published a series of articles entitled 'The Royal Road to Bridge', each feature filling between a quarter and a third of a page.[11] Comparisons were made with other authors, Captain Beasley (later Colonel Beasley, of whom you will read more) and William Dalton.[12] Reference was made to 'Robertson's Rule', a point-count method for assessing a hand suitable for no-trump.[13] Using 'Robertson', an ace was worth 7 points, a king 5, a queen 3, a jack 2 and a ten 1. A hand with 24 points, and three suits guarded, was suitable for no-trump, although the writer suggests that a 'good dealer' required only 21.

The game experienced a surge of popularity around that time. In 1906, the first Irish bridge publications appeared. A twenty-page booklet, *Essentials of Sound Bridge*, whose author used only his initials, 'O'F., E.', and *The Grand Slam – A Modern Bridge Guyed*, a fifty-six-page work whose author used the pseudonym 'Revoke', were published in Dublin. In Belfast, *Abecedary of Nublo, The Improved Bridge*, a thirty-four-page pamphlet by J. McTear, went on sale. McTear also produced a two-page pamphlet, *The Improved Bridge, Synopsis of the Game*, around the same time.

Bridge was not universally well received. An outraged reader of the *Irish Times* wrote to the editor in January 1909, protesting 'against the growing evil of bridge playing in Dublin'. Signing himself 'Pro Bono Publico',[14] he suggested that 'just as it is in London, it has become a veritable craze here also'. Echoing the sentiments expressed in the *Irish Golfer* five years earlier, he considered it 'a demoralising sight to see young ladies . . . being taught the game'. He laments that some people 'come away heavily in debt, with the result that their tradesman often has to wait a considerable time before he can get a penny'. The gentleman concludes: 'society is on the downgrade'. The letter, redolent of class division, makes it clear that tradesmen did not play bridge with gentlemen.

Despite reservations about them taking part, ladies continued to play the game in increasing numbers. A new item of ladies' fashion appeared in the winter catalogues in 1907: the bridge coat.[15]

NOT THE SAME BRIDGE AS TODAY

The game played then was not the one we know today. There was no auction. Dealer declared the trump suit, or no-trump, and made as many tricks as he or she could. Alternatively, dealer could leave it to partner (dummy) to decide the denomination. The scoring was: spades 2 points per trick; clubs 4, diamonds 6, hearts 8, no-trump 12. Doubles, redoubles and double again were permitted up to a maximum of 100 points per trick. If you made sufficient tricks to yield 30 points, that was game. Furthermore, there were additional points, a multiple of the trick value, for holding honour cards. The rubber was, as it remained with later developments, the best of three games.[16]

Duplicate bridge was not unknown. The penultimate piece in the 'Royal Road to Bridge' series explained how duplicate was organised. The method of arranging tricks was an innovation. In rubber, the player winning the trick gathered in the four cards; in duplicate, the card was placed vertically or horizontally in front of the player, denoting a winning or losing trick. Players were asked to reshuffle their cards at the end of the deal. It was suggested that a 'master of ceremonies' – what we now call a tournament director – was necessary to make the arrangements, collect scores, and so on. The writer concluded: 'when the game becomes better known . . . I expect to see it quickly establish itself in popular favour'.

Howell and Mitchell movements had been inherited from whist, and some English publications referred to trays on which the cards were placed before being moved to the next table,[17] but I have found no records of duplicate being played in Ireland during the first three decades of the twentieth century. Rubber bridge would continue to be virtually the sole form of the game in this country until the 1930s.

The same *Irish Times* article described another form of the game which experienced some popularity but did not survive the test of time. That was progressive bridge, described in the *Irish Times* as 'less serious . . . more social'. It was ideal for mixed pairs, and two or four boards were played at a table. The winning pair (based on total points scored) left the table, the lady going up one, the gentleman down one. At the end, when the players' points were added up, there was a lady winner and a gentleman winner. 'Progressive' competitions remained popular for a while, and the Contract Bridge Association of Ireland ran some 'progressive' tournaments during the early 1930s.[18]

AUCTION BRIDGE

That necessity is the mother of invention was nowhere better exemplified than in a distant station of the British Empire in India in 1902, when three devotees of bridge, unable to find a fourth, came up with the idea of bidding for the right to play the dummy hand. Thus the auction – and a new form of the game, auction bridge – was devised. In the 'Royal Road to Bridge' column on 2 March 1907, auction bridge was introduced to readers as 'a fascinating form of the game which is likely to become popular', but there is no evidence that Irish players immediately took to it. Indeed, the writer betrayed some scepticism on the subject when he stated: it 'seems to be a sporting sort of game, even if it is not to be compared with the parent game'. A review of *Auction Bridge*, by Vane Pennell,[19] which appeared in the *Irish Times* in May 1908, suggests that it had some following by then. By 1909, auction bridge had become so widespread in Great Britain that the Bath and Portland Clubs drew up a set of laws relating to it.[20]

In auction, the scoring scale consigned spades to a virtually worthless state, merely providing dealer with a cheap call. With competitive bidding, that issue no longer arose, so a new call, that of 'royal spades' (as distinct from 'ordinary spades') was introduced. 'Royal spades' – or 'lilies', in the table parlance of the time – ranked between hearts and no-trump. Indeed, the term 'royal' came to be applied to the game itself. From 1912, books on royal auction bridge and royal spades auction bridge appeared,[21] one of them a tome of 346 pages written by Robert F. Foster. In 1914, a new scale of trick values, more appropriate to the competitive nature of the auction, was adopted. 'Ordinary spades' disappeared. No-trump, spades, hearts, diamonds and clubs were scored at 10, 9, 8, 7 and 6 points per trick, respectively.[22] Game was still 30 points.

In the course of time, auction bridge took over from the old game. British army officers helped to spread the new version in Ireland. Alfie Hanratty is a case in point. While serving as a doctor in the British army, he learned to play. On returning to his home in Collon, County Louth, after the First World War, he introduced it to his family and their friends.[23] Before that, the game had taken root in garrison towns the length and breadth of Ireland.

Bridge was not confined to mature or elderly citizens. John Joe Ryder, from a County Sligo bridge-playing family, supplemented his income by playing auction while he was a student at University College Galway around 1920.[24] The family produced competent players who went on to compete successfully in 'duplicate'.[25] Around the same time, Eamonn O'Sullivan, the future GAA personality from Killarney, played auction while he was studying medicine at University College Dublin.[26]

2

THE IRISH TIMES BRIDGE COLUMN

The growing popularity of auction bridge is evident in the fact that on Saturday 9 June 1923, the *Irish Times* introduced a fortnightly column, the unknown writer using the pen-name 'Palomar'. A prize of two guineas – a substantial amount, exceeding the weekly wage of many workers – was offered for solving a problem. The fact that the winners' addresses, published in the paper, were spread across the country demonstrate the extent to which the game was enjoyed.

Retired British army personnel, from captains to brigadiers general, won frequently. The solver of problem No. 9, on 6 October 1923, was Mrs Holmes Wilson of Sandymount, Dublin – the wife of a lieutenant colonel. Her name would appear several times in the column. H. G. Freehill from Clontarf was a winner too. Holmes Wilson and Freehill were destined to play crucial roles in the organisation and development of bridge during the 1930s.

The column in the *Irish Times* would indicate that the game had a widespread following among the Protestant community. It is significant that it first appeared a fortnight after the ending of the civil war. Few who played bridge would have been actively involved in the armed struggles of the previous four years,[1] but everyone's lives had been disrupted. Now that these conflicts had ended, bridge enthusiasts could enjoy weekends of uninterrupted leisure, which included solving the puzzle in the *Irish Times*.

In the 1920s, 'North–South' and 'East–West' were not yet used to designate the four players at the table. Instead, it was 'YZ' v. 'AB', as used in whist. Many of the playing techniques we use today would have been familiar then, including fourth-highest leads, and the high-low signal to show an even number of cards. The bidding element of problems looks strange to the modern player, since it was not necessary to bid 'game' to make game. You simply had to make the required number of tricks to score 30 points.

The column continued until 20 July 1929, when problem No. 150 was followed by an editorial notice:

> We much regret that in a recent issue Palomar's article on Auction Bridge infringed a copyright which is vested in the form of Messrs Allen and Unwin of London. The problem posed was originally by Mr Sidney Lenz, the well-known American authority on the game.

Palomar had pinched his puzzles from previously published sources. The column abruptly ended.

Evidence shows that the number of auction-bridge players was continually increasing. Reviews of bridge books and advertisements for bridge sets and bridge stationery appeared regularly in newspapers.[2] The dance and bridge tournament became a popular social phenomenon, usually as a charity fundraiser. As young people glided across the floor of the Aberdeen Hall in the Gresham Hotel, Dublin, the older generation played bridge on the balcony. Reports of those occasions often included lists of attendance, frequently headed, in the late 1920s, by titled ladies and, in the 1930s, by government ministers and their wives.

Auction bridge was in vogue. It was mentioned in gossip columns. Novels and memoirs contained references to the game.[3] Hotels saw it as an activity to attract patrons.[4] Experts offered tuition. Newspapers and magazines carried titillating stories about the game. The Bennett case in Kansas City, Missouri, was reported in both the *Irish Times* and the *Irish Independent* on 2 October 1929. The story is well known. It will be sufficient to remind readers that Myrtle Bennett shot dead her husband, John, after he went down in a four-spades contract, having first called him 'a bum player'. She was not convicted of homicide – a salutory lesson, perhaps, to husbands who would partner their wives at the bridge table.

An English vicar[5] condemned 'the evils of bridge drives. They engender envy and jealously, friendships are broken, families divided'. A bishop drew attention to a widening scandal, namely 'well-to-do women who play bridge from two o'clock in the afternoon until the early hours of the morning'[6] – much like current complaints about young people spending all their time playing computer games.

Articles were published about the conflict between the American laws of the game and those of London's Portland Club.[7] Those who had a radio receiver, or 'wireless', heard a bridge broadcast from the BBC in June 1927. The four hands were announced to the listeners, who heard the Countess of Ossery, Viscount and Viscountesse Masserene and Ferrard, and Viscount Castlerosse bid and play, followed by analysis by 'a leading expert'. The broadcast itself was the subject of newspaper reports.[8] A visitor to Bray in 1928 wrote a letter to the editor of the *Irish Times* complaining that there was 'no opportunity for a rubber of bridge' in the town.

During the late 1920s, ladies' bridge coats reappeared in the catalogues. Leading fashion stores advertised them from late autumn. These coats continued in use for many years. Dorothy Peart, whose husband, Noel, was one of the leading players of the 1940s, remembered the bridge coats: 'They were necessary,' she said, 'there was no central heating. The hostess usually took the warmest place, with her back to the fire; those furthest away would be frozen. The bridge coats were simply to keep us warm.'[9]

A NATIONWIDE TOURNAMENT

A nationwide bridge tournament was organised by the Soldiers, Sailors and Airmen's Family Association between November 1927 and January 1928. Promoted as 'the Hostess Bridge Tournament', it was played in Athlone, Athy, Bagenalstown, Baltinglass, Carlow, Castlecomer, Enniskerry, Galway, Greystones, Kildare, Monasterevin, Kilkenny, Malahide, Mullingar, Naas and Rathfarnham (which was then a village outside Dublin), as well as five centres in Dublin city. Participants paid 2/6 each.[10] Later it was reported that £200 was raised – a sum, if we allow for expenses, representing more than 1,600 participants. Titled ladies were among the organisers. (Bridge, while growing in popularity, was still associated with supporters of the regime which had ended in 1922.) The same body continued to organise an annual tournament into the late 1930s, but never again on the scale of the first one.

THE FIRST BRIDGE CLUBS

Though mainly a drawing-room pastime, the game was played in establishments such as the Kildare Street Club and the St Stephen's Green Club and, as we have observed, in golf clubs. Given the number of players, it was inevitable that clubs catering exclusively for bridge would come about. The Regent in Dublin, founded by F. T. (Fred) Quin in 1925,[1] is Ireland's oldest.

THE REGENT

Quin responded to a newspaper advertisement inviting people interested in playing bridge to come to a meeting, following which he took the initiative and hired a room in the County Hotel in Harcourt Street. A few doors away at the Abbotsford, another keen player, John Morgan, resided.[2] Two bridge-playing dentists, Lionel Wigoder and Joe Rubenstein, had their surgeries on the same street.

Among the Regent's founding members, as well as Quin, Morgan and Wigoder, were Mrs Frances Lee, who later married Morgan; Charlie O'Neill; William Butler, a future treasurer of the CBAI, and his wife, Eileen; Hugh Hackett; Hubert Prost, of Maison Prost hair salons, and probably his wife, Jackie, who became a fine player; Kathleen Bowles; Mrs Colgan; the Ebrill brothers, Brian and Willy; Bernard Williams; and Harold Williams. (The last two were not related.) Stewart and Clare Fitzgerald, Alf Kibble, the well-known professional singer Gerard Crofts and his wife, Mairéad, were probably at the inaugural meeting and were certainly early members of the club.

The Regent's first address, an annexe to 42 Harcourt Street, was also that of Lionel Wigoder's surgery. After a brief period there, the club moved to No. 13, where Quin resided. It went up the street to No. 84 in 1937 and remained there until it relocated to 25 Waterloo Road, its present address, in 1953.

The unifying power of bridge is nowhere better manifested than in the membership of the Regent during the 1920s. Protestant, Catholic, Dissenter and Jew, republican and unionist, met in cordial competition at 42 Harcourt Street. John Morgan, a British army war veteran and a recipient of the Military Medal, sat down with 1916 revolutionary Gerard Crofts, with cards as their only weapons. Indeed, Croft's wife, Mairéad, and Morgan went on to work closely together for the advancement of bridge for many years.

WATERFORD

Waterford Bridge Club was founded on 27 February 1927. That the date is known is due to a fortuitous circumstance. While watching the St Patrick's Day parade in the city in 1985, Billy Kervick showed Michael Brennan an old diary in which the inaugural meeting of the bridge club was marked. Brennan, a man with an interest in history, took note – luckily, because the diary went missing following Kervick's death.[3] The club played initially at the Adelphia Hotel and was still active when the Contract Bridge Association was established five years later.

KILKENNY

Kilkenny Bridge Club had its origins in Butler House – the Dower House of Kilkenny Castle – the home of Mrs Henrietta Duggan, who organised a game there in 1929. She was president of Kilkenny Bridge Club until it moved to the Club House Hotel. When the game became organised nationally in the 1930s, the city assumed its role as the natural hub around which activities in the south-east revolved. Elaine, Lady Bellew, was a leading figure in the bridge scene in Kilkenny. The competition for the cup which she donated became the major bridge event for the area.

During the late 1920s, a revolution which would change the game of bridge was gaining momentum on the other side of the Atlantic.

4

Contract Bridge

Great events can have humble beginnings, and while it may not be accurate to describe a cruise from California to the Caribbean as a humble exercise, contract bridge was nevertheless conceived in an unpretentious manner on such a cruise between November 1925 and January 1926.[1] There was a fortuitous aspect to the creation of the game. When the ship reached Balboa, at the entrance to the Panama Canal, the passengers were told that they could not go ashore, for quarantine reasons. At least one of the passengers had a good idea as to how to fill the time.[2]

Harold Sterling Vanderbilt, a former wartime naval commander, was to win yachting's blue riband, the Americas Cup, three times in the 1930s. One of the new breed of American aristocrats whose status was founded on business success, the railroad king was brother-in-law to the Duke of Marlborough, a man of substance and influence who, on the fateful evening while the *SS Finlandia* was docked at Balboa, introduced a new card game to his friends.[3] It was not bridge but a game closely resembling it called 'Plafond',[4] which he had played in Paris.[5] By the time the ship had returned to California, contract bridge had been born and a set of rules for the game had been drawn up. From Plafond, he took the idea that only tricks contracted for are scored towards game.[6] He devised the scoring table which, with some modifications, is used to this day.

Although there is wide acceptance that contract bridge dates from Vanderbilt's cruise, nevertheless Plafond, from which Vanderbilt got his idea, was in fact a game of contract. In the French game, you contracted to make a certain number of tricks; if you did not bid game, you could not make game. That was the essential advance from auction bridge.

Alan Truscott, long-time bridge editor of the *New York Times*, suggested in a March 1987 article that contract originated in Poona, India, in

1912, where four Englishmen – Steven, Allison, Church and Clayton[7] – developed an improvement on auction and called it 'SACC', from the initials of their names. In SACC, overtricks did not count and there was a bonus for successfully playing at the five-level. There was a 500-point bonus for a small slam, 1,000 for a grand. Truscott suggests that the rules of SACC, published by Hugh Clayton – a civil servant and later Commissioner of Bombay – in 1914 in the *Times of India*,[8] could have given the French the idea for Plafond, which was introduced to Paris shortly after Armistice Day, 11 November 1918.[9] It seems that the contract concept was becoming well known, because in 1918 Colonel G. G. J. Walshe (who from 1925 would write a bridge column for the London *Sunday Times* under the pen-name 'Yarborough'), described SACC. He was not enthusiastic about the idea of contract, and thought that the majority of auction players had no desire to see the element of luck reduced in favour of skill. It is notable that this view was espoused by a leading figure in the game. SACC retained the old auction form of scoring, with hearts the highest-ranking suit and spades the lowest.

However accurate or inaccurate it may be to credit Vanderbilt with having created contract bridge, he certainly introduced his hybrid to the New York clubs in 1926. Contract bridge's popularity spread from there, until it eventually displaced auction bridge.

ELY CULBERTSON AND THE BATTLE OF THE CENTURY

It was not Vanderbilt who most actively promoted the new game but a hitherto unknown adventurer, Ely Culbertson, born in Romania to a Russian mother and a Scottish father.[1] Vanderbilt's book, *Contract Bridge Bidding and the Club Convention*, the first textbook on the new game, was published in 1929.[2] Before that, Culbertson had begun the process which, by the mid-1930s, would result in his name becoming synonymous with contract bridge.

Culbertson was the right person in the right place at the right time, a man with flair and a hard neck, living in America just before the Great Crash. Americans were rich; they would buy anything. Culbertson decided that he would sell them the game of contract bridge. When he and his wife, Josephine Dillon Murphy,[3] discovered contract in 1927, he was frequenting the New York clubs, supplementing the family income with his winnings. She was one of New York's leading auction-bridge teachers.[4] Culbertson had published a book on auction in 1924, but he recognised the potential of Vanderbilt's creation, applied his own theories to it and set about spreading them. He wrote articles for magazines, gave lectures and spoke on the new radio stations.[5] In October 1929, Culbertson launched a magazine, *Bridge World*, into a competition-free market: *Auction Bridge* magazine had gone bankrupt in September. The new magazine was an instant success.[6] He recruited teachers – 3,000, it was said – who, with the authority of Culbertson's diploma,[7] spread the good news about what would soon become his kingdom.

Culbertson understood mass psychology. The bridge table was the great leveller: servant and master were equals; women achieved equality with men – indeed, could become men's superiors. Bridge was also a social necessity. If you played well, you were invited to places and met the right people. If you did not, you were a social pariah. His system could equip you to claim your place in society. The sweetheart-and-lover image which Ely and Jo projected was deliberate and successful. He promised publication of his *Blue Book*, which would reveal his secrets. Month by month, his magazine whipped up anticipation for this book.[8]

Culbertson needed a touch of luck, and he got it. In Britain, Colonel Walter Buller declared American methods unethical in principle and worthless in practice. He boasted that any reasonably good British four would easily beat the Americans. Culbertson took the Colonel's bombast as a challenge. He would play the Colonel over 300 duplicate deals. His team would use his approach-forcing system.[9]

That autumn was a quiet time for English sport, so the event was welcomed by the press and, borrowing the term from cricket, was referred to as a test match. Buller helped to raise patriotic fervour through the pages of *British Bridge*. He lampooned Culbertson's system, calling it 'the cumbersome system' and describing it as consisting of 'artificial stunts'. He continued: 'the sooner we cut out this nonsense, the better'. He was convinced 'that the British people are the greatest natural players [of bridge] in the world'. In a pre-match press conference, Culbertson gave reporters what he figured they wanted. 'What do you think of British bridge?' he was asked. 'Look, fella, let's keep the party clean,' he replied. He went on to tell the assembled journalists that the British had no chance because they did not use his methods.

The match began at Almack's Club in London on 15 September 1930. Culbertson's *Blue Book* was published in America on the same day. With Ely and Josephine were Baron Wulsemar Von Zedtwitz, a German who had taken American citizenship, and Teddy Lightner, who gave his name to a type of double. Their opponents were Buller, Mrs Alice Gordon Evers, Dr Nelson Wood-Hill and the Irish-born Cedric Kehoe. The Americans won by 4,845 points. Later they defeated a team from Crockfords Club led by another colonel, Henry Mountifort Beasley. Before he left England, Culbertson received a telegram from New York. The *Blue Book* had sold out of its initial run. The message ended: 'You are rich.'[10]

The effects of Culbertson's visit to London were great, immediate and lasting. From it, we can date the birth of system bidding and the adoption of duplicate contract bridge in Great Britain and Ireland. The *Blue Book* was published in London before the end of the year.[11] The system would dominate Irish bidding into the 1950s. Other authors cashed in on the new form of the game, and other books on the same subject soon appeared in the shops.[12] Indeed, plots of popular novels of the day were punctuated by references to contract bridge.[13]

Buller too had a flair for publicity. Three weeks after the match ended, it was reported[14] that he had undertaken to teach the game of bridge to the novelist Hugh Walpole, in three days. The enormity of the colonel's task and, by inference, his own ability as a teacher, was emphasised by a quote from Walpole: 'Thousands have tried to teach me but failed.'

Between them, Buller and Culbertson did much to stimulate interest in bridge, nowhere more so than in Ireland. However well the public received Mr Culbertson, the game's establishment did not – and not just in Great Britain. In the US, he expanded his enterprise and recruited additional teachers. The game's leading experts, including F. Dudley Courtenay, who developed the losing-trick count, and Milton C. Work, who introduced the 4, 3, 2, 1 point count, joined forces to launch *The Official System of Contract Bridge* in March 1931 and to form the American Bridge League. Embodying the collective wisdom and experience of America's acknowledged greatest players, it was the bastion of the old order.[15]

Culbertson resisted efforts to induce him to join the new organisation. His response – that there was room for only one – was a virtual declaration of war. Only a shoot-out in true American tradition could resolve the battle for supremacy. Culbertson targeted Sidney S. Lenz, a man who carried an aura of genius and invincibility. He was, like his antagonist, a multilinguist; in the realm of sport, it was said that he could give Bill Tilden a good match on the tennis court[16] and stretch Walter Hagan at golf.[17] It was reported that he had trained with Mickey Walker when the latter was preparing for his world-title fights.[18] He was also accomplished at bowls, shooting and table tennis, and played chess against Capablanca.[19] On top of that, he was a member of the American Society of Magicians. Having made a fortune from timber, he had retired in his early thirties. In 1931, at the age of fifty-eight, he was regarded as the world's best bridge player.[20] To Lenz is attributed, among a number of technical advances in bridge, the introduction of the high-low signal to show an even number of cards.

The 'Culbertson-Lenz Marathon', billed as 'the Bridge Battle of the Century', began at the Chatham Hotel in New York on 8 December 1931. Following the Christmas break, the contest resumed on 28 December at the Waldorf Hotel, and eventually ended on 7 January 1932. The conditions of the contest put a phenomenal strain on the two leading protagonists. The match, unlike the London events which had been contested as duplicate teams, was played over 150 rubbers. Culbertson and Lenz played throughout. At least seventy rubbers had to be played with a designated partner. Ely played eighty-eight with Josephine, and the remainder with Lightner, Von Zedtwitz, Howard Schenken or Mike Gottlieb. Lenz played 103 rubbers with Oswald Jacoby and the rest with Commander Winfield Liggett Jr. The tournament director – or referee, as he was then known - was Alfred Gruenther, who, years later, became Commander-in-Chief of the Allied Forces in Europe. Colonel G. G. J. Walsh, bridge correspondent of *The Times* and a future president of the Northern Ireland Bridge Union – and the man who, in 1918, had been cynical about contract – was an observer.[21]

Culbertson employed every trick – some of them unethical, at least by today's standards – to upset his opponents. He arrived late. He played slowly, to exasperate Lenz, who was fast. He took breaks to send out messages to the press. One evening, his two children came in attired for bed to say goodnight to their parents. The occasion was carefully staged and there were press photographers at hand. That night, Lenz misplayed a hand – for the only time in his life, it was said. That attracted news headlines too. Josephine announced that she was taking a break to do her Christmas shopping with the children, and the papers had another story.[22] Culbertson's stamina was phenomenal. He did a nightly broadcast and wrote daily articles for newspapers for the duration of the 'marathon'. When it was over, his team had won by a convincing margin.[23] In the public eye, he was the supreme master of the game.

The match was followed with interest in Europe. The very concept of a bridge contest lasting a month was enough to attract the attention of the news media. All three Dublin dailies – even the recently launched *Irish Press* – carried reports of the event. At least one account was cynical in tone: 'The American contract bridge marathon has come to an end,' reported the *Irish Times* on 11 January, 'Most people on this side of the Atlantic will rejoice, having already lamented that it ever began.' The brief article ended with a caustic cut at Culbertson: 'The result of the contest will bring prestige and profit to the Culbertsons. In such circumstances bridge ceases to be a game, and is simply a business.' The writer was clearly of the Buller school of thought, which saw bridge as a game for gentlemen, and not to be tainted by commerce. Nevertheless, the contest had helped fuel the excitement which the game was generating.

CULBERTON'S FOUR-FIVE NO-TRUMP CONVENTION

In reviewing the Buller, Beasley and Lenz matches, Culbertson had detected a weakness in slam-bidding methods. By 1933, he had devised the four-five no-trump convention.[24] This convention was put to the test in London in July of that year, when he challenged Colonel Beasley to a duplicate match for what he termed the 'World Championship'. Lightner and Gottlieb were the other half of his team, against Beasley, Lady Rhodes, Percy Tabbush, Sir Guy Domville and Captain Graham Mathieson. Culbertson performed another Herculean task. During the match, he wrote a daily column for a newspaper, did live broadcasts to the US – which, in order to avail of peak-time listening in America, went out at midnight – and wrote a 400-page book on the tournament. The match, which the Americans won easily, ended at 2 AM on 23 July. The book was in the shops thirty-six hours later.[25]

THE FIRST EUROPEAN CHAMPIONSHIP

Two months earlier, a more low-key event had been staged at London's Grosvenor House: the first European championship was contested by Austria, Belgium, Denmark, Great Britain, the Netherlands and Norway. The event, won by Austria, was run under the auspices of the International Bridge League, which had been formed the previous year with A. E. Manning Foster as president. The organisation embraced not only Europe but also the US. However, it was with the American Bridge League, not the Culbertson organisation, that Manning Foster had allied himself. Whatever lapse of judgement or fit of naivety he had suffered, he invited Culbertson to the championships as an observer. The brash American, in a press conference, was, to put it mildly, less than magnanimous about Manning Foster's organisational efforts. The contrast between the understated European championship and the ostentatious

Culbertson–Beasley match at Selfridges two months later could not have been greater – and did nothing to promote good relationships between the old guard and the new.

The events of May and July 1933 in London widened a rift which had already opened between different groups in England, the effects of which were felt right up to the outbreak of World War II, and into which Irish interests were dragged. Foremost in Culbertson's mind when he took on Beasley was to unveil his four-five no-trump convention to the British public. The British establishment, led by Manning Foster, denounced Culbertson's methods and equated them with cheating. Buller condemned Beasley as a traitor because the latter had gone over to the approach-forcing system. The Portland Club declared the four-five no-trump convention to be unethical and barred all artificial conventions.[26] Culbertson's response was: 'The millions of players who are utilising these methods will not be deterred by the thoughts of fogeys who do not understand them.'

Apart from Beasley, Culbertson had other prominent supporters in England, chiefly Hubert Phillips, who edited *British Bridge World* magazine and promoted the American's system. Indeed, Phillips had edited and written a preface to the London edition of the *Blue Book*.[27]

By this time, while factions in England denounced each other, duplicate contract bridge had become a nationally organised game on the other side of the Irish Sea. When the time came for international contact, it was with Phillips rather than with Manning Foster that the new organisation in the Irish Free State would ally itself – and with good reason.

THE CONTRACT BRIDGE ASSOCIATION OF IRELAND

Nineteen thirty-two was an eventful year for the ten-year-old Irish Free State. De Valera's Fianna Fáil Party entered government for the first time in March. In May, Ernest Walton, a native of Dungarvan, County Waterford, split the atom at Cambridge University[1] and Lady Augusta Gregory, founder, with Yeats, of the Abbey Theatre, died. The new government's protectionist policy was signalled with the introduction of widespread import duties. The Eucharistic Congress of the Catholic Church opened on 19 June; a week later, as the congress closed, the second Tailteann games began in Croke Park. By then, contract bridge had been organised as a national competitive game.

On the evening of 25 February, a group of people met at Mrs McMunn's bridge club at 8 Fitzwilliam Street in Dublin.[2] The meeting, which had been called by three women – Erina Holmes Wilson, Kathleen Lambert and Constance Maxwell Henry – unanimously passed a resolution to form an organisation known as the CBAI. Thus the Contract Bridge Association of Ireland, the governing body for bridge in the Irish Free State, later to become the Republic of Ireland, was born. Its aims were to foster the game of contract bridge and to improve the standard of play.

Given the demands for space during the post-election period, when the country anxiously speculated whether the Labour Party would support Fianna Fáil in the Dáil, the occasion might have been ignored by the newspapers, but the *Irish Times*, in a brief article, announced the birth of the new body the following day. The women mentioned above became the first president, secretary and treasurer, respectively, and headed a committee of fifteen[3] to guide the infant association through its early days. The three figureheads were well known in Dublin society. Erina

Holmes Wilson was the wife of a British army lieutenant colonel;[4] Constance Maxwell Henry's husband, James, was a fellow of Trinity College, Dublin; and Kathleen Lambert was married to Septimus Drummond Lambert, a prominent solicitor. Mrs Lambert had been the prime moving force in the creation of the new organisation. It was she who, the year before, had interested her friends in the new game of contract bridge.[5] The nucleus of the association was already functioning prior to the meeting in February.

The CBAI was among the world's earliest national bridge organisations. In Europe, only those of Austria (founded in 1929) and the Netherlands (1930) pre-date it for certain. Belgium, Czechoslovakia, Germany and Norway also had national governing bodies in 1932 but, taking account of winter conditions on mainland Europe, it is doubtful if any of them had formed before the end of February. Such strongholds of the game as France and Sweden did not establish national associations until 1933. The CBAI came into being long before the national bridge unions of Northern Ireland, Scotland, Wales and England. (The British Bridge League, founded in 1931, was essentially a private organisation.)

Mrs Lambert and her friends had probably been prompted to set up the association by recent events in London and New York. The Culbertson–Lenz marathon, which had ended only seven weeks previously, had been covered by the Dublin papers – extensively so by the *Irish Independent* – after Christmas.[6] Sidney Lenz's book on contract bridge had been in the Dublin bookshops since June 1928.[7] Mrs Lambert et al would have known about Culbertson's bidding system: the London edition of the *Blue Book* was in circulation in Ireland. They were convinced that the future of Irish bridge lay in duplicate. Joseph O'Neill, writing in 1948,[8] credited the three women with having introduced duplicate bridge to Ireland. Clearly, their founding of the association resulted in the development and growth in popularity of this form of the game.

At this time, bridge was still widely regarded as the pursuit of upper-middle-class and professional people, and was associated especially with those who would not have felt uncomfortable under the pre-1922 political regime. A majority of the founders of the CBAI were members of the Church of Ireland congregation. There were Presbyterian and Jewish members too.[9] Nevertheless, there were signs that Catholic nationalist Ireland was taking to the game. On 7 January 1932, the *Irish Press*, the recently launched organ of de Valera's Fianna Fáil Party, reported that a bridge drive and dance had been held the night before at the Gresham Hotel in aid of the party's election fund. 'Nearly five hundred attended,' the newspaper reported. The following Monday, the paper reported victory for Culbertson's 'approach-forcing system of bidding' over Lenz, who was described as 'the champion of the one-two-three variation of the official bidding'. The fact that the paper used such technical terms is indicative of informed interest in the game among its readers. Votes of bridge players were important in the forthcoming election. The message was that Fianna Fáil in power would not pose a threat to the class of people who played bridge.

Seán Lemass's use of bridge as a diplomatic tool while he was on an official visit to Ottawa in August was well publicised. There had been tension between the Dublin and Westminister governments following de Valera's announcement that he would discontinue payment of land annuities to Britain.[10] The payments, provided for under a provision of the 1921 Anglo-Irish Treaty, derived from financial loans granted to Irish tenant farmers to enable them to purchase lands under the Irish Land Acts during the previous half-century. While in Ottowa, Lemass, the Minister for Industry and Commerce, played bridge with the British representative, J. H. Thomas. The Anglo-Irish bridge games were the talk of the town.[11] When a quick-witted journalist asked Lemass, 'Is it true that J. H. Thomas has won back for England a large proportion of the land annuities?', Lemass replied: 'Ireland doesn't owe Britain any more money. Jimmy has won it all from us.'

EARLY COMPETITIONS

Initially, the CBAI was Dublin-centred and played its competitions at Jury's Hotel, at that time situated on College Green. It wasted no time in getting competitive duplicate started, nor did it hesitate to demonstrate where its inspiration lay. On 2 March, teams were invited to enter 'an open American bridge tournament'. In April, a competition which attracted eighteen teams was won by Mrs Holmes-Wilson, Mrs Revington, Mrs H. Brown and Mrs W. McCormick.[12] The winning team received a cup, which had been presented by Dr Lionel Wigoder to the association at its inaugural meeting.[13] The Wigoder Cup continued to be contested as a national championship until 1962.

A women's pairs championship in 1933, with sixteen competing partnerships, was won by Mrs McMunn and Miss Leech. Among the participants were Mrs Hickey and Mrs Crofts, each of whom – albeit under different names – were destined to play major roles in Irish bridge. There was a Mrs Spiro too, but it was not Elvina – who would represent Ireland with distinction in later years – but Mabel Spiro who donated the trophy for the CBAI mixed pairs. Elvina and Mabel were married to two brothers, Harold and Joseph, both of whom also played bridge. The family business was IMCO Cleaners and Dyers.[14] In the women's pairs championship for 1933–34, a field of eighteen pairs played a qualifying round, leading to a ten-pairs final on 5 December 1933, when Mrs Miley and Miss Kelly took the title. The following year, Harry and Miss Jackson[15] donated the cup which had been named after them – and which is still awarded annually to the winners of the competition. Nineteen thirty-three saw the first open pairs championship, for which the Davidson Cup later became the trophy. Some twenty-six pairs took part in the inaugural contest, won by Mrs Sharpe and Dr Leonard Abrahamson.[16]

The format for the Wigoder Cup in October 1933 – its third running – was indeed worthy of a national championship. The entry of eighteen teams, paying ten shillings per team, was divided into three sections of six. Each group played a round-robin. The winners of each, plus the best runners-up – teams captained by Miss Leech, D. R. Pigot, F. T. Quin and Miss Baker – went on to the semi-finals, in which Quin beat Leech and Pigot beat Baker. In the final, played on 30 January 1934, D. R. and Mrs Pigot, with Mr and Mrs Stewart, beat F. T. Quin, H. Smith, C. O'Neill and J. Morgan. This is the first time that the name 'Pigot' appears in the annals of bridge. David Pigot was destined to become an influential figure in the game, not only in Ireland but also further afield. His sons, Peter and Edgar, would represent Ireland too, as would his grandson, also named Peter.

A 1933 individual event illustrates the different way in which the early CBAI approached its championships and other competitions. The event, with an entry of forty players, began with a qualifying round, after which the field was reduced for a final. Miss Gertie McMeekin won from joint runners-up Mrs McCormick and Miss F. Williams. The championship format is even more clearly illustrated in 1934. Two tournament directors, Harold Williams and Harry Freehill, were exempt from the first round. The remaining forty players were divided into two groups of twenty, with the first nine from each joining the exempted players in the final. The two-session final, held on 6 and 13 February 1934, resulted in a win for Joseph O'Neill, with Muriel Leech coming second. The exempted pairs justified their special treatment by finishing fourth and sixth. Championships were multi-session events and true tests of ability over large numbers of boards.

Nineteen thirty-four also saw the start of the inter-club competition, which, in later years, developed into the inter-county championship. Eight teams entered the inaugural contest, all from the greater Dublin area: Regent, Mrs McMunn's Club, St Stephen's Green Club, Valentine, United Services Club, Foxrock Golf Club, Dun Laoghaire Golf Club and Herbert. Matches were staged on a knockout basis. Herbert, represented by Kathleen Lambert, Bernard Williams, Mairéad Crofts and Joseph O'Neill, beat St Stephen's Green in the final.

Fourteen teams contested the President's Cup on 8 and 15 May 1934. The cup, which was donated by the president, Mrs Holmes Wilson (and still bears her name), is awarded to the winners of the CBAI open team championship. The first winners were Kathleen Lambert, Bernard Williams, Joseph O'Neill, Mairéad Crofts and Harold Williams. The following year, when Mrs McMunn, Muriel Leech, Mrs Bowles and Mrs Colgan won, the competition was again referred to as the President's Cup.

In 1938, there was a nationwide, inter-club, team-of-four competition for the 'Fingal Cup'. The *Meath Chronicle* reported a 'big entry from provincial clubs'; Navan Bridge Club had participated in the competition. The *Kerry Champion* stated that 'each club was entitled to enter one team'. Hands were set. Scores were awarded for the correct call, opening lead, result and so on. The winners have not been traced but Tralee tied for third place.[17] However obscure the competition may seem behind the clouds of history, it indicates flair and imagination on the part of the CBAI organisers, and seemingly widespread participation.

REPRESENTATIVE MATCHES

The infant association was scarcely on its feet when it organised trials to select a team to play against an English side – Colonel Walter Buller, Colonel Henry Mountifort Beasley, Captain Graham Matheison and Alice Gordon Evers – in Dublin in November 1932. At the Royal Hibernian Hotel in Dawson Street, Mrs H. J. Brown, Mrs W. McCormick, J. B. Short,

Dr Gerald Tierney, Bernard Williams, Harold Williams, Mrs Holmes Wilson and Mrs Shortt, with non-playing captain H. G. Freehill, lost by 6,490 points to their more experienced opponents. Holmes Wilson and Shortt had replaced Mrs Bowles and Mrs Colgan, who had been chosen for the team but had cried off.

An encounter in any sport against England during the 1930s attracted attention, and the Buller match was no exception. Newspapers carried reports and articles about the contest throughout the following week. Harold Williams's[18] report in the *Irish Times* on 30 November contains the first full deal from a bridge game in an Irish newspaper. A clever play by Williams's partner and namesake, Bernard (Barney) Williams brought forth profuse expressions of admiration from Colonel Buller (see Chapter 37). The prevailing attitude towards psychic bidding is revealed. Harold Williams admired the visitors' propensity to psyche. 'The superiority of the English team was no more clearly demonstrated than in psychic bidding,' he wrote. It is clear that the psyche was a normal ploy, to be used by partnerships. It is scarcely correct to say it was part of the bidding system because the English players decried systemic bidding. Their method was 'natural' or 'original', not systemic. One report described Buller's method as 'a common-sense method of bidding'. It added 'the higher the class of player, the more effective the common sense'.[19] The Colonel was not lacking in self-esteem. The Irish used Culbertson's system. Buller, who never missed an opportunity to castigate American ideas, suggested in an after-match statement that the Irish might have done better had they not been 'in the habit of playing the American stunt conventions'. He suggested that 'no bridge player should play with any artificial conventions whatever'.[20]

At the Royal Hibernian Hotel on 21 and 22 April 1934, Dublin, represented by J. P. Morgan, C. O'Neill, H. L. Williams and H. G. Freehill, beat a team from Belfast – Tom Shanks, Mrs Deans, W. McCallum, W. McCaughey, George and Mrs Allen – by 3,110 points over forty-eight boards. Williams's *Irish Times* report demonstrated how quickly Culbertson's methods were catching on. On one deal, a Belfast pair used Culbertson's 4NT, the bid that had been used for the first time in competition only nine months previously in London. Unlike Blackwood, introduced in the United States, also in 1933, it was not an asking bid. It was descriptive, showing either three aces, or two aces plus a king of a bid suit, while the partner's ongoing call showed a particular feature. The deal gave the unnamed Belfast pair an opportunity to use the new bidding tool.

The CBAI took on a British Bridge League team at the Shelbourne Hotel on St Stephen's Green on 15 and 16 December 1934, in a David-and-Goliath encounter. BBL captain Richard Lederer had been on the British team in the 1933 European championships. He and his partner, Willie Rose, had just won their second BBL Gold Cup. L. W. (Leslie) Dodds, who partnered W. Grew, was at the start of a career which would bring him four European gold medals. The story did not have the same ending as that of David and Goliath, however. Harold Williams, Harry Freehill, Bernard Williams and Frank McMenamin, with non-playing captain James Hogan, lost the hundred-board match by 4,300 points.

Travel was not all in one direction: Irish players went to England too. In April 1933, Constance Maxwell Henry, Mrs Kennedy, Mrs Gough, Mrs F. G. Sharpe, Lady Brook and Janet Jackson were in London at the invitation of the ladies of Crockfords, headed by Doris Lady Rhodes and Mrs Evers. The London ladies won by 3,060 points.

Walter Buller's admiration of Barney Williams during the match in November was sincere. The Colonel invited him to play for Southern England against Northern England in Newcastle-on-Tyne in May 1933. Williams was in good company. The team, completed by Mrs Evers, Captain Mathieson, Richard Lederer and C. H. Collingwood, beat Ewart Kempson's team comfortably. Buller also invited Williams to play against a Northen Ireland selection in Belfast in November. Although billed as the first international bridge contest to be held in the North, it could hardly claim such status. There was still no national governing body for bridge in either Northen Ireland or England in 1933. Buller became ill and did not travel; Mrs Evers, who became unwell during the first session, was replaced by Constance Maxwell Henry. So it was really an England and Irish Free State combination which overcame the home side – Professor Alan McKinnon, Mrs Stephens, Mr Lloyd, O. P. Phillips and G. B. Hanna – by 2,260 in the hundred-board match.

Culbertson launched his bridge Olympic, a world par contest, in 1932, and Ireland featured among the prize winners. Messrs Lawler and Bolger (Bunclody) and O'Malley and Bolger (Enniscorthy) were second North–South and East–West respectively, in the worldwide competition – evidence that there were not only subscribers to *Bridge World* in the two County Wexford towns, but also organised games with players of good standard. The Dublin branch participated in 1935 and 1936, while in 1939 Birr-Banagher was the only centre in Ireland to take part, resulting in its members, D. A. Houlihan, T. C. O'Gorman, T. J. and Mrs O'Meara taking the national prizes. (Incidentally, the Olympic bears no relationship to the later World Bridge Olympiad.)

Joseph O'Neill accidentally acquired fame in the 1936 competition. Before dispatching the set of sixteen deals for the competition, Culbertson and his staff analysed and checked every hand until they were satisfied that each deal was susceptible of only one correct solution. While defending with a particular hand, O'Neill lost concentration and inadvertently ruffed his partner's winner. That turned out to be the only successful defence, and one which Culbertson had not considered. The effect of O'Neill's accidental brilliance was that Culbertson had to send out apologies around the world and cancel the scoring for that deal. The war put an end to the competition.

7

The CBAI Spreads

From the start, the founders of the CBAI were industrious in their efforts to win over auction players to contract. Constance Maxwell Henry opened a bridge school in Clery's restaurant on O'Connell Street. Mrs Maxwell Henry was rare among her contemporaries. The wife of a Trinity College Dublin academic, she was a well-qualified person herself, holding MA and LLB degrees. In addition, she was a certified teacher of the Harold Thorne Bridge School. Thorne, author of several books on contract, had been converted to Culbertson and was one of the leading bridge teachers in England. He was in Dublin on 21 May 1932 lecturing on the game, and was present when the Maxwell Henry school opened two days later.[1]

Erina Holmes Wilson wrote a manual, *Short Cuts to Contract Bridge*.[2] Divided into seventeen short lessons for the beginner, it included 'tit-bits of information on the play of the hand'. She also established a bridge club at her home in Monkstown, which continued into the 1950s.

Branches

Press reports of bridge tournaments in aid of various charities offer evidence that there were large numbers of players throughout the country. Just before Christmas 1932, it was reported that 1,500 people had taken part in a tournament at the Gresham Hotel to raise funds for Irish athletics.[3] The personalities present included Dr Pat O'Callaghan from Clonmel, who, earlier that year, had retained his Olympic hammer title. Allowing for exaggeration in the report, it was still quite a gathering.[4] It was clear that such functions were many and frequent – and that bridge had a large and widespread following at this time.

Taking the number of players in the country into account, the association can hardly be said to have made great headway in terms of recruiting during its first two years. The second annual general meeting of the CBAI, held in September 1933, was told that membership was now 'almost two hundred, fifty more than last year', but a plan was put forward to form branches all over Ireland and to have inter-county and inter-town matches. There was a further aim 'to establish permanent premises for the association' – an objective which was not realised for another sixty-six years. A pattern of activity emerged: a visit from Dublin players became the catalyst for establishing a branch. The founding members certainly did not spare themselves.

LIMERICK

In the autumn of 1933, Harold Williams and Harry Freehill were invited to Limerick, where Willliams's brother Billy was a prominent auction player. Following a meeting at the Stella restaurant, where the two men from Dublin explained duplicate, the first branch of the national body outside of Dublin was founded.[5] Initially, they played over the Imperial bakery in Sarsfield Street. Numbers increased, necessitating a move, Cruise's Hotel seemingly the obvious venue. However, a Garda chief superintendent warned that if they attempted to play cards on licensed premises, he would have them arrested. They remained at the Stella, and later went to the Savoy, before eventually moving to Cruise's. There is no record of arrests. Limerick celebrated with an at-home – twenty-four boards followed by dinner – in December 1934, when they entertained teams from Dublin, Ennis and Cork. This was the first of many such occasions.

The branch quickly made its presence felt. In 1938, Dr Denis Corboy became the first CBAI president from outside Dublin. He and his wife, Mary, were the first non-Dublin pair to win the national pairs championship in 1939. They donated the Thomond Cup for the Munster pairs. Ten years later, Dr Hubert Roche-Kelly, another founding member, also became president. Jack and Eileen O'Sullivan left Limerick in the autumn of 1936 to become one of the strongest pairs in Dublin, before moving to Tralee. They later became distinguished international players.

TULLAMORE

In November 1933, Kathleen Lambert, Joseph O'Neill, and Mairéad and Gerard Crofts played a forty-eight-board match in Tullamore. The locals, Jack and Mrs Williams, Mr and Mrs Murray, Mr and Mrs Maguire, Mrs O'Hara and J. B. Moorhead, were no match for the visitors, but the encounter heralded the setting up of a branch in the town.

GALWAY

In December 1933, Kathleen and Septimus Lambert, Constance and James Maxwell Henry, and Muriel Leech went to Galway, where the home team – Dr Sandys, Mr Furlong, Dr O'Malley and P. Arkins – beat them over forty-eight boards. Thus the Galway branch began, with H. T. Vernon as honorary secretary.

WATERFORD

On the weekend following, Harold and Barney Williams, Harry Freehill and B. Thornhill were in Waterford, at the invitation of J. W. O'Loughlen, who, along with Dr Nicholas Purcell, W. N. Cleary, Mrs Carew and Mrs Fitzgerald, beat the visitors over fifty boards. However, no branch was formed, and Waterford remained outside the association. There had been a club in the city since 1927 but there was no enthusiasm for joining the CBAI. It is the only recorded failure, on the part of the executive, to persuade local players to form a branch.

PROVINCIAL PLAYERS IN DUBLIN

The dinner and matches organised by the CBAI on 6 February 1934 at the Metropole restaurant in O'Connell Street, Dublin, where visitors from Cork, Kildare, Limerick, Sligo and Tullamore were entertained, was part of its strategy for promoting the association. The *Irish Times* reported that the Dublin sides had an advantage, as they were used to duplicate, whereas the others were not. Limerick gave the Dublin players the closest match. Although the Cork players had never before, as a team, competed in a duplicate competition, Cork organised a return meeting the following month, when players from Dublin, Sligo and Limerick travelled to the Munster capital. This time, Sligo fielded two teams, one of men, the other of women.

SLIGO

Dr Bourke and Mr Lyons from Sligo had been among the invited guests at the Metropole Hotel in February. They in turn invited two teams of Dublin players to Sligo two months later. This was the catalyst for establishing the Sligo branch, which was certainly operating by April, despite their two teams – 'A' consisting of Mr Higgins, Dr Bourke, A. Lyons and Dr McCarthy, and 'B' of Mrs Higgins, Mrs C. Lyons, Mrs Connolly and Miss Burke – losing their matches to the Dublin visitors. The field for the 1935 CBAI individual championship included Dr Michael Martin from Sligo.

ENNIS

A branch was formed in Ennis towards the end of 1934,[6] following a visit from the Limerick players Robert Walker, Billy Williams, Larry Byrne and Mr McGarry, to the Old Ground Hotel, where they explained duplicate. James O'Regan, the hotel's proprietor, had become interested in the new form of the game when he bought a copy of Culbertson's book and introduced the American's ideas to his friends.[7] O'Regan became branch secretary.

Ennis became a most active unit, with good players. As early as January 1935, Captain Vesper represented the branch in the CBAI individual championship in Dublin. Victor Roughan and T. D. Cooper went close to international selection on a number of occasions: they were the reserve pair for the Welsh match in July 1937. During the same season, Molly O'Donnell and Nan O'Mara ended Dublin's monopoly of the women's pairs championship when they won the Jackson Cup, held that year in Limerick. In 1938, Roughan, Cooper, Dr Patrick Moylan and Molly O'Donnell reached the final of the Kelburne, only to lose to the holders – a team captained by Kathleen Lambert. Later, Roughan and Tom McCarrick went close to getting places on the Irish team in the European championships.[8] In January 1941, Dr Nora O'Dwyer and J. Degnan made the arduous journey to the Shelbourne Hotel in Dublin to contest the national pairs championship. The leading provincial pair in the competition, they tied for the last remaining place in that year's panel test, but the tie was split in favour of Johnny Morgan and Charlie O'Neill.[9]

At-homes were highlights of the social calendar. For example, in April 1936 the Limerick, Fermoy, Cork, Tralee and Dublin branches were guests of the Ennis branch. Forty-eight-board matches, held over Saturday and Sunday, were followed by dinner. Dress was formal. One particular Ennis at-home was considered sufficiently newsworthy to warrant a large photograph in the *Irish Independent*.[10] On such occasions, two names recur during after-dinner speeches, in relation to their contribution to the development of the game in both Limerick and Ennis: Robert V. Walker and F. W. Williams.[11] On one occasion, Walker was described as 'the father of the Ennis team' and Williams as 'the godfather'. In presenting the Jackson Cup in Limerick in March 1938, Mrs Maxwell Henry, the CBAI president, praised Walker for his work in popularising the game.

From the start, Ennis players, keen to improve their play, frequently issued challenges to other branches. In January 1935, less than two months after the branch had been established, Roughan, Cooper, P. F. Moloney and Miss Frances Walker defeated a Dublin team which featured three future national champions.[12] In July 1937, a Belfast quartet consisting of future Camrose competitors was invited to Ennis.[13]

The Ennis branch was outward-looking too, and helped to advance the game beyond its own immediate area. In March 1935, members were in Tipperary taking on players from Cappamore, Doon, Pallas, Lattin and Emily. Ennis won the match. There is no evidence of clubs existing in those villages.

The game made remarkable progress in the catchment area of the town. In the autumn of 1936, less than two years after the formation of the branch, a winter league was organised, involving ten teams. In order to involve as many players as possible, entrants were divided into two pools, from each of which two players were drawn to make up a team. In June 1941, the branch organised what it termed an 'end-of-season intercounty pairs'. Competitors from Dublin, Galway and Limerick joined the County Clare players at the Falls Hotel, Ennistymon, where Dr M. J. and Mrs Hillary (Milltown Malbay), the parents of the future president of Ireland, Dr Patrick Hillery, were the winners.

When Ennis Bridge Club celebrated its diamond jubilee in 1994,[14] it was really the founding of the branch that was commemerated. It remained a branch until 1948, at which point it became a club.

ENNISCORTHY

In Enniscorthy, in December 1934, John Bolger's selection defeated a team from the town's rugby football club over twenty-four boards. The report on the match stated that among those taking part were the winners of the Culbertson Zone Cup[15] – from which we can conclude that contract duplicate bridge competition was already well established in the area.

DUN LAOGHAIRE

There was a branch in Dun Laoghaire by early 1935. Teams from Cork, Dublin, Dun Laoghaire, Limerick and Sligo took part in a tournament in Jury's Hotel, Dublin, on the weekend of 23 and 24 April. Dun Laoghaire players Mrs Brown, Mrs Revington, Mrs Miley and Miss Kelly were members of the Dublin branch as well. There would always be duplication of membership between the capital and its satellite town.

DROGHEDA

Kathleen Lambert, James Hogan, and David and Violet Pigot assisted in getting the Drogheda branch off the ground when they played a match against Willie Berrill, Mrs Fox, Mrs P. J. Gallagher and T. Rohan towards the end of October 1935. Local players had been practising duplicate from the previous May. The branch, which was founded probably in September,[16] predates the Gate Club in the town, which started in 1936.

TRALEE

Dr Eamonn O'Sullivan (Killarney) claimed that the Tralee branch was founded before Killarney Bridge Club. That is not possible. O'Sullivan wrote his notes in 1965; his memory, on that point, was not accurate. Killarney started in 1932. The CBAI decision to form branches was not made until the AGM of September 1933. There could have been a club, as distinct from a branch, in Tralee before that. Tralee branch was founded probably in 1935. Even by then, only two years after the CBAI executive's decision to foster branches, there was a certain ambiguity about the distinction between a 'branch' and a 'club'. Tralee branch ran a 'club' pairs championship in 1935, won by R. J. Keating and Mrs. Quinlan.[17] By 1937, a reporter, using the pen-name 'Grand Slam', was regularly writing accounts of 'Tralee bridge club' competitions in the *Kerry Champion*. Whether it was a branch or a club, the membership was quite big. In February 1938, a novel form of match was played: sixteen women versus sixteen men. Although the club frame of mind was quickly adopted, the branch identity was not totally abandoned. On 20 March of that year, Tralee was 'at home' to teams from the Limerick, Dublin and Cork branches. On that occasion, some of the locals acquitted themselves well, beating strong Dublin and Cork sides. Tralee is a good example of how the concepts of branch and club became blurred and how quickly the club outlook became dominant. Tralee's season was remarkably short, coming to a close at the end of March.

KILKENNY

On 14 November 1936, the *Irish Independent* reported that a branch of the national association had been established in Kilkenny, with W. F. McGarry as honorary secretary.[18] It was the last recorded branch of the CBAI to be formed. The game had been organised in the city since 1929, when Henrietta Duggan started a regular game in her home.

AT-HOMES

'At-homes' originated in earlier times, when ladies or gentlemen opened their homes to friends or groups of people on specified days or evenings. Inevitably, bridge became a fitting activity for such gatherings.

The adoption of the at-home idea by branches of the CBAI played a significant role in spreading the game, raising awareness of the association and promoting team competition. Sometimes there was a single match between two branches; more often, guests were invited from a number of neighbouring branches, or occasionally from further away. Arguably, they were the embryos from which congresses later developed. They were thoroughly civilised affairs, with bridge and dinner – for which, usually, the guests dressed formally. Drinks flowed liberally, with gin and tonic or whiskey and soda (from a syphon) being popular choices. Friendships and camaraderie were established among those who took part. An extraordinary example of this was when Mrs Aldritt, a leading personality in the game in Portlaoise, invited the 1938 Kelburne Cup finalists, from Dublin and Ennis, to play the match in her home.

Despite the unstinting efforts of the founders and the consequent addition of several branches, total membership of the CBAI barely exceeded 300 by September 1935. However, this figure is misleading, as it represents only registered players – those who wished to play in CBAI competitions. The actual number of players who had been won over to contract is impossible to gauge. Members of clubs were not included in the total. The primary aim of the CBAI leadership seems to have been to set up branches in order to increase the number of registered players. They were concentrating on developing the serious competitive aspect of the sport.

CBAI CONGRESS AND THE CREATORS OF ACOL

The success of CBAI at-homes (like the one held in the Shelbourne Hotel in January 1936, when sixteen visiting teams from the provinces played matches against Dublin sides) and developments in Britain undoubtedly influenced the decision to organise a congress at the Royal Marine Hotel, Dun Laoghaire, in June 1937.

By this time, congresses were well established on the neighbouring island. Harrogate in Yorkshire was one of the biggest, but in March 1934 it had been abandoned following a threat from the police similar to the one issued by the Gardaí in Limerick. Bridge was a game of chance, according to the police, and therefore prohibited in the hotel – a licenced premises. By 1937, Harrogate was running unhindered by the law. Two key CBAI personnel, Kathleen Lambert and Geraldine McConkey, the honorary treasurer, led a team there,[19] not merely to compete but to obtain first-hand experience of how a congress worked. They also engaged in a public-relations exercise on behalf of their own event, which was scheduled to take place in three months' time.

The main feature of the CBAI congress in Dun Laoghaire was an invitational team competition, won by an English squad: Maurice Harrison Grey, S. J. Simon, J. H. C. Marx, Ben Cohen, Terence Reece and

Hubert Phillips. A more formidable line-up can scarcely be imagined. Significantly, it consisted of the players who pioneered the Acol bidding system. Marx and Simon had created Acol[20] a short time previously; Harrison Grey was one of the first to adopt the new system;[21] Cohen and Reece, by writing about it, largely in Phillips's magazine, brought it to the attention of the public and assisted in its spread. Marx and Simon were using Acol in competition at that time. It is almost certain that it was used for the first time in Ireland on that occasion.

Marx, Simon, Cohen and Phillips also won the congress teams event from a north of Ireland four: George B. Hanna, Eric Goldblatt, Bertie Vard and R. J. McKee.[22] The women's team winners were the Mrs Holmes Wilson, Shortt, Crofts and O'Sullivan – the last-named not long arrived in the capital from Limerick. Congress pairs were not run as they are nowadays. The winners of open pairs competitions went forward to a final, which was won by Mrs and Miss Roantree.

The congress was repeated in October 1938 and again in 1939, but minus the English stars. A Wexford quartet – Moreen McCarthy, Paddy Carson, Dr N. Purcell and W. N. O'Leary – won the teams competition in 1938 from the Purcell brothers, Des and Gerry, playing with two young lawyers, Noel Peart and Rex Mackey. This was one of the rare occasions when Mackey's name appears among the prizewinners. His fame rests on a book, *The Walk of the Oysters*, one of the best-written volumes on bridge.

CLUBS

Clubs pre-date the CBAI but the association chose to establish branches when it moved to embrace the players of the nation, and it was through the branch that it decided to recruit participants for its national competitions. One of the association's aims was to improve the standard of play, so the branch sought to enrol competent players. The branch was focused on the national body and was keen to get involved in inter-branch activity; whereas the club was inward-looking, its members happy to enjoy what is referred to as a 'social game'. At the risk of over-simplification, it is not inaccurate to state that rubber remained the staple game of the club, while the branch promoted duplicate. Branch members were the more competitive elite players. A club played regularly, usually weekly, in a fixed location. Some branches, for example the Dublin one, did not have a regular place to play but moved their games from hotel to hotel as rooms became available. Branch formation was pushed by the CBAI founders in Dublin, but it was invariably the action of a local individual that led to the formation of a club.

The Ennistymon club was founded in 1932 by Dr Denis O'Dwyer from Lahinch. Auction bridge was popular and widespread in County Clare, as evidenced by the county board of the National Athletic and Cycling Association organising a bridge drive to raise funds in 1930.[23]

Killarney Bridge Club was founded in 1932, by Sir Maurice O'Connell and Anthony McGillicuddy at O'Connell's home in Fossa. When the house was converted into the Lake View Hotel in the late 1930s, the club moved to the town and, after brief sojourns in the Great Southern and the Lake Hotels, settled in the Intercontinental Hotel for some years. Dr Eamonn O'Sullivan remembered that Killarney played duplicate from the outset, and he recalled that members from Tralee and Killorglin attended reglarly.[24] Evidently the game was well established in that part of the county. Further evidence of the advanced level of organisation of the game in Kerry is seen in a county individual championship in January 1938, won by Killarney founding member Anthony McGillicuddy of Flesk Castle.

There was a club in Westport in 1936, and it may have been founded earlier. Clubs were established in Athlone, Monaghan and Roscommon in 1935. The Gate (Drogheda) and Wicklow came in 1936; Ardee, Castlebar, Tullamore and Wexford all in 1937; and Edenderry and County Longford in 1938. By 1941, clubs in Athlone, Clonmel, Mullingar, Naas, Navan, Portlaoise and Thurles were competing in the inter-club championship, and the following year the entries included Athy, Balbriggan and Dundalk. A number of clubs existed in Dublin.

It is likely that there were other clubs throughout the country, but evidence of their origins has not been uncovered. By 1941, branches had become indistinguishable from clubs and, even though the constitutional change did not come for another seven years, from that year branch and club were, for practical purposes, synonymous.

MONAGHAN

A game held in the home of Dr Edward McNally in 1935 led to the formation of a club in Monaghan. Dr William Coyne, medical officer at St

Davnat's Hospital, and two local bank managers, P. J. Walshe and Mr Cox, made up the four. When McNally suggested that they form a bridge club, it transpired that Coyne had been thinking along the same lines. However, the first organised game, held shortly afterwards in the courthouse, was greeted with hostility from Monaghan County Council, which banned the use of the courthouse for the playing of bridge.[25] One member of the council suggested that 'these bridge players are a lot of snobs'. What the councillors failed to understand – or chose not to – was the fact that bridge was a unifying influence in the border town, where differences between the communities were marked and significant. Among the members of the bridge club were Joseph Corr, Dr P. B. Cusack, Reverend Professor Patrick Flanagan, Dermot Kelleher, M. C. R. Lardner, Mrs McWilliam, W. E. Morgan, A. Rudd and Luke Skeath – people representing both sides of the religious divide.

The club found accommodation in the offices of the *Northern Standard*, the local newspaper, whose proprietor, Harold Swann, was a keen player. It moved to the Westenra Hotel in 1937. Two or three tables of rubber were the norm, with stakes ranging from a penny to sixpence a hundred. Garda Superintendent John Ryan, on his arrival in the town in the early 1940s, introduced duplicate.

THE GATE, DROGHEDA

In August 1936, four people – bank manager William Behan, fashion-store proprietor P. J. Gallagher, dentist Joe Liddy and Josephine Carberry – while playing in Doherty's Hotel in Baltray,[26] were distracted by noisy patrons. They resolved to look for a place where they could have a regular game in peace. A fortnight later, a Mr Farrell, in a local newspaper, advertised rooms to let at 23 Laurence Street, a few yards from St Laurence Gate. It was there that the appropriately named 'Gate Club' met for the first time on 25 September. Behan became its first president.

Even though the club was founded on the initiative of bridge players, other card games were played as well, and table tennis and debating were also popular in the club. Indeed, the official opening night, 16 October, was a whist drive. As in bridge clubs in other towns, the membership was comprised of professional and business people, with the bank manager at the helm. To be accepted as a member of the Gate meant inclusion in the top echelon of the town's society. In a short time, under the influence of people such as Willie Berrill, Joe Stanley and Eddie McArdle, bridge took over. Berrill, self-taught by reading authors such as Culbertson and Hubert Phillips, became an accomplished all-rounder: a good player, teacher, tournament director and administrator. When he died in 1978, an annual open competition was inaugurated in his memory. The Willie Berrill Cup remains a popular event.

BALBRIGGAN

Bridge was widely played in the area encompassing north County Dublin and south Meath. Following a meeting in the Carnegie Library, Balbriggan, addressed by Fred Quin and Harry Freehill, in late October or early November 1936, a club was formed in the town, with Dr P. W. McGowan as president and Mrs Warner as honorary secretary. That a club, not a branch, was the result of the executive members' visit is evidence that the branch concept was on the wane.

CASTLEBAR AND WESTPORT

A letter from Harry Freehill,[27] honorary secretary of the CBAI, dated 23 February 1937, to Mr R. Kilkelly, Main Street, Castlebar, has survived. In response to a request from Kilkelly as to how to form a club, Freehill refers him to Mr P. V. Plunkett, the honorary secretary of Westport Club, which was already affiliated with the association. Plunkett, he suggests, would help to get the Castlebar club started. The letter explains the affiliation system, stating that it merely committed a club to recognising the CBAI as the national governing body. Fees were five shillings for clubs with less than twenty members, and ten shillings for bigger clubs. Affiliation did not confer association membership on the club member. Those who wished to compete in national championships had to pay an individual fee of five shillings. Members of clubs were deemed to be associate members.

WATERFORD

On 13 November 1937, the *Irish Independent* reported that 'Waterford bridge club has been formed recently'. In fact, the club had started ten years earlier. The match played against CBAI players from Dublin in December 1933 would indicate that the club was still functioning then, but it disbanded soon afterwards. Billy Kervick, who had been present at the inaugural 1927 meeting, disclosed to Michael Brennan in 1985 that there were 'initial difficulties between the club and the CBAI'. The members 'refused to have any truck with the new crowd in Dublin'. What those difficulties were remains a mystery. This is the only instance from the period of a negative attitude towards the new national association. It is possible that Waterford was simply reluctant to adopt contract bridge – auction remained popular in many places for a number of years – but the tone of Kervick's remarks, almost half a century later, suggests a more deep-rooted hostility to the organisation. By late 1937, attitudes had changed. Dr d'Abreu[28] and Louis Doolan[29] were foremost among the group that revived the club, which, soon after its rebirth, affiliated to the CBAI.

GALWAY

A branch of the CBAI existed in the city for at least three years before Galway Bridge Club was founded, in late 1936 or early 1937. The club's first honorary secretary was J. Henry Daly, an official of the National Bank, who did much to further the game in the various towns to which his profession brought him.[30] Daly was a future president of the CBAI and was succeeded in that office in 1951 by a fellow founder of the Galway club, Dr W. J. McHugh. A good model for a club in a large urban area, the Galway club showed itself to be among the most progressive in the country when, in 1940, it organised the West of Ireland Congress,[31] which has continued uninterrupted to this day. Club records are extant from 1952, by which time the weekly game was routinely established at the Warwick Hotel in Salthill and the congress at the Great Southern Hotel. By the early 1950s, friendly matches were taking place against Limerick, Tuam and the Corrib club, Galway's local rival.

WEXFORD

Wexford Bridge Club, founded in late 1936 or early 1937, was lucky to have players of the first rank: Moreen McCarthy and Paddy Carson would in time win national championships and gain international 'caps'. The fact that Wexford formed a club, rather than a branch of the CBAI, indicates that the branch idea had been well and truly abandoned. Branches had been built around players of the calibre of McCarthy and Carson, and it is not surprising to see Wexford contending for national prizes from the beginning. In 1939, they reached the final of the Kelburne Cup.

THE CARLTON CLUB

The Carlton Club, with premises initially on Lower Leeson Street[32] and later at 118 St Stephen's Green, was Dublin's leading club during the 1930s. Although not one of the eight clubs participating in the first inter-club championship in 1934, it quickly came to the fore: not surprisingly, given that players of the calibre of Kathleen Lambert, Mairéad O'Neill, Geraldine McConkey and Ina Hickey were among its members. There was, of course, a degree of overlapping with other clubs, notably the Regent, but the Carlton set a standard not merely of play but also of organisation. It won the inter-club championship in 1936 and again in 1940; the Regent did not succeed in winning the prestigious title until 1942. Carlton's 1940 victory was celebrated with an at-home.

The club hosted a Dublin v. Belfast match at the end of October 1936, when the home side was victorious. The visitors used the Kempson system and the Dublin players Culbertson, according to a report.[33] Carlton got involved in imaginative tournaments which attracted the attention of the press. Mairéad Crofts was behind a unique event in January 1937, when ten elite players were invited to compete in an eighty-one-board contest over three sessions.[34] Among those invited were four members of the Jewish Social Club, an institution which remained to the fore of the national bridge scene for the next two decades.

KELLS

In November 1932, the *Meath Chronicle* wrote that 'bridge was becoming a favourite game in Kells, with increasing attendances and drives'. There had been thirteen tables at a recent tournament in the St Vincent de Paul Hall. The results suggest that a 'progressive movement' was used, as there were prizes for best lady and best gentleman. The paper speculated that 'a bridge circle will probably be formed in the town'. In the late 1930s, the town was not represented in the North-East League. In March 1939, however, two teams of Kells players visited Navan for a match[35] – which suggests that there was a club in the town at this time. By 1948, Kells had affiliated to the CBAI.

CLARA AND STRADBALLY

The villages of Clara, County Offaly, and Stradbally, County Laois, probably did not have enough players to form clubs, but there were certainly enthusiasts of the game in both villages, as evidenced by the presence of competitors from the two localities at an open pairs competition held in Portlaoise in April 1939. In any event, whoever sent the report to the *Irish Independent* thought it worth mentioning the fact.[36]

Regionalisation

The division of the country into regions evolved during the late 1930s, driven by practical considerations on the part of the CBAI executive in relation to national championships. At the same time, local committees emerged to initiate and oversee activities in their respective areas.

The introduction of the inter-club and national team championships, both knockout competitions with open draws, gave rise to territorial divisions, to avoid the possibility of teams from either end of the country meeting in the early rounds. By 1936, when the Kelburne Cup was launched, provincial players were competing in significant numbers. Entrants were divided into two sectors: Southern – a vast geographical area stretching from Kilrush, County Clare, to Wexford – and Eastern (in practice, Dublin and northward to Drogheda). Invariably, a Dublin team and a provincial side fought out the final. Galway, Sligo, Boyle and Tullamore, all of which had branches, did not take part in pre-war Kelburne Cup competitions.

The inter-club championship attracted entries from a wider area. Entrants for the inaugural inter-club contest in 1934 were from the greater Dublin area, so travel was not a consideration. By 1936, clubs throughout the country were keen to take part. By 1938, participants were divided into four areas: Western, South-eastern, North-eastern and Dublin. The respective area winners – Roscommon, Thurles, Balbriggan and Regent – went forward to semi-finals, in which Roscommon defeated Thurles, and Balbriggan beat the Regent, to set up the first championship final without Dublin players. Roscommon's Patrick Ballantine, William Hourican,[1] and James and Mrs Hurley were victorious. The following year, when forty-eight teams entered the competition, the executive announced that the competition would be divided into areas to 'minimise travel'.[2] The 'regional' divisions were not the same as in the previous year. In a new Southern sector, Tralee and Waterford met in the final.

The national pairs championship was also attracting provincial competitors by 1936. Eliminators were run by the branches. By 1937, preliminary qualifiers led to Southern and Eastern zonal contests, from which sixteen pairs qualified for the final in Dublin.[3] The following year, entrants were grouped into 'geographically convenient' areas, but the elimination rounds led to what were termed 'regional championships', with twenty-two pairs advancing to the final.[4] There was an incentive for aspiring players to compete: the leading pairs gained admission to the panel tests, from which teams for the home-international championship were selected. In fact, the 1937 championship was promoted as a 'medium to find new talent for the 1938 national teams'.[5]

'Area secretaries' were appointed by the CBAI during this period. On 6 November 1937, the *Irish Independent*, in a report on the state of the game, informed readers that 'area secretaries are having a busy time and the policy of the Executive Committee of the CBAI in creating these offices for the better organisation of the game has been fully justified'. Only one area secretary has been identified: John P. Morgan, whose duties covered a slice of the east coast, including Dublin and Drogheda. The *Meath Chronicle*, in January 1938, mentions that he had helped the secretary of Drogheda Bridge Club, Mrs Gallagher, organise the North-east league.[6] The only other reference to 'areas' is a certificate which hangs in Mullingar Bridge Centre and which attests to the fact that, in 1940, Mullingar became an affiliated club in 'Area 5' of the CBAI.[7] The area number does not coincide with the subsequent 'regional' number: while zonal and regional divisions were drawn up for the convenience of participants in national championships, the 'areas' had to do with administrative tasks – pursuing affiliations, collecting fees, assisting local officers in organisational matters, and so on.

Local activities were important when it came to determining regional boundaries. George N. Jessop (Portlaoise)[8] was behind the South-east Cup, a competition which, in 1938, attracted an entry of twelve teams. These twelve were divided into four groups of three: Athlone, Tullamore and Edenderry; Birr-Banagher, Thurles and Clonmel; Athy, Portlaoise and Kilkenny; and Wicklow, Wexford and Waterford. Teams of eight – consisting of 'A' and 'B' sides from each club – played round-robins of forty-eight-board matches, twenty-four home and twenty-four away, the winners decided by the cumulative scores of the clubs' two teams. This led to semi-finals and a final. In 1940, following George Jessop's death, the cup was renamed the Jessop Cup. Henceforth, the final would be in Portlaoise.

A league was organised in the north-east over the winter of 1938–39, with Ardee, Balbriggan, Drogheda Commercial, Gate Drogheda (two teams), Dundalk, Monaghan and Navan competing for the North-East Shield. Matches were home and away there too.

Two examples serve to illustrate the ad hoc, indeed pragmatic, basis for the territorial divisions implemented by the CBAI. Balbriggan was in the North-eastern zone for the inter-club competition, but in the Dublin-Eastern for the Kelburne Cup. Thurles took part in the South-east Cup in 1938 but the following year played in the South-midland's inter-club cup. What was emerging was a 'regional' way of thinking, and it was happening as a club frame of mind was taking over from the branch idea. Local organisational machinery was already in place, ready for the introduction of formal regional boundaries.

1940 CHANGES

Two important changes occurred in August 1940. From the commencement of the following season, associate members would be entitled to play in CBAI championships. Before that, only club members could play in the inter-club competition. They still had no voting rights, nor could they serve on the executive committee. Such a change would have required an amendment to the constitution, but granting permission to take part in CBAI competitions was an executive function. It was also within the executive's remit to map out regional boundaries. Regions, which had been evolving, were formalised. A new CBAI regulation read:

> Affiliated clubs in various parts of Ireland will be grouped into convenient regions, and activities of the CBAI . . . shall be controlled and organised in each such region by a regional committee elected by the affiliated clubs of that region.

The administration of the game was decentralised. Control was transferred from Dublin to the provinces. Regional boundaries were drawn up as follows:

No. 1: Mayo, Sligo, Leitrim, Roscommon and Longford
No. 2: North County Dublin, Meath, Louth, Monaghan, Cavan
No. 3: Galway, Westmeath and Offaly
No. 4: Laois, Kildare, Carlow, Kilkenny, Tipperary and Waterford
No. 5: South County Dublin, Wicklow and Wexford

Munster, where a regional committee already existed, was referred to simply as 'the Munster region'. It consisted of Clare, Limerick, Cork and Kerry.

Temporary honorary secretaries were appointed to convene regional committee meetings: Superintendent John Ryan (Boyle) for Region No. 1, Joseph M. Stanley (Drogheda) for No. 2, J. Henry Daly (Galway) for No. 3, Miss M. White (Portlaoise) for No. 4 and Moreen McCarthy (Wexford) for No. 5.

It is notable that neither Donegal nor Dublin was included in the new regional structure. Dublin continued to be governed by the original founding branch, and the CBAI executive was centred there. Donegal was the only county without an affiliated club. 'When Donegal becomes bridge-minded, the CBAI is ready to receive it and plan for the organisation of the game there,' a report read.[9]

Inaugural regional meetings took place in September. Executive members were supportive in getting the regions under way. Constance Maxwell Henry attended the inaugural meetings of Region No. 1, where P. A. Arkins (Longford) and Superintendent Ryan (Boyle) were elected chairman and honorary secretary respectively, and Region No. 3, where Superintendent Doyle (Ballinasloe) and J. Henry Daly filled the same positions. Daly, the convenor of the latter meeting, was embarrassed when he discovered that, due to an oversight, Edenderry Bridge Club, far distant from Daly's base in Galway, had not been informed of the meeting. Joseph O'Neill represented the executive at the No. 4 regional meeting, where L. Doolan (Waterford) and Miss F. Slaney (Portlaoise) became chairman and honorary secretary respectively. There was a tone of optimism in statements released by the executive in Dublin. Affiliations were expected to increase, and it was suggested that 'it may be necessary to further subdivide regions'.[10]

Activities in Munster from the mid-1930s had given rise to a regional way of thinking there. The Limerick branch had taken the initiative and organised a Munster pairs championship in December 1937.[11] The allocation of the CBAI women's pairs championship (the Jackson Cup) to the city in the same year suggests the presence of a competent administration there. It was the first national competition to be held outside Dublin.

It seems strange to find Tipperary placed in Region No. 5 rather than in Munster. The explanation for this state of affairs lies in the fact that the players of Clonmel and Thurles, the leading bridge towns in the county, had more of an affinity with Waterford and the adjacent counties on the Leinster side and were taking part in the South-east Cup. Waterford, having more in common with closer neigbours, also remained outside of Munster.

Regionalisation had an immediate effect on participation in the national pairs. In January 1941, a majority of the twenty-two pairs in the final were from outside the capital. Places had been allocated as follows: Dublin area plus Region No. 2, ten pairs; Munster region, seven pairs; regions No. 1 and 3, three pairs; regions No. 4 and 5, two pairs.[12]

By 1941, the effects of the Emergency period were beginning to bite, especially with regard to travel, making organisation of regional qualifiers for national events impossible, except in Dublin and Munster. Things continued in the same vein throughout the wartime period. On 25 October 1947, the *Irish Independent* published new conditions for the pairs championship, for which the Davidson Cup had, by then, become the trophy. It was, the newspaper announced, 'the first year that regions, other than Munster, have taken a direct part in national championships'. Under new conditions, entry to the Davidson Cup was 'through finals of regional and Dublin pairs championships'. Places were allocated as follows: Dublin, five; Munster, five; regions No. 1, 2, 3 and 4, three each. Region No. 5 had disappeared altogether. Wexford had ben assimilated into Region No. 4, while Wicklow had become part of the Dublin Metropolitan area.

THE METROPOLITAN REGISTER

The Metropolitan Register, established in 1943,[13] was more or less a continuation of the original Dublin-based CBAI. It had developed into the first branch of the association, and its area of jurisdiction initially stretched from Portmarnock, in the north, to Dalkey, south of the city. The register was a list of members, within its boundaries, who wished to participate in CBAI competitions. The Dun Laoghaire branch of the association was subsumed into the metropolitan body, as was most of County Wicklow. It had become an elite group with disproportionate representation on the CBAI executive. At the 1948 AGM, six of the seven elected members of the executive were from Dublin: G. Commins, C. H. Day, Dr P. P. Donovan, F. T. Quin, Cleo Roy and R. Sheehan. The seventh, Joe Stanley, lived in Drogheda. That situation derived, perhaps, less from a bias in favour of Dublin players than from the convenience of having the executive members close to each other. Travel in immediate post-Emergency Ireland was a troublesome undertaking. Distance was an inhibiting factor when considering national office. Noel Byrne, who was elected honorary treasurer of the CBAI in 1951, relinquished the position when his bank transferred him to Carlow. Prominent officials of the CBAI were also at the helm of the Metropolitan Register. David Pigot, for example, was chairman of the executive committee of the former and president of the latter.

ADMINISTRATIVE AND STRUCTURAL CHANGES

A new affiliation system was introduced in 1946. This was the first change in the method of collecting revenue since the foundation of the association. A fee of one shilling per member replaced the old levies of five shillings for clubs with less than twenty members, and ten shillings for bigger clubs. It was not a popular change. The records of Wexford Bridge Club reveal how it was affected, and probably reflect how news of the increase was received throughout the country. With thirty-six members that year, Wexford's commitment to the CBAI went up to thirty-six shillings, from ten shillings the previous year – an increase of 260 percent. Following a debate at the AGM in October, the club decided to remain affiliated, but under protest.[14]

In return, club members, who were still regarded as mere associate members of the national body (and outnumbered registered players), were to be given a voice in the affairs of the association. Work on a new constitution began in 1946. It aimed to rectify the anomaly caused by the existence of branches as well as clubs, and especially the huge imbalance in power favouring the branches, which still provided the delegates to the AGM, which, in turn, elected the executive.

The draft constitution was approved at the CBAI's AGM in September 1947, to take effect from the day preceding the following year's AGM. The major changes were as follows: (a) associate members became full members; branches, in effect, became clubs; and membership was open to anyone who made direct application to the association; (b) new regional committees, to which clubs sent delegates, were to be formed. In addition, the regions would appoint delegates to the national executive.[15] The latter provision had not been a factor in the initial regionalisation in 1940.

RESIGNATIONS

Both the president, Joseph O'Neill, and vice-president, James E. Hogan, resigned shortly before the AGM of 1948. Hogan, a dental surgeon, had been president of the CBAI in 1937; he was the first man to be elected to the position after the three female founders had taken their turns in the highest office. He was the association's second vice-president, succeeding Harry Freehill in 1942, and retained the office until 1948. Hogan had been non-playing captain of Camrose teams in 1937. O'Neill was a leading personality from the foundation of the association and had played a prominent role in the Duplicate Bridge Control Board, the body which had initiated the home-international championship.

That such men should resign from the two highest positions in the association would indicate the existence of an issue of some magnitude. Their action resulted from their failure to secure the support of a special general meeting for a resolution to do with the new constitution.

Having been approved at the 1947 AGM, the constitution and rules came before a special general meeting on 10 July 1948. An article, which defined the business of the AGM, gave rise to debate. The AGM, according to the section in question, would (a) receive reports from the honorary officers, (b) elect a president and (c) appoint auditors. The rule went on to state that 'no resolution shall be proposed except such as may be directly related to (a), (b) and (c) above or such motion of sympathy, courtesy etc as the chairman may see fit to accept'.[16] Notices of motion could come only before special general meetings.

O'Neill, who had a major input into the drafting of the constitution, had, in his view, good reason for what seems, nowadays, a strange situation with regard to the AGM: that is, it would not take notices of motion. Throughout the 1940s, there had been few provincial representatives at AGMs: petrol was still scarce in 1948. As O'Neill saw it, the AGM 'is practically in the hands of Dublin members, who find it convenient to attend'.

He regarded the removal of notices of motion from the agenda of the AGM as a means of redressing the imbalance of power between Metropolitan and provincial members. He had a point: the entire CBAI executive had, from the foundation of the association, been comprised of Dublin-based members. The new constitution would remedy that flaw, but he knew that not many country delegates would travel to the capital for the AGM. In his opinion, a special general meeting, to which delegates would be more likely to travel – because they were 'special' – was the place for notices of motion. Of course, it was accepted that the AGM would be held in Dublin: there was relatively easy access to Dublin by rail and bus.

At the meeting of 10 July, an amendment to the constitution was adopted. 'Other business' was added as an item on the agenda of the AGM. The change, brought about by a thirty-two-to-twelve majority vote, seemed to broaden the opportunities for ordinary members to raise issues, but O'Neill saw it as consolidating the power of Dublin members.

Another special general meeting was held on 7 August, at which O'Neill moved a resolution, seconded by Hogan, to rescind the decision which had been taken on 10 July. The attendance at this meeting far exceeded that of the July meeting – a fact which adds weight to O'Neill's theory about special meetings. The issue took more than three hours to resolve. When it was put to the meeting, O'Neill and Hogan's motion was defeated by eighty-four votes to twenty-four. The president and vice-president regarded their failure to get the support of the association for what they saw as an issue that was vital to the democratisation process as being serious enough to warrant their resignations.

O'Neill, in the leading article in the *Irish Bridge Annual* that year, displayed a thorough grasp of the difficulties facing the association and the direction in which he thought it should go. He forecast problems. Expenditure had increased, from £208 in 1934 to £1,106 in 1947, and would continue to rise. Inflation for the period was minimal, so the increase was substantial. He observed that there was a limit to the amount of work that could be demanded from honorary officials. In 1940, the workload of the honorary secretary had increased to the extent that an assistant secretary was appointed. With a five-and-a-half- or six-day working week and long hours being the norm, people had little time to devote to voluntary work. By 1948, the workload had increased, and there was a new and costly commitment to European competition. O'Neill suggested that the acquisition of permanent offices, or at least office equipment, had become essential.

Along with the constitutional changes in 1948 there came another big increase in affiliation fees, from one shilling to half a crown per member. As had happened two years earlier, there was outcry in Wexford; if the debate there is anything to go by, there was heated discussion around the country. The 150 percent increase came on top of the 260 percent rise for that club only two years earlier. Wexford again considered whether it should remain affiliated to the national body. It decided to stay in but J. H. Daly,[17] the regional representative on the CBAI executive, was instructed to protest and to ask for a reduction.[18]

1948 REGIONAL BOUNDARIES

There was a major redrawing of boundaries in 1948. Midland and Munster, two huge geographical areas, were each divided in two, between north and south. Tipperary went back where it belonged, into Munster, and Donegal – which seems to have become 'bridge-minded' at last – augmented by clubs in Derry city and some players in Limavady,[19] became a separate entity.

In all, eight regions were created: North-midland, South-midland, North Munster, South Munster, Western, North-western, North-eastern and Northern. The Greater Dublin area continued to be governed by the Metropolitan Register. The Kelburne Cup competition took on a new format. It was still a knockout contest from start to finish, but for the first time one team came through from each region, the result of qualifying competitions. Incidentally, North-western was unable to field a team for this competition in 1949.[20]

THE NORTHERN IRELAND BRIDGE UNION

Bridge was as popular in Northern Ireland as it was in the Free State. During the 1920s, among the winners of the auction bridge quiz in the *Irish Times* were enthusiasts from Armagh, Belfast, Bangor, Enniskillen, Limavady and Omagh. The presence of a Belfast team in Dublin in April 1934 was a sign that the game was being played on an organised basis in the northern capital. In fact, that match may well have been a factor influencing northern players to form their own national governing body.

The NIBU was founded some time in the autumn of 1934. There is no official record of its beginnings, but its formation was referred to in both the *Irish Times* and the *Irish Independent.* Captain R. G. McCall, who was associated with the Culbertson International Bridge Studio, frequently lectured in Dublin. On one of those occasions, 8 October 1934, in Brown Thomas on Grafton Street, McCall told press reporters that Culbertson would like to see a contest between the Irish Free State and the Bridge Union of Northern Ireland, which had been 'recently formed'.[1]

A match between the NIBU and the CBAI duly took place over the weekend of 11 and 12 May 1935, at the Imperial Hotel, Belfast, with eight players from each side taking part in the first official meeting between the two bodies. All of the participants would become well known in the years that followed. Neither the length of the contest nor the score were recorded, but the NIBU, represented by Professor Alan McKinnon, Mrs Sephens, G. B. Hanna, E. Goldblatt, J. Davis, Tom Shanks, A. Fletcher and A. Frame, beat their southern opponents, Mrs Boles, Mrs Colgan, Mrs Lambert, Mrs McConkey, David and Violet Pigot, John P. Morgan and Charles O'Neill. The match had been arranged by NIBU honorary secretary George Allen, who, with his wife, had participated in the Dublin v. Belfast game held in April of the previous year.

In March 1936, a return match took place in Dublin. H. S. Lindsay[2] and H. G. Miles[3] were added to the NIBU squad, while the CBAI fielded a completely new line-up, consisting of E. O. Barry, P. Quinn, Dermot Murphy, T. O'Grady, H. L. Cowan, H. Freeman, Professor James and Mrs Maxwell Henry, H. G. Lindsay and H. Williams. The NIBU won the sixty-board encounter by 1,300 points.

By the following year, the home-international championships had been launched, and the annual match became part of the Camrose series.

INTERNATIONAL AFFAIRS – THE 1930s

The International Bridge League was founded, with Britain's Albert Edye Manning Foster as president, in Scheveningen, the Netherlands, on 10 June 1932, three months after the CBAI had been established. Ireland had no representation on the International Bridge League. Manning Foster, the bridge correspondent of *The Times* and publisher of *Bridge* magazine, had founded the British Bridge League[1] in 1931. The BBL was a commercial, non-elected and non-representative body to which some area associations in the UK gave their allegiance. With presumptuous effrontery, Manning Foster assumed the right to represent Great Britain and all of Ireland in the International Bridge League. Thus it came about that Ireland did not have representation in European championships in the 1930s, except insofar as Irish players might gain places on British teams. None did. Not surprisingly, more than a decade after the foundation of the Irish Free State, this was not acceptable to the CBAI.

THE DUPLICATE BRIDGE CONTROL BOARD

National bridge unions were formed in Scotland, Wales and Northern Ireland in 1934. Consequently, a demand arose for international competition. A meeting in Belfast in April 1936 drew up a draft scheme for a controlling body for the two islands. The national associations of the Irish Free State, Northern Ireland and Scotland were represented but English delegates in Belfast came from area associations in Yorkshire, London and the Home Counties, the north-east and the National Bridge Association (which did not represent all of England).[2] There was still no national governing body for bridge in England as such. Colonel Beasley, Lord Tollemache, Lady Milne, Colonel G. G. J. Walshe, Hubert Phillips and others had founded the National Bridge Association of Great Britain during the summer of 1933, as a rival to Manning Foster's organisation. However, the Irish and the Scots would not recognise either of those bodies as representing England. Colonel G. G. J. Walshe wrote in the *Sunday Times* on 30 May 1936:

> Scotland and Ireland insisted on preserving their national character to the extent that their relations should be with a united England and not with a number of English associations.

That insistence put pressure on interested parties in England to come together: they formed the English Bridge Union on 23 May 1936. It appears that National Bridge Association people were not averse to the new English national body. Hubert Phillips was involved in the English Bridge Union from the start. Delegates from the five home unions met in Liverpool on the same day, presumably immediately after the EBU's inaugural meeting, and adopted a constitution for a new federal body, the Duplicate Bridge Control Board (DBCB).[3] One of the aims of this body was to organise and regulate matches between the five unions. Another of its stated functions was 'the representation of Great Britain and Ireland upon such international bodies as may be recognised by the Board'. That was a direct challenge to Manning Foster's British Bridge League.

RIVAL ORGANISATIONS IN ENGLAND

The British Bridge League continued to dominate the game in England. The rivalry between it and the National Bridge Association was not just a conflict for power between controlling bodies but was also a battle for magazine sales: Manning Foster's *Bridge* magazine versus Phillips's *Bridge World*. The conflict, however, spilled over into the DBCB, and Ireland was reluctantly dragged into English affairs. The rivalry between the two British factions hindered the development not only of the English Bridge Union but also of the newly formed home-international organisation.

Indirectly, Ely Culbertson contributed to the problem. The American was anathema to Manning Foster and the English bridge establishment. He had shown them to be inept as organisers and inferior as players. Furthermore, anybody who showed the slightest partiality towards the

American was expelled. This included Phillips, who, in his magazine, was favourably disposed towards Culbertson's system, and wrote a preface to the London publication of the *Blue Book*.

Phillips made efforts during 1937 and 1938 to have the Duplicate Bridge Board of Control recognised by the International Bridge League, but without success.

CAMROSE

Constance Maxwell Henry and Joseph O'Neill represented the CBAI at a meeting of the DBCB held in Liverpool in January 1937, when it was resolved to run a home-international championship, to be decided on a round-robin basis. Whereas the result of each hundred-board match would be decided by cumulative total scores (international match points and victory points still lay in the distant future), the overall contest was decided by awarding two points for a win, and one for a tie. The first match was played at the Shelbourne Hotel, Dublin, on the weekend of 20 and 21 February 1937. The Irish Free State, represented by Kathleen Lambert, Geraldine McConkey, Kathleen Boles, Mrs Colgan, David Rivlin and Harry Fine, with James Hogan as non-playing captain, beat Scotland by 3,560 points.

A match between the Scots and the Irish had been planned before the new championship was launched. The previous November, the CBAI had invited Scotland to Dublin for a game before Christmas, but this was postponed. The CBAI held trials, when thirty-two players[4] 'who had distinguished themselves in competition' were selected to compete for places on the team to face its Scottish counterpart. The DBCB's decision to organise a championship simply raised the status of the already planned Ireland–Scotland encounter.

There was Irish optimism when the Free State and England, both unbeaten, met in the decider in Blackpool in October. However, the Irish players failed to make games, overbid to bad slams and, overall, performed poorly. England won by 2,830 points.

William Berry, the Right Honourable Viscount Camrose, proprietor of the *Daily Telegraph*, presented his trophy for the competition the following year.

Tensions

There were tensions on the board, but these were not, as might be expected, due to the CBAI's desire to go it alone in Europe: that fact was known to the neighbouring unions, and there was no serious disagreement on this point. It was the situation in England which gave rise to problems. The home-international championship had gone ahead only because the powerful 'bridge unions in England had composed their differences and agreed to submit to the control of a parent body, the English Bridge Union' (EBU).[5] In England, acceptance of the EBU as the parent body did not last long. It appears, from records of the eighth – and, as it turned out, last – meeting of the DBCB, held on 19 November 1938, that the EBU had by then, in effect, ceased to function. Phillips, in the chair, was the only English person present. The delegates – all but one of them men – were as follows:

> Scottish Bridge Union: Manson, McCurdie, McKerrow, Rowan;
> Contract Bridge Association of Ireland: Freehill, Quin, Mrs Maxwell Henry;
> Welsh Bridge Union: Perry, Lewis;
> Northern Ireland Bridge Union: Maver;
> English Bridge Union: no delegate.

Extant correspondence is revelatory. The Scots were unhappy with developments in England. They wanted Scotland, Wales, Northern Ireland and the Irish Free State to form a new board, to arrange a series of matches without England, and later to allow the British Bridge League to join on behalf of England – as soon as the BBL altered its constitution to the satisfaction of Scotland. The very idea of a Camrose series without England seems preposterous, but that is exactly what the Scots proposed. Following the meeting, Harry Freehill, in a letter to Joe O'Neill, indicated that he had adopted an aggressive attitude at an informal meeting with the Scots and had warned them that

> their plans did not meet with our wholehearted support. They would be unwise to count on our co-operation.

The letter ends:

> when we formed the Board we allied ourselves with Phillips and his crowd and I don't feel happy about deserting them.

Irish Compete for England's Pachebo

and Tollemache Cups

There was a close affinity between the CBAI and Phillips's National Bridge Association. Irish players competed in the NBA's Tollemache and Pachebo Cups.[6] In January 1938, E. O. Barry, Philip Quinn, Harry Fine and David Rivlin won their first-round match of the Tollemache; they subsequently travelled to Holyhead to meet a Liverpool team. There was a Dublin qualifying section for the Pachebo. In March 1938, Rivlin's team – probably the same four who had competed in the Tollemache – beat Dr Bethel Solomon in the section semi-final, the winners to meet E. Bruce Parker for the right to play in the final in London.[7] There are no records of Irish participation in those competions in other years, but they possibly took part in 1939. The close relationship between the respective governing bodies and the players started only the year before, with the Camrose matches. The following year, war put an end to all competitive bridge in Britain.

The English Bridge Union: A Phantom Organisation

By late 1938, it would appear that 'Phillips and his crowd' no longer represented the English Bridge Union. At the November meeting, Phillips expressed embarrassment at the absence of English delegates. Major J. Vaughan (England), the honorary secretary and treasurer, had resigned. There were financial problems. Welsh subscriptions were in arrears. Perry stated that the contributions for 1936–37 had been paid to Mr Lederer (England), from whom the money should be recovered. The EBU was also behind in its payment. Perry pointed out that it was known

> that the subscriptions of the EBU were paid directly by its constituent bodies and since at least three of these had seceded from the EBU it was reasonable to assume that the EBU had not the funds available to meet its obligations.

Scottish delegate McCurdie said that

> the SBU had held the opinion for a long time that the EBU was merely a phantom organisation and to all extents and purposes it was now defunct.

Perry supported that view. Phillips promised to take steps to have the EBU arrears paid. Phillips then announced that he found himself in an anomalous situation. He had not been a member of the EBU for the past year. Since he therefore could not be a delegate, his position as chairman was irregular. Freehill, having been elected to the chair, invited Phillips to remain at the meeting, he being the only link with English bridge.

McCurdie outlined three possible courses of action:

That the Board should expel the EBU and endeavour to find a really national English organisation which could be invited to join the Board;

That the EBU should resign gracefully, thus leaving the Board in a position to invite some really national English organisation to take its place;

That the Scottish, Welsh, Irish and Northern Irish should secede from the Board. (The object of this step would be to form another body which would incorporate at some later stage a representative English organisation.)

Freehill pointed out that the first course was unconstitutional and that the second was impracticable because of the absence of English delegates.

The meeting then transacted routine business so that a record would be available. F. T. Quin acted as secretary. Phillips gave an account of unsuccessful negotiations which he had had with the BBL on the question of the selection of teams to represent Great Britain and Northern Ireland. He seems to have assumed that the CBAI would want to be a separate entity on the international field.

Perry asked for instructions as to the disposal of the Camrose Trophy, which was in his possession. He was advised to retain possession of it until the conclusion of the current international series, by which time the future of the board would have been settled. The EBU was congratulated on being the first holder of the trophy. That belated felicitation, coupled with the fact that the trophy obviously had not been presented to the winners, and bearing in mind that this meeting took place in November 1938, more than a year after the first Camrose series of matches had been completed – as well as Phillips's admission that he had not been a member for the past year – all support the validity of

McCurdie's charge that the English Bridge Union was indeed a phantom organisation.

As to the future of the Board, Freehill faced the obvious and the inevitable:

> although the withdrawal of the SBU and WBU would be deplored, he felt that the Board would be a valueless body unless all the bridge organisations belonged to it. The CBAI would therefore relinquish membership should the Scottish and Welsh secede.

Maver, on behalf of the NIBU, made a similar statement. McCurdie told the meeting that the Scottish delegates had plenary powers, and he therefore formally announced that from that moment, the Scottish Bridge Union relinquished its membership of the Duplicate Bridge Control Board. Perry made a similar statement on behalf of the WBU. The Scottish and Welsh delegates retired from the meeting, and the Chairman adjourned the meeting *sine die*.

Harry Freehill, in a letter to Joe O'Neill, was angry about the outcome of the meeting:

> The Scottish bastards are happy. Having wiped out the board without consulting any of us . . . and I cannot but feel that while their view of the EBU is correct we are, to put it bluntly, selling them out . . . it sticks in my gullet.

It is interesting to read that the CBAI was England's closest ally. Nevertheless, the DBCB, the body which had first organised the Camrose, ceased to exist.

THE DUPLICATE BRIDGE BOARD OF THE

UNITED KINGDOM AND ÉIRE

After Rowan and Perry had investigated the position of the EBU, as requested by the board, it appeared that the board could be re-formed. The EBU was resuscitated and early in 1939 representatives of the five controlling bodies met in Liverpool, where it was agreed that the Duplicate Bridge Control Board was defunct but that a new body could be formed, with the assets to be transferred to the new organisation.

O'Neill, Perry and Stapleton Harris (England) were appointed to draft a new constitution. Printed headed notepaper of 'The Duplicate Bridge Board of the United Kingdom and Éire' shows F. E. Perry as honorary secretary, with an address at 35 West Bute Street, Cardiff. The new board had a brief existence. The Camrose went ahead in 1939, its schedule not affected by the problems within its governing body. In England, a power struggle was in progress. When that was finally settled, there would be a shift in the balance of the control of bridge in the two neighbouring islands.

MOBBS'S INITIATIVE

Mr A. Noel Mobbs, OBE (later to become Sir Noel), chairman of the Portland Club, succeeded Manning Foster as president of the British Bridge League in January 1939. At a general meeting of the BBL held at Bexhill in May 1939, he set out proposals for ending the rivalry between bridge organisations in England and aimed at unifying the administration of bridge for the two islands. Mobbs proposed that the BBL should become a federal body, replacing the existing Duplicate Bridge Board of the United Kingdom and Éire. Its president would be the chairman of the Portland Club (incidentally Mobbs himself) and it would have five vice-presidents, representing England, Scotland, Wales, Northern Ireland and Éire. This body would represent Great Britain and Ireland internationally and would be the supreme governing body on all matters of common interest. Each country would retain its own organisation; in England, that would be the English Bridge Union. The BBL would cease to have any national functions but would run the Camrose, international matches and the Gold Cup, which would be open to all five countries.

Following the Bexhill meeting, Mobbs took an initiative that forced events. He invited Stapleton Harris and Bearn (England), Perry (Wales) and Miles (Northern Ireland) to spend the second weekend in June at his home in Stoke Park, Slough, where he ran his extensive business interests. The object of the meeting was to work out the details of the merger between the DBB and the BBL. Harry Freehill, chairman of the DBB, was not invited, nor was anybody from the CBAI. In his letter to Miles, a copy of which still exists, Mobbs suggests that a full-time secretary might be appointed to the reorganised BBL and that this person might also act as secretary to the EBU.

NORTH–SOUTH COOPERATION

The close co-operation between Northern Ireland and the South in the 1930s comes across in the fact that, on receiving Mobbs's invitation, Harold Miles wrote to CBAI hononary secretary John Morgan on 31 May. Miles, interpreting the proposed merger of the DBB and the BBL as an absorption of the former by the latter, wanted to know, before he went to Slough, what the CBAI's position was on the question of the DBB. He asked directly if the CBAI, in the event of the merger of the DBB and the BBL, wanted separate membership of the International Bridge League.

On 5 June, Freehill replied to Miles's letter. He described the new proposals as a bombshell, although not surprising. He said that Miles's letter – and the report in *Bridge* magazine, which he received at the same time – was

> the first intimation we had that the SBU and the WBU were preparing to sell out the DBB, and us in particular.

Freehill saw the CBAI's exclusion from the informal meeting in Slough as 'exclusion from the BBL's family party'. He emphasised that the CBAI was 'still anxious to co-operate with the other countries in all matters of mutual interest'. He set down the CBAI's policy with regard to membership of the International Bridge League:

> we consider everyone of the five countries should individually be members of the IBL, but that for convenience and to avoid expense the Board should supply the delegates to the meetings of the IBL.

The view that England, Scotland, Wales, Northern Ireland and the Irish Free State should each have separate teams competing in European championships had been unacceptable to the other members of the old board – the DBCB – but the CBAI had accepted their stance. Regarding the new arrangement (that is, Mobbs's idea for a new BBL), Freehill did not regard it as being disadvantageous to the CBAI: 'subject to our right . . . to join the IBL separately and provided our rights in the Camrose Trophy are not threatened'.

He made the CBAI's position clear:

> We would not, in any circumstances, agree to be included in the new arrangements. . . . since we have built up our own organisation

71

without outside help of any sort, there is no reason why we should even consider accepting a subordinate position to the BBL, which has never done anything for bridge in this country.

Alluding to Mobbs's get-together in Slough, Freehill adds:

Since we have been so pointedly excluded from the new organisation, it is to be presumed that the BBL will not oppose our application for membership of the IBL.

He then asks Miles to secure a statement on this point from Mobbs. With regard to the Camrose:

As this was presented for competition among the five countries, it does not seem proper that its control should be given to a body which does not represent the five countries. As you point out, we have equal rights in the competition and do not require permission to take part. However, this is a matter for the DBB to decide before its dissolution.

All-Ireland Body Suggested

Freehill follows with a suggestion for an all-Ireland body – the first time the idea was articulated:

Would there be any chance of [an] Irish Bridge League meeting with approval up there? Such a body would, of course, have two constituent associations and would be mainly concerned with representing Ireland as a whole in internationals and in negotiations with other bodies. If approval were likely, this might be a good time to start discussions.

Meanwhile, Perry (Wales) and Stapleton Harris (England) together had written a letter to Joe O'Neill on 1 June enclosing a copy of a press report of Mobbs's speech at Bexhill. The letter is a reply to O'Neill's of 15 April, which no longer exists, and gets to the crux of the matter. England, Scotland, Wales and Northern Ireland would go along with Mobbs's proposal

principally because Scotland, Wales and Northern Ireland never really wanted or expected to be separately represented in any international tourney or on the International Bridge League.

Neither Perry nor Stapleton Harris saw a problem with the CBAI wanting separate representation internationally while at the same time continuing to participate in the Camrose:

> If the projected scheme makes progress, then the opportunity for Éire to compete in the Camrose must be provided for in any event.

In his rejoinder of 6 June, O'Neill is scathing in his attack on what he sees as 'a deep-laid plot to submerge the DBB and surrender to a commercial organisation'. 'It would seem,' he wrote, 'that the Welsh and the Scottish Associations are becoming specialists in breaking up Control Boards – this is the second one they are prepared to walk away from, without any consideration of their obligations to other members.' He was scornful of the willing acceptance of Mobbs's proposals: 'I am sure the national organisations are delighted they would be allowed to remain in control of their own country.' Although he emphasises that the views expressed are his own, he nevertheless did not have the slightest doubt 'about my association refusing to become a subsidiary body of the BBL'.

Harold Miles informed Perry on 6 June that the NIBU would not be sending a representative to Slough. He was surprised by the nature of the agenda, at a time when the constitution of the new DBB was still being drafted. He pointed out that Perry's interpretation of the CBAI's view on the matter was not accurate. Miles took 'the greatest exception to a manoeuvre to bring about such a result unconstitutionally, for example by exclusion of one of the five national bodies from full participation'.

Miles wanted any proposals which might be mooted at Slough to be put to a meeting of the DBB. He referred to a discussion with Manning Foster in December 1938, when he had got the definite impression that there was no question of an understanding being reached between the BBL and the DBCB except by the complete obliteration of the DBCB and the unquestioned acceptance of the BBL's terms. Miles is clear on the terms he would accept vis-à-vis the BBL: the constitution of the BBL must be changed to provide for its governance by representatives of the five national bodies, and he wanted

> every effort to be made to meet objections or modifications put forward by the CBAI in order to retain that very active and valuable Association within the Bridge Councils of these islands.

Assuming that Miles's letter reflected the official policy of the NIBU, this indicates the close affinity between the northern body and the CBAI at the time.

Meeting in the Shelbourne

A meeting of the DBB was called for the weekend of 15 and 16 July in Dublin. Perry, in a letter to Freehill on 14 June, thought the concept of the new BBL to represent a considerable advance towards the ideal of a unified control of bridge. He suggested that delegates might arrive in Dublin on the morning of 15 July for informal discussions preparatory to the official meeting the following day. There were two items on the agenda:

(a) To receive a report from the Constitution Sub-Committee (Stapleton Harris, O'Neill and Perry)

(b) To receive a report of the offer made by the British Bridge League to merge their activities with the five national bodies.

In further correspondence with Freehill dated 19 June, Perry mentions that neither he nor anyone else in Wales had had any contact with the BBL directly or indirectly in the last twelve months. He thought that the same situation applied to Scotland. No proposals by Mobbs had been put to any country, except perhaps England, before they were invited to Slough. He admitted to knowing the probable proposals, having heard them second-hand from Stapleton Harris. Those who had been invited to Slough were to submit Mobbs's proposals to their respective councils and in turn express views at a meeting of the board.

Freehill's reply to this letter on 4 July shows that Mobbs's failure to invite someone from the CBAI still rankled, but he indicated that Perry's letter told a very different story from that of Mobbs's speech as reported in *Bridge* magazine and in various letters which had passed between O'Neill, Mobbs, Perry and Miles.

On 7 July, Perry circulated a report preparatory to the meeting in Dublin on 15 July. Covering the period of the old DBCB as well as the DBB, it admits that at the end of 1938 the only important activity of the board was the Camrose. It refers to Mobbs's speech at Bexhill, informal meetings between Mobbs and representatives of the EBU, and Mobbs's personal invitation to Miles, Rowan,[8] Perry, Bearn and Stapleton Harris to Slough. Mobbs's proposals formulated at Slough are recorded:

> That the Countries should approve of one Central Body to act for Duplicate Bridge in the same way as Cricket, Rugby, Tennis or Golf are controlled by their respective organisations, and that as far as England is concerned there should be only one authority in England.

> As regards the 'National Body' in England, the BBL (as operating in the past) would cease to exist.

> The EBU would take over all internal activities previously carried out by the BBL.

> That the Constitution which Harris, Perry and O'Neill were preparing for submission to the other countries should be revised to comply with the following:

> 1. The name of the Control Board shall be the British Bridge League (and thus permit its association with the IBL and with America to continue without any break).

> 2. The DBB (renamed BBL) shall be controlled by
>   Chairman: nominated by the Portland Club
>   Committee: England 4, Scotland, Wales, Northern Ireland, Éire, 2 each.

> 3. The new BBL would probably run the Gold Cup and two Congresses, open to the five countries, the benefit accruing therefrom to be for funds for the BBL.

> 4. A full-time paid secretary would probably be appointed with offices in London, part salary paid by the BBL and part by the EBU. Comdr. Foote and Mr Cecil Lane have been mentioned as possible Secretaries.

> 5. Each country retains full authority to control its internal affairs being subject only to the governing body in matters which cannot be classed as internal domestic affairs.

Perry then suggests that the principal objects of the meeting in Dublin should be

To receive any further explanations which may be required;

To consider the proposed Constitution;

If the Constitution is approved in principle, to authorise Mr Noel Mobbs to have the position confirmed by the old Council of the BBL and by the Card Committee of the Portland Club.

Mobbs wrote to Harry Freehill on the day on which Perry circulated his report. He conceded

> that the new constitution proposed for the British Bridge League can hardly be likely to be as satisfactory to Éire as it is to the other Contract Bridge Associations. . . . I was advised that there was no possibility of Éire agreeing to become a member of the British Bridge League.

Later in the letter, he states:

> I could, I feel sure, get the International Bridge League to agree to Éire having separate representation on the League, if the present arrangement by which the British Bridge League represents the whole of Great Britain and Ireland were cancelled.

So when the meeting of the DBB was held in the Shelbourne Hotel on 15 July, Manning Foster's old 1931 British Bridge League was about to be consigned to the history books and a new body of the same name, with democratically elected delegates, but which would exclude the CBAI, was virtually a fait accompli. The CBAI's right to participate in the Camrose was not in question, and even Mobbs saw no obstacle to the CBAI obtaining separate representation on the International Bridge League. As far as European championships went, the NIBU, however, could compete only as part of a UK team.

That was in mid-July. The lazy days of late summer and the holiday season followed. On 1 September, Hitler's armies marched into Poland. That changed everything.

11

THE 1940s

There are no extant CBAI or NIBU records for much of the 1940s, so there are gaps in the available information on bridge in Ireland during these years. Scarcity of paper supplies and the consequent reduction in the size of newspapers – the *Irish Times*, for example, was reduced to four pages for much of the period – resulted in a reduced amount of news on bridge, although, fortunately, the *Irish Independent* chronicled a number of important developments.[1] Despite transport restrictions, bridge players were extremely active. Many local and regional cup events, as well as congresses, had their origins during those years, and national championships were held in various parts of the country.

During July 1942, on Friday evenings, Noel Peart, a leading bridge player and barrister, had a weekly fifteen-minute *Bridge Talk* programme on Irish radio. In September of the following year, he broadcast an account of a match between North and South, and there was a programme entitled *Build Up Your Bridge*, almost certainly presented by Peart too, around that time. Of course, few people owned a radio, and programmes were aimed squarely at the middle classes. Producers of the time obviously considered bridge to be a topic that would attract listeners.

The Second World War altered the courses of many lives and left permanent reminders of the time in at least one Irish bridge club. In 1940, a Danish ship, the *Liliana*, docked in Drogheda port and had to remain there for the duration of the war. The captain, C. Hjortmar, and the first mate, Farup-Gregerson, were welcomed into the Gate Club, where they played regularly during their enforced sojourn in the town. At the end of the war, when they were leaving, the two men, to show their appreciation for the kindness of the members, donated two trophies, the Viking Cup for a pairs competition, the Danish Cup for an individual contest. The latter trophy is now awarded annually to the Gate's player of the year.[2]

By the start of the decade, auction bridge was losing ground to contract. Duplicate had become established for competitive tournaments, although rubber was still the standard game. The battle for system supremacy had hardly begun, and Acol had not yet had an impact on Culbertson. The variety of bidding systems used in the semi-final of the inter-club championship between Athlone and Dublin's Carlton Club, in August 1940, is indicative of the widespread experimentation with new methods that was talking place at this time. The Athlone pair, Miss Geoghegan and Miss Cullen, used Dr Paul Stern's Vienna system.[3] Their teammates, Mr and Mrs Cohen, played Acol, while the Carlton players, Ina McMenamin, Frances Morgan, E. O. Barry and Philip Quinn, employed the two-club method with Acol variations.

A number of leading Irish players wrote bridge books. Ina Hickey and Noel Peart collaborated on *Modern Contract Bridge, Bidding Made Easy*, published in 1944.[4] Around the same time, Peart launched another slender volume, *Sixpence a Hundred*. Superintendent Charles B. Heron wrote *The Heron Club System of Contract Bridge*, published in 1947,[5] and Harry Freehill's *The Squeeze at Bridge* (mentioned in Chapter 37), came out in 1949.[6] Dorothy Peart remembers her then young fiancé's efforts at writing. 'He did it to make some money,' she freely admitted. 'As a young barrister, after paying his train fare and hotel bill there wasn't much left of his fee when he came home.' It is unlikely that any of the authors made much from their literary efforts.

Heron, a Garda superintendent stationed in Balbriggan, had developed a new bidding system. While it did not attract a wide following, it helped him and Mrs Heron to win back-to-back Kelburne Cups in 1949 and 1950.[7] The Heron Club was not a strong club system. You opened 1♣, holding only certain narrow-ranged hands: eleven or eleven and a half high-card points and less than thirteen suit points, which were calculated by the length of the trump suit. Much of the theory concerning suit openings, over-calls, strong-hand bidding, and so on, was standard.

It is when he deals with psychic bidding that Heron surprises the modern reader. 'Psychic bids,' he writes, 'are for the expert . . . as they require understanding between partners.' The very idea of partnership understanding on psyches is anathema to present-day players. Psychic bids are not illegal, but partnership understanding about them certainly is. That was not the case in the 1940s.

IMPORTED FROM LONDON

Ideas travelled fast, especially in the immediate post-war world. A report, published in the *Irish Times* on 12 November 1946, of the Ireland v. Scotland Camrose match, included the following:

> J. C. H. Marx . . . has recently produced a series of artificial bids . . . to explore . . . a major suit contract after an opening bid of 1NT.

The article featured a deal in which a response of 2♣ to a 1NT opening bid asked if partner held a four-card major. We recognise the bid as 'Stayman'. However, Sam Stayman did not create the convention that bears his name. It was devised in the USA by his partner, George Rapee, but around the same time, Jack Marx, in London, came up with a similar idea. Stayman was the first to write about the new convention – in *Bridge World* (Culbertson's magazine) in June 1945 – and his name stuck to it. By late 1946, the convention was being used by tournament players in Ireland, but the idea had been imported from London, not the United States.

DONEGAL AND COLONEL BEASLEY

Jack Marx was not the only Englishman to influence Irish players. In around 1940–41, Dr Joseph Ward, the County Registrar for Donegal, and an enthusiastic bridge player, picked up a copy of *The Beasley Contract Bridge System*. Ward digested the book's contents and decided to preach the Beasley gospel in Raphoe. It spread over the County Donegal. The Beasley in question was the same Colonel Henry Mountifort Beasley, DSO, who had played against Culbertson in London in 1930 and who had been a member of Buller's team in the CBAI's first representative match in November 1932. The founder of Crockford's, one of London's more sophisticated card-playing clubs, his contribution to bridge was significant. In 1905, just as the new game of auction bridge was reaching the United Kingdom, he had written *London Bridge and How It Is Played*, which is described as having made a major contribution to the technical development of the game.[8] An expert player, he won the British Bridge League's inaugural Gold Cup in 1932. He was bridge correspondent for the *Daily Mail*; it was the Lord Northcliffe-owned Associated Newspapers that, in 1935, published the work that fired Joe Ward's enthusiasm.

Donegal was not the only, nor indeed the first, place in Ireland where Beasley found disciples. A March 1938 report in the *Kerry Champion*[9] stated that Messrs McGillicuddy and Hilliard, winners of the weekly competition in Tralee, used the Beasley system. Presumably, since McGillicuddy lived in Killarney, it was known there too.

The essential difference between Beasley and many other systems is that no simple response to a one-level suit opening bid is forcing. Responder with more than ten points has to jump the bidding. According to accepted modern wisdom, the system is inefficient and outdated, a relic of times past. But it is still used to good effect by some of Donegal's best players. As recently as 2000 and 2001, Denis Ellis and John Joe Doherty won back-to-back IBU inter-club pairs championships using Beasley. Donegal may well be the only place in the world where the system is still regularly, and profitably, employed.

New Clubs

New clubs were appearing all over the country. Mullingar and Navan had already formed as the decade began, and the game was popular with members of the Donaghmore Club in Clonmel and in Wicklow Lawn Tennis Club. Carrickmacross was founded in 1941, Nenagh in 1942, Blackrock (Dublin) in 1944. The creation of the Civil Service Club resulted from an advertisement that was placed in the *Irish Times* on 7 November 1946, inviting civil servants who played to meet at 15 Harcourt Street the following Sunday. Across the border in Newry, during the winter of 1944/45, Mrs Blaney, wife of the town surveyor, Charles Blaney, and Mrs J. H. Collins, wife of a solicitor, invited Geraldine McConkey, then living in Dundalk, to give lectures on the Acol system to rubber-bridge players in the town. From that nucleus, a club was formed in February 1945. The fact that bridge was still a popular pastime among military people is evident from the founding of a club in Collins Barracks, Cork, in 1947 and from the presence of one in the Curragh Camp.

The origins of the game in Clonmel are obscure although, given Clonmel's status as a garrison town, it is fair to assume that British army personnel played a part in its introduction there. In the early 1940s, there was a good standard of play in that part of south Tipperary. Donaghmore, although not primarily a bridge club, nevertheless had good players and made a heroic effort in the inter-club championship of 1941, almost pulling off an act of giant-killing. E. G. Ryan, J. F. Jennings, A. H. O'Sullivan and T. O'Brien came through the early knockout rounds, beat Athlone in the semi-final, and faced the might of Portmarnock Golf Club – Des and Gerry Purcell, Frank McMenamin and C. Casey – in the forty-eight-board decider at the Hibernian Hotel in Portlaoise. However, Donaghmore proved to be no match for the Dublin players. Clonmel Bridge Club also made a valiant effort to win a major title that year, when Dr and Mrs Russell, Mrs Binchy and Mrs Reidy won through to the final of the Kelburne Cup, only to lose to virtually the same team that had beaten Donaghmore. (The Dublin side that beat Clonmel was arguably stronger than the one that had beaten Donaghmore, with Ina Hickey having replaced Casey.)

EDDIE BURKE AND NENAGH

Eddie Burke, principal of the town's primary school,[10] was the driving force behind bridge in Nenagh. An athletic man, he is reputed to have once taken legendary amateur golfer Joe Carr to the twenty-first hole in the South of Ireland golf championship.[11] He had a talent for art too, studying painting under Seán Keating, and had an abiding interest in archaeology: he was cited in at least one learned journal for his part in the excavation work on the neolithic site at Ardcroney.[12]

Bridge was a life-long passion of Burke's. His wife, Eimer (née Walsh), played too, having come from a card-playing family in Tulla, County Clare. Her cousin, Augusta Murphy, also from Clare, came to teach in Portroe in 1939. At weekends, she cycled to the Burkes' home in Nenagh, and another teacher, Roddy Bent, was invited over on Saturday nights, when the four would play bridge. They must have been enjoyable evenings – bridge being secondary to Eimer and Eddie's efforts to play cupid to the two unattached young people – but Nenagh bridge club evolved from those Saturday-night games.

There were other bridge enthusiasts in the town, including Nellie Herriott from the chemist's shop; Mr McNaughton, an engineer with the county council; and Mrs Ryan, who owned O'Meara's Hotel. Eddie Barry, one of the country's top players, came to work at the Munster and Leinster Bank in Nenagh in July 1940. When he married a few months later, his wife, Grace, who was also a fine player, further enhanced the standard of the game in the town. Burke soon had the nucleus for a club. In 1942, he wrote to a friend in Dublin, Tom Boden,[13] to find out what methods were in use in the capital. Boden sent on the fundamentals of the relatively new Acol system.[14] Burke invited the known players to O'Meara's Hotel in September: Nenagh Bridge Club was up and running. Among the attendees on the first night were the Burkes, the Barrys, Roddy Bent, Augusta Murphy, Mrs Ryan, her sister-in-law Bridie Ryan, Nelly Herriott, Mr McNaughton, Barney Stewart, a bank official, and Mr Forde, manager of the maltings mill.[15]

For the record, the Burkes' efforts at matchmaking failed. Augusta married Daniel Shouldice, gave up her teaching job, became part of the Shouldice business in Portroe, and later ran the post office until she retired in 2003 at the age of eighty-three.[16] She died in 2007.

Eddie Burke's contribution to the development and spread of the game in north Tipperary was enormous. For years, he travelled the county teaching classes. He solved the problem of integrating beginners with established players by setting up new clubs following series of lessons. His name lives on in the Burke Cup – the trophy for the IBU's inter-county championship.

CONGRESSES

Although the CBAI organised congresses in Dun Laoghaire in 1937, 1938 and 1939, the congress is really a development of the 1940s. Galway's West of Ireland congress is the oldest in the country. There are conflicting claims about the year of its origin. The 1948 *Irish Bridge Annual* states that it was first held in 1940, whereas the *Irish Bridge Journal* of March/April 1959 claims: 'This year's congress will be our twenty-first'. If true, this would place the first one in 1939. The congress committee's own brochure in recent years would indicate that 1939 is correct: the brochure for 2008 advertised the seventieth running of the event. However the *Irish Independent*, on 5 April 1941, carried notice of 'the second annual West of Ireland congress' about to take place. On 14 April 1941, the *Irish Times* carried the results from 'the second annual West of

Ireland congress, which opened in the Great Southern Hotel on Saturday'. Furthermore, the 1940 event was promoted as 'Ireland's first provincial congress'.[17] The first was held over Whit weekend, 10–12 May 1940, when Ina Hickey, Frank McMenamin and the Purcell brothers, Des and Gerry, won the team event.[18]

Mrs Cross, who conceived the idea for the congress and donated the cup for the team competition,[19] planned to bring over English international players, but the war led to this idea being shelved.[20] Nevertheless, some London players did take part in 1940.[21] J. Henry Daly, whose banking career led him to many parts of the country and who played an important role in promoting bridge wherever he went, was congress secretary. Unlike the CBAI congress in Dun Laoghaire, Galway's organisers did not permit wartime difficulties to hinder its continuity. The second West of Ireland congress, in 1941, was held at Easter. It has had venue problems over the years but it continues annually at Easter to this day.

The Regent Club in Dublin organised a September congress at its premises in Harcourt Street from 1940 to 1946. It attracted widespread support from the provinces.

The East of Ireland congress was first held at Greenore over the Whit weekend of 1942.[22] When she went to live in Dundalk, Geraldine McConkey[23] breathed new life into competitive bridge in the area. She became secretary of the congress, which attracted such large crowds that it outgrew the Greenore venue and moved to Dundalk in 1945 – where the congress was held around St Patrick's Day. The date was moved back to the Whit weekend in 1948, and it went to Ballymascanlon for a while during the 1960s before making its final return to Dundalk. When the public holiday was fixed at the first Monday in June, it kept that date until 2007, when in was put back to November.

The South of Ireland congress in Killarney, which dates from 1944, was the brainchild of Dr T. P. Magnier of Fermoy, who had been elected president of the CBAI the previous year. Magnier, inspired by the successes of the West of Ireland and East of Ireland ventures, felt that the south should have a showpiece congress too. Some Munster people saw Cork as the obvious venue but the Fermoy-based doctor, conscious of the tourism potential of the event, fixed his eye on Killarney. He put his plan to Dr Eamonn O'Sullivan, resident medical superintendent of St Finian's Psychiatric Hospital. Dr O'Sullivan was quite a hero in County Kerry: he had successfully trained all-Ireland-winning football teams and had been instrumental in developing Fitzgerald Football Stadium and Killarney Golf Club. He was a man who got things done – and was the dominant figure in Killarney Bridge Club.[24]

Together, Magnier and O'Sullivan formed an ambitious plan for a nine-day event aimed at attracting cross-channel visitors. In 1944, travel from abroad was impossible, but the following year eight British visitors attended. By the third running of the congress, in 1946,[25] overseas visitors were sufficiently numerous to facilitate the addition of a novel unscheduled team contest to the programme: a match between Irish and visiting players, the latter coming from all over Britain – England, Scotland and Wales. Even the Irish side included visiting players: E. T. C. and P. V. M. Cotter and Colonel George Walshe, all of whom were Irish-born but living in London.[26]

From the start, the South of Ireland congress adopted a festival atmosphere. One session of bridge a day – 8 PM to midnight, originally – allowed time for fishing, golf or sightseeing. Close of play each night was followed by impromptu entertainment. The congress, which was initially an autumn festival, moved to June in 1948. The original format, with its emphasis on fun and friendliness, has been retained, giving the Killarney congress a unique quality which continues to attract numerous contestants from abroad.

Competitors from England and Scotland took part in NIBU congresses in Portrush in 1945, Belfast in 1946 and Newcastle, County Down, in 1947. Rosslare's first congress took place over the Whit weekend of 1946.

Dr Joseph P. Brennan obtained the support of the Dun Laoghaire Borough Corporation and Business Men's Association for a congress to be held in the Royal Marine hotel from 1 to 6 October 1947. This congress, like the one in Killarney, attracted cross-channel competitors. By the time the second congress came around the following year, Brennan had become an important public figure, having been elected to the Dáil. He used his new-found influence well. Among the speakers at the opening of the congress in Dun Laoghaire town hall were the Minister for Foreign Affairs and leader of Brennan's party, Seán McBride; Lord Rugby, the UK representative in Ireland; future Taoiseach Liam Cosgrave, then a parliamentary secretary (junior minister); and Sean McEntee, representing the opposition.

OPEN CUP COMPETITIONS

A number of open cup competitions have their origins in the late 1930s and early 1940s. The Father Doris Cup, named after one of the founders of Ardee Bridge Club, was on the calendar by 1941.[27] The McQuillan Cup, played in Drogheda, was also a popular competition. In Limerick, the Thomond Cup, for the Munster pairs championship, was virtually on a par with national competitions: the winners and runners-up qualified for the national panel test. The Lady Bellew Cup in Kilkenny, the Jessop Cup in Portlaoise, the Stafford Cup in Wexford, the Red Island Cup in Skerries and the Connacht Cup, organised by the Strandhill club in Sligo, all became well-supported competitions during the decade.[28]

Imaginative strategies were devised to circumvent wartime travel difficulties. In May 1941, twenty-six teams from clubs in Counties Kildare, Laois, Kilkenny, Tipperary and Waterford took part in a competition by post. Twenty-one boards were dealt by CBAI officials in Dublin and sent to the participating clubs, where the boards were opened at the commencement of the matches. This was the first of a number of simultaneous events held during the Emergency period – an approach forced upon organisers by the circumstances of the times. If the players could not come to the competitions, the competitions would go to the players. Towards the end of 1942, Drogheda and Ardee Bridge Clubs ran their respective McQuillan and Father Doris Cup competitions in similar manners. Score sheets were sent to CBAI headquarters, where the winners were determined. Clubs in Ardee, Ballybofey–Stranorlar, Carrickmacross, Drogheda, Dublin, Dundalk and Tullamore took part in the Father Doris Cup, without having to walk – or cycle (there was no petrol for cars) – farther than their own clubs. The winners were Dr Moran and J. C. Kieran (Ardee).[29] The Drogheda contest, for which T. C. O'Gorman[30] received the entries, also attracted contestants from far and wide; it was won by P. V. Carson and W. O'Leary (Wexford).

Major championships left the capital and were held in a number of different venues, including the Revington in Cork in March 1941,[31] the Spiro in Ennis in November of the same year,[32] and in Drogheda in November 1943.[33] The fact that a sufficient number of players were willing to undertake long, cold train journeys, together with the core of local competitors, ensured the success of those competitions.

There are examples of withdrawals from national competitions due to travel difficulties. Ennis and Longford, for instance, pulled out of the inter-club championship in 1942.[34] John Morgan, in his CBAI honorary secretary's report in 1944, recorded that 'growing city membership compensated for enforced absence of those who were unable to compete owing to lack of transport facilities'. Serious disruption of competitions was occasioned by the 'big snow' of 1947. The fixtures affected included Kelburne Cup matches in the south, and in March a Grattan (Galway) v. Tullamore match had to be cancelled.

VARIETY OF CBAI CHAMPIONSHIPS

During the 1940s, an imaginative variety of championship events was staged. The Wigoder Cup continued as a team-of-four league, with entries divided into sections, leading to knockout play-offs. Although the CBAI was committed to promoting duplicate, it introduced a rubber-bridge, knockout team-of-four championship during the 1941/42 season, for which Roddy Carroll, a native of England living in Dublin, donated a trophy. The Carroll Cup had a fate resembling that of the Wigoder and was last contested as a national competition in 1958.

Individual competitions were popular. In fact, there were two individual championships staged by the CBAI. An open-entry event – first played in 1933, when Gertie McMeekin won – continued annually until 1947, when the future international Babs Hooper took the title. Kathleen Lambert donated a cup for the competition in 1942. When the individual contest was dropped from the calendar, the cup was awarded to the winners of the secondary-pairs championship, which had been initiated in 1944. This championship was open to all except the top finishers in the national pairs championship and recent winners of major cups. This was the pre-master-point era, hence the title 'secondary pairs'. Nowadays, entry to the Lambert cup is limited by master-point holding.

Another individual championship, for the Davidson Challenge Cup, was introduced during the 1941/42 season. To ensure the highest possible standard, it was confined to winners and runners-up in the main CBAI pairs and team events, as well as the first five in the national individual competition. The Thomond Cup in Munster also qualified pairs for the new super-individual competition. The Davidson Challenge Cup was contested for only three seasons: it was won in the inaugural year by

Fred Quinn and in the two years following by Charlie O'Neill and Harry Day. In 1944/45, the trophy, donated by Andrew H. Davidson, was diverted to the national pairs championship.

A once-off championship event was organised by the CBAI in 1942, 'in order to compensate provincial clubs for the temporary abandonment of their regional pairs championships'. Each affiliated club entering the competition arranged its own eliminator, after which it sent representatives to compete in a national final on 22 November.[35] The winners of the event, held at the Central Hotel in Dublin, were Geraldine McConkey and Mrs McHugh (Dundalk). Among the particiapting clubs were three from Donegal: Stranorlar, Buncrana and Letterkenny. This is an indication of how quickly the county had become organised: two years earlier, it did not have a single affiliated club. Dublin clubs were excluded, as the competition aimed 'to compensate provincial clubs'.

COLONEL WALSHE CUP

International competition was suspended for the duration of the war but the CBAI continued to hold panel tests – the equivalent of modern trials – entry to which was by performance in the major championships. Although war raged across Europe and around the world, there was the continuing hope that the conflict might end and that normal international relations would be resumed. The only representative competition possible was one between the CBAI and the NIBU. The first such wartime match took place in March 1943, at 20 Merrion Square, Dublin, when the visitors, Professor A. McKinnon, Norah McKee,[36] Professor B. L. Lloyd, E. Goldblatt, W. McCallum and B. Vard, beat their southern opponents, May McNulty, Dr A. H. Davidson, E. O. Barry, Philip Quinn, C. H. (Harry) Day, P. Powell, Mrs Ina Hickey and Dr Frank McMenamin, by 1,560 points over a hundred boards.

The following September, a return match, which the NIBU also won, took place at the Grand Central Hotel in Belfast. An account of this match was broadcast on Radio Éireann by Noel Peart on 30 September. On 11 and 12 November 1944, the NIBU defeated the CBAI by 600 points at Dublin's Royal Hibernian Hotel. The following year, the match officially became an annual affair when Colonel G. G. J. Walshe donated a cup for the contest, between the respective team champions of north and south. The winners of the Kelburne Cup represented the CBAI. The competition continued until 1950, when cordial relations between the neighbouring associations were suspended. The Colonel Walshe Cup is now awarded to the winners of the annual Camrose match between the two associations.

The results of those encounters suggest that at that time there was a better standard of play north of the border. Of the nine matches played between 1943 and 1950, the NIBU won eight to the CBAI's one – and that one by a margin of only 420 points. All matches were over a hundred boards, except the 1948 meeting, which was reduced to eighty-four because of a late start.

The 1948 defeat was particularly painful for the southern players. With one deal remaining, the CBAI led by 1,780 points. On the last board, Drew Davidson, when his right-hand opponent opened the bidding with 1♠, overcalled 2♦, holding K Q 7 x x x in the suit. When his partner, May McNulty, bid hearts, he bid his anaemic diamonds again. McNulty bid 3NT, which was doubled, and Davidson removed the unbeatable game to 4♦, which was doubled, and went for –800. Unfortunately, Davidson ignored his ♣ A J 8 x on the second round. His partner held ♣ K Q 10 x. Goldblatt and Gordon bid and made six clubs at the other table, for an aggregate of +2,170 for the NIBU on the board. Truly, the unfortunate Davidson snatched defeat from the jaws of victory.

In 1949, a 'junior' contest – perhaps 'B' international might be a more accurate term – was added to the cross-border meetings. In 1950, Bertie Vard presented a cup, won by George and Sheila Doyle and J. Henry and Helen Daly (CBAI), after four extra boards. The Vard Cup was never contested again.

Despite increasing political tension between the two divided jurisdictions during the war years, the bridge-playing fraternity maintained friendly relationships. There was a great deal of cross-border inter-club activity. For example, in the early 1940s members of Monaghan Bridge Club frequently travelled across the border to play Enniskillen in the RAF officers' mess.[37]

12

POST-WAR INTERNATIONAL ACTIVITIES

The Camrose resumed in March 1946 under the auspices of the new British Bridge League: Northern Ireland defeated the CBAI at the Royal Marine Hotel, Dun Laoghaire. In Stockport in November, Ina McMenamin, T. D. Purcell, the Bastow brothers, Jimmy and Bobby, and the Cork father-and-son partnership, Bill and Barry O'Connell, with Dr P. J. O'Dowd as non-playing captain, recorded the CBAI's first victory over England.

The CBAI faced England again at Dublin's Central Hotel in May of the following year, when Dermot Egan and Ina McMenamin became the first and only brother-and-sister combination to play on an Irish team, although not in partnership. The English had a score to settle. The defeat in Stockport the previous November still rankled, even though it did not prevent them from winning the Camrose. The CBAI led by 640 after the first session. A vulnerable game swing could turn that around. Starting the last period, England led by thirty points: a mere overtrick in a major-suit contract would level it. Neither P. J. O'Dowd nor C. H. St Ingram, the respective captains, were pleased with their players' performance. The Bastow brothers doubled 2♠, made by the English declarer, and also missed two games. For England, Boris Schapiro and Adam 'Plum' Meredith bid a hopeless 3NT, down four. The Irish led by 550 points. O'Dowd sent in Ina McMenamin and Des Purcell to join Eddie Barry and Dermot Egan for the last eight boards. England's captain took more drastic action, splitting the offending partnership. Schapiro was paired with Terence Reese. It is claimed that this was the first time that Reese and Schapiro had played as a pair in international competition.[1] (The two men were among the best players in the world and went on to achieve fame – and court infamy – during their long careers.) When the last board had been played, England was ahead by 1,950 points.

IRELAND IN EUROPEAN CHAMPIONSHIPS

The Emergency period[2] represented merely an inconvenient interruption to the CBAI's efforts to achieve recognition in Europe. Thanks mainly to the efforts of Harry Freehill and Joseph O'Neill, Ireland's place on the European stage had been assured in 1939, its entrance merely postponed by the war.

In January 1947, informal talks were held in London with a view to restarting European competition. In the aftermath of the war, there were difficulties to be overcome before agreement could be reached on the constitution of the new international body. British delegates did not want their enemies in the recent conflict to be part of such a body. There was a positive outcome from the London meeting, as far as the CBAI was concerned. Joe Stanley,[3] its delegate to the conference, reported that the CBAI would be accepted in whatever new European body would emerge. Scotland and Wales would not. Following an international convention in Copenhagen in April, the CBAI received a formal invitation to join the European Division of the International Bridge League, the body which later became the European Bridge League.

COPENHAGEN

Participation in the first post-war European championships in Copenhagen should have been an occasion for celebration, but it was marred by controversy over team selection. The CBAI decided to enter for the open championship but not for the women's competition.

What seems astounding to the modern player is that the team was not comprised of regular partnerships. John Burke, Dermot Egan, Ina McMenamin and Noel Peart had all won their way, through competition, on to the national panel, but none of their respective partners were select-ed. Neither Paddy Carson from Wexford nor Geraldine McConkey had even qualified for the panel. No two of the six players were regular part-ners. Selecting players as individuals, however, was not unusual at that time; the practice continued well into the 1950s. The failure to appoint a non-playing captain probably points to a lack of finance.

Questions were raised about team selection. At the AGM in September, when the championships were over, John Lane from Skerries commented that 'the best team did not travel . . . only those . . . who could best afford it'. In the press coverage of the event, there was another hint of controversy, concerning the youngest member of the team, twenty-two-year-old John Burke from Clonmel, a student at Trinity College. On 2 July, Philip Quinn wrote in the *Irish Times*: 'The outstanding player in the Irish team was J. G. Burke, about whose selection there were some misgivings.' Quinn praised Ina McMenamin for coping with the burden of being player and captain. Nothing was written about the other players. No words were needed. The team finished eighth of the ten participating nations. Neither Germany nor Italy took part, although Italy competed the following year.

In one respect, the Irish team caused a sensation in Copenhagen. At that time, it was unheard of for women to play in the open championship. Ireland had two women on its team, and one of them was the captain.

In 1949, the selectors woke up to the fact that there were more than two talented women players in Ireland. Geraldine McConkey, Elvina Spiro, Ina McMenamin, Moreen McCarthy, Eileen O'Sullivan and May McNulty, with non-playing captain Cleo Roy, went to Paris, where they came fifth out of the nine competing nations – a better performance than that of the open team, which finished last out of eleven.

Ina McMenamin, Geraldine McConkey and Elvina Spiro are the only women to have played on both an Irish open and a women's team in European or world championships. McMenamin and McConkey achieved the feat in successive years.[4]

The CBAI continued to represent Ireland until 1954. During that period, Irish women's teams emphatically outperformed the male-dominated open selections, gaining silver and bronze medals, and three creditable fifth places. The best finish for an Irish team in an open championship was tenth of thirteen, and that was on home ground, in Dun Laoghaire, in 1952.

First Republic of Ireland Team

The CBAI Camrose match against Wales, in Collins Barracks, Cork, on 23 and 24 April 1949, marked the first appearance of a team representing the

Republic of Ireland. The act which brought about the Republic had become law the previous December and came into effect on Easter Monday, five days before the Camrose contest. The team – Paddy Paul Donovan, David Rivlin, Jack Kelly, Joe Harold, Moreen McCarthy and Eileen O'Sullivan, with non-playing captain Geraldine McConkey – won by 3,480 points. The *Irish Times* reported: 'Mrs McCarthy and Mrs O'Sullivan . . . were brilliant in the closing stages' – further evidence of the quality of women players of the period. As was usual during the 1930s and 1940s, there was a Saturday-night radio broadcast on the match, with Noel Byrne commentating.

Imps

The 1940s ended with the introduction of international match points – 'imps' – for team competition. The first time imps were used to score a match in this country was on 3 and 4 December 1949, in a Camrose match in Dun Laoghaire. The CBAI team, of Donovan, Rivlin, Kelly, Dick Belton, Moreen McCarthy and Paddy Carson, with non-playing captain Dermot Egan, lost to Scotland by 40 imps. For some time, the new scoring method was described as the European system of match pointing. The conversion scale, different from the one which is currently used, was as follows:

0–10	= 0	400–490	= 7
20–30	= 1	500–590	= 8
40–60	= 2	600–740	= 9
70–100	= 3	750–1,490	= 10
110–180	= 4	1,500–1,990	= 11
190–290	= 5	2,000+	= 12
300–390	= 6		

It would be modified the following year, and again after that.

13

Bridge at the Turn of the Half-century

Noel Byrne and Joseph O'Neill jointly published *The Irish Bridge Annual* from 1948 to 1950. The publication gives the impression of an association teeming with activity all over the country. In 1948, it listed sixty-nine clubs in the provinces affiliated to the CBAI: twenty-nine in Leinster, sixteen each in Connacht and Munster, and eight in Ulster. In addition, there were twelve registered clubs in the Metropolitan area. (Half of these were not bridge clubs as such but consisted of bridge-playing groups within golf clubs and other establishments.)

The small number of registered clubs in Dublin is surprising. There were others in the capital and its suburbs throughout the 1940s: Alexander, Blackrock, Cambridge, Carlton, Herbert, Norwood, Teachers', United Services, Valentine and York Bridge Clubs, as well as the Mad Hatters' Club in Dun Laoghaire. Bridge was played in golf clubs too (including the Castle, Grange and Howth), and there were clubs which took their names from the women who ran them: Mrs McDevitt's, Mrs McMenamin's, Mrs McMunn's and Mrs Roantree's. Furthermore, we know that the game was played in various clubs – St Stephen's Green, Kildare Street, Mount Street, Fitzwilliam Tennis, United Arts and RAF – and that most of them took part in the inter-club championship.

It is tempting to jump to the conclusion that the Metropolitan executive was negligent in pursuing affiliations, but it was simply not necessary for a club to be affiliated for its members to compete in national championships. An individual competitor merely had to pay a registration fee. The thrust of the effort in Dublin was to secure the registration of individuals rather than the affiliation of clubs.

In 1948, there were still six branches of the CBAI: Cork, Ennis, Fermoy, Limerick, Drogheda and Commercial Travellers. Under a new constitution, they were given the same status as clubs. Two years later, the pattern had changed. The number of registered clubs around the capital had almost doubled, from twelve to twenty-two. Affiliations in the rest of the country had increased by just two, from sixty-nine to seventy-one.[1] If four former branches, now regarded as clubs, are taken into account, there was a net loss of two clubs throughout the provinces, despite eleven new affiliations.

Donegal showed a remarkable resurgence. The county which, ten years earlier, had not been considered bridge-minded, had brought in four new clubs: two in Letterkenny, Swilly Bridge Club and Letterkenny Social Club, in addition to the existing Letterkenny Bridge Club. Strabane, which straddles the border on the road between Omagh and Letterkenny, also joined, as did City of Derry, which for practical purposes belonged to Donegal and indeed was part of the CBAI's Northern region. However, it was not all progress in the county. Carndonagh was no longer part of the association, nor was another Letterkenny club, CYMS. The latter may well have merged into one of the new clubs. That the town could accommodate three clubs in 1949/50 is remarkable; that it could have four is difficult to envisage.

Roscommon added two new clubs: Ardcarne–Boyle and Castlerea. In County Wexford, Enniscorthy and Gorey joined the association. Wexford town, however, had lost two clubs: CYMS and Chamber of Commerce. Listowel, Mountmellick and Tuam had also become affiliated.

Thirteen clubs had cut their links with the national association, including Westport's two, and two of Galway's: Corrib and Grattan. Carrick-on-Shannon, Cashel, Clonmel and Wicklow had also disaffiliated. The loss of clubs is likely to have been the result of the 150 percent increase in affiliation fees imposed by the executive in 1948. One of the old branches, Drogheda, had disappeared during the previous two years, being swallowed up by the Gate Club. In Dublin, eight golf clubs were now affiliated: Castle, Donabate, Dun Laoghaire, Edmonstown, Elm Park, Milltown, Portmarnock and Royal Dublin, as well as two branches of the CYMS organisation, Dolphin's Barn and Harrington Street. Newly affiliated groups included the Teachers' Club and Neptune Bridge Club, 9 Clarinda Park, Dun Laoghaire. The former Commercial branch continued as a club.

As the second half of the twentieth century began, the game was in a healthy state. The loss of some key clubs in the provinces was only a temporary setback, as the overall membership continued to increase. The CBAI's well-organised regional structure was geared to catering for the expected intake of new players as the country entered a new phase of its history following the ending of the Emergency. The main competitions were well supported. The knockout team contests, the Inter-club and Kelburne Cups, engendered a spirit of friendly rivalry among clubs and camaraderie between participating players. The *Irish Times* and the *Irish Independent*, through the pens of their respective correspondents, Philip Quinn and Joseph O'Neill, gave generous space to the game. The regions were in the hands of competent and enthusiastic secretaries: Dick Tierney (Galway), T. J. Hamilton (Sligo), Dick Twomey (Cork), Eileen O'Sullivan (Tralee), T. Mullally (Letterkenny), Willie Berrill (Drogheda), E. C. Maguire (Tullamore) and Mrs Drea (Kilkenny) – the last three pioneers of the 1930s branch era. O'Sullivan, better known as a player, was destined to soon add to her already considerable fame in European competition.

The CBAI had achieved membership of the European Bridge League – and now had the best of both worlds with regard to the home international championships. Without being a member of the British Bridge League, it had secured its place in the Camrose competition. With a pool of talented players, the future looked bright. However, there was a dark cloud on the horizon.

14

CONFLICT

One of the outcomes of the CBAI's affiliation to the European Bridge League was the isolation of the Northern Ireland Bridge Union as far as European competition was concerned. Theoretically, the North could compete in Europe as part of a UK team. In practice, Northern Ireland players remained in the wilderness – where the whole island had been during the 1930s.

The two neighbouring governing bodies had been close before 1940, and cordial relations continued during the war years. There was a two-way flow of competitors between the organisations. The annual match for the Colonel Walshe cup was a highlight of the calendar.

A sudden and dramatic deterioration in the relationship between the CBAI and the NIBU occurred in 1950. To understand what happened, it is necessary to appreciate the political climate during the years immediately following the Second World War. Wartime coolness between the governments of Belfast and Dublin was reflected in the population: in particular, the Free State's policy of neutrality during the war was deplored by northern unionists. The citizens of the Free State took seriously their constitution's claim to jurisdiction over the whole island: it was taken for granted that the border was but a temporary inconvenience. Northern Protestants would have nothing to do with a Catholic southern state. Events, influenced by opposing ideologies, were about to cast a cloud over Irish bridge – a cloud from which the CBAI would not emerge for almost half a century.

In the spring of 1950, David Pigot and Cleo Roy attended a meeting of the European Bridge League at which the chairman, Sir Noel Mobbs – who was also chairman of the British Bridge League – raised objections, lodged by representatives of the NIBU, to the CBAI playing in

European championships as 'Ireland'. Pigot objected to the chairman raising matters on behalf of the NIBU because that body was not a member of the EBL. Besides, the CBAI claimed to represent all of Ireland and indeed had members in the North. Having briefly left the meeting to confer privately, the Irish delegates returned, and Pigot informed the chairman that 'the matter was one on which there could be no compromise'.[1]

Pigot's report on the meeting to his association's AGM in Galway in May 1950 – the first to be held outside Dublin – gave rise to an instantaneous outburst of anti-NIBU feeling. Fred Daly (Tramore), brother of incoming president J. Henry Daly, proposed that the CBAI 'should withdraw from any competition in which the NIBU are allowed to compete'. Dick Tierney (Galway) seconded the proposal. The CBAI's honorary treasurer, William Butler, drew attention to the fact that there had been no notice of motion and questioned the legality of the proceedings. When Pigot, who was chairman, overruled him, shouts of 'up the Republic' and 'Munster knows how to vote' mingled with the applause.[2] Among the delegates who spoke in favour of withdrawing were Joseph O'Neill and Noel Byrne (Dublin), Superintendent J. Murphy and Captain B. Kiely (South Munster), Dr Roche-Kelly (North Munster), Jim Wynne (Western), Stephen Bergin and James Hurley (North-western), Liam Barry (South Midland) and Paddy Paul Donovan (Dublin), who would become honorary secretary of the CBAI the following year. The proposal was carried on a show of hands, by thirty-four votes to twelve. Pigot pointed out that this could not be a directive, only 'an expression of opinion'.

Donovan then proposed that the executive should be directed 'to make further efforts to secure unification of Ireland with regards to the European Championships by means of an approach to the NIBU'.[3] This proposal was carried, with only two unnamed dissenters. Thus, at the very moment of greatest anti-NIBU feeling, the seed of unity was sown.[4] Donovan's proposal made no reference to the home international championships for the Camrose Trophy. Of course, the aspiration of the majority of the delegates was to replace both the NIBU and the CBAI with one all-Ireland team in that competition. It would be naive to suggest now, with the benefit of hindsight, how futile were the wishes in the Republic that northern players should give up their place in the Camrose – or that the British Bridge League should support such a move. The Irish

Republic was just a year old in 1950, and the South had cut connections with the Commonwealth.

The CBAI executive, placed in a difficult situation, held a special meeting on 6 July to consider 'matters arising out of the feelings expressed at the AGM'. A special general meeting was called for 14 October 1950, at 84 Harcourt Street, Dublin. At this meeting, CBAI delegates took a decision which was to keep their players out of Camrose and Lady Milne competitions for the next forty-seven years. There were two motions on the agenda, both with similar intent. The first, in two parts and worded rather cumbersomely (proposed by Joseph Honan and seconded by Maisie Cooper[5]), was withdrawn. The second, 'that the CBAI take no further part in any competitions in which the NIBU take part as a unit', was carried by a large majority. The attendance, estimated at two hundred, was the largest recorded at an Irish bridge meeting; it was not a matter of a small number of extremists exerting a dominating influence, as one commentator has suggested.[6] Five months had elapsed since the AGM. In the interval, the issue had been debated: By October, the delegates had had time to reflect on the seriousness of the issue and opinion had hardened. The *Irish Times* reported that of the sixty-seven duly accredited delegates, only ten voted against the resolution.[7]

There is a certain irony in the fact that the proposer and seconder of the motion were drawn from the civil and military guardians of the new Republic, namely Superintendent J. L. Murphy of the Gardaí, from Cobh, and Captain Kealy of the Southern Command of the national army. In proposing the motion, Murphy reminded the delegates that 'when playing in Belfast, a toast to the King was honoured' – a ceremony which irritated nationalist sensitivities. The chairman, David Pigot, reported that a subcommittee had informed northern representatives of the 'urgent wish . . . to have no border in the field of contract bridge in Ireland'. The CBAI wanted 'united control [of bridge] for the whole country' so that all-Ireland teams would compete in Camrose matches as well as in European championships. Pigot reminded the meeting of the CBAI's obligation to fulfil its Camrose commitments for the current season.

15

THE IRISH BRIDGE UNION

There are gaps in the official records of the CBAI over the next four years, but there is evidence of communication between the CBAI and the NIBU. At the CBAI AGM, held in Limerick in May 1952, the incoming president, Dr Frank McMenamin, referred to correspondence with the NIBU but no details of this correspondence are recorded. Dr Joseph Brennan, who became president of the CBAI in 1954, emerges from the historical mists as a key figure in the move towards reconciliation between the two organisations. His aim during his year of office would be the unification of the control of bridge in Ireland. Hands of friendship were extended – but not always grasped. The British Bridge League declined an invitation to send a team to the An Tóstal international event in Galway in April of that year; England, Scotland, Wales and Northern Ireland did not send teams either. In effect, the CBAI was being ostracised by its former Camrose colleagues. But not all of the approaches met with negative responses. In July, there is reference in an NIBU record of 'informal discussion . . . regarding the desirability of renewing former relations with the CBAI'. The feeling was that the first move should come from the South. Attitudes were softening; doors were opening.

There is another factor which helped in the reconciliation process: the various close personal friendships between prominent players in the Republic and others, both over the border and in England. For instance, Des Purcell was a friend of Colonel George Walshe, 'Yarborough' of the *Times* and president of the NIBU. Walshe, who frequently partnered George B. Hanna, the key bridge personality in Northern Ireland, in competition, lived over the Hamilton Club in London and invited Purcell to play there.[1] Purcell's circle included Paddy Donovan,[2] a nationalist-minded Gaelic-speaker who would be one of the CBAI's negotiators in talks with the NIBU.

In December 1951, an unofficial two-day match, billed as 'Dublin v. London', took place in the Shelbourne Hotel. The visitors – Dr S. Lee, S. L. Booker, A. Meredith and L. Dodds – included some of Britain's most eminent players. The Dublin team included Donovan and Purcell.[3] The Jewish communities of Belfast and Dublin played their part in maintaining harmonious cross-border relationships, with the annual match between Belfast's Jewish Institute and Dublin's Jewish Literary and Social Club being an important focus for such relationships. In May 1952, for example, the match took place at the Dublin club: the home side won the Aaron Hool Memorial Cup. Participants included former and current Camrose players.[4]

Noel Byrne, the leading Irish tournament director, and his wife, Kay, were friendly with the English director, L. Pritchard Robinson, and his wife, Faff. The Robinsons and Colonel Walshe[5] were among the few cross-channel visitors to Galway's 1954 An Tóstal event. Byrne, a member of the CBAI executive, was influential in Irish bridge circles. The selection of him as a delegate to the inaugural IBU council meeting was probably influenced by the strength of his contacts.[6]

The effect of friendships of this kind should not be underestimated. Officials may not have met formally but there were plenty of off-the-record discussions and unofficial meetings – and a genuine desire among tournament players on both sides of the border to meet in competition.

The process of reconciliation culminated in a meeting between representatives of the CBAI – Brennan, Donovan and Paddy Fitzgerald – and of the NIBU – Larry Bradley, Norman H. Douglas and George Sloane – at Ballymascanlon on 27 January 1955. Agreement was reached on proposals for a union between North and South. At its meeting on 26 February, the CBAI executive was not willing to accept the original proposals,[7] but Brennan, anticipating objections, was prepared. Aware of NIBU thinking on the matter, he suggested various modifications, and these were accepted, bringing to an end almost five years of division.

Both sides moved fast. Special meetings of both the CBAI and the NIBU were held simultaneously on 26 March, with a single item on their respective agendas: 'the proposed agreement negotiated between the CBAI and the NIBU'.

There were sizeable minorities on both sides of the border against the union. There is a perception among some observers of history that Dublin's professional and business class – the very sections of society which played bridge – were, in some way, less hardline in their national-ism than other citizens of the Republic. This was not the case in 1955, when the strongest opposition to the union with the NIBU came from the capital. A meeting of the Dublin regional committee in mid-March, while welcoming efforts to achieve unity, nevertheless unanimously passed the following resolution:

> Unless both organisations agree not to field separate teams in interna-tional and other competitions, including the Camrose Trophy, that any such agreement would be futile and against the principle accepted at the annual general meeting in Galway.[8]

To impose a condition that the NIBU would withdraw from the Camrose in favour of an All-Ireland team was tantamount to sabotaging the union. South Munster region, at a meeting on 19 March, passed a similar resolution.

It appeared that advocates of the union might have a difficult task ahead of them. However, Dr Joseph Brennan was persuasive, and a week later, at the Four Courts Hotel in Dublin, the agreement was ratified by forty-one votes to twenty. Among those who voted against were D. R. Pigot, J. P. MacHale, J. M. O'Sullivan, J. Wallis (Dublin), Mr Logue (Derry), D. A. Houlihan (Birr) and R. A. Tierney (Galway).

The NIBU meeting also ratified the agreement – the actual vote is not recorded – although the delegates needed to be assured that 'such a union did not mean that a composite team would in future compete in the Camrose competition'. The Irish Bridge Union was established at those two parallel meetings on that day, 26 March.

It has been suggested that one of the compelling factors which made the northern delegates vote for the union was that they had virtually no hope of getting into the European championships as part of a UK team, whereas they had a realistic chance of becoming part of an All-Ireland squad – as indeed proved to be the case.[9] Pigot, MacHale and O'Sullivan may have been mandated by their region to vote against the union, but it was also in their own interests to do so. They could hardly have been overjoyed at the prospect of NIBU members competing for places on the Irish team. A fellow international, D. A. Houlihan (Birr), was also against the union.

In deference to his role in bringing about the union, Brennan was authorised by the CBAI executive to appoint the delegates to the first IBU Council.[10] He nominated himself, Donovan, Alderman Stephen Bergin (Sligo), Noel Byrne (Carlow), Paddy Fitzgerald (Cork, but living in Dublin) and George Doyle (Dublin). Doyle withdrew, and his place was taken by Brian O'Kennedy (Dun Laoghaire). Less than five years earlier, Bergin, Byrne and Donovan had been among those who were in favour of severing connections with the NIBU.

The first meeting of the Irish Bridge Union took place at the Midland Hotel, Belfast, on the evening of Good Friday, 8 April, 1955.[11] George B. Hanna was invited to chair the proceedings, which he opened by describing the background to the historic occasion as 'the unfortunate difference of opinion existing for some time now'. He set the tone for the new body. 'We must remember,' he said, 'that this union was designed for the advancement of the game of bridge, and bridge alone.' Political differences were left outside the meeting room – and have remained outside it.

There were six delegates from each side: from the CBAI, Brennan, Fitzgerald, Donovan, Bergin, Byrne and O'Kennedy, and from the NIBU, T. J. McAfee, W. Robb, G. Sloane (Portadown), Norman H. Douglas, L. Bradley and J. E. Arnott (Belfast). Also in attendance were Major George Jackson and Michael Dorgan, both from Dublin, as well as the Right Honourable George B. Hanna. Dr Brennan was elected president, Sloane vice-president. (The presidency continues to alternate annually between North and South.) Paddy Paul Donovan and Norman H. Douglas were appointed as joint honorary secretaries.

In accepting the presidency, Brennan referred to 'the great pleasure which Colonel Walshe . . . has expressed at the formation of the union'. Walshe, the permanent president of the NIBU and a man who had served bridge for more than forty years,[12] was not involved in the negotiations and was never a delegate to the IBU council, but his benign influence behind the scenes was acknowledged.

Since the CBAI was still the body affiliated to the EBL, it was mandated to select the teams for European championships until such time as the CBAI's affiliation was superseded by that of the IBU. However it was decided that, for the forthcoming championships in Amsterdam, the CBAI should nominate two pairs and the NIBU one, for each team, with each organisation providing a non-playing captain. The question of delegates to the EBL was left, for the moment, in the hands of the CBAI.

At a NIBU meeting a few weeks later, on 19 May, the chairman, T. J. McAfee, and the other delegates to the inaugural IBU meeting felt that it was 'only fitting that at that first meeting the CBAI representatives should be our guests'. So the costs of the inaugural meeting of the IBU, including the expenses of the southern delegates, were met from NIBU funds. It was a generous gesture and a symbolic act of friendship.

ALL-IRELAND CHAMPIONSHIPS

The primary change resulting from the founding of the IBU – indeed, the very reason for its establishment – was that, henceforth, Irish teams in European championships would represent the whole island. In addition, All-Ireland championships were organised. Dermot Egan's death coincided with the founding of the union. His sister, Ina McMenamin, donated the cup which bears his name. First contested in 1957, it is awarded to the winners of the IBU's team championship, qualification for which is by winning CBAI and NIBU competitions – four in the South, two in the North.

It might have been called the Fitzgerald Cup. At the IBU inaugural meeting, Paddy Fitzgerald, a man of some personal wealth, 'intimated that he would donate £100 to provide a cup'. One of the three CBAI representatives trusted with the delicate negotiations with the NIBU, he was non-playing captain of open teams in Europe in 1954 and 1955. Norman Douglas, joint honorary secretary, in his annual report in May 1956, mentioned the union's debt to Mr Fitzgerald 'for generously presenting a cup'. However, at an IBU meeting three months later, Denis Jackson, newly elected joint honorary secretary, reported that Fitzgerald had withdrawn his offer. Instead, 'Mrs McMenamin had offered to provide a cup to commemorate the memory of her late brother'. Fitzgerald, having played a role in the negotiations that brought about unity, was probably disappointed when he was outvoted by Liam Barry in the election to succeed Donovan as CBAI honorary secretary at the 1955 AGM. He never attended an executive meeting again. There was another factor which may have influenced Fitzgerald's decision to withdraw his offer of the cup. According to Noreen O'Grady (a long-time member of the Regent Bridge Club), 'something happened between Fitzgerald and Denis Jackson around that time'.[13]

The Moylan Cup, donated by Dr Patrick Moylan from Ennis in 1943, had traditionally been awarded to the winners of the panel test. Now that the tests, or trials, were to be organised by the IBU, the cup was transferred to the all-Ireland body. It was awarded to the winners of the trials in 1956. However, the IBU council meeting of 26 August 1956 decided to hold team trials to select representatives for Vienna the following year. The cup became the trophy for a new All-Ireland pairs championship, inaugurated in 1957, and it is still presented annually to the winners of this competition.

The inter-club championship, which had become an inter-county event for the 1955/56 season, was taken over by the IBU the following season, when Antrim became Northern Ireland's first winner. The inter-provincial competition was transferred to IBU control in 1957/58.

16

UNLIKELY ALLIES

George Boyle Hanna, a founder of the Northern Ireland Bridge Union in 1934, was the most influential person in northern bridge. A regular Camrose participant, he was well known on the British tournament circuit. He was described as a physically massive figure who dominated the table with his presence.[1] He became a member of the Northern Ireland parliament following a by-election in Duncairn, Belfast, in November 1949. In October 1953, he was appointed minister of home affairs. His attitude to the Republic did not soften with time. Speaking in Stormount on 29 November 1955, he referred to 'the wisdom of our fathers in refusing to join with the south'.[2] In 1956, in a paper published by the Northern Ireland government, he outlined reasons why Northern Ireland could never be united with the Republic.[3]

The Right Honourable George Boyle Hanna, therefore, seems an unlikely person to have brought his influence to bear on the founding of an all-Ireland organisation, but he chaired the first meeting of the Irish Bridge Union, which united north and south. Dr Joseph Brennan, the first president of the IBU, acknowledged that had it not been for Hanna, 'it is quite probable that the union would not have come about'.[4]

Dr Joseph Brennan was an unlikely ally of Hanna. A founding member of the Clan na Poblachta Party in 1947, he was elected to the Dáil for Dun Laoghaire–Rathdown the following year. He was close to the party leader, Seán McBride, a former chief-of-staff of the IRA.[5]

At the first annual meeting of the Irish Bridge Union, held at the Royal Marine Hotel, Dun Laoghaire, on 27 May 1956, George Sloane suggested that Brennan should continue as president. The gesture was a token of the respect and affection in which he was held. However, he was no longer a delegate. Having achieved his aim of unifying bridge on the island, he bowed out. Neither he nor Hanna attended a meeting of the IBU again. Hanna's political and judicial duties took precedence. He was appointed Minister for Finance in April 1956; in September, he was appointed County Down Court Judge.

The two men made one further – and lasting – contribution to Irish bridge. In 1958, they jointly presented the appropriately named Friendship Trophy for competition amongst Irish universities. When first contested, in February 1960 at Queen's University Belfast, with Professor Alan McKinnon as tournament director, Queen's, UCD and Trinity each had two teams. The result was a win for UCD.[6] The president of Queen's, F. H. Newark, CBE, presided at a dinner in the great hall. Among the guests were Brennan and Hanna.

That Hanna and Brennan, men of diametrically opposed political and ideological convictions, could come together in the formation of the Irish Bridge Union says much for the effectiveness of the game as a unifying force. It also says much about the two men's deep interest in bridge. They remained political enemies but personal friends, and played together occasionally. Brennan invited Hanna to the Dun Laoghaire congress, where, in 1957/58, they featured among the team prizewinners.

17

THE GOLDEN AGE OF IRISH WOMEN'S BRIDGE

If the intrusion of politics brought discord in the early 1950s, the period was also marked with success – for women players. The group consisting of May McNulty, Ina McMenamin, Geraldine McConkey, Eileen O'Sullivan, Elvina Spiro, Ruth Giddings, Eileen O'Doherty, Alice Mahon, Doreen Cairnduff and Anne Quinn – and perhaps a few more – all Dublin-based, and Moreen McCarthy (Wexford) represent arguably the largest body of good players from any period.

Players from the group won European bronze and silver medals in 1952 and 1954 respectively. The failure of the CBAI executive to send a women's team to Helsinki in 1953 (discussed below) quite likely robbed them of another medal. The need on the part of the newly formed Irish Bridge Union to make a politically correct decision with regard to team selection in 1955, and the combining of open and women's trials in 1956, probably deprived them, and the country, of further honours. Two fifth places in Europe, in 1957 and 1958, confirmed that they were still serious contenders. Essentially the same group won bronze in Torquay in 1961[1] and Beirut in 1962.[2]

Some of Dublin's leading women players used to meet regularly in Switzers of Grafton Street. They met at noon in deference to May McNulty, a single woman of independent means who never surfaced before that time. The Switzers set were close friends. They practised together, played rubber bridge together, took part in club, regional and national duplicate events, joined together in pairs and teams – and dominated women's domestic competition and international selection for a number of years. Mostly, they were typical wives of professional men: they had time for leisure activities. That is a factor which should be taken into account when comparing today's women players with those of former times. Nowadays, women have careers, and many come home to children and housework as well; it should not surprise us that their performance sometimes falls short of their potential.

Many factors combine to make a top-quality bridge player. Talent is one. The school in which the talent is nurtured is another. Those women developed their skills and temperament in the rugged environment of men's rubber bridge, in which making mistakes costs money. Some of them – McNulty, McMenamin, O'Sullivan and Giddings, for example – played much of their tournament bridge with good male partners. Their names are engraved on trophies open to men and women.

A STRANGE DECISION

The executive's decision not to send a women's team to Finland in 1953 seems astonishing in retrospect. At the executive meeting at which the decision was made, only Noel Byrne (Carlow) dissented, despite the fact that three prominent women delegates, Geraldine McConkey, Eileen O'Doherty and Eileen O'Sullivan, were present. The other delegates who took the extraordinary decision were Stephen Bergin (president, Sligo), David Pigot (chairman), Paddy Donovan (honorary secretary), Eoin O'Riordan (honorary treasurer), John Morgan, William Butler (Dublin), John Lane (Skerries), E. Sonneschein (North-western region) and Joe Honan (Limerick).

The following year, the executive once again debated whether to send one or two teams to the European championships. The wisdom of supporting a team for the open championship was not questioned, but Eoin O'Riordan was not in favour of sending a women's team, as this would result in a financial deficit. He was strongly supported by Paddy Donovan. Fortunately, the two officers did not have their way: the women's team went on to win the silver medals in Montreux, while the open team[3] finished eleventh of the fifteen participants.

The secretary and treasurer had their way when it came to the question of grants, however. A ceiling of £300 was placed on the sum voted to the two teams of six, plus two non-playing captains, travelling to Montreux, with a maximum of £25 per person. The total, divided by fourteen, gave each person a subsidy of £21. Playing for your country was an expensive business then, as indeed it remains today.

The CBAI was not the only national governing body to shy away from sending women participants to Helsinki. Only five women's teams took part – host nation Finland, Sweden, Netherlands, Great Britain and France – the smallest entry in the history of the championships. The eleven teams in the open championship – one more than in the first post-war competition, held in Copenhagen in 1948 – also represented a poor turnout. Cost was a factor: Finland had the highest standard of living in Europe, with correspondingly high prices.

In March, the executive had decided that it would send two teams to Helsinki. The old system of trials was abandoned, and teams-of-six trials were announced. However, the notice of the trials in the newspapers carried a puzzling rider: 'It is doubtful if more than that number (i.e. six) will be prepared to spend the time and money on a trip so far afield. It is possible therefore that the proposed competition (i.e. the team trials) will not materialise, in which case a sole entry in the two events will earn the right to go to Helsinki' – hardly an encouragement to take part. In the event, there were no trials. The players themselves would have to contribute a large portion of the cost – a factor which may have put off potential participants.

During the ten-year period from 1950 to 1959, women more than held their own in the major domestic events open to both sexes. Women won the Holmes Wilson Cup seven times,[4] and the Davidson, Kelburne, Moylan and Inter-County championship five times each during the period. The women who shared those successes were not all from the elite group mentioned above. For example, the first team to win the Holmes Wilson without a Dublin-based player included Mrs Cohen from Cork, who partnered her husband and the O'Connell brothers in 1954. The all-Galway team that won in 1957 included three women: Mrs S. Barry, Mrs A. Sandys and Mrs K. Braund.[5] There were others who were good enough to upset the expectations of the top players. In 1956, Frances and Maura Jennings (Dundalk) became the first sisters to play for Ireland. With them on the team were Mary Clare Riordan (Callan) and Kathleen Hanley (Fermoy). In Dublin, Jackie Prost (whose playing career began in the 1920s), Rita McNally, Lily McDonagh, Sheila Doyle, Cleo Fellowes, English-born Charlotte Fowler, Babs Hooper and Molly O'Carroll all gained international selection and won national championships. Clearly, it was a good time for women's bridge – and a relatively weak period for male players.

The 1950s – An Eventful Decade

Lady Milne Trophy

The inaugural women's home-international team championship for the Lady Milne Trophy was held in May 1950. The trophy dates back to 1934, when Lady Milne, the assistant secretary of Hubert Phillips's National Bridge Association, presented it to the winners of an open English women's team competition organised under the auspices of that body. The event later became a British Bridge League competition, but it was not until 1950 that it became the international contest that we know today.

In 1950, it was a requirement that participants should be the current holders of their own national women's team championship. Coincidentally, 1950 was the inaugural year of the CBAI women's team competition. So the association was represented by Jackie Prost (captain), Doreen Cairnduff,[1] Rita McNally and Sheila Doyle. In fact, Lily McDonagh had been McNally's partner when the team won the McMenamin bowl in March, but McDonagh, a primary-school teacher, was not free to travel. The team was not successful, but the winners, Scotland, beat them by only four imps. This was the only team from the Republic of Ireland to take part in the championship until 1998. Northern Ireland, where the organisation of women's bridge was not well advanced, did not take part in the Lady Milne competition during the early 1950s.

YOUNG MALES

The period saw the emergence of some promising young male players. Marcus Shrage and Michael O'Connell, the younger of the Cork brothers, made their international debuts in 1951; Gerry Read and Joe MacHale did the same in 1953. Nine years would elapse before MacHale won his second cap. Barry O'Connell, who had played Camrose in 1946, first competed in the Europeans in 1955. The Read–Shrage partnership began towards the middle of the decade. The two men were on the Irish team a number of times, as were the O'Connell brothers. However, the fact that a total of twenty-nine other players got places on Irish open teams during the 1950s indicates that no group consistently dominated. John Burke, still in his twenties, settled in London in 1954 and was lost to Irish bridge.

Older champions were nearing the end of their careers. Eddie Barry made his last international appearance in 1952. Des Purcell secured a final international cap in 1959 and continued to win in domestic competition into the 1960s. However, the leading players in general – and they included players of the calibre of Paddy Donovan, Jimmy Bastow, Jack Kelly, Dick Belton and Jack O'Sullivan – failed to make an impression abroad.[2] Donovan was unable to command a regular place on the team after 1952, probably because of the difficulty he experienced in attracting partners, and had to wait until 1959 for his next cap. Joe MacHale was not yet the force he later became. The lack of talent – or perhaps of commitment – is reflected by results in Europe: eighth of eleven competing nations in Brighton in 1950 was the best of a clutch of poor performances; tenth of thirteen on home ground in 1952 was probably the most disappointing.[3] Ireland finished last of fourteen in 1951 and last of sixteen in 1956.

THE 1952 EUROPEAN CHAMPIONSHIPS

The European championships were held in Dun Laoghaire from 19 to 27 September 1952. David Pigot, a member of the European Bridge League executive, was responsible for bringing them to Ireland, but he had the driving force of CBAI president Dr Frank McMenamin behind the organising team. Dr Joseph Brennan, with his substantial political and business clout, mobilised valuable support in Dun Laoghaire. Both the Royal Marine Hotel and the town hall were used as playing areas; the banquet at the end was held in the more distinguished Gresham Hotel, in the city centre.

Germany, whose participation in international competition had been resisted by some of its wartime enemies,[4] competed for the first time since the war, as did Lebanon. In the open championship, the thirteen competing teams were divided into two pools, each playing a round-robin of forty-eight-board matches. Scoring was by imps – then referred to as 'European match points'. However, the overall positions were decided on the basis of two points for a win, one for a tie. The leading two from each group qualified for the semi-finals. Ireland, drawn in Section B, lost to Great Britain, Norway and Switzerland, tied with Iceland and defeated Lebanon and Austria, the eventual bronze medallists.

An aspect of the non-playing captain's strategy, which seems extraordinary to the modern player, was the practice of changing partnerships from match to match. For example, Eddie Barry and Paddy Donovan played together against Austria – incidentally, Ireland's best result – while Barry partnered Dermot Egan to oppose Switzerland. Such changes of partners during major events were not unusual during this era;[5] indeed, this approach was facilitated by the fact that all members of the team played Culbertson's system.

Those who failed to reach the knockout stage competed for the minor placings. Ireland performed poorly and could finish only tenth, disappointing the large numbers of supporters who turned up every day to watch. Sweden and Italy met in the final, having disposed of Austria and Great Britain, respectively, in the semis. Austria won the third-place play-off by five imps. The final produced an exciting climax to the competition. After ninety-five of the ninety-six boards, the Italians led by one imp. On the last, a seemingly innocuous part-score deal, the Swedish South, Jan Wohlin, made two spades while the Italian North went down one in three clubs. The scoring of the day gave the Swedes a gain of three imps, and the gold medals. The winning margin of two imps remains the smallest in the history of the European championships.

The women's event, with seven competing nations, was decided by a round-robin of fifty-six-board matches. Great Britain won all its games and the gold medals. With the final round to be played, Ireland and Norway were fighting for the minor places. Ireland beat Germany, and Norway overcame Denmark, resulting in a tie for second. However, in the head-to-head clash, the Norwegians beat the Irish. The home team had to be satisfied with bronze – still a good performance, and the first international bridge medals for the country.

Something had gone badly wrong when Ireland met Norway in the third round. The Irish women dominated for most of the match and led by twenty-eight imps after thirty-two boards. Then, in six boards, numbers thirty-seven to forty-two, they gave it all back, and the sides were level. The Norwegians continued their momentum and picked up another nine imps to win. Having lost to Great Britain by twenty-six imps in the previous round, the Irish seemed unlikely to win medals at that point. However, they regained their composure: defeating Denmark, France and Germany, and displaying the resolute character, as well as the skills, which would bring many honours in the decade that followed. Ireland's heroines in Dun Laoghaire were Ruth Giddings, May McNulty, Geraldine McConkey, Eileen O'Sullivan, Ina McMenamin and Elvina Spiro, with Moreen McCarthy as non-playing captain.

There was drama away from the table, too, when a British player, Louis Tarlo, was rescued from drowning, providing a story for the media. Tarlo was watching twelve-year-old Peter Fell – son of Britain's non-playing captain, Geoffrey Fell – fishing from Dun Laoghaire pier. As Fell junior cast his line, Tarlo, in a reflex action, overbalanced and fell into the sea. The young fisherman jumped in and rescued the unfortunate – or perhaps lucky – Tarlo, who was taken to St Michael's Hospital. He played no further part in the championships. The accident may have cost Great Britain a medal, as it was narrowly beaten into fourth place.

ENNIS PAIR OVERLOOKED

The members of Ennis Bridge Club were not impressed by the methods employed to select Ireland's open team in 1952. As early as January,[6] they expressed indignation at the treatment of two of their members, Tom McCarrick and Vic Roughan, who had finished second to Eddie Barry and Des Houlihan (Birr) in the panel test. Ennis supporters thought that that performance should earn their men automatic places on the Irish team. In fact, the team was not selected until April, when the leading pairs on the panel, including McCarrick and Roughan, formed two teams of six to face each other in a final trial. Players were selected as individuals, and three players from each side were chosen. Alas, there was no place on the team for Dun Laoghaire for the Ennis players.

THE HELSINKI QUINTET

Unusually, a team of five players represented Ireland at the Helsinki European championships in 1953. The players changed partnerships from match to match.[7] Jack O'Sullivan, with Camrose appearances and two previous Europeans behind him, was the veteran of the team. Joe MacHale, who was making his international debut, was better known as a tennis and squash champion. Gerry Read and Phil Purcell won their first caps too; John Burke had played for Ireland once before. The team performed poorly in the Finnish capital, finishing ninth of the eleven participating teams.

Phil Purcell (no relation to the better-known Des Purcell) went to Yorkshire shortly afterwards, where he practised as a vet. Helsinki was his only appearance on an Irish team. For many years afterwards, he returned for competitions and frequently attended the South of Ireland congress. During the mid-1960s, one of his partners at Killarney was Raymond Brock, who became one of Britain's great bridge players.

John Burke, a native of the Clonmel area of Tipperary, was arguably the most interesting member of the team; at least his subsequent career made him so. Having studied engineering in Trinity College Dublin, he was only twenty-two when he was selected for the Irish team to compete at the first post-war European championships, in Copenhagen in 1948 – becoming one of the youngest people to play on an Irish open team. On his way home from Helsinki,[8] he stopped over in London and liked what he saw. He continued to play in Ireland during 1954, but he was drawn to the British capital, where he eventually settled. Destiny ordained that he should play a hand in events which led to a change in the gambling laws of the United Kingdom.

Burke, a tall, handsome, quiet, well-spoken man, fitted easily into post-war London society. He helped John Aspinall[9] organise *chemin de fer* games in select and ever-changing venues in fashionable London (ever-changing because gambling was illegal). Taking a percentage of every winning pot, the organisers made a great deal of money. In January 1958, Aspinall and Burke were raided by the police and charged, under the 1854 Gaming Act, with using an apartment for unlawful gaming. Following the hearing, during which an expert witness from Crockford's admitted to running illegal poker games at the famous club, the case was dismissed. It seems that every club in London was breaking the law, which was proved to be antiquated and inadequate. Shortly afterwards, the Macmillan government introduced new gaming legislation.

In 1962, Aspinall opened the Clermont Club in Berkeley Square, with Burke as manager. They cultivated an elite clientele. Wealth and good breeding, although both were essential, were not sufficient for a person to be accepted as a member at the Clermont: you also had to have a reputation for paying up when you lost. Members of the club included Lord Derby; the Duke of Atholl; Bernard van Cutsem, the queen's racehorse trainer; Ian Fleming, the creator of James Bond; and the ill-fated Lord Lucan, John Bingham. The club prospered – but not enough to satisfy Aspinall's financial needs.[10] An ingenious scheme to cheat the players was devised: cards were bent very slightly at the corners and were capable of being read only by trained experts, who spent hours practising. The scam went into operation successfully in January 1964. About a year later, Burke parted company with Aspinall. Burke revealed his secrets to author Douglas Thompson only recently.[10]

A report in the *Sunday Times* on 18 May 2008 revealed that Martha Fiennes had bought the rights to Thompson's book, *The Hustlers*, with a view to making a film. 'HIGH SOCIETY STING TO GET A HOLLYWOOD TWIST,' ran the headline.

DUBLIN REGIONALISED –

END OF THE METROPOLITAN REGISTER

In the summer of 1953, the Greater Dublin area had not yet become part of the regional bridge structure. At the CBAI executive meeting of 23 July 1953, Dun Laoghaire was granted regional status. On 10 September, the boundaries of this region – then known as Dun Laoghaire and Wicklow – were approved. George Doyle was its first delegate, at the 22 October meeting. The next meeting, 19 November, fixed the name as the Eastern region.

The Metropolitan Register, then reduced to 135 members and entitled to five delegates to the AGM, exerted an influence out of proportion to its size. There was no resistance to its demise.[11] On 27 July 1954, the CBAI executive approved the formation of the Dublin Region. Although Dr P. J. O'Dowd was welcomed as its first delegate to the executive on 17 December, the region did not officially come into being until 1 January

1955. To celebrate its formation, Dublin invited the other nine regions to an at-home in Jury's Hotel on 13 February. A social weekend of the first magnitude, it began with players attending the Ireland–England rugby match the day before and included a competition for the thirty teams that had accepted invitations.

THE 1954 AN TÓSTAL INTERNATIONAL TOURNAMENT

In 1953, the Irish government promoted a national festival, An Tóstal, around Easter to boost tourism and lift the spirits of a people weighed down by unemployment and emigration. Communities were encouraged to organise cultural events by way of celebration. Bridge clubs played their part, with An Tóstal tournaments being organised throughout the country.

Galway, not for the first time, was to the fore. The annual congress of 1954 was extended to a week and incorporated an An Tóstal international team contest. This was a period of strained relations between North and South. The CBAI's seccession from the home international championships had alienated it from its UK neighbours, with the unfortunate effect, for Galway, that England, Scotland and Wales did not accept invitations to participate. Teams from Belgium, Italy, the Netherlands and Sweden did compete. The CBAI was represented by John Burke, Gerry Read, Alice Mahon, Eileen O'Doherty, Marcus Shrage and Elvina Spiro. The competition, which was run off at intervals throughout the week beginning on 19 April, was won by Belgium on a split tie from Sweden: the Belgians had won the head-to-head match.[12] The Irish could manage only fourth place.

The young Swedish team[13] – it was said that the average age of the players was twenty-one – won the congress teams for the Cross Cup. Only Ina McMenamin and her brother Dermot Egan prevented a clean sweep by the visitors when they won the congress pairs, beating Belgium's Jacobs and Pollack into second place. Northern Ireland visitors were scarce that year, but the redoubtable Johnny McRobert from Crossgar, County Down, with his partner, W. J. Stewart, came third.

Youghal was one of the many bridge clubs to organise an An Tóstal competition. It continues annuallly to the present day – long after the festival has ceased to be celebrated nationally.

ALL-IRELAND TEAMS IN EUROPEAN CHAMPIONSHIPS

Delegates to the inaugural meeting of the Irish Bridge Union in April 1955 amicably agreed that, for the Amsterdam European championships in July, the CBAI should select two pairs and the NIBU one pair for each of the two teams, open and women. So Larry Bradley and Maurice Gabbey from Belfast lined out on the open team, with Gerry Read and Marcus Shrage from Dublin and the O'Connell brothers from Cork, under the captaincy of another Corkman, Paddy Fitzgerald. The state of the women's game in Northern Ireland was reflected by the fact that it could produce only one player, Norah Bradley, who joined Elvina Spiro, Ruth Giddings, May McNulty, Babs Hooper – all from Dublin – and Moreen McCarthy from Wexford, with Professor Alan McKinnon from Belfast as non-playing captain, providing political balance.

The Irish teams may have made history, but they made no impression on the competitions, the open team finishing tenth of thirteen, the women eighth of ten. The latter result was a particularly disappointing performance, in view of the fact that two medals had been won in the previous three years.

FIRST ALL-IRELAND TEAM

A month earlier, an international invitational team tournament organised by the Italian Bridge Federation at Lake Como passed almost unnoticed. The event featured the first team to represent the whole of Ireland in competition; ironically, the team was captained by the Ulster Unionist politician George B. Hanna. The Italian invitation, which had been put before the inaugural meeting of the IBU, would have come to the CBAI, the internationally accredited body. Placing it on the table at the first IBU meeting was, therefore, a gesture of goodwill from the CBAI towards its new partner. Six players – three from the CBAI (Anne Lenihan, R. McLennan and J. O'Gorman), and three from the NIBU (G. B. Hanna, A. McKinnon and W. H. Smyth) – were guests of the Italians from 9 to 13 June.[14]

The Mrs Lenihan who played at Lake Como was from Athlone. During the 1950s and 1960s, she was one of the better players in the midlands. In 1951, in partnership with Mrs Sharpe, also from Athlone, she won the Lambert Cup, and her name frequently appears high on the leaderboard of major competitions. Mrs Lenihan was a regular competitor in trials – most frequently with Mrs W. O'Farrell (Longford) – and in 1966 she and Maureen Ryder (Galway) reached the last eight. She won an inter-provincial medal with Leinster in 1974 but her claim to fame rests less on her bridge-playing prowess than on her position as matriarch of a political dynasty. Her husband, Patrick Lenihan, was a member of Dáil Éireann. Her son Brian and her daughter Mary O'Rourke – the latter, incidentally, also a bridge player – became government ministers, as did her grandchildren, Brian and Conor Lenihan.

Team member W. H. Smyth reported briefly on the Lake Como tournament to the IBU meeting of 23 July with the cliché that the team 'had acquitted itself very creditably'.

Visit to Lebanon

The bridge association of Lebanon had appreciated the hospitality which had been extended to its team during the European championships in 1952. So much so, in fact, that Frank and Ina McMenamin, Dick Belton and Des Purcell were invited to be its guests at a twelve-day international tournament in Beirut in July 1955. They finished third in the team competition, a leisurely event played over five days, while Belton and Purcell were fourth in the pairs.[15]

'No Mixed Pairs Shall Apply'

Given the relative strengths and successes of the respective sexes, one could be forgiven for interpreting as churlish the attitude of the male players who objected to mixed partnerships taking part in trials. Gerry Read, in a letter to the CBAI executive in February 1956, expressed the opinion that 'mixed pairs should not be allowed to compete for places in the open panel test'. International selection was, of course, a matter for the Irish Bridge Union, but each of the two constituent bodies was allocated a quota for the panel tests (trials) and each could make its own decision regarding the composition of its quota. Read was supported by Dick Belton and David Pigot. Laur Sheeran was the only delegate to support the cause of mixed pairs, even though three women – Geraldine McConkey, Nellie Faul (Dundalk) and Eimer Burke (Nenagh) – were at the meeting.[16]

In 1956, the IBU made a curious decision to run combined trials to select open and women's teams. Not surprisingly, the match-pointed pairs test threw up strange combinations. The open team consisted of six new European 'caps'; the women's side featured four first-timers. In Stockholm, the open team finished last of the sixteen competing nations, the women eighth of ten. The NIBU, it seems, had no objection to mixed pairs competing, as the trials were won by Norah and Larry Bradley. However, they did not take their places on the team.[17]

THE INTERPROVINCIALS

The interprovincial championship, a round-robin of 100-board matches, each contested over a weekend, was introduced under the auspices of the CBAI in 1952. It got under way on 22 and 23 March, when Leinster, represented by Alf Bloom, Phil Purcell (Dublin), Tom Brick, John Lynch (Enniscorthy), John Lane and Andy Butler (Skerries), with non-playing captain Philip Quinn, beat Ulster – T. Dunbar, F. McConnell (Derry), J. Ryan, J. J. Kennedy (Monaghan) and the Jennings sisters, Frances and Maura (Dundalk) – by 3,950 points. Imps scoring had been introduced in 1949, but administrators were slow to implement new ideas, so the old total-points method was used. The winner of the series, however, was decided on the basis of two points for a win, one for a draw. In the event of a tie, the cumulative total score was the deciding factor.

The competition was inaugurated during the period of the cold war between North and South. So, since the interprovincials were a CBAI competition, NIBU players were excluded from Ulster teams. Clubs in Derry were affiliated to the CBAI. We can but speculate as to whether Ulster teams would have been representative of the whole province if relations between North and South had been affable. It is interesting to see that Dundalk was considered to be part of Ulster for the purpose of team selection.

In May, Leinster defeated Munster by 7,400 points and, while the result of the Leinster v. Connacht game has not been found, it is reasonable to assume that the western players, even if they had won the game, would not have succeeded by a sufficiently wide margin to prevent Leinster from becoming the first interprovincial champions. Connacht certainly did not win the competition.

The restricted geographical area from which Ulster could select its team did not prevent the province from winning the second running of the championship in 1953 – on a split tie from Connacht. Teams of exclusively Monaghan players lost to Connacht but beat Munster. An all-Derry combination beat Leinster.

The shield which is awarded to the winning province was introduced in 1954. Hundred-board matches, one province against another over a weekend, continued until 1960, when the format which is in use today was first put into practice: that is, three teams from each province playing the sides from the other provinces in turn, at one venue over one weekend. Total-scoring continued to be used to decide matches until 1959, as was two points for a win, irrespective of the margin of victory.

Munster, despite the existence of large groups of strong players in Cork and Limerick especially, has been the least successful of the provinces. Three of its four championships were achieved over a four-year period, 1963–66. Extraordinarily, the winning squad of eighteen in 1966 differed completely from the successful group two years earlier. Ulster won five championships between 1968 and 1973, including four in a row. However Leinster has had several periods of dominance and has won more titles than the other three provinces combined. Connacht had to wait until 1982 for its first victory but since then has successfully challenged Leinster's supremacy; for the last twenty-five years, the two provinces have had roughly an equal number of victories.

Inter-club Becomes Inter-county

In 1956, the inter-club championship became an inter-county competition. Members of a team still had to belong to the same club – a rule that continued until 2002 – but each county entered one team, which was selected following a qualifying competition. Most counties took part, the format being long knockout matches. Reading accounts of activities from the period, one senses a feeling of competitiveness around the country that has since been lost. In County Laois alone in 1956, fifteen teams entered the county knockout qualifier, with clubs in Portlaoise, Mountmellick and Mountrath to the fore.

The CBAI's Twenty-fifth Anniversary

Nineteen fifty-seven was the CBAI's silver jubilee year, but its celebration was a year late. Only in July was it decided to invite teams from England, Scotland, Wales and Northern Ireland to take part in a commemorative competition. This competition did not take place until March 1958, by which time the association was twenty-six years old. England's Harold Franklin, Louis Tarlo, Dr Sidney Lee and Graham Mathieson, with captain Reg Corwen, won, with Scotland second. Gerry Read's team was the best of the Irish, taking third place on a split tie from Geraldine McConkey.[18]

1957 Challenge Match, Dublin

Prior to the official jubilee tournament, Dr Frank McMenamin invited a team of English and American players to play an eighty-eight-board match against an Irish selection at Dublin's Shelbourne Hotel in November 1957. The visitors, Ewart Kempson and Geoffrey Fell (England), with Americans Charles Goren and Helen Sobel, defeated Jimmy Bastow, Dr Richard Belton, Jack Kelly, Ina McMenamin, Des Purcell, Gerry Read and Marcus Shrage by 3,840 points. Kempson wrote a book about the match, detailing the bidding and play of all eighty-eight boards.[19] It was 'a dull match' according to Ruth Giddings, who was present.

World Records

As the decade drew to a close, students in Belfast and Dublin attracted publicity for the game with attempts on the world bridge marathon record. In Belfast in December 1958, twenty-year-old Desmond Deery, with fellow Queen's University students Michael Trevitt, Jestyn Phillips and Peter Blackwood, set out to beat the existing record of fifty-one hours. No sooner had they started than they were told that the record, which had been set by students in Birmingham the previous year, in fact stood at fifty-seven hours.[20] Undeterred, they played for sixty-one hours.

The record stood for eleven weeks. Early in March 1959, Glynn Cochrane and Duncan White from UCD, with Eamonn O'Higgins and

Patrick Lim from Trinity College, played for sixty-three hours twenty-eight minutes. The Dublin students demonstrated a talent for promotion and attracted considerable media attention. Northern Ireland BBC television showed the play of the first deal on the evening of 4 March. The students began the marathon in a show window of Joe Malone's car-hire company and moved back and forth between there and the Hibernian Hotel, continuing to play in the back of a Joe Malone car as they travelled. Walter Smithwick, of the brewing company, supplied them with a barrel of ale. They raised a considerable sum for the National Council for the Blind of Ireland. On 7 March, attired in evening dress, their photo, together with an account of their achievement, made the front page of the *Irish Times*. Of all those young players, Deery alone went on to be a top-grade player.

Forty-seven years would pass before the next Irish attempt on the record, in February 2006. Olive Rose, Eileen Hurley, Deirdre Walsh, George Hayes, Mary Horgan, Brian O'Neill, Ann Bailey and Mary Quinlan, at the Trident Hotel in Kinsale, set a new record of seventy-five hours ten minutes, played 1,153 deals and raised €38,450 for the Cork ARC Cancer Support House.

The Best of Them All?

'Donovan was the best of them all,' Eoin O'Riordan once remarked.[1] Eoin's opinion was to be respected. No mean player himself, he competed for Ireland and, during his long career, met all the great Irish players at the table. Subjective assessment is useful but it may be tainted by admiration: O'Riordan was Paddy Paul Donovan's ally on the CBAI executive, and a friend of his.

'Big Paddy' Walsh, as he was affectionately known around Templeogue to distinguish him from other players of the same name, told me that he had read that the legendary Italian player Giorgio Belladonna, when asked who was the best player he had ever faced at the table, had replied: 'Paddy Donovan of Ireland.'[2] I have been unable to verify the claim but the anecdote illustrates the myth that grew around Donovan. 'He never made a mistake,' said Wesley Burrowes, who played with him many times.[3] Statistically, Donovan's achievements are not hugely impressive. The winner of thirteen major domestic events, he played for Ireland in four European championships and for the CBAI in fourteen Camrose matches. He was 'a difficult man, hard on partners,' O'Riordan added.

Wherever he ranks in the hierarchy of great players – and he was certainly one of the best of his era – Donovan was an unforgettable personality. When his name is mentioned, there is invariably an emotive response. In London in December 2003, I met Dermot Hunt, whose father, A. G. Hunt from Cavan, had been president of the CBAI in 1964/65. Hunt could not bring himself to mention Donovan's name: 'that mad man from Galway who took us out of the Camrose'. It was an unfair remark, since Donovan did not become an officer of the association until seven months after the CBAI had pulled out, but it was typical of the responses prompted by mention of his name.

Dr Paddy Paul Donovan – his doctorate was in the field of chemistry – divided his working life between Dublin and Galway, where he was public analyst for the county. Born in Cork, he played for Munster in the interprovincial championship in 1954, and later for Leinster. He was elected honorary secretary of the CBAI in May 1951, having opposed the incumbent, Cleo Roy, who withdrew, thereby obviating the need for a ballot. Donovan was not universally popular. Although he was returned unopposed the following year, in 1953 he had to see off a challenge from Alice Mahon, whom he defeated by sixty-seven votes to twenty-six. In 1954, he beat L. O'Callaghan from Cork sixty-nine votes to twenty-five. The recording of the votes is significant: Donovan wrote the minutes, and on each occasion the size of the majority is flattering to himself. He was not a candidate in 1955, when Liam Barry, of Tramore, defeated Cork-born, Dublin-based Paddy Fitzgerald. The vote, on that occasion, was not recorded, nor was it afterwards in elections of officers.

During Donovan's tenure, the CBAI rented office space, first at 32 Graham Terrace, Seville Place, and later at 31 Aungier Street.[4] The four years during which he was honorary secretary – 1951–55 – were a fateful period for Irish bridge. When he took up office, relationships between North and South were at an all-time low. Undoubtedly, nationalist attitudes of the kind which Donovan espoused contributed to the problem. However, by the end of his four years in charge, the rift had been healed – permanently. He was one of the CBAI's negotiators in the talks with the NIBU which led to the formation of the Irish Bridge Union. Indeed, it was he who proposed, in May 1950, that an approach should be made to the NIBU with a view to bringing about unity.[5] Like many patriots in the Republic at the time, he saw the formation of the IBU as a stepping stone to all-Ireland participation in the Camrose, an aspiration which would never become a reality.

Donovan was frequently involved in conflict. In 1953, he submitted the names of Irish team members for the Helsinki European championships in the Irish language to the Finnish organisers. IBU chairman David Pigot pointed out that he had not been given authority to do so, and Pigot was supported by executive members. Donovan inserted a note into the minutes:

> The sending of names in Irish was expressly not objected to. He had no apology . . . he considered the sending of names . . . in the language

of their country a . . . normal procedure. He was prepared to let his action be judged by the general body of the association and if the majority . . . disapproved . . . he would have no desire to continue as Chief Officer [sic].

The minutes end with the honorary secretary presuming that there was no objection to writing in Irish. Donovan had his way.[6] Furthermore, when the *Irish Times* pubished the names in English, he wrote to the paper correcting them: the names, in Irish, appeared in the newspaper on 23 August. At the October meeting, he informed the executive that he had put the title of the association in Irish and English on the programme. So the Irish translation of CBAI, Comhlachas Cor-Bheiriste na hÉireann, appears on the association's 1953/54 annual programme for the first time. Both Irish and English versions of the title continue to be used to this day.

When the team returned from Helsinki, Donovan, on behalf of the executive, wrote a congratulatory letter, in Irish, to the captain, Gerry Read. The latter replied, also in Irish, that neither he nor his team could accept the executive's congratulations. It seems that Read, who had a similarly touchy temperament, suspected that the message, since it was in Irish, was from Donovan himself and not from the executive. The point-scoring exchange of letters ended when Donovan wrote an acerbic reply – in English – stating that it was indeed the executive's desire to congratulate the team on its excellent performance.[7] The 'excellent performance' was to finish ninth of the eleven participating teams; they had not won a match.

Minutes of meetings reveal clashes between Donovan and various prominent bridge personalities. He wrote to Geraldine McConkey asking why a letter addressed to him had been opened by her and retained for a week before being forwarded to him.[8] She had done so inadvertently; nonetheless, raising such matters at executive meetings did not endear him to his colleagues. Eileen O'Doherty questioned his conduct in breaching the confidentiality of a tournament committee meeting by not only disclosing the actual voting on a controversial issue but also divulging how each individual had voted. The same committee quarrelled with Donovan again when he asked for the detailed minutes of a meeting. Eileen O'Sullivan, a committee member, described him as 'false, malicious and mischievous in intent'. Tensions between himself and people such as David Pigot and Frank McMenamin emerge from between the lines of written records. Certainly there were few dull moments while Donovan was honorary secretary of the CBAI.

A crisis arose in 1954 in connection with the Kelburne Cup competition. Jack Kelly and his team – Dick Belton, Des Purcell and Jimmy Bastow – had neglected to pay their annual subscriptions by the date specified in the constitution, 31 December. Technically non-members of the association, they could not play in the Kelburne. A special executive meeting was called on 11 March to consider the matter. Kelly received widespread support but Donovan, backed by O'Riordan, pointed to the obligation to enforce the rules. It was accepted that the failure of Kelly and his team-mates to affiliate was an oversight; nevertheless, rules could not be ignored.[9]

The impasse was broken when Frank McMenamin and Geraldine McConkey proposed a special executive meeting, at which a motion could be tabled calling for a special general meeting which could amend the constitution by changing the date by which subscriptions were due. However, the special general meeting, held at the Four Courts Hotel on 10 April, rejected the motion. The matter did not end there: an executive meeting of 29 April suspended standing orders, to allow the election to the association of the four whose membership had lapsed. Donovan may have felt he had a score to settle with Kelly. With Bastow and Purcell, he had previously won the Kelburne twice. Was Donovan piqued because Belton had replaced him on the team? People who knew him testify to his lack of malice, and it is more likely that it was Donovan's obsession with upholding the rules which led to the unpleasant incident. By 1954, Belton and Kelly had become a regular pair.

At the end of his four years as CBAI honorary secretary, Donovan clashed with Liam Barry[11] (Tramore). At an executive meeting in June 1955, Donovan drew attention to two circulars issued by Barry in connection with the position of honorary secretary. The circulars, it would appear, were critical of Donovan, and he asked the authority of the executive to seek legal advice as to whether they were of a defamatory nature. The following month, at the first meeting of the new executive, Barry, who replaced Donovan as honorary secretary, pointed out that counsel's opinion had not been forthcoming. He explained that, in view of Donovan's tendency to consult the law, he had revised the alleged inflammatory circular, which, lawyers had assured him, was quite innocuous.

The rivalry between Donovan and Barry continued after the former had left office. At the executive meeting of 11 November 1955, Mrs McConkey drew attention to the condition of the Aungier Street office and the stocks stored there. Barry reported that the stock was damaged. He had salvaged whatever was saleable and sold it to clubs at a bargain price. The revelation pointed towards neglect on Donovan's part, and items were missing, according to Barry, who had written to Donovan on the subject. Donovan replied, not to the honorary secretary, but to the president, Nellie Faul, claiming no responsibility for any damage or missing items. The meeting agreed not to pursue the matter. O'Riordan, still honorary treasurer, reported that renting of the Aungier Street premises had ceased.

At the European championships in Amsterdam in 1955, a daily news bulletin was published for the first time.[12] Copies which participants brought home introduced novel bidding methods to Irish players. Philip Quinn featured one of those, the Marmic system, used by an Italian pair, in his *Irish Times* column.[13] Donovan liked the system and used it in competition. This led to a clash with Denis Jackson, a man who also liked to implement rules – or indeed, as in the story that follows, to make rules to enforce his will.

In a regional competition played in early 1958, Jackson, as tournament director,[14] refused to allow Donovan and his partner to use Marmic.[15] There was no regulation forbidding the use of the complex system, and Donovan used every avenue of appeal, right up to the CBAI executive. Jackson, as CBAI honorary secretary, was in the position of power, and the incident led to the executive deciding that 'any system or convention, of which a published English version is not readily available in Ireland, may not be used'. The decision continued: 'Players using generally recognised systems or conventions in conjunction with their own variations may do so provided the variations are explainable in a few moments.' Those strictures applied to pairs competition. In team tournaments, 'such a system may be used provided a complete English version is submitted to the other competing teams at least seven days before a match'. That rule, introduced by the CBAI at Jackson's instigation to curb Donovan's use of Marmic, is still in force.

Despite having disagreements with many people, Donovan was acknowledged to be a large-hearted and generous man who did not bear malice. Many whom he irritated had affection for him. Ina McMenamin was forced to withdraw from the 1955 European championships because of illness. Her granddaughter, Deirdre Fitzpatrick, is in possession of a letter, from Donovan to Ina, expressing his regret that she was unable to play, but wishing her well, 'despite some conflict between us'. That she retained the letter betrays her affection for him. Ruth Giddings probably best summed up how people felt towards him: 'Paddy was a great pal of mine,' she said, before adding, 'of course, I never agreed with him.'

Paddy Paul Donovan died suddenly in April 1977 following a game in the Regent Bridge Club. Playing with Ruth Giddings, and needing a part-score to win the rubber, the auction began 1♥ from Ruth, 1♠ from Donovan. Ruth's rebid of 2♥ would normally have ended the auction, but Donovan insisted on playing the hand, and bid 2♠. He made the contract and in typical good humour went to the bar for a drink. Returning to Ruth's table laughing, he playfully teased her: 'Oh, I couldn't let Ruth play that hand.' These were his last words before he fell at her feet.[16]

20

MASTER-POINTS

The use of master-points was introduced in September 1958. The topic was first raised at the inaugural meeting of the Irish Bridge Union three years earlier, in the context of raising revenue. After the idea of a capitation levy on clubs was dismissed, Larry Bradley suggested a master-points system similar to the one used in America.[1] Details of this scheme could, he believed, be had from Alvin Landy in New York. The first subcommittee of the IBU, consisting of Bradley, George Sloane and Wilfie Robb, all from Northern Ireland, was appointed and asked to submit recommendations on the matter. No helpful information came from across the Atlantic, and the committee failed to come up with anything concrete.

The subject was next discussed by the CBAI executive in July 1958, when it was agreed that what had proved to be successful in other countries should be tried in Ireland. The task of preparing a scheme was entrusted to the committee of the Dublin region, with the honorary secretary, Denis Jackson, also being involved. The Dublin committee worked over the summer, and one of the most speedily and efficiently expedited plans in the history of Irish bridge went into operation in September, with Rita McLoughlin as master-points secretary. The mixed-pairs championship for the Spiro Cup, run in Tramore in November, was the first national competition for which master-points were awarded, with the winners, Ina McMenamin and Gerry Read, each receiving four 'B' points – the equivalent of modern national points. The runners-up got three points each, the third-placed players two, and the fourth- and fifth-placed one.

At the CBAI executive meeting of 2 May 1959, Geraldine McConkey, president of the Dublin region, reported that the scheme had been 'a tremendous success', having raised £126 for the CBAI. A meeting on 28 November was told that since the previous April, the sale of master-point books had realised £214. In March 1960, £200 was transferred to the coffers of the CBAI, and in July 1961 an additional £288 was handed over.

Master-points were used to raise revenue for the CBAI. Following the example set in Great Britain, clubs purchased, from the association, certificates, which were issued to members who earned them in competition. Except in the case of national championships, where points were automatically credited to the winners, the individual was responsible for registering points with the secretary of the master-points committee. There was no compulsion to register.

Players were classified as various levels of 'master'. At the end of 1959, Miss McLoughlin reported that there was one master and fourteen regional masters, twenty-nine local masters, 113 club masters and a total of 200 registered players. Names of holders of the various ranks were not recorded.[2]

Thereafter, the master-points secretary, with an eye to promotion, regularly published lists of the leading master-point holders. At the end of 1961, by which point the scheme had been in operation for three years, there were twenty-seven masters – players with fifty or more points. Only five were from outside Dublin: Gordon Holmes and Mrs M. Hurley, Limerick; Eddie Barry, Waterford; Moreen McCarthy, Wexford; and Enda Boland, Bray. Eighteen of the Dublin-based masters were past or future internationals; the other four were Mrs R. H. Watchorn, Kevin Fowler, Mrs W. Dunne and Miss V. Dunne. There were contradictory figures published with regard to the total number of competitors who had registered for points,[3] but the total can be estimated at between 11 and 15 percent of the total membership.

By October 1963, two players – Ruth Giddings with 211 points, and Peter Pigot with 150 – had attained the rank of national master. Thirteen one-star masters were listed in the order of their points holding: Ann Quinn, Geraldine McConkey, J. P. MacHale, J. A. Kelly, M. F. O'Connell, Doreen Cairnduff, Eileen O'Doherty, Alice Mahon, G. A. Holmes, M. Shrage, May McNulty, Lily Maguire and Ina McMenamin.

Rita McLoughlin was the key figure in the pioneering work in this area. In preparing the scheme, she received help from the English Bridge Union, whose system had been operating for the previous two years. From September 1958, she was in regular attendance at executive meetings, reporting on progress or on difficulties encountered. The first contentious point arose following Denis Jackson's writing to the EBU's master-point committee with a view to mutual recognition of master-points between the two governing bodies. The EBU rejected the suggestion. The Dun Laoghaire congress, with which Jackson was associated, had advertised that points won at the congress would be accepted by the EBU, but no agreement on this matter was reached.

From its inception, and into the early 1960s, the scheme was almost always an item on CBAI executive agendas. The scheme was not without problems. Some clubs were slow to implement it. For instance, Galway still had not issued master-points by the end of October 1959, fourteen months after the introduction of the scheme. On 28 October, on Dick Tierney's suggestion, the club decided to issue master-points for its weekly competitions (but only for two nights per month) as well as for its major club competitions.[4] Elsewhere, there was confusion as to how the system should be organised. At Wexford's AGM in October 1964, a Mr Murphy stated: 'it is now essential to issue points certificates to winners. Hitherto only a few members accepted the points certificates and paid for them.'[5] It is clear from this remark that members had to pay for their certificates – hardly an incentive to promote the scheme, and definitely not what Rita McLoughlin and her committee intended. Wexford decided that in future the cost of the certificates should be a charge on the club. Also that year, the executive yielded to a request from the North-eastern region to waive the 1,000-point qualification to play in the Spiro, as a courtesy to the president, Gerry Hunt from Cavan. One can infer from the request that the region had not been enthusiastic in implementing the scheme.

In September 1960, Michael Hurley from Limerick proposed modifications to the system aimed at making it attractive to smaller clubs. Hurley's idea was that all clubs should rank equally, each to hold one weekly competition, for which master-points would be awarded. He suggested an increase in the top award at all levels – club, region and congress – and that lower allocations should be abolished. In January, Rita McLoughlin reported that the revised scheme, largely based on Hurley's suggestions, was in operation.

David Pigot saw the challenge matches against Harold Franklin's English team in March 1960 as a stimulus to the master-points scheme. Entries to regional trials, to select teams to play against Franklin, were confined to master-point holders. This, the first attempt to use master-points as a standard of entry to competition, did not work: some trials participants held no points. However, there was a tightening up afterwards. Two and a half years after their introduction, master-points were proving successful, and not solely for raising money. They were perceived to be an objective measure of standard, and players considered them to be of value.

Rita McLoughlin kept tight control over the administration of the scheme. In September 1964, it was reported that neither Sligo nor Dundalk congresses had awarded points. Although there was no obligation on individual players to register points, congresses, clubs and regions were obliged to issue certificates. Indeed, as late as 1977, following complaints, the honorary secretary, Marie Gleeson, issued a directive to congress committees on the subject.[6]

The scheme continued to be run for the association by the Dublin region until the summer of 1963, when the CBAI appointed a master-points subcommittee, to which every region nominated a member. Rita McLoughlin continued to carry out the routine work. The involvement of representatives from the provinces seems to have had an effect on the scheme. During the committee's first year, £369 was raised, compared with £252 the previous year – an increase of nearly 50 percent.

Miss McLoughlin retained the position of master-point secretary until illness forced her to resign in 1969. Gerry Deignan reported to the executive, on behalf of the committee, on 30 March of that year and was duly appointed in her place. In 1969, the scheme generated £490 for the CBAI. The woman who had devised the original master-point scheme and administered it for its first eleven years is commemorated in the McLoughlin Cup. The cup was awarded originally to Dublin region's intermediate 'A' pairs champions, and on the division of the region in 1989 it was assigned to Dublin North. Gerry Deignan was no less assiduous when he took over the master-point administration, keeping handwritten records of the continually increasing number of players registering points. The practice was continued by his successor, Frank Kirrane, until computerisation was introduced in the 1980s.

Master-points have been used as a discriminating tool, especially in determining entry to international trials. When intermediate grades were introduced, master-points were a ready-made tool for determining the various divisions.

THE EXCITING 1960s

For bridge in Ireland, the 1960s were punctuated by a series of visits by groups from abroad. These visits began in March 1960, when a team led by British expert Harold Franklin played a hundred-board match in Athlone against a selection from the North-western, Western and North Midlands regions. The three-region trials to pick a team to play the visitors had attracted an entry of twenty-eight pairs.[1]

FRENCH VISITORS

The announcement in July 1960 that the recently crowned World Olympiad champions, France, would tour Ireland the following spring stimulated widespread interest. The visit was Gerry Read's idea and he approached Messrs Murray Ltd, the manufacturers of Craven A cigarettes, who agreed to sponsor the visit. David Pigot, who was friendly with the perfume magnate Baron Robert de Nexon (who was president of the French Bridge Federation and of the world and European governing bodies), was instrumental in making the arrangements.

The visit affected Irish bridge in a number of ways. It provided a focus and an aim for the top players in the months leading up to it. It also afforded the CBAI executive an opportunity to promote the master-point scheme. The increased press coverage stimulated public interest in the game. Following the decision to play matches in Limerick, Athlone and Dun Laoghaire, trials to select teams to play against the visitors were held in November in those three centres. The trials drew from wide catchment areas. For example, entries for the Athlone trials were sought from the North Midlands, Western and North-western regions. It was required that trials participants should have a specified minimum number of master-points. On 22 March 1961, master-point secretary Rita McLoughlin reported to the executive that the visit of the French had resulted in additional clubs adopting the scheme, so that their members could earn enough points to enter the competitions from which selections were made.

The French arrived in March 1961. De Nexon brought with him a formidable line-up, including three of the Olympiad-winning team: Rene Bacherich and Roger Trezel; Pierre Ghestem, creator of the over-calling convention to show a two-suiter hand;[2] Louis Malabat, Robert Mantilla and Nadine Alexandre, one of France's leading women players, completed the team. They played a hundred-boards match in Cruises Hotel, Limerick, on 13 and 14 March, when a local side proved no match for the world champions. The next day, the French travelled to the Shamrock Lodge Hotel in Athlone, where Des Houlihan and Laur Sheeran (Birr), Tom Gleeson and Tom McCormack (Athlone), and Maureen Ryder and Mrs N. Stewart (Galway) caused a major upset by beating their opponents over fifty deals. It was an extraordinary feat by the Midlands and Western players: apart from Houlihan, none of them had experience with that calibre of opponent. A year later, in March 1962, the achievement in Athlone appeared even better when Trezel and Pierre Jais won the gold medal at the first world pairs championships in Cannes, with Ghestem and Bacherich taking the bronze.

The visit ended at the Royal Marine Hotel, Dun Laoghaire, on 16 and 17 March with another hundred-boards contest. There the visitors faced the strongest Irish team of the tour: Ruth Giddings, May McNulty, Eileen O'Sullivan, Cleo Fellows, Joe MacHale and Peter Pigot. The home side held the visitors for the first half of the match, after which the French pulled away, winning easily.

POLISH TOUR

In the 1960s, Poland was not yet the great bridge nation it subsequently became.[3] To the rest of the world, the state of the game was largely unknown in that country, which was then cut off from Western Europe by the Iron Curtain. Its first venture into European championships, in Vienna in 1957, was not impressive: it finished second-last of the seventeen competing nations. The Poles did not compete again until four years later, when, in Beirut, they climbed to seventh – four places ahead of

Ireland. When they won the bronze medals in Baden-Baden in 1963, the bridge world took notice. By then, the 1966 European championships had been allocated to Warsaw. Poland was about to move centre stage.

Enda Boland, who was constantly searching for ways to improve the standard of Irish bridge, became president of the CBAI in 1963 and invited Poland to send a team to Ireland. The Poles were reaching out to the West: in 1963, a Polish cycling team had won the eight-day, multi-stage road race the Rás Tailteann, proving that, in at least that sport, the Irish had some ground to make up.[4] The Poles were to make a similar point with bridge, only more emphatically.

Six Polish players and three officials arrived in Ireland on 5 February 1964, to begin an eleven-day tour during which they would play – and win – eleven matches. Eight of the CBAI's regions in turn hosted the visitors.[5] Dublin fielded two squads. In addition, the Poles played against the recently selected Irish open and women's teams that were due to take part in the New York Olympiad in May. A match against Northern Ireland, included in the original schedule, was cancelled.

Most of the contests were over forty-eight deals. Only two teams succeeded in putting up real opposition to the visitors. North Munster, represented by four of the Irish open team which had played in Baden-Baden – Coman, Fitzgerald, Holmes and O'Connell (the latter on loan from South Munster), augmented by Mrs M. Quaid and Mrs MacMahon – held the visitors to twenty-one imps in Tipperary, after the lead had changed hands a number of times. The Irish women's team, which had been selected for the Olympiad – Ruth Giddings, Barbara Seligman, Lily Maguire, Beatrice Titterington, Nellie Cotter and Sheila Kirwan – lost by only seventeen points, in Dublin, having led narrowly with one eight-board segment remaining.

Elsewhere, the Polish players exposed the poor standard of the Irish game. South Midlands suffered the heaviest defeat, by 127 imps over forty boards, in Kilkenny. The Irish open team was humiliated in Dublin, losing by ninety-three imps. Bearing in mind that the visitors played forty-eight boards most days and faced long journeys daily from venue to venue, as well as being wined and dined by their hosts in every town they visited, the tour was a triumph for them and a reminder to Irish players that they were a little short of the top European standards. The Polish players introduced bidding methods which were new to most of their Irish opponents, including transfers in response to a 1NT opening bid.

135

In view of the heavy defeat of Ireland's national open team in Dublin, it was surprising that the result was emphatically reversed in the first round of the Olympiad in New York just eleven weeks later. Under the revised international victory point scale, the Irish beat the Poles – substantially the same side that had toured in February – 5–2. Ireland beat Poland again the following year in Ostend.

The Polish tour differed from that of other groups that came to Ireland during the 1960s, because the visitors were not confined to meeting the top-grade players exclusively: every region got the opportunity to select teams to play against the visitors. Apart from North Munster, Eastern and Dublin regions, those chosen were not internationals, nor were they likely to be. For most of the Irish participants, it was a once-in-a-lifetime opportunity to meet players from abroad. The teams that opposed the Poles are listed in Appendix J.

English–Swiss Team

Enda Boland was also behind the invitation to a team of six world-class players – Ewart Kempson, Geoffrey Fell, Tony Priday, Claude Rodrigues (England), Jeanne Besse and Dara Hakimi (Switzerland) – who played three matches in Ireland in February 1965. In Dun Laoghaire, they defeated Boland, J. J. Bailey, J. A. Kelly, G. F. Read, M. Shrage, J. P. MacHale and P. J. Pigot by eighty-four imps over forty-eight boards. In Tipperary, the visitors played two matches against Boland, J. Fitzgerald, F. W. and M. F. O'Connell, E. O. Barry and G. A. Holmes, with John Coman as non-playing captain. On 13 February, the English–Swiss combination won a thirty-two-board match by sixteen imps, while the next day they were victorious again in a shorter encounter, of twenty-four boards, by a margin of forty-one points.

Irish in Czechoslovakia and Austria

Boland also organised a two-week visit to Czechslovakia, starting at the end of April 1967. He and Dick Belton, Jim Fitzgerald, Michael O'Connell, Sonya Britton and Lily Maguire began the tour in Prague, where they lost an eighty-board match to the Czech national team, 154–175 imps. At the Marienabad international congress, they finished third in the congress teams: Fitzgerald and O'Connell won the main pairs event, and Boland won the individual contest. The following year, Boland again brought a party to Czechoslovakia. With him were his son Fergal, Jim Fitzgerald, John Coman, Laur Sheeran, Ann Quinn, Maura Kirby and M. W. Broderick. In addition to participating in the Czech international bridge week, they crossed the border into Budapest, where Boland, Sheeran, Coman and Fitzgerald played two matches against the Hungarian national team. In August 1969, Boland, Wesley Burrowes, Arthur Kavanagh, Risteárd De Barra, John McIlhinney and Conor O'Hara attended the Austrian international bridge week in Wachau.

ENDA BOLAND

Enda Boland made an enormous contribution to bridge and was the first great mentor of younger players. To Bray, where he taught and directed the club for many years, as well as founding a congress, he left the legacy of the 16–18 no-trump opening. He came from one of the country's most influential political families. His father Gerald and his brother Kevin were ministers in Fianna Fáil governments. His uncle, the ill-fated Harry Boland, took the republican side in the civil war and was killed by Free State government forces in July 1922. Given his background, it would have been understandable had Enda adopted a hardline attitude towards Irish participation in the Camrose. However, in 1978 he supported Laur Sheeran's motion to seek re-entry to the Camrose and his appeal to keep politics out of bridge. His first wife, Eilish, achieved some fame as a songwriter. Her best-known composition, 'Oh To Be in Doonaree', became a hit for Ruby Murray, Vera Lynn and others. On Eilish's death, Enda married Zlata, whom he had met in Czechoslovakia.

LAUR SHEERAN AND HIS TWO-DIAMOND CONVENTION

Laur Sheeran from Birr, an engineer by profession, was a life-long bridge fanatic and one of the heroes of the victory over the French in Athone in 1961. In 1960, he and local solicitor D. A. Houlihan won the CBAI men's pairs championship for the Revington Cup.

Sheeran served on the executive of the CBAI and on the Irish Bridge Union council. North Midlands region nominated him as CBAI president, an office he took up in 1974. At a time when it was not popular to do so, he tried to persuade the association to apply for re-entry to the Camrose.

In 1961, he formulated his 2♦ convention. It remained popular for more than twenty years and was a standard option printed on convention cards into the mid-1980s. The 'Sheeran 2♦' lent itself to accuracy when holding certain balanced hands facing a 1NT opening bid. In response to 1NT (twelve to fourteen),[6] 2♦ showed eleven high-card points; 2NT showed twelve. Few players explored the convention further, but there was more to it.[7] 'Sheeran' got around the loss of a 2♦ natural response by going through Stayman: 1NT: 2♣; then, following any reply from opener, responder's 3♦ was the weak take-out in diamonds, but a level higher than the direct natural bid. Of course, one needed a six-card or longer diamond suit.

Sheeran also used Stayman to distinguish between game-forcing major responses and invitational major bids. 1NT:3♥ (or 3♠) was forcing. Starting with 1NT:2♣, responder's jump to 3♥ (or 3♠) when opener replied 2♦ was invitational. It was possible to find a 4–4 major fit. Following 1NT:2♦, opener's 2♥ showed fewer than fourteen points, four hearts and possibly four spades also. Opener's rebid of 2♠ showed four spades, denied four hearts, with fewer than fourteen. Responder then decided the contract. Following the same initial sequence, 1NT:2♦, opener's 3♣ was game-forcing, following which the responder bid 3♦ to show both majors or made a Stayman-like bid to show other hand shapes.

The 2♦ response was used also with hands of seventeen or more points to elicit vital information concerning the strength and composition of opener's hand. A slam could then be explored.

'Sheeran' was more comprehensive than the outline sketched above, but few played the convention in its entirety. Its simplest bids, 2♦ to show eleven points, 2NT to show twelve, were widely used, largely thanks to George Ryan, who featured them in his best-selling book *The Bones of Bridge*. As bidding methods became more sophisticated, especially with the increasingly widespread use of transfers, the popularity of 'Sheeran' declined. Nowadays, it is used by a mere scattering of partnerships.

Laur Sheeran never achieved a full international cap, although he did take part in friendly matches like the ones against the French and the Hungarians mentioned above, and he went on a tour of Poland in 1972. The closest he came to international recognition came only weeks after the French visit. He and Des Houlihan (Birr), with Eddie Barry and

Gordon Holmes, led the trials until the last match, in which they went under to the only Northern Ireland quartet to win an Irish team trial: Aidan Lennon, Jim O'Dempsey, Sonny Diamond and Monty Rosenberg (Monty's first All-Ireland cap). A third pair was added to the team but it did not include Laur: the nod went to Cork's O'Connell brothers. In 1964, Sheeran and Houlihan again went close when, having led throughout the first weekend of the final, they dropped to fifth over the last couple of matches. In 1967, the Birr pair finished fourth under the Butler scoring system, but they were not really close, as the leading three pairs were a long way clear.

Laur died suddenly at his home near Navan in August 2007. His lifelong friend, George Ryan, paying tribute to him in the *Irish Bridge Journal*, admitted that he owed his life to Laur. Both men had been addicted to alcohol, and it was Laur who had persuaded George to take the step that returned him to health.

THE BONES OF BRIDGE

George Ryan wrote *The Bones of Bridge* in 1966, having left his primary-school teaching job for a period to teach bridge professionally. Travelling the length and breadth of the country to conduct his classes, he saw the need for a concise, conveniently sized book as a way of following up on his classroom instruction. Cleverly designed to fit into a woman's handbag or a man's pocket, Ryan's little volume was an instant success. The biggest-selling Irish bridge publication of all time, it went through several print runs and sold all over the English-speaking world. Its last edition came out in the late 1980s. George followed up with *Some of the Flesh* in 1967.

HELVIC

Eoin O'Riordan devised 'Helvic', a convention which, although it did not achieve the popularity of Sheeran's creation, nevertheless outlived it. The manner of its introduction is testimony to O'Riordan's sense of humour. In 1968, he played in the trials[8] with Wolfgang Heidenfeldt – who was also a chess master. The fastidious German refused to use Eoin's creation because it was not a recognised convention: it did not even have a name.

O'Riordan told Heidenfeldt that it was 'all the rage on the Continent'.

'What is it called?' asked Heidenfeldt. 'It must have a name.'

'I don't know,' replied Eoin, 'but I'll find out.'

That night he randomly chose a volume of an encyclopedia from his bookshelves and randomly selected a page. The first word he saw was 'Hellvic'. Thus the convention was named. His partner was happy. One of the 'L's was dropped during a printing of convention cards, so it became 'Helvic'.[9]

THE ANTHEM AND THE FLAG

Although politics remained outside of Irish Bridge Union meetings, potentially explosive topics were occasionally raised. The minutes of the CBAI executive meeting of 2 September 1961 record that a proposal for 'an alternative flag and anthem for the Irish teams in Torquay, submitted by the general-purposes committee of the NIBU', had been withdrawn following correspondence between Denis Jackson and Norman Douglas, the joint honorary secretaries. Four members of the Irish open team were from Northern Ireland. There was an awareness that the Tricolour and the anthem of the Republic might be offensive to some Northern players. Douglas had obviously taken soundings on the subject. The decision not to pursue the matter may have been taken out of common sense. The open team was unlikely to end up on the podium in Torquay, while the women, who did in fact take third place, were all from the South.

However, the meeting, presided over by Dick Tierney, agreed that 'some steps must be taken at the next IBU meeting to safeguard the position should such a matter be raised again'. There is a hint of rumblings beneath the surface in David Pigot's undertaking to raise the matter at the European Bridge League with a view to having the the position restated 'in the event of dissolution of the IBU and an application by the CBAI to rejoin the EBL, as arranged at the time of the formation of the IBU'.[10]

Nonetheless, the matter was not raised at the next IBU meeting,[11] nor subsequently (or if it was, nothing on the subject was recorded). Douglas wrote the minutes of IBU meetings. Jackson, the difficult and overbearing man that he was, nevertheless seems to have been astute in avoiding potentially delicate political issues.[12]

ISRAEL IN, SCOTLAND OUT

Occasionally, the wider world of politics impinged on the relative tranquility of Irish bridge. In 1963, the Irish Bridge Union council unanimously directed David Pigot to support Israel's application to join the European Bridge League.[13] Two years earlier, the council had sat on the fence with regard to Scotland's application to join the EBL as an entity separate from Great Britan. While the IBU expressed sympathy with the Scottish application, it was left to Pigot to decide how to vote at the EBL meeting.[14] While Pigot's views are not known, he nevertheless reported to the next meeting that 'Scotland's application had met with great opposition and had been defeated by a large majority'.[15]

WORLD PAIRS, CANNES

The Irish Bridge Union held trials in March 1962 to select three pairs to contest the world pairs championship in Cannes. One hundred and sixty-two pairs entered. Preliminary qualifiers were played in different centres, leading to a semi-final of forty-eight pairs and a twenty-four-pairs final. Gordon Holmes and Jack Kelly, Joe MacHale and Peter Pigot, and Barry and Michael O'Connell took the first three places. However, taking into account Irish women players' recent performances in international competition, it seems extraordinary that no Irish representatives were chosen to contest the women's pairs. Only five months earlier, Ireland's women had won the bronze medal in the team championships in Torquay. Ruth Giddings and Barbara Seligman finished fourth in the trials and, although Seligman was at the start of her career and as yet untried at the top level, it was astonishing that they were not sent to Cannes for the women's event.

At the IBU meeting on 26 November 1961, at which the world pairs event was discussed, the women's championship was not even mentioned. Denis Jackson, the joint honorary secretary and who would have received the relevant correspondence from the World Bridge Federation, informed the meeting of a mixed-teams competition, a kind of curtain-raiser in Cannes. It appears that he did not inform the meeting of the women's competition, however. The delegates present[16] were not all unaware of the programme. David Pigot, a member of the EBL and WBF executives, certainly knew about it.

141

The failure to send women to Cannes becomes reprehensible when we discover, in the minutes of the meeting of 15 April 1962, that Ruth Giddings had written to the IBU asking if she and her partner, Barbara Seligman could play in Cannes at their own expense. Northern delegates Des Deery and Norman Douglas proposed that Giddings and Seligman, along with the pairs who had finished fifth and sixth in the trials, should be invited to play on Giddings's terms. This proposal was rejected by eight votes to five. The delegates present were: from the CBAI, Mrs McConkey, R. A. Tierney, D. T. Waldron, Mrs Faul, T. Murray, D. R. Pigot, E. McArdle and D. G. Jackson, and from the NIBU, S. Blaney, D. A. Cohen, H. S. Diamond, M. Rosenbery, B. Vard, Deery and Douglas. It is interesting to note that even at this time, a mere fortnight before the event began, the women's championship was not mentioned. Giddings and Seligman, it seems, were willing to take their chances in the open competition. There was no mechanism for appeal against the IBU council's blind indifference to the talent of Ireland's leading women players; and if there was any protest, it was not recorded.

In September in Beirut, women would highlight the IBU council's injustice by taking another bronze medal in European competition, with Giddings and Seligman on the team, as the men finished a sad second-last.

MacHale and Pigot – the latter would not win his first full cap for another three years – did well in Cannes, reaching the thirty-six-pairs final.[17] Holmes and Kelly had a moment of jubilation, when they too were declared to have qualified in thirty-fifth place, but the discovery of a misboarding, and the resulting adjusted score, meant that they were relegated.

VICTORY POINTS

The choice of pairs trials to pick the teams for the Europeans in Baden-Baden in 1963 was influenced by the poor team entries of the previous year.[18] The open team which emerged went on to become the first to finish in the top half of a European championship, while the women, although they looked strong, with four former European-medal winners in the line-up, had their worst result in fourteen years.

The 1963 trials were the first Irish competition in which the victory-point scale was used. The scale, which had been employed in European championships, looks strange to the modern player. It would undergo modifications as time passed. Six victory points (vps) was the maximum per match. An imp difference of 0–3 was converted to a 3–3 draw, 4–8 was a 4–2 win, 9–16 won 5–1, while a difference of 17 or greater translated to the maximum 6–0 victory points.

EROSION OF ECCLESIASTICAL POWER IN GALWAY

The control exercised by Catholic Church authorities was taken for granted in the conservative and conformist city of Galway, where Bishop Michael Browne was a domineering presence. Holding the annual West of Ireland congress over the Easter weekend had the potential to bring the organisers into conflict with ecclesiastical power. The congress committee invariably yielded to the bishop's will, although it took the risk of quietly running open pairs on the evening of Good Friday. In 1956, it was announced that the playing time would be 'restricted by the extension of the Lenten ceremonies'. There would be no competitions on Easter Saturday. The Faller Cup (for congress pairs) was held over two sessions, of thirty-two and thirty boards, on the Sunday.

The following year, the congress committee, in order not to clash with Easter Saturday church ceremonies, decided that there should be no major competition that evening. The Faller Cup was held on Saturday afternoon and Sunday afternoon, with the team-of-four championship for the Cross Cup being contested on Sunday evening and Monday. Over the next decade, the congress committee became braver, a more secular attitude crept in, and eventually, during the early 1960s, a session of the pairs was played on the Saturday evening.

However, at the AGM of the club on 13 December 1967, the Reverend Éamonn McInerney, a local priest and a club member, suggested that holding a session of a major competition on Saturday night deprived some members of the opportunity to take part in the competition. In his view, they would attend the church ceremonies rather than play in the congress pairs. Mild opposition to this proposal was led by Dick Tierney, until McInerney asserted his authority and proposed a motion, seconded by future club president James O'Dowd, 'that this meeting directs the committee in charge of organising the Easter congress will not hold a session of a major competition on Easter Saturday night'. This was a proposal from the floor. There was no notice of motion on the matter before the AGM. Indeed, it was hardly a fit motion. Such subtleties did not deter McInerney, nor did Gerald O'Donnell, who presided, rule him out of order. Predictably, the proposal was carried by a substantial majority.

Balances of power were shifting everywhere in the 1960s, however, and the reverend gentleman did not have the last word. A month later, on 17 January 1968, an extraordinary general meeting which had been called on foot of a requisition by twenty-four members rescinded the decision.[19]

DAVID PIGOT

David R. Pigot died unexpectedly in 1965. A well-known Dublin solicitor, he was, at least in his younger years, renowned as a cricketer and was a leading figure in the Phoenix Club. He and his wife, Violet – nicknamed 'Copper' because of her glowing, light-auburn-coloured hair – became the first husband-and-wife Irish bridge internationals when they were selected for the CBAI's second Camrose match, against Northern Ireland, in April 1937.

Pigot acted as non-playing captain in four further pre-war Camrose contests. In 1949, he was playing captain of Ireland's open team in the second post-war European championships in Paris. However, it was as an administrator that Pigot stood above his contemporaries. On the formation of the Dublin Metropolitan Register in 1943, he became its president, remaining so for the ten-year existence of that body. He was elected president of the CBAI in 1945. When the office of vice-president was abolished in 1948, Pigot was elected to the new position of chairman of the executive committee, an office he held until it, in turn, was abolished in 1954. Two years later, he became vice-president, the first of the long-term incumbents of that office, who were retained in the position for the sake of continuity and stability.

As Ireland's delegate to the European Bridge League, Pigot quickly made an impression on his European colleagues, and he was elected to its executive committee in 1952. On the formation of the World Bridge Federation six years later, he became a member of its executive too. His legal background was probably a factor in his appointment to the laws and ethics committee of the world body. In that position, he had input into the drafting of laws.

When Pigot died, there was debate as to how best to commemorate him. The European Bridge League presented the opportunity to honour his memory when it introduced junior bridge (age-related) in 1968. When the first European junior championship was fixed for Prague that year, a fund was established in Ireland – North and South – to purchase a trophy for the event. The young participants in Prague in August 1968 competed for the David Pigot Trophy, donated by Ireland to perpetuate the memory of a man whose contribution to the game has been surpassed by few. (Ironically, Ireland has never won the David Pigot Trophy. The closest an Irish team came was in Copenhagen in 1974, when Nick FitzGibbon, Adam Mesbur, Michael McGloughlin, David Scannell, John McKeon and Donal O'Donovan took the silver medal. The championship was held in Dun Laoghaire in 1970 and won by Denmark.)

Pigot is also commemorated in his native Dublin. The Pigot Cup, originally awarded to the old Dublin region's team champions – the qualifier for the Kelburne – went to Dublin South in the division of the region in 1989.

22

THE CONGRESS DECADE

The 1960s was the decade of the bridge congress, although of course a number had been held before that. The Butlin's Holiday Camp congress in Mosney, County Meath, was first held in 1954[1] and continued annually until 1959. The novelty of the event, which was held at the end of the holiday season, lay in its location at the popular resort, where participants could book accommodation. The success of the CBAI's belated jubilee celebrations in Jury's Hotel in January 1958 may have given the Dubin region committee the idea for a congress in the heart of the capital. Whatever the inspiration, a congress took place in Jury's in January 1959, and again the two following years, before being dropped.

The 1960s saw a dramatic increase in the number of congresses. Until 1969, new congresses appeared on the calendar every year. The big, established events, the West of Ireland, South of Ireland, East of Ireland and Dun Laoghaire congresses, continued to thrive. Tramore, established in 1951, had by this time joined the elite festivals, its location in the Majestic Hotel overlooking the great strand being part of its attraction.

The Dun Laoghaire congress attracted phenomenal attendances. Although there was a falling off in cross-channel competitors from 1958, overall participation soared as the decade progressed. Its main pairs and team championships attracted what could be considered very good entries, but huge numbers took part in open pairs. In 1955, there had been an impressive fifty-seven open pairs competitions. Two years later, there were seventy-eight. In 1961, there were eighty-five; the following year, eighty-eight. In 1963, there were ninety-two, and in 1965, 101. By 1969, the congress had introduced open pairs for the new junior grade, and it reached a peak of 109 sessions: a hundred normal open pairs, and nine for juniors. The figures are all the more impressive when it is taken into account that they were all Mitchell movements, with first and second prizes for both North–South and East–West. Assuming an average of eleven to twelve tables in each section, 5,000 players sat down to open pairs at the 1969 congress. Over its nine days' duration, this represents twelve competitions involving 550 players daily. The Royal Marine Hotel was unable to accommodate all the competitors, and some events, including the junior pairs, with fifty-two partnerships, were held in the nearby Ardeen Hotel.

In 1968, Dun Laoghaire congress committee awarded a special prize to Michael and Mrs Delaney from Liverpool. What was extraordinary about the couple was that they were both blind. He had lost his sight in the Glen of Imaal explosion in 1941,[2] she during wartime bombings in London. They had brought with them a set of Braille-marked cards and played throughout the congress in open pairs. There have been few accounts of blind people playing bridge. The Dun Laoghaire congress in 1968 may well be the only example of Braille-marked cards being used in duplicate competition in this country.

Bray Bridge Club, with the driving forces of Enda Boland and Roddy Connolly behind it, organised its first congress in 1960. It lapsed for a time but was revived in 1967.

Newry's congress started in 1962 at Ballymascanlon and remained there until it moved to the Great Southern Hotel, Rostrevor, in 1968. Sligo's 'Yeats Country' congress got going in June 1963, and three new congresses appeared in 1964: Ballybunion, Clonmel and City of Derry. Clonmel introduced a novel competition confined to married couples, with a flitch of bacon as the prize. This competition attracted an initial forty-four pairs. 'The Flitch', as it was known, remained popular for many years.

Ballybunion congress was the result of an initiative by three members of Listowel Bridge Club: Maurice O'Sullivan, Shay O'Reilly and Eddie Hanrahan. The congress represented an effort to prolong the tourist season and thereby keep hotel staff occupied until the start of the Listowel Races. Michael and Marjorie Lynch (Limerick) ran the congress from the start. Michael remained the principal tournament director until Billy Mullins took over.[3]

In 1965, Limerick opened at Cruise's Hotel, and Malahide, sponsored by John Player cigarettes, opened at another ideal venue, the Grand Hotel. The same year, Limerick hosted the Opera Festival of Bridge. Organised by Riordan's travel agency and supported by Arthur Guinness & Son, it was repeated the following year before disappearing from the calendar.

Dublin's Intercontinental Hotel sponsored a congress in November 1966, probably inspired by the fact that the hotel had been booked for the European championships the following August. Glenalbyn Bridge Club organised a two-day congress in July 1967 as a fund-raiser for the European event.

Cahir held what was termed a 'mini-congress' – over two days – in March 1968, a week before the first Bankers' congress in Dublin. Later that year, Cork had its first congress, and Blackrock College Club opened its congress for junior players, with Roddy Connolly helping Harry Devine with the planning.

Two congresses were introduced in 1969: there was the Kingdom in Tralee and, at the other end of the country, the Irish Bridge Union organised a week-long event in Newcastle, County Down. The latter was repeated a year later but, unlike other congresses, it was poorly supported and was not run again.

The introduction of new congresses year after year, and their success in attracting patrons, reflected the growing number of people taking up the game across the country.

23

Junior and Intermediate Grades

In 1964, the CBAI recorded membership figures for the first time[1] but, since clubs paid affiliation fees according to a sliding scale based on the number of club members, the total of 5,600 is an approximation. Membership was steadily increasing. By 1967, there were almost 7,000, and the three biggest regions – Dublin, North Munster and South Munster – each had affiliations exceeding 1,000. In 1970, the total reached 8,700, with Dublin exceeding 2,000.

As membership increased, the gap in standards between the established players and those who had joined recently widened, creating a problem for competition organisers. The presence of a dominating group, which monopolised the prizes in national, regional and congress events, discouraged participation. In 1965, for example, only fifteen teams contested the CBAI men's championship for the Geraldine Trophy, and eleven women's teams competed for the McMenamin Bowl. There was no incentive for inexperienced players to take part.

Owen Rowe, one of the country's leading bridge teachers, and his wife, Nancy, honorary secretary of Dublin region, were more aware than most of the problems facing beginners and novices and pioneered confined competition. The Rowes were behind the organising of a junior league over the winter of 1964/65, for those 'who have played little competitive bridge'. They defined junior as 'not having finished first or second in an IBU or CBAI regional or major event'. Seven clubs took part.[2] The league ran from mid-December to mid-March, with a heat in every one of the seven participating clubs. Des Purcell donated a cup, the first holder of which was the Regent, represented by Mr and Mrs P. D. McCarvill, Mrs R. Mulcahy and Mrs D. Young.[3] They won narrowly from a quartet of Trinity College students.[4] Master-points were awarded. The

149

following year, twenty-seven participating teams, representing twelve clubs, were divided into three sections, with the leading four from each going forward to a play-off.

The Rowes's example was quickly followed. Dun Laoghaire congress added a junior team competition to its programme in 1965. The following year, Dublin region ran a team-of-four competition for players 'of intermediate standard' and Dun Laoghaire and Malahide congresses had 'junior' pairs competitions on their programmes. The Eastern region organised what it termed a 'limited event' in January 1967. In April of that year, a Dublin 'intermediate' pairs championship attracted forty-seven pairs. The Civil Service Club ran a 'junior' team contest the same month. A number of clubs introduced 'junior' sections. Of course, the terms 'junior' and 'intermediate' had not yet been defined, but 'junior' was not related to the player's age, despite the fact that many of the prizewinners were still in their twenties.

In a further effort to promote 'junior' bridge, the Rowes donated a cup for a pairs competition. First contested in March 1966, the Rowe Cup was won by a young husband-and-wife pair from Trinity College, Diana and Peter Stocken. On graduating, the Stockens returned to their native England, but many years later Peter was to prove himself a good friend to Irish bridge (see Chapter 30).

Participation in the Rowe Cup over the next few years emphasised the void that had existed before the Rowes's initiative. Sixty-eight pairs competed in 1967; eighty-seven the following year. In 1969, the Rowe Cup attracted ninety-eight pairs and was won by the Rowes's daughter, Aileen, and her fiancé, John O'Keeffe, who, when they married shortly afterwards, kept up the family tradition of teaching bridge.

In addition to their other activities, the Rowes formed a club, New Deal, in which many future champions gained their first competitive experience. They were not alone in wanting to meet the needs of the growing new membership. In North Munster, Michael Hurley raised the question several times.[5]

The success of the pioneering work in the capital resulted in the CBAI executive, in 1967, asking the Rowes to submit proposals for a nationwide scheme for junior and intermediate competitions. The proposals came before the executive in September 1967, were accepted and immediately implemented. The 'intermediate' grade was defined by master-point holding, 'junior' by the length of time spent playing.

Dick Tierney from Galway donated a cup for junior teams, the first winners of which, in 1968, were Aidan and Ena Cleary, Teresa Breslin and John Cunningham, all of whom subsequently became well known. Nick FitzGibbon got his name on the trophy in 1969, Pauline Maguire in 1970, Michael MacDonagh in 1971 and Donal Garvey in 1973 – and all four were destined to win more prestigious trophies and to represent their country.

Two of Dublin's leading clubs came forward with cups: Bankers for the intermediate teams, Civil Service for junior pairs. The first winners of the Bankers Trophy were from Longford: S. Gallagher, J. O'Donnell, and J. J. and Mrs Murphy. John Murphy, a future CBAI president, became a champion of the new grades in the North-western region and donated a cup for a national junior mixed pairs championship.

The list of early winners of some of those trophies makes interesting reading. For example, in 1970 a Mrs Ó Briain from Dublin, with her two young sons Pádraig and Micheál, and Nora Browner, won the Bankers Trophy. The following year, future women's internationals Elva Gannon and Pauline Maguire were on the winning side, while in 1974, a young Paul Porteous got his name on the trophy. The future general secretary of the CBAI had a precocious career as a junior and intermediate player. As well as the Bankers Trophy, he won the Kervick junior pairs in 1973 and the New Ireland, direct-entry intermediate pairs in 1974, all in partnership with Denis O'Connor. The Ó Briain brothers demonstrated that they could win without their mother when, in 1971, they took the same New Ireland Trophy, while their parents won the Hagerty Trophy in the same year.

The novice grade was not introduced until 1979, when the junior mixed pairs event was discontinued. At this point, the J. J. Murphy Cup was transferred to the novice pairs championship.

The introduction of junior and intermediate grades constituted one of the most significant developments in the game since the founding of the national governing body in the 1930s. Inexperienced players no longer felt intimidated or overawed. The innovation facilitated the continuous and accelerating increase of membership in the late 1960s, 1970s and through the 1980s. In 1964, when Nancy Rowe, as Dublin's regional secretary, launched the junior league, CBAI membership was 5,600; twenty years later, it had swelled to 22,246.

The two Dublin universities, TCD and UCD, enthusiastically participated in the bridge activities of the city, especially in the junior events.
The inter-university championship for the Friendship Trophy, first contested in 1960, had given the students an annual goal. In addition, during
the 1960s the two Dublin colleges had an annual match for the Davidson-
Barniville Cup.[6] Some of the students quickly moved up in the ranks. In
1967, Trinity's Peter and Diane Stocken, John Royds and Robert Woods
reached the final of the regional teams championship, for the Pigot Cup,
only to be defeated by Jack Kelly's team of heavyweights.[7]

Northern students made headlines too. In June 1962, Queen's
University Belfast, represented by Des Deery, M. J. Coppel, Nick Percival-
Price and Keith Singleton, won the 'British Isles' Universities' champi-
onship for the Waddington Cup, beating London University in the final.
The following week, Deery and Percival-Price paired up with Enda
Boland and Aidan Lennon, respectively, to contest the IBU trials, which
resulted in twenty-four-year-old Deery gaining his first international cap
at the European championships in Beirut.

An inter-varsity pairs championship was added to the students' calendar in 1969 when five graduates – Marcus Shrage, Des Deery, Eoin
MacNeill, Risteárd De Barra and Michael O'Connell – representing five
different colleges, presented a trophy, the Varsity Cup. First competed for
in December that year, it was won by C. McHugh and V. O'Brien (UCD),
with the Ó Briain brothers from the same college, coming second.

The term 'junior' presents some difficulty for the researcher. While
Owen and Nancy Rowe were promoting competition for inexperienced
players and referring to them as 'juniors', Enda Boland and others were
championing the cause of young players. There was encouraging support
for the latter. In a novel team competition in the Victor Hotel, Dun
Laoghaire, in July 1964, twenty-eight players under thirty each partnered
a master. On the winning team, partnering Eileen O'Sullivan, was Jimmy
Powell, a future national-tournament director. Gerry Read presented a
cup to the Trinity College Club, and the students competed for it annually. In 1965, the Irish Bridge Union introduced an under-thirty-five all-
Ireland pairs championship, which continued annually for ten years.

There is evidence to suggest that Ireland's promotion of youth competition had an influence on the European Bridge League's decision to
initiate a European junior championship. In July 1967, it was reported

that the Czech Bridge Union had offered to organise a European junior competition in Prague the following year. It was hardly coincidental that the offer was made only three months after Enda Boland's visit to that country. The second running of the championship, in 1970, was allocated to Ireland.

As has been noted, Boland was the first great mentor of young players. Denis McGrath followed in his footsteps in the 1980s, when he guided and inspired the young, talented competitors who came through University College Cork. Many successful top-level performers have acknowledged their debt to him.

24

DENIS JACKSON

When invitations to the banquet at the 1991 European championships in Killarney were being discussed, it was suggested that Denis Jackson should be asked to attend.[1] The man who had been chief organiser of the European championships in Dublin in 1967 was, in some people's view, entitled to an invitation. Besides, he had been a member of the European Bridge League executive, one of only two Irish people to hold that position. In the end, Jackson was not invited to Killarney. In researching material for this book, I have not found a more small-minded act. Having delved into the records and spoken to people who knew him, I still do not condone the refusal to invite him – but I do understand it better.

Denis Jackson, a civil servant, lived in Churchtown in south Dublin, although his activities were centred in the adjacent Eastern region, where he became regional secretary. He was elected honorary secretary of the CBAI and joint honorary secretary of the IBU in 1956. As a tournament director, he ranks among the best ever, and he was certainly the foremost such person in his day. In 1959, he was appointed a delegate to the European Bridge League, accompanying the incumbent, David Pigot. When Pigot died in 1965, Jackson was elected a member of the EBL executive, and he became prominent on its tournament and play committee. Michael Lynch described him as 'a very able man, one of the best secretaries of the CBAI, but arrogant'.[2] That arrogance attracted enemies, who gradually closed ranks, finally ousting him at the CBAI AGM in Sligo in 1972. Jackson was rarely far from controversy but two particular incidents alienated him from players across the country.

The Baden-Baden Business, 1963

A suggestion by David Pigot at an IBU meeting in Ballymascanlon on 19 May 1963 led to a clash with Jackson and a rift opening up between the latter and representatives of North Munster. Because the Europeans were to be held in Ireland in 1967, Pigot thought it would be wise to send an observer to the championships in Baden-Baden in July 1963. Pigot suggested (and the meeting agreed) that Joe Honan from Limerick, a former president of both the CBAI and the IBU, be sent. Honan was also duly elected as second delegate to the European Bridge League meetings, to join Pigot at the German resort.

The IBU's decision seems to have taken Jackson by surprise. A week later, on 26 May, an emergency meeting of the IBU council, presumably called at the instigation of the joint honorary secretary, was held to further consider the sending of representatives to Baden-Baden. The meeting unanimously agreed to a second observer – Jackson – on whom it was felt that the major part of the organisational work in connection with the 1967 event would fall. He agreed, provided that he would be able to rearrange his annual leave from his job in the land-registry office. Although he had already been elected as second delegate, Honan surrendered that position and proposed Jackson instead. There was unanimous agreement at the IBU council. It seemed that the business had ended with all parties satisfied. Not so.

A routine report from the IBU was read at the CBAI executive meeting the following week. Time did not permit a discussion of the report, so a special meeting was called on 30 June, at which Pigot took the chair in the absence of the president, Dr Eveleen Arkins.

The atmosphere was tense. A letter addressed to Dr Arkins from the honorary secretary of North Munster challenged the validity of the meeting. A copy of the letter had been sent to all regional secretaries but, pointedly, not to Jackson, whose notice had failed to mention the reason for the meeting. Pigot, having examined the constitution, found that the honorary secretary was not obliged to give the reason. There was no basis for the challenge.

Jackson had allies. Dick Tierney (Galway), supported by Tom Gleeson (Athlone), complained that Pigot had proposed Honan as observer without consulting the members of the CBAI. He felt that the matter could be resolved by asking Honan to withdraw. Jackson expressed concern for the organisation of the 1967 European championships. These were four years away, and he felt it was right to send a younger man. He thought that Owen Rowe, Michael Hurley or Michael Lynch would be suitable observers.

A defensive Pigot regretted what he called 'the misunderstanding'. He said he had no wish or intention to cause pain to anyone, especially the honorary secretary. He referred to a long conversation he had had with Jackson, in which most of the misunderstandings had been straightened out. The meeting unanimously adopted the resolution

> that the honorary secretary of the CBAI be asked to communicate with Mr Honan and ask him to withdraw from the post of observer for the IBU at Baden-Baden and that a copy of this resolution be sent to the joint honorary secretary and the president of IBU.

Jim Fitzgerald from Tipperary seems to have been the only one who grasped that the resolution was an attempt by the CBAI executive to usurp the powers of the Irish Bridge Union. Appointing delegates, observers or whatever to the EBL was a matter for the IBU. The CBAI, apart from the fact that its executive might direct its delegates in regard to voting – and it had not done so in this instance – had no function in the matter.

Jackson's minutes of the CBAI meeting end with:

> The . . . matter was discussed in a . . . friendly and cordial atmosphere. There was no suggestion . . . of a witch-hunt . . . and no attempt made to pillory any individual or group. It resulted in clearing the air . . . and restoring matters to the position which pertained before the incident under discussion.

The position which pertained before the incident was that Denis Jackson was in control.

At the 6 July meeting of the CBAI executive, North and South Munster delegates objected strongly to the wording of the resolution and to the letter which had been sent to Honan. They requested that the CBAI delegates to the IBU be instructed to support the nomination of Mr Honan as observer.

A letter from Honan informed the next meeting of the IBU council on 14 July that he was not withdrawing as observer. Jackson informed the same meeting that he was unable to change his annual leave arrangements after all, and as a result could not go to Baden-Baden. Time and expense had been wasted, and people had been distressed to no purpose. Honan did go to Baden-Baden, and his report as observer was read to the IBU meeting of 25 August at Ballymascanlon. As a result of the incident, Jackson made enemies in North Munster.

There are clues as to what motivated him in pursuing the matter. It may have been a power struggle between him and Pigot, although the latter's position at home and in both the EBL and the World Bridge Federation was secure. Jackson did have an old score to settle with both Pigot and Honan, however. The World Bridge Federation's first World Olympiad had taken place in Turin in 1960. In November 1959, the IBU council had debated whether Ireland should compete in the event or not. Pigot was in favour of participation; Jackson was not. A vote resulted in a tie, but Honan, the president, exercised his casting vote and decided that Ireland should send a team to Turin. A defeat at CBAI or IBU meetings was a rare experience for Jackson. He did not like it, nor did he forget it.

Two years before that, Jackson had changed the date of a CBAI executive meeting, apparently without informing most of the delegates. Honan had been president at the time and, apart from him and Jackson, only four delegates turned up. Whereas the minutes, written by Jackson himself, record merely that the meeting felt that it was not desirable to hold meetings without informing delegates, and that the honorary secretary was asked to write to the other delegates to inform them of the position, it is nevertheless clear that the meeting, with Honan in the chair, rebuked Jackson for his unilateral action. Pigot was also present.

THE IBU PRESIDENCY AFFAIR, 1967

Jackson was at the centre of the controversy surrounding the IBU presidency in 1967. Dr John O'Sullivan from Cork, president of the CBAI from July 1966, normally would have stepped into the office of president of the IBU the following year. However, Jackson and the steering committee for the European championships, which were scheduled for Dublin in 1967, wanted Dr Richard Belton in the role. There were good reasons for choosing Belton. His political and business connections made him the ideal person to attract support. A wealthy man, well known for his generous hospitality, he could afford to entertain visiting VIPs. Furthermore, he had international experience, having played in three

European championships and a World Olympiad. Delegates from South Munster did not see things that way, however. The attempt to sideline O'Sullivan was seen as an insult to their candidate and an affront to the players of the province.

At a CBAI executive meeting in Cork on 6 November 1966, South Munster delegate William McBratney first raised the question. The people in the south were angry. A special meeting, in Athlone on 26 November, required sensitive handling. In the circumstances, neither O'Sullivan, the president, nor Belton, the vice-president, could chair the meeting. Jim Ennis, a solicitor from Rhode, County Offaly, who had made a good impression when he had been president of the CBAI the previous year, and, importantly, was seen as impartial, was asked to take the chair. He agreed, provided that his selection was unanimous. It was. Ennis invited McBratney to open the proceedings but it became obvious that a solution would not be easily found. Ennis called a recess to allow delegates to meet in groups and discuss the matter at leisure. After the meeting had resumed, it was agreed that Ennis should talk separately to both parties, but no progress was made.

At the executive meeting on 19 March, O'Sullivan and Belton left the meeting while the item was being discussed. Ennis took the chair and reported 'complete failure to reach any sort of agreement'. P. C. Kiely, from Mitchelstown, threatened serious consequences if Dr O'Sullivan was not elected. In an interview in 2005, Kiely said that at the time feelings in South Munster were such that there was a possibility of the region breaking away from the CBAI if a solution satisfactory to them was not found.

A note at the end of the minutes of that meeting refers to 'minutes of later meeting taken by M. Lynch [being] attached'. When the later meeting was held is not known, and there is no copy of Lynch's minutes attached to the minute book. The fact that a further meeting was held indicates the entrenched positions taken by the two sides, and especially the tenacity with which the Munster delegates fought for their man.

A further special meeting was held in Athlone on 16 April 1967, with Ennis again in the chair. By then, as a result of informal talks, a compromise had been agreed. Belton would assume the office of president of the IBU at the annual meeting and hold it for the duration of the European championships. Then, after the lapse of a decent interval, he would resign and Dr O'Sullivan would take over as president for the remainder of the year. The meeting recommended, by way of consolation to O'Sullivan, that he should be nominated as non-playing captain of the open team. It transpired that Des Deery was appointed captain by the IBU, but O'Sullivan was given the position the following year for the Olympiad in Deauville.

The episode was an unfortunate one, with the affable Dr O'Sullivan caught in a dispute which was not of his own making; it required six executive meetings, including three special ones, to bring it to an end. Belton proved generous during the championships. As president, he was provided with a suite in the Intercontinental Hotel, but he hired a second one at his own expense to ensure that additional hospitality was available. The Irish players were disappointing, finishing thirteenth of twenty in the open, eighth of thirteen in the women's championship. When it was over, John Coman, from Tipperary, the new president of the CBAI – a friend of Paddy Kiely, and on the Munster side of the dispute – referred to the outstanding success of the championships and generously thanked Jackson and Belton. In accordance with the April agreement, O'Sullivan took over the IBU presidency in October. There was good reason to thank Jackson. Due to his efficient management, there was a surplus of £800 in the coffers of the IBU.[3]

The episode may have been over, but it had repercussions. From a Munster perspective, Denis Jackson was the villain who had deprived their man of the honour of presiding during a major international occasion. Michael Lynch and Paddy Kiely, when I spoke to them in 2005, agreed that the Munster people were out to get Jackson from then on.

SOUTH MUNSTER CENSURED

Two years later, Jackson gave South Munster further cause for complaint when the executive censured the region for changing the date of the men's pairs championship to clash with the women's pairs being held in North Munster. Major events were allocated to the regions by the executive on application. Nobody seems to have questioned how the Revington and Jackson Cup competitions, entries to which are mutually exclusive, could possibly affect each other. Nevertheless, the executive decided that South Munster would not be allocated any national competition for two years. It was an executive decision but it was felt that Jackson was behind it.

In 1970, when George Ryan started with the *Irish Times*, Jackson approached him with a blunt warning: 'I will not allow you to score over the *Irish Independent*.' Mairéad O'Neill, correspondent for the *Independent*, got on well with Jackson, but there was never any rivalry between her and Ryan, with whom she worked in close co-operation. Minutes of several meetings record objections to the presence of press people. Ryan believed that Jackson was behind moves to have the press excluded.

In the provinces, Jackson was seen as favouring Dublin players. Michael Lynch recalled an alleged incident when Jackson, as tournament director, ordered a re-deal after Anne Quinn and her partner had played a hand the wrong way round. It seems a strange decision, and the truth was probably distorted in the telling, but stories like that went around, further blackening Jackson's image.

DEMOCRATIC WISH FOR CHANGE

It is difficult to persuade someone to stand against a strong incumbent officer, and it took time to find a candidate to oppose Jackson. Eventually, Lieutenant Colonel Dick Dalton agreed to do so. Jackson's old enemies mustered, and old scores were settled at the CBAI annual general meeting held in Sligo on 25 June 1972, when Dalton defeated Jackson in a ballot. Nobody was allowed to sit on the fence in Sligo. According to Michael Lynch, every region had mandated their delegates to vote one way or the other. Even the Dublin region had instructed its delegates to vote for Dalton.[4] P. C. Kiely claimed that Munster delegates were to the fore in organising opposition to the outgoing honorary secretary.[5]

When the result of the ballot was announced, Jackson walked out. Dalton paid tribute to the efficiency of his predecessor and said that the result should not be viewed either as a victory or a defeat but as a democratic wish to effect change. His reference to Jackson's efficiency was rightly made, and the result did indeed reflect a wish for change. Nevertheless, it was a defeat for Jackson, and a victory for the many enemies he had made over the years.

A EUROPEAN

When David Pigot died in 1965, Jackson was elected to the vacancy on the executive of the European Bridge League. National governing bodies have no right to a place on the EBL executive, whose members are chosen by delegates from member countries. Jackson's election is indicative of the favourable impression he had made on his EBL colleagues during the preceding six years.

Even though he no longer had an official position in Irish bridge after July 1972, Jackson nevertheless continued to be the IBU's delegate to the European Bridge League. As he would be attending EBL meetings as a member of its executive, the IBU council, at its meeting of 3 December 1972, decided that he should continue as the Irish delegate. As such, he attended IBU meetings.[6]

Jackson presented a report on his EBL activities to the IBU annual meeting on 22 July 1973 at Ballymascanlon. This, his last contribution to a meeting of a national body, shows the amount of work he had done in Europe. During the past year, he had attended eight meetings of the league, which consisted of twenty-five countries. The report contains surprising revelations. For example, the EBL was opposed to the use of bidding boxes, on the grounds that a revision of the laws might be necessary.[7] Israel, host of the 1974 European championships, would make bidding boxes available but their use would not be mandatory.

The EBL had challenged the winners of the American women's championship to a match to be played at the same time as the Bermuda Bowl. This would be the first Venice Cup, first contested in Venice in 1974. A decision had been taken to hold the European team championships every two years to fit in with the Bermuda Bowl schedule. Jackson was involved in all of these EBL executive decisions.

In 1973, the IBU council again appointed Jackson as delegate to the EBL. Jackson's last attendance at an IBU council meeting came on 21 October 1973 in Athlone, when, having reported on EBL meetings in Ostend, he announced that he was resigning as delegate. His detailed reports on EBL affairs would lead one to believe that Jackson kept Irish colleagues informed. That was not always the case. That last meeting did not go without a final caustic remark aimed in his direction by the joint honorary secretary, John Grummitt,[8] who complained that although he had been joint honorary secretary of the IBU for five years, he had never seen any communication from the EBL.

Jackson may have resigned as Irish delegate but he was still a member of the EBL executive. In July 1974, he was still chairman of its tournament committee, submitting suggestions on how European championship costs might be reduced and how the use of various systems might be regulated. On the question of cost, he was blunt: he argued that where a country was unable to provide the total financial outlay and sufficient manpower to run the championships efficiently, an application from that country should not be considered.[9] When the European championships next came to Ireland in 1991, Jackson's successor as chief organiser, Joe Moran, took a different view.

Jackson also believed that some measure of control in the use of systems and conventions should be exercised. He deplored the use of screens and bidding boxes. He felt that controlling the use of systems would go a long way towards removing suggestions of unethical conduct.

The bitterness Jackson betrayed when he left the meeting in Sligo remained with him for the rest of his life. He declined an invitation to the CBAI's golden jubilee celebrations in 1982.[10] Apart from that, he was shunned by the association in general, even though he continued to play a role in bridge locally. Barry Hogsett befriended him towards the end of his life and it was to Barry that he left papers which have been helpful in writing this book. When he died, his old adversary George Ryan attended the funeral, as did local bridge players, but there was no officer of the association present.

Even his enemies admitted that Jackson was an able administrator. He was a product of an authoritarian age, when to be in control was considered to be fundamental to doing a good job. His administrative skills were crucial in the progress made during his term of office, which saw unprecedented growth and key innovations. At the AGM in Virginia, County Cavan, in 1965, he suggested that the CBAI should acquire premises which would accommodate a head office and a club where major competitions could be staged. The idea would have to wait thirty-four years to become a reality.

Michael Lynch had a certain admiration for Jackson and recognized his contribution to bridge. 'In a way I was sorry to see him go,' he said. 'He was a very efficient man.'[11]

25

The Communist and the
Bourgeois Game of Bridge

There is an incongruity about the founder of the Communist Party of Ireland promoting the bourgeois game of bridge, but that is part of the enigma that was Roddy Connolly. Son of James Connolly, the executed 1916 revolutionary, Roddy became honorary secretary of the Eastern region of the CBAI, a member of the national executive and of the IBU council, and a founder of two congresses.[1] In addition, he was a tournament director, bridge teacher and journalist.

Roddy Connolly was only fifteen when he acted as his father's aide-de-camp in the General Post Office during the Easter Rising. A few days later, while detained in Richmond Barracks, he displayed a budding interest in mind sports when Seán MacDiarmada[2] taught him to play chess by scratching out a board on the floor and using bits of fruit peel as pieces.[3]

He joined the Socialist Party of Ireland in 1917 and became its secretary. Visits to Russia in 1920 and 1921, when he became close to Lenin, inspired him to play a role in founding the Communist Party of Ireland in October 1921. He edited its newspaper, *The Workers Republic*. The Communist Party of Ireland was dissolved in 1924, but two years later Connolly helped found another Marxist organisation, the Workers Party of Ireland, and edited its journal, *The Hammer and the Plough*. The WPI, too, was dissolved, and in 1928 Connolly joined the Labour Party. Elected TD for County Louth in 1943, he lost the seat the following year but regained it in 1948.[4] He lost the seat again in 1951 and did not stand again. He was party chairman from 1971–78 and a senator from 1975–77.

From the mid-1950s, when his level of political activity decreased, Connolly became active in bridge. He was drawn to the game by the fact

163

that his wife, Peggy, a native of Glasgow, was a keen player and a member of Bray Bridge Club. Besides, the calculations which a competent command of the game demanded appealed to his mathematical brain. They were frequently among the prizewinners in Bray, Blackrock and Dun Laoghaire, although they rarely played together. Connolly seemed unable to play a passive role in any organisation to which he belonged, and he became actively involved in the CBAI, first with Bray Bridge Club and later with the Eastern region. He succeeded Denis Jackson as regional secretary in 1956 and retained the position for four years. He was a close ally of Jackson and frequently assisted him in directing major championships before becoming a national director himself.

Connolly was somewhat eccentric, and in his capacity as director he devised his own movements. When Connolly taught beginners in Bray during the late 1950s, he devised a new count method. His *Aids to Beginners* included the following gem of pedagogical wisdom: 'The Rule of Two and Two: Count your honour points. Divide by two. Add one point for every card over three in each suit. Divide again by two. The answer is the number of tricks your hand will probably win with the suit bid as trumps.' Using this formula, he recommended that the minimum requirement for an opening bid of one of a suit was four tricks, although 'allowing half a trick for insurance against error, the normal opening should show four and a half tricks'.[5]

It would be easy to deride such an approach, but Connolly seems to have had a mania for figures and formulas and, of course, bridge is a fertile field for such manias. It would be unfair to suggest that he did not understand the principles of teaching: he was a teacher by profession, working in Bray VEC for thirty-three years.[6] He gave his students easy-to-memorise jingles to help them assimilate his formulas. For example, his rule of 'two and two' became: 'Take half, add long cards, take half again.'

Opinion is divided as to whether eccentricity or principle was behind Connolly's actions in Poland in 1966, when he caused embarrassment for certain Polish officials while reporting on the European championships in Warsaw for the *Irish Independent*.[7] The authorities, aware of his background, treated him with due respect. During a visit to a steel mill, the Irish visitors were being ushered into the executive dining room for lunch when Connolly asked: 'Where do the workers eat?'

'In the canteen,' came the reply.

'Then I also will eat there,' said the founder of the Irish Communist Party. He subsequently led the way to the canteen, where the members of the Irish party and their Polish hosts sat and ate with the steel workers.[8] Michael Lynch believes that it was more mischievous fun than socialist principle behind the action. Des Deery, who was a member of the Irish team in Warsaw, viewed the incident as 'a bit of stage play by Connolly, understandable given his background . . . merely a gesture'.[9]

If there was any serious intent behind Connolly's gesture, it may have been an effort to make a point to the Polish authorities, who had tried to insist, with the support of the European Bridge League, that all travel and accommodation in connection with the championships be made through a Polish state agency. There was a hint that there could be difficulties in obtaining visas if participants tried to make other arrangements. This was viewed by the IBU council as blackmail, because direct booking could be made for approximately £50 less per person. Connolly had been one of the delegates at the IBU council meeting which had decided to withdraw its teams rather than give in to the demand. Both the Polish Bridge Federation and the European Bridge League were informed of the IBU's intention.[10] When the IBU's letter was read at the next meeting of the EBL executive, other countries supported the Irish stand. The Poles were forced to give way.[11]

Although Connolly took up bridge too late in life to get to the top as a player, he nevertheless became proficient in many aspects of the game. A founder of Bray congress in 1960, he also helped Harry Devine start the Blackrock congress for junior players in 1967. The journalistic talent which he had first employed in the cause of communism was put to the service of bridge, not just in his work for the *Irish Independent* but also in his writing for the short-lived *Irish Bridge Journal* in 1959 and his editing of a CBAI bulletin. (At least two issues of the latter were published in 1966.)[12] In June 1967, he was appointed to a subcommittee, which included fellow journalists Jack Kelly and Mairéad O'Neill, to examine the possibility of producing another publication. If anything resulted from their efforts, no record of it has survived.

Roderick J. Connolly, 'a very amiable, nice person', in the words of Michael Lynch, died in 1980.

The Buenos Aires Affair

and Other Irregularities

In 1965, the world of bridge was stunned by what became known as the Buenos Aires affair. While representing Great Britain in the Bermuda Bowl in the Argentinian capital, Terence Reese and Boris Schapiro were accused of cheating by using their fingers to signal the number of hearts they held. They denied the allegation. However, the executive of the World Bridge Federation found them guilty and referred the matter to the British Bridge League. The British non-playing captain, Ralph Swimer, accepted the finding and conceded the match against Argentina – which the British had won easily – and the one against North America, which Britain was leading narrowly with twenty boards to play.

The affair was followed closely in Ireland, where it received considerable press coverage. Reese, in particular, was well known to Irish players, due to the popularity of his books. He was also personally known to many of the leading competitors and was an occasional visitor to Northern Ireland congresses. It is not surprising then that the Irish were supportive of the British pair. Indeed, the tone of press articles on the subject hinted at American paranoia brought on by the successes of European players, especially the Italians: it had been eleven years since the Americans had won the world championships. The *Irish Times* reported:

> This has been hard for the top Americans, enmeshed in the snares of their outdated bidding methods, to bear, and so the allegations that all the top Europeans cheated began to be heard. When the Italians beat the Americans year after year, all sorts of bridge detectives were employed to break the code; finally even the most aggressive of the accusers had to admit that the Italian methods, although complicated,

were beyond reproach. . . . The Americans claim to have a dossier of irrefutable evidence. . . . It now remains to be seen whether the BBL accepts or refutes the accusations.[1]

The British Bridge League set up an inquiry, headed by Sir John Foster QC, which did not find the American evidence to be irrefutable. Foster ruled that Reese and Schapiro were not guilty. The tone of the announcement in the *Irish Times* on 10 August 1966 was one of relief. In December, Jack Kelly published a favourable review of Reese's *Story of an Accusation*,[2] which gave the British players' side of the story.[3] The same newspaper featured the book again the following February, when Paul McWeeney's review portrayed the Americans 'aflame with jealousy and frustration'. Swimer, the non-playing captain, who in Buenos Aires had accepted his players' guilt, had been 'omitted as a player from European and World tournaments'. Therefore, 'his jealousy of Reese and Schapiro exceeded that even of the Americans'. Geoffrey Butler, the president of the BBL and a member of the WBF executive, was accused of betraying British national solidarity. As the *Irish Times* noted: 'Swimer and Butler jumped eagerly into the opposing camp, followed by Truscott for strictly personal reasons.'

Alan Truscott, European team-championship winner in 1961, who was English-born but had settled in America, wrote his version of the affair, *The Great Bridge Scandal*,[4] often referred to as 'the case for the prosecution'. The 'personal reasons' mentioned by McWeeney refer to Truscott's close relationship with American team member Dorothy Hayden, whom he later married. (Hayden was one of the players who had brought attention to Reese and Schapiro's behaviour.)[5] The French chief tournament director, Irénée Bajos de Heridia, was quoted as saying: 'The need for scandal is stronger than the need for justice.'

Given that kind of media coverage, it is not surprising to find that the Irish in general supported the Reese account rather than that of Truscott. Most of Europe did too. The Irish Bridge Union council meeting on 30 April 1967 was informed by Denis Jackson that the European Bridge League delegates to the next meeting of the World Bridge Federation had been instructed to support the findings of the Foster report and its endorsement by the British Bridge League.[6] The IBU adopted Jackson's report.

It transpired that the European representatives did not follow the directive at the WBF meeting, which took place in Miami in May, but 'found it expedient to vote in favour of reaffirming the Buenos Aires decision'.[7] Reese and Schapiro were still guilty in the eyes of the WBF, which henceforth would not accept entries from them to its competitions. In retribution, Great Britain refused to take part in the next WBF championships, the Olympiad in Deauville in 1968.

When the EBL executive met in Dun Laoghaire in September 1967, 'it regretted that its delegates did not insist' on the EBL's point of view. A motion to that effect was passed in Dun Laoghaire by nine votes to nil but there were nine abstentions, presumably including the EBL's representatives who had been to Miami. Although it was not recorded how individuals voted, there is no doubt but that Denis Jackson would have taken the Reese–Schapiro side in the controversy. Reese was welcomed to Dun Laoghaire during the European championships. Prior to the competition, on 3 September, he and Harold Franklin, together with two Swedish players, Berglund and Rosengrün, played an exhibition match against MacHale and Pigot, Read and Shrage in Iveagh House.

The controversy was slow to die. In February 1969, a libel action, brought by Ralph Swimer against Rixi Markus,[8] reached the High Court in London. Markus, in the October 1965 *Bridge* magazine, had been scathing of Swimer's conduct as captain. Swimer defended his honour vigorously in court. In his view, the Foster inquiry had reached 'a mistaken verdict'. He asserted: 'I saw them cheating with my own eyes.' Markus was appalled that Swimer had been 'the chief accuser and chief witness against his own team' – a situation that was 'without precedent in any sport'. She compared the incident with one that had occurred in Palermo in 1959, when 'a British captain had threatened to withdraw his team if allegations of cheating [were not] withdrawn'. Swimer, she thought, was the 'dupe of others . . . a tool of those conspiring to accuse Reese and Schapiro'. Markus 'did not intend her article as a personal attack on Mr Swimer' but rather as 'a criticism of his conduct as captain'.

The *Irish Times* followed the case in great detail throughout the ten-day hearing, at the end of which the jury failed to reach a verdict. The two principals presumably had to meet large costs, but the case kept bridge in the news in Ireland as well as Britain.

Reese did not play international bridge again. Schapiro returned to the international arena only when seniors' competitions were introduced. He won the world seniors' pairs title, with Irving Gordon, in 1998, at the age of eighty-nine.

The Buenos Aires affair jogged memories of other allegations of cheating. At the Bermuda Bowl in Como in Italy in 1958, an American player, 'chagrined by defeat', according to a newspaper report, had made allegations, which he later withdrew, about an opponent's method. In 1960, the French Bridge Federation held an inquiry into allegations of cheating by a pair during the French trials prior to the Olympiad in Turin, where the pair in question represented France.[9]

Throughout his long life, Alan Truscott remained convinced of Reese's and Schapiro's guilt. In *The New York Times Bridge Book*, he offered the opinion – and indeed some compelling evidence – that before the introduction of screens in 1975, cheating was endemic. Writing in 2002, he stated: 'Of the twenty-six teams that won world titles up to and including 1975, all but five are tainted by indications of cheating.'[10] The person chiefly involved in investigating and putting an end to the unsavoury practices was Jaime Ortiz-Patino, now the owner of the Valderama Golf Club in Spain. Ortiz-Patino represented Switzerland at bridge and became president of the World Bridge Federation. Before that, as a young man, he had spent many hours sitting at bridge tables, observing and taking notes on suspect practices, and afterwards presenting evidence to the authorities, who were reluctant to take action.

Two important developments of the mid-1970s aimed to reduce or eliminate cheating. The bidding box, developed in Sweden, was first used in international competition in Herzlia (Haifa) in Israel in 1974. Screens (above the table only) were used for the Bermuda Bowl in Bermuda in 1975. Initially, two monitors, one on each side of the screen, verbally repeated the bids made by the players who placed bidding cards on the table. This development was refined in 1976, when the tray carrying the bidding cards under the screen came into use. That year too, screens were extended down to the floor. Since then, according to Truscott, results of major championships have been, by and large, above suspicion.

A final twist in the Reese–Schapiro saga came in 2006, when David Rex Taylor revealed that Reese, some years earlier, had admitted to having cheated. Taylor claimed that Reese had told him that he and Schapiro had been experimenting in order to see if the authorities would notice. Finger signals were not new in 1965. Twelve years earlier, Roald Dahl featured a couple in a short story who had perfected the practice while playing rubber. One wonders if Reese's and Schapiro's literary interests embraced Dahl.[11]

In Ireland, there have been no proven cases – and few direct accusations – of cheating. That is not to suggest that Irish players have been paragons of virtue. In the course of interviews in connection with this book, a number of players voiced suspicions about certain top-level partnerships of the past. Misgivings there may have been, but proof there is none.

Many irregularities are committed innocently. Peadar Murnane (Ballybay) tells of a story going back to the late 1960s or early 1970s, relating to a certain regular partnership in the town. Defending 3NT, the male partner held ♠ K Q J 10 9. His partner did not lead a spade. She got in twice and still a spade did not come. The contract was made. Afterwards, he remarked that he wanted a spade lead or switch. She had none, of course, and remarked, good-humouredly, that the only place she could have got a spade was in Corrie's – a hardware shop in town. During the next round, again defending, as his partner pondered her lead, he wondered aloud if Corrie's was still open.

In Monaghan Bridge Club, Rosaleen McGowan, partnering Jimmy Swift, was on lead against 3NT when Jimmy asked her if she had been in Lurgan recently. She did not recognise the cue: there was a factory in Lurgan which manufactured spades!

Peadar Ó Ceallaigh and his wife (Kells), both well known on the tournament circuit in the north-east, developed an unorthodox signalling system. Eoin O'Riordan, a man with an impish sense of humour, eventually cracked the code after long observation of their methods. Once, during an auction in an open cup competition, Eoin reached out his leg and gently tapped Mrs Ó Ceallaigh on the foot. She passed. Her husband, who had not given his foot signal, had expected her to continue the auction. O'Riordan, his head down, smiled as a heated exchange ensued. I had heard the story from another source before asking Eoin if, in fact, the incident had taken place. He confirmed that it had.[12]

There is a humorous element in anecdotes of that kind. Indeed, remarks such as those made by Jimmy Swift may be taken as being part of a night's fun. In most cases, the people concerned would be horrified if it was suggested that they had been cheating. However, seemingly innocuous incidents can give rise to serious repercussions, and some have ended in courts of law.

LITIGATION

The *Dundalk Democrat*, on 31 March 1979, reported a case which had come before the circuit court the previous week and which contained a salutary lesson for bridge clubs. The dispute began simply enough, as a difference of opinion as to how many tricks a declarer had made. The declarer in question, Kevin Smyth, was honorary secretary of the Riva 77 Club. Smyth claimed to have made his 3NT contract, but the plaintiff in the circuit court, Mrs Rita Campbell, and her partner, Mrs Carroll, disagreed and stated that he had gone one down.

As reported in the newspaper:

> Mr Smyth was adamant, and after some examination of the cards he informed them that he was the tournament director and proceeded to resolve the issue in favour of himself and his partner.

Having completed the round and moved on, Smyth 'returned to inform the plaintiff and her partner that he was reporting them to the club committee'.

The committee met, and decided to expel Mrs Campbell from the club. Smyth, as honorary secretary of the club, communicated the decision to her in writing. She was 'immediately expelled from the club for breaches of the laws of international bridge and for discourteous behaviour, without any right of appeal'.

Although Judge T. F. Roe had been unable to come to a decision as to who was right regarding the dispute about the cards, the real issue was whether the club committee was entitled to expel Mrs Campbell. Judge Roe had

> absolutely no doubt that the decision of this committee must be held to be invalid, void and contrary to natural justice. From the beginning

the bridge club were entirely in the wrong. Mr Smyth ought to have called another tournament director, as he was a player in the dispute, and the bridge club will have to take the consequences of Mr Smyth's action. Furthermore Mrs Campbell ought to have been given an opportunity of defending herself at this committee and the committee also should have heard the evidence of Mrs Carroll.

The judge warned the committee that it 'would be taking a grave risk to hold a further enquiry into this affair'. They were entitled to hold a further meeting, provided that they gave proper notice to Mrs Campbell and Mrs Carroll, but the committee would seek to ensure that, if a tournament director was playing in a game when a dispute arose, another director, not involved in the incident, should act to resolve the dispute. Mrs Campbell did not ask for damages but the judge awarded her costs.

MULHALL SAVES THE CBAI FROM

POTENTIAL EMBARRASSMENT

The question of disciplinary action by a club, or indeed by any constituent part of an association, against members requires careful wording in a constitution and sensitive handling in practice. In June 1994, the CBAI was saved from putting itself in danger of possible litigation when, at an extraordinary general meeting in Athlone, it convened to approve a new by-law on conduct and discipline, Dublin delegate Dave Mulhall – an administrator in Trinity College – drove the proverbial coach and four through the draft. The meeting adjourned without approving the new by-law. A new committee, which included Mulhall, was appointed to work on the document. The work of that committee culminated in the adoption of a new constitution at the AGM of 22 June 1996. Separate rules of conduct which cover procedures to deal with disputes owe much to Mulhall and the committee convener, Peter Flynn.

MacHALE v. MACLACHLAN

A dispute following an incident in the CBAI mixed pairs championship (Spiro Cup) at the Bloomfield Hotel, Mullingar, in November 1994 also reached the circuit court. MacHale v. Maclachlan was set to proceed on

14 November 1996 but Maclachlan's solicitors, Arthur McLean and Company, succeeded in having the plaintiff's notice of trial struck out. The case did not go ahead. However, two years of correspondence between the solicitors, and efforts on the part of a mediator, followed what had seemed, at the time, to be a common breach of Law 16 of *The Laws of Duplicate Contract Bridge* and a routine ruling by a tournament director.

Walter Maclachlan sat North, Joe MacHale was West. Maclachlan opened the bidding with 1NT. MacHale's partner, East, asked what no-trump they were playing and, on being told 12–14, passed. The bidding went around to MacHale, who, holding ♠ K x ♥ J x x x x ♦ K x x x ♣ x x, bid 2♥. This was alerted and explained as showing hearts and a minor. Advancing the auction, MacHale's partner bid 2NT, asking MacHale to bid his minor. He bid 3♦. South, who held a nine-points hand opposite her partner's opening 1NT, doubled. Maclachlan called tournament director Joe Murray and reserved his rights.

Reserving one's rights does not entail accusing opponents of impropriety. It merely gives notice that, in the event of an infringement of a law resulting in damage, redress may be warranted. MacHale made 3♦ doubled. Murray returned to the table and awarded an adjusted score, +90, 1NT making, to Maclachlan.

What happened up to this point was a normal procedure under Law 16, which deals with unauthorised information:

> After a player makes available to his partner extraneous information that may suggest a call or play, as by means of a remark, a question, a reply to a question, or by unmistakable hesitation, unwonted speed, special emphasis, tone, gesture, movement, mannerism or the like, the partner may not choose from logical alternative actions one that could demonstrably have been suggested over another by the extraneous information.

Murray, in effect, ruled that East's question made extraneous information available to her partner. MacHale, who had a logical alternative action available, i.e. to pass, could not choose to bid 2♥.

Sometimes, in a situation like that, it is not clear whether a player might or might not have bid. In that event, the director approaches a number of players and puts the bidding sequence to them (but without mentioning the extraneous information), before asking them what call they would make. If a majority would bid, then the score stands. If a majority would pass, the director adjusts the score in favour of the non-offending pair. Joe Murray, the most senior and most experienced director in the country at the time, considered this a clear-cut violation and adjusted the score without further consultation.

Joe MacHale tended to be aggressive in the auction. He would bid, especially in the protective position, when others would pass. Throughout his long and well-documented career in partnership with Peter Pigot, he was renowned for competing for part-scores. Rarely did he allow opponents to play at the one-level. He may well have bid in this case even if his partner had not asked the question, but the question may have influenced his action, and that is enough to create a doubt. When there is doubt, the director must find in favour of the non-offending side. Few, if any, experienced players would disagree with Murray's ruling.

MacHale appealed, as was his right. The appeals committee upheld the director's decision. So far this is a routine story. Law 16 is frequently infringed.

Some time after the incident, Walter Maclachlan, in a brief conversation with MacHale's partner, expressed the opinion that MacHale's bid amounted to cheating. The comment was relayed to MacHale. A proud man, he felt slandered by the allegation and sought the aid of his former teammate Gordon Holmes, a leading solicitor. At length, the antagonists, seeking a way out with dignity, agreed to Joe Moran acting as mediator. His intervention may have been instrumental in the decision to settle the case just short of the courtroom.

A few years later, MacHale asked Maclachlan for a game in an attempt to extend a hand of friendship, but the latter declined. However, Walter turned up to pay his respects at Joe's funeral in July 2005.

SPLIT IN BRIDGE CLUB ENDS IN COURT

The case which came before the local circuit court in Kells, and which was reported in the *Meath Chronicle* on 15 February 1974, was of a different nature. Around September 1972, following differences between members of Kells Bridge Club, a group including John Whaley, Mrs Sheila Woods and Miss Ellen Smyth left the club and, with other persons, formed a new one which was also named 'Kells Bridge Club'. As a result, for a brief period there were two clubs in the town with the same name.

In March 1973, at a special meeting, the original club amended its constitution and, among other changes, adopted a new name, Headfort Golf Club Bridge Club.

The dispute, which came before Judge Kenneth Deale in the circuit court, largely had to do with ascertaining which club was the successor of the original, and therefore entitled to the assets of the old club. The plaintiffs, Patrick Coyne, Patrick Hopkins and Mrs Anne Marie McGlynn – president, captain and secretary, respectively, of Headfort Golf Club Bridge Club – 'claimed a declaration that the assets, property and funds of the Kells Bridge Club are the property of the Headfort Golf Club Bridge Club and its members'. The defendants – Whaley, Woods and Smyth – 'counterclaimed that Kells Bridge Club, of which they were president, captain and secretary respectively, is one and the same club as the club which existed in Kells under that name since 1956'. They also claimed that 'the name of the club was never changed to Headfort Golf Club Bridge Club' and that the meeting which was alleged to have taken place on 7 March 1973, when the name of the club was changed, was not a valid meeting. They further claimed that the club's funds and other assets, which included the trophy known as the Kells Cup, were the property of Kells Bridge Club. They sought an injunction 'restraining the plaintiffs and members of Headfort Golf Club Bridge Club from holdng the Headfort Golf Club Bridge Club out as being the successor of the Kells Bridge Club'.

Under the terms of a settlement reached by the opposing parties, who asked that it be made a rule of court binding on both parties, the assets, including about £180 in cash and £30 worth of prize bonds, and the minute book of the original club, became the property of Headfort Golf Club Bridge Club. The Kells Cup went to Kells Bridge Club. As of and from the date of its affiliation to the CBAI in 1972, 'the present Kells Bridge Club shall be entitled to the sole undisputed use of the name "Kells bridge club"'.

The dispute in Kells was typical of what can happen in a small town, where rivalries can easily give rise to conflict. As in all cases where the law is called on to intervene, the episode proved to be expensive. Each side had to bear its own costs in relation to the proceedings.

Bridge has a longer history in Kells than the story of the dispute would indicate. As outlined in Chapter 7, the game was popular in the town during the era of auction bridge.

A PERIOD OF DISQUIET – THE 1970S

A note of discord interrupted the usual harmony of Irish Bridge Union council meetings over the venue for the 1970 European junior championships. Southern delegates assumed that the championships would be held in Dublin. However, at a meeting in Ballymascanlon in August 1969, joint honorary secretary Desmond Deery proposed that they be held in Belfast. Queen's University had already agreed to provide accommodation at a nominal cost. Owen Rowe claimed to be able to get better and cheaper accommodation in Dublin. The capital of the Republic, he argued, was the natural centre for bridge, and there were many junior players there.

A tension not previously experienced at IBU meetings developed. The NIBU delegates withdrew, to allow the CBAI representatives to consider the question in private. When the meeting resumed, a vote was taken, but it was tied: eight for the proposal, eight against. The decision rested on the president, Moreen McCarthy. Deery rescued the situation by withdrawing his proposal 'in order to spare the president the invidious duty of using her casting vote'.[1]

The situation seemed more serious than it probably was. A CBAI executive meeting on 20 September, having agreed that the present allocation for the Moylan Cup – twenty pairs from the South, eight from the North – should remain, went on to decide that 'if, however, the NIBU decide to secede from the IBU, the number [is] to be reduced to twenty-two'. The fear of an NIBU secession, and the consequent break-up of the union between North and South, was exaggerated, but it was present in the minds of some CBAI personnel.

At the next IBU council meeting, held on 2 November 1969 in the Royal Marine Hotel, Dun Laoghaire, Denis Jackson drew attention to an article in the *Belfast Telegraph* which had suggested that the two constituent bodies were in conflict on a political issue relating to the choice of venue and that this meeting had been called in an attempt to settle it. The Dublin press, as a result, were expecting a statement from the IBU. The *Telegraph* article was deplored by the delegates. However, it had the effect of concentrating minds, and ranks were closed in defence. A statement was released:

> The reports which appeared in the press did not emanate from the IBU and were not in any way official. The decision, to stage the junior championships in Dublin next year, was reached after a full discussion of the matter at the AGM of the union, and the decision had been accepted by both constituent members of the union. In the earlier discussion, no political consideration was taken into account, and today's meeting of the IBU is a normal meeting, called to discuss the day-to-day running of the IBU.

Another press announcement was referred to; this claimed that a steering committee for the junior championships had been set up by the CBAI – giving the impression that the southern body was taking over the event. Consequently, a committee consisting of four representatives from each side of the border, comprised of Belton, Lynch, Rowe, Jackson, Deery, Robb, Sloane and Grummitt, was appointed.

The *Belfast Telegraph* article had, in fact, been written by Deery. He was writing regularly for the paper at the time and wrote the piece as 'an anonymous bit of mischief'.[2] He calculated, correctly, that the Dublin newspapers would pick up the story and, sure enough, three Dublin reporters arrived at the IBU meeting on 2 November. Deery, who was reprimanded by George Sloane and Wilfie Robb – two of the NIBU's senior delegates – for his frivolity, is quite certain, to this day, that there was never the slightest chance, or 'even thought', of the NIBU seceding from the IBU.

The episode prompted CBAI representatives to examine their collective conscience with regard to allocating venues for events held under the auspices of the union. Until then, no major championships had gone to the North: Dublin had hosted the 1967 European open and women's championships. The Northern Ireland bridge community felt that it deserved to get the minor prize of the junior event. The northern delegates were further annoyed that the NIBU had contributed more per capita to the funding of the 1967 occasion than the CBAI.[3] The next IBU meeting, in November, agreed that the NIBU should be allocated one all-Ireland championship every year. Thereafter, the Egan Cup was held in Northern Ireland.

Ten nations competed in the junior championships in Dun Laoghaire, 21–28 August, when Denmark became the second holder of the David Pigot Trophy, with Italy second and Sweden third. Ireland seemed to have a strong team – Rex Anderson, Pat Barry, Nick FitzGibbon, Alan Johnson, Maria Nolan and David Scannell – but they finished eighth. Enda Boland was non-playing captain.

IRISH BRIDGE UNION CONGRESS

The IBU council, with the support of Grand Metropolitan Hotels Ltd (with which British expert and tournament director Harold Franklin was associated), organised a ten-day congress, held from 7 to 16 March 1969 at the Slieve Donard Hotel in Newcastle. It was 'modestly successful: numbers were fair at the weekends; midweek events depended almost entirely on the support of local players'.[4] The congress was repeated the following year, again in March. The second was no more successful than the first. Strangely, there is no reference to the congress in the minutes of the two preceding IBU council meetings – a fact which leads one to suspect that it did not receive the wholehearted support of the council members themselves. The sponsor had brought Tony and Jane Priday, two of Britain's best and most popular players, to Ireland as part of a team to play an exhibition match against an Irish side. That, however, had little impact. Furthermore, there were clashing events in the South which, it was thought, took away from the attendance at Newcastle. The fears expressed that Grand Metropolitan Hotels Ltd might not again support the venture proved to be well founded.

BRIDGE AFFECTED AS VIOLENCE SPREADS

The time was not favourable for a congress that depended on cross-border support. The civil-rights march from Belfast to Derry, which had ended violently at Burntollet Bridge, had taken place in January 1969. The battle of the Bogside, after which the Republic's Taoiseach, Jack Lynch, had made his 'We will not stand idly by' speech, occurred the following August. There was political unrest in the two states. British soldiers were deployed on the streets of Belfast. In Dublin, government ministers were about to go on trial, charged with illegally importing arms. In the North, people were dying in riots and shootings. In the Republic, in February 1972, the British embassy was burned in retaliation for the Bloody Sunday deaths in Derry. In such an atmosphere, Southern bridge players were reluctant to cross the border.

The CBAI found it difficult to get teams to travel to Rostrevor, County Down, for the Egan Cup in 1974. John Grummitt appealed to his southern colleagues. 'The NIBU, in the present circumstances,' he said, 'needed all the support it could get from its partner.' In March 1976, when captains of CBAI teams wrote letters expressing their unwillingness to travel north, CBAI delegates showed their solidarity with their northern friends and did not insist on changing the venue. Monty Rosenberg assured the CBAI delegates of the northern players' appreciation.[5]

LEBANON'S STANCE REJECTED BY IRELAND

Politics elsewhere in the world found a place on the IBU agenda. At its meeting in Athlone on 23 May 1971, Denis Jackson reported that the EBL had to determine the problem posed by Lebanon's refusal, on political grounds, to play against Israel in European championships, the next of which was coming up soon in Athens. Following the 1952 European championships in Dun Laoghaire, friendships had developed between Irish and Lebanese players, culminating in an exchange of visits. Nevertheless, Wilfie Robb proposed, Tom Gleeson seconded, and it was resolved that the IBU would support the view that Lebanon's entry could not be accepted on those terms.

In Dublin in 1967, the Lebanese had refused to play against Israel. A newspaper report revealing that the four Israeli players who lined out for the match had been veterans of the Six-Day War the previous June might have caused readers to conclude that that was the reason for the Lebanese protest.[4] However, Lebanon had been refusing to play against Israel since the Israelis had been admitted to the European Bridge League in 1963 and, despite the Irish attitude, would continue to participate in the championships. Whenever the two countries are drawn to play against each other, the Israelis turn up and sit at the two tables for an appropriate period to ensure that they are credited with the points for a walkover.

THE GLEESON ERA

Marie Gleeson was elected honorary secretary of the CBAI at the association's AGM on 28 June 1975 in Athlone, defeating Jim Agnew (Dublin) in a secret ballot. She became joint honorary secretary of the IBU a month later. Following three years of the more laid-back, secretarial style of Lieutenant Colonel Dick Dalton, there was once more a strong administrator at the helm.

Marie did not work alone: she and her husband, Tom, were a team, and for sixteen years they ran the CBAI and the IBU from their home at 17 Beech Park, Athlone, as unpaid, virtually full-time officials. From 1959 to 2002, a period of forty-three years, one or both of them were central to the organisation in the North Midlands region. Marie, the epitome of the efficient secretary, was centre stage; Tom organised things behind the scenes. Having neither family nor other interests, they invested heavily, in terms of time, energy and commitment, in bridge. The European Bridge League conferred its award of merit on Marie Gleeson in 2000, in recognition of her service to the game.

As a young army officer, Tom had been a capable cross-country runner. Even then, he had displayed the cunning and guile for which he was later noted. Once, in order to ensure team victory in a cross-country race, Tom hatched a plan. A strong frontrunner, he led the field from the start. When the runners reached a fork in the course, Tom led the wrong way. His teammates knew the right track and gained sufficient advantage to achieve their aim. Tom was good enough to double back on to the correct course, make up the ground and contribute to the team's points total. He revelled in such escapades. He was nicknamed 'the Glee'.[1]

The story illustrates not just Tom's deviousness but also his commitment to team effort. He was certainly an effective committee man.

Important work was done away from meetings, testing how individuals felt on sensitive matters and convincing others to see his way of thinking. For instance, he persuaded Joe Moran to let his name go forward for the presidency of the IBU in 1987, a position which Raymond O'Leary (Cork), as CBAI president two years earlier, might have expected to fill. In 1991, he prevailed upon Johnny Kiely to stand for the same position and secretly campaigned for the Cahir man, who went on to defeat Kay Downes in a ballot.

The name 'Gleeson' first appears in an official record at the AGM of North Midlands region in Tullamore courthouse on 9 November 1956,[2] when Captain T. Gleeson was elected as one of the region's delegates to the CBAI AGM. A regular at regional meetings thereafter, Gleeson became secretary in November 1959. Three years later, he was treasurer as well. He retained both offices until his death in 1991, when Marie took over the secretarial work; she remained in this role until retiring in 2002.

Marie's involvement began at the regional AGM in Tullamore, on 24 October 1963. Tom's skill at manipulation can be detected in the meeting's decision that a second delegate to the CBAI executive would be nominated by himself and also that the choice of delegates to the AGM be left to him and the president, Mr M. Burke. Gleeson and Burke attended the CBAI executive meeting in Athlone on 23 November, but it is no surprise to find Commandant and Mrs Gleeson representing the region at the meeting of 22 March 1964. Thereafter, the Gleesons were at the centre of CBAI affairs. By the end of the 1960s, it became routine, in the region, for Tom Gleeson to select delegates to the CBAI AGM, and sometimes to the executive as well. From 1970, the Gleesons represented the CBAI at IBU council meetings.

Marie Gleeson's administrative skills have never been in question. The whole range of tasks, including arranging the calendar of events, writing press releases, organising championships, collecting affiliations and carrying out the myriad other assignments which might arise following meetings or competitions, was carried out with efficiency and promptness. Minutes of meetings were written immediately, and letters answered by return. Tom also displayed a similar effectiveness in administering the affairs of the region. The North Midlands region was repeatedly the first to pay its affiliations, submit its master-points and meet targets when funds were collected for specific purposes. In the eyes of the national executive, it was the model region – an image that the Gleesons took pride in projecting.

However, Marie Gleeson, like Denis Jackson before her, belonged to an authoritarian age. Tom did too; indeed, his career as an army officer was based on a hierarchy of command. Like Jackson, who in many respects was her tutor, Marie lacked public-relations skills, and she could be curt with those who were outside her circle of favourites. An examination of the growth in CBAI membership, since figures began to be recorded in 1964, shows that North Midlands had the lowest percentage increase of all the regions between then and 1991, the year Tom died and Marie ceased to be honorary secretary of the national association.

Marie Gleeson was a competent tournament director. (Only one woman before her, Rita McLoughlin from Dublin, had directed national championships.) Marie began by assisting Denis Jackson at events held in Athlone during the 1960s; she could scarcely have had a better instructor. As Gleeson became more involved in CBAI and IBU affairs throughout the 1970s, she took responsibility for an increasing number of competitions. By the time classification was introduced in the 1980s, she was the only woman to be assigned to the highest category of national director. Nuala Spillane, from Limerick, subsequently achieved that status by passing the CBAI's examinations.

The practice of holding the CBAI AGM in the outgoing president's region was discontinued in 1981. John Murphy, North-western region, was outgoing president but instead of the AGM being held in his home town of Longford, it became a fixture in Athlone for the next eighteen years. The pattern was broken in 1999, when it took place at the new bridge centre in Templeogue. CBAI executive and IBU council meetings, as well as most IBU competitions and a good number of CBAI ones, were held in Athlone during the Gleeson era, invariably at the Shamrock Lodge Hotel.

Conflict arose over the venue for the 1990 CBAI AGM, when outgoing president Kay Downes, the last president from the old Dublin region, wished to have the AGM in the capital. Marie Gleeson would not agree. The general-purposes committee, which decided on matters of that nature, did not support its president. When her proposal was put to the meeting of 28 April 1990, only one member of the committee, Marie Cummins, the Dublin regional secretary, supported her. The episode was an emphatic reminder of who was truly running the association. It was not until 2001 that management, once again, saw the value of moving the AGM around the country.

The Gleesons were responsible for bringing the European championships to Ireland in 1991. Before Marie applied, on behalf of the IBU, to the European Bridge League, she and Tom had made up their minds as to who was going to organise it. From their experience of attending major world and European events, they understood the magnitude of the organisational task – and they knew there would be a huge financial commitment. Marie, as joint honorary secretary of the IBU, would, in the normal course of events, head the organising team. However, she was no Denis Jackson, and she and Tom knew it. They set their sights on Joe Moran. Only when he agreed to head the organising team did the IBU apply to the EBL.

Sadly, Tom Gleeson did not live to see the event that he and Marie had brought to Ireland. He died from prostate cancer in February 1991, four months before the championships opened in Killarney. A good player, he won seven national titles and played for Leinster many times. When smoking was the norm at bridge tables, he used his cigar to effect – a practice which irritated opponents. Marie rarely played in the major events but in 1997, towards the end of her career, she won her sole national competition: the IBU inter-club pairs championship, with Eddie Fitzgerald, who, like Tom, was an army officer.

Tom accompanied his wife to European and world championships, where Marie was the IBU's official delegate to the EBL and the WBF. For many years up to and including 1990, he reported on those events for the *Irish Times*.

Marie Gleeson, after more than forty years' service to bridge, passed away in 2004. Her huge and unstinting contribution to bridge was acknowledged by the large attendance, from all over the country, at the removal of her remains to the church and at the funeral the next day.

THE LONG ROAD BACK TO CAMROSE

Soon after the CBAI's withdrawal from the Camrose competition, following the completion of the 1950–51 series of matches, moves began which aimed to ensure the organisation's return to the championship. What happened in 1950 must be viewed in the light of contemporary political moods. The reasons for the withdrawal were deep-rooted. Following the Government of Ireland Act of 1920, the nationalist population had never accepted the partitioning of the country as a permanent arrangement. The claim to jurisdiction over the whole island enshrined in the 1937 Irish Constitution was taken seriously by the majority of the Republic's citizens.

The NIBU's objection, in 1950, to the CBAI competing in Europe as 'Ireland' touched a nerve south of the border and prompted a spontaneous and widespread outburst of nationalistic fervour whose wrath was visited on the NIBU. The same fervour lay behind divisions in a number of sports in the Republic at the time, notably athletics and cycling.

The founding of the Irish Bridge Union, the result of an extraordinary and swift process of reconciliation, less than four years after the CBAI's last Camrose match, while it opened a gate to European competition for northern players, nevertheless raised false hopes in the South for all-Ireland participation in the Camrose. For the next quarter century, when the question of a return to the home-international championships was discussed within the CBAI, it was in the hope, if not the expectation, that an all-Ireland team would replace Northern Ireland in the championship.

The invitation to teams from the other four unions to the CBAI's silver jubilee tournament in February 1958 signalled a desire for good relations and might be viewed as a step towards appeasing the other governing bodies. Joe Honan and Donal Waldron, presidents in 1958 and 1959, respectively, tried to organise meetings with the NIBU on the subject but without success.[1] At an executive meeting on 28 November 1959, 'a discussion regarding the possibilities of re-entering the Camrose matches concluded the meeting', but the minutes reveal nothing more.

Donal Waldron, at the 1962 AGM in the Warwick Hotel, Galway, tabled a resolution 'that the CBAI re-enter the Camrose'. He saw a contradiction in playing against NIBU players in the Egan Cup but not in the Camrose. However, the association's decision in 1950 had been to withdraw from any competition in which the NIBU took part 'as a unit'. The debate on Waldron's motion went to the heart of the problem: a majority in the CBAI still aspired to an all-Ireland team in the Camrose. A Mr O'Farrell opposed Waldron's motion, stating that it would be possible to take part 'if only four countries competed and if the competition was called anything else other than Camrose Trophy'.[2] There were people who did not feel comfortable playing for a trophy carrying the name of a British viscount.[3] Munster delegates were not in favour of returning to the Camrose. Michael Hurley from Limerick 'felt that coming out of the Camrose had done no great harm'. William McBratney from Cork, 'speaking for South Munster', said that his 'region was completely against the resolution'. Joe Honan (Limerick) thought that the NIBU was 'the barrier', a view supported by David Pigot. Dick Tierney (Galway) felt 'that sufficient efforts to solve the problem had been made and we had eaten enough humble pie'. Geraldine McConkey, a former Camrose competitor, felt that the CBAI should compete 'but only when they approach us'. (By 'they', whether she meant the British Bridge League or the Northern Ireland Bridge Union is not clear.) Honorary secretary Denis Jackson, whose opinion on the Camrose question was never revealed in minutes, saw the futility of continuing the discussion and, following his suggestion, Waldron withdrew the resolution.[4] The matter was again raised at the 1964 AGM but the honorary secretary merely recorded that 'various views were expressed'.

At the AGM on 29 June 1968 in the Royal Hotel, Tipperary, Laur Sheeran tabled a motion on the matter, seconded by Desmond Houlihan (Birr). Sheeran explained that his aim in returning to the home-international championships was 'in the interest of fostering competitive bridge'. He appealed to the delegates to eliminate politics from the discussion.

The widely held view that the nationalist attitude which had taken the

CBAI out of the home international championships was predominately based on feelings in the provinces was, not for the first time, exposed as a myth when, on the Tuesday prior to the CBAI AGM, a meeting of the Dublin region instructed its delegates to oppose Sheeran's motion, unless it was amended, with the aim of an all-Ireland team entering the competition.[5] Indeed, the very origins of the Camrose seem to have been forgotten in the South. Jack Kelly, writing in the *Irish Times* on 29 June 1968, stated that the Camrose had originally been a competition between England, Scotland, Wales and Northern Ireland and that the CBAI had been allowed to participate for a period, 'in association'. That was incorrect. The home-international championship had been the collective undertaking of the governing bodies of the five members of the Duplicate Board of Control. Not only had the CBAI been a full member of the body that had sponsored the championship, but its representatives had been chairman and honorary secretary of that body as well.

At the Tipperary meeting, Dublin delegate Owen Rowe proposed that the amendment 'that the CBAI take steps to have the question of an Irish team, or teams, being entered in the Camrose under the auspices of the IBU [be] put forward for discussion at the annual meeting' of the all-Ireland body. He was supported by Maureen Ryder from Galway and Michael Hurley from Limerick. Enda Boland supported Sheeran. Jackie Kneeshaw from Clonmel deplored the unnecessary heat being engendered by the discussion.[6] The honorary secretary's recording in the minutes of Kneeshaw's interjection is an eloquent statement with regard to the quality of debate. Sheeran's appeal to eliminate politics from the discussion was premature: the membership was not yet ready for that. Rowe's amendment was carried by 44–30, and Sheeran's motion was defeated by the same margin. Of course, there was a certain futility about the exercise. The NIBU would never give up its position in the Camrose to go into an all-Ireland team in the competition; the CBAI was sticking to a head-in-the-sand approach. Nevertheless, the margin of the vote was reduced from the May 1950 three-to-one majority in favour of discontinuing competition with the NIBU.

Rowe himself was a CBAI delegate when his proposal appeared on the agenda at the IBU annual meeting in Ballymascanlon on 4 August. Incoming IBU president Wilfie Robb expressed the views of the NIBU delegates as follows:

The NIBU delegates welcome any movement to enable the CBAI to re-enter the Camrose. They will recommend to the NIBU, and that the NIBU should recommend to the BBL, that a NIBU team and a CBAI team should be entered for the Camrose Trophy under the auspices of the IBU . . . and that in the event of any future suggestion of one team only representing Ireland in the Camrose Trophy, then this right should automatically revert to the NIBU.[7]

The defeat of Laur Sheeran's motion in Tipperary precluded the CBAI from trying to re-enter the Camrose by making a direct approach to the British Bridge League. Indeed, as a matter of principle many CBAI members would not do so. As the minutes of the IBU annual meeting record: 'The best chance of persuading the BBL to accept two teams from Ireland without the direct re-entry of the CBAI would be along the lines of the NIBU recommendations above.' Rowe and the two joint honorary secretaries, Denis Jackson and John Grummitt, were appointed to a subcommittee to explore the matter further.

IBU council meetings of 10 November and 27 April of the following year were told of meetings of the subcommittee but no progress was reported. The next annual meeting, on 24 August 1969, heard Rowe state that there had been no formal report from the subcommittee. It would appear that they had done nothing and there the matter remained for two years.

Yet again, at the AGM in Galway in June 1971, another motion appeared on the agenda, proposed and seconded by two past presidents, Dick Tierney and John Coman, who articulated the old aspiration to get back into the Camrose 'not as the CBAI but as Ireland'.[8] Eddie Burke from Nenagh, opposing the motion, referred to the Republic of Ireland's imminent entry into the European Economic Community and suggested that a decision should be deferred until after that time. The motion was passed, and delegates to the IBU were instructed to press for its implementation.

On 4 July, at the annual meeting of the IBU, Dick Tierney submitted the following resolution on behalf of the CBAI:

That the IBU enter two teams for the Camrose Trophy with equal representation from each of the bodies comprising the union. The appointment of non-playing captains to be by the NIBU and the CBAI.

Discussion was deferred until the NIBU considered the matter. A letter from the Northern Ireland Bridge Union, read at the executive meeting on 18 December 1971, made it clear that the NIBU was 'not prepared to assist on the terms proposed but would give every assistance to facilitate entry if CBAI decided to apply for re-entry on the original terms'.[9] The original terms, of course, were that the CBAI and the NIBU would enter the home-international championships as separate governing bodies representing separate political entities. It hurt republican sensitivity to recognise the existence of Northern Ireland, and that attitude pervaded the CBAI. Getting into the Camrose under the umbrella of the IBU, an all-Ireland body, would have soothed the collective nationalist conscience.

Attitudes had changed by the time the question was next raised – at the June 1978 AGM in the Killeshin Hotel in Portlaoise. At the end of the meeting, under 'any other business', Dick Tierney proposed from the floor 'that the incoming executive should reconsider re-entering the Camrose'.[10] This was seconded by Tierney's colleague from Galway, Paul Scannell, one of the younger delegates. There was general agreement – Emer Burke (Nenagh) was the only dissenting voice – and the executive took action.

Una Walsh presided at a special general meeting in Athlone on 29 April 1979, when the sixty-eight delegates in attendance considered the resolution from the executive 'that the CBAI re-enter the Camrose Trophy'. This time, the aim was simply to go back into the championships alongside the NIBU as an equal. For the first time, politics were kept out of the discussion. Significantly, Tom Burke from Drogheda, a man known for his strong nationalist views, proposed the motion and pledged the support of the North-eastern region. One after another, delegates followed on behalf of their regions: Paul Scannell, Western; Peter McLoone, Northern; Tom Gleeson, North Midlands; Denis McGrath, South Munster; J. Coleman, North-western; Maeve Devine, Eastern; J. Spencer, South Midlands; Jackie Kneeshaw, North Munster; and Marie Cummins, Dublin. Eddie Burke (Nenagh) was alone in sticking to the old line and asked to have his disagreement put on record.[11]

Sonya Britton informed the meeting that she had been in contact with some officials of the British Bridge League. She saw 'no difficulty, as they would all welcome our application'. Michael O'Connell, one of the players who had missed out on the top-level competition which the Camrose would have provided, expressed the mood of the moment when he said he was 'delighted with the mature decision taken today, and considered it a most happy occasion for the association'.[12]

There was no reply from the BBL prior to the AGM on 23 June. That was not surprising. The British Bridge League, if it had met at all, would scarcely have had time to deal with the application in the interval. However, from information received, it seemed unlikely that the CBAI would be included in the 1979/80 competition. Still, the mood was jubilant. Treasurer Michael Lynch transferred money to the current account in anticipation of the expected additional expenditure.

During the twenty years or so during which the association discussed the matter of returning to the Camrose, it does not seem to have occurred to anyone that the British Bridge League might not accept the CBAI back into the competition. Between 1951 and 1979, there is no record of the matter having been raised either formally or informally with the British Bridge League. Apart from Sonya Britton's statement, there is no record of approaches having been made to officials of the other unions, or indeed of contact with their delegates to the British Bridge League. There is no evidence that the CBAI carried out exploratory or preliminary preparation at any time. During the 1970s, when the political unrest in Northern Ireland was carried across to mainland Britain, there was little contact between players from either side of the Irish Sea. Irish participation in British tournaments was minimal, and Killarney congress was the only one that attracted British competitors to the Republic.

The 1980 AGM at Ely House in Dublin was told that the British Bridge League had turned down the application. The rejection, in view of the major turning point that the passing of the motion at the April 1979 special meeting represented, was a disappointment. The honorary secretary, Marie Gleeson, reported that 'the English Bridge Union had obstructed our entry into the Camrose'.[13] It was ironic that the EBU, the very body which had been forced into existence by the Celtic nations so that England might be able to participate in the competition, was the one that blocked the CBAI's return. Long forgotten was the fact that when the Scots and the Welsh wanted to expel England from the Camrose, it was the Irish Free State representatives who had been sympathetic to England's situation.

For much of the 1970s, the Irish in Britain were subject to bad press. British casualties in Northern Ireland and the extension of the IRA's bombing campaign to mainland Britain engendered anti-Irish feelings. In late 1979 and 1980 especially, Ireland was not exactly England's favourite sister nation. On 27 August 1979, Lord Louis Mountbatten (an uncle of the queen's husband, Prince Philip), was the victim of an IRA bomb placed in his boat at Mullaghmore, County Sligo, where he had a summer home. In the long-troubled relations between the two nations, English hostility towards its neighbour was at an all-time high.

The question of participation in the Camrose was dropped, for the moment, from the CBAI agenda. Good relations between the CBAI and the NIBU had long been restored; and now there was a need to build bridges between the CBAI and the other constituent members of the BBL. The English and Scottish Bridge Unions were invited to take part in the golden jubilee competition in 1982. Both declined. However, unofficial teams from England and Scotland did take part, at the invitation of Sonya Britton, the president. The Sonya Britton Trophy, awarded to the winners, was intended as a perpetual prize, but the competition failed to establish itself as an annual event. The trophy did not sit idly on a shelf for long. When the first official CBAI v. NIBU contest in almost forty years took place in Newcastle in August 1989, it was awarded to the winners.

Not long afterwards, relationships between England and the Republic changed for the better. The Irish Bridge Union received, and accepted, an invitation to take part in the 1988 Lederer Memorial Trophy in London. Britain won the open championship at the Europeans in Killarney in June 1991, and the president of the British Bridge League, Raymond Brock, attended the banquet. Shortly afterwards, the CBAI sought to have a schools' team entered in the BBL's Peggy Bayer Trophy. However, the CBAI's general-purposes committee meeting on 14 December 1991 was informed that 'it was not feasible to include a CBAI team this year', but at Brock's suggestion a formal application, which would be discussed by the constituent members of the BBL in the new year, had been made to have a team included in the future. Just before that, the English Bridge Union had invited a CBAI schools' team to be its guests at the EBU London congress at the end of December to play a sixty-board practice match against the English Peggy Bayer team. Four girls from Laurel Hill College, Limerick – Fionnuala Langford, Alison Levins, Deirdre McNulty and Lizanne White – who had won the All-Ireland schools' title in March, accompanied by their coach, Gordon Lessells, became the first Republic of Ireland team to play against an English side since 1950.

In the late spring of 1992, John Williams, secretary of the English Bridge Union, wrote to the CBAI suggesting the possibility of matches being played between the two national bodies. Shortly after that, Joe Moran had a key meeting with Williams at London Heathrow Airport. Williams thought that the time was not yet right for the CBAI's return to the Camrose, but friendly matches would be welcomed. The process that led to the annual match for An Corn Cairdis, and ultimately to the CBAI participating in the Camrose again, had been initiated.

The EBU board of directors' meeting, held on 22 July, accepted Williams's proposals for an annual friendly match. Initially, open, women's, juniors' and officials' teams would be involved. The original Irish proposal was that the trophy should be called the Friendship Cup. Peter Stocken, the EBU's vice chairman, experienced some pleasure in pointing out to the Irish that they already had a 'Friendship Trophy'. Indeed, he had represented Trinity College in the annual inter-university championship forty years earlier. So, CBAI president, Tom Burke, gave it its Irish name – An Corn Cairdis – the inaugural contest for which was played in Dublin on 27 and 28 February 1993. Similar matches followed against Scotland in 1995 and Wales in 1996.

The CBAI formally applied to the British Bridge League for readmission to the Camrose in October 1996. The application was discussed at the EBU board of directors meeting on 16 January following. Stocken was now chairman of the EBU; David Harris, who also favoured the Republic's return, was vice-chairman.

The CBAI's application posed problems for the BBL and its constituent members. It coincided with changes proposed for the BBL itself. England, Northern Ireland, Scotland and Wales would have to find additional weekends in already crowded calendars. However, those were minor, largely logistical problems. The Northern Ireland representative on the BBL council had made a strong appeal for the CBAI's inclusion, and Scottish and Welsh delegates had also supported the application. Only the lack of an English endorsement stood in the way of the CBAI's return. An EBU board meeting on 20 March 1997 was told that both the Republic and Northern Ireland were completely opposed to an all-Ireland team.[14] The ghost which had haunted previous CBAI ambitions to return had been exorcised. However in England, the EBU council, not its board of directors, would decide how its delegate to the BBL would vote. Council had instructed its tournament committee to examine the technical and financial implications. Peter Stocken was apprehensive prior to the council meeting of 9 April:

> I was very apprehensive about this meeting, sufficiently so to attempt to drum up support beforehand. I knew the background to Eire withdrawing from the Camrose but I could not believe that, nearly half a century later, our council delegates could possibly object to Eire re-entering. However, there were those who had been at previous council meetings where Eire's application had been turned down and I was warned not to expect an easy ride. I need not have worried – I was pushing at such an open door that I was practically blown over by the draught. The handful who voted against it had their own private agenda anyway.[15]

A proposal, 'that Eire's re-admittance to the Camrose series be pursued', was carried by a substantial majority. It remained merely for the BBL to solve the organisational problems.

The CBAI women's team was the first to return. On the first weekend of June 1998, Maria Barry, Ann Montwill, Grainne Barton, Rosemary Ennis, and Aileen and Rebecca O'Keeffe, with CBAI president Marie Cummins as non-playing captain, went to Cardiff to compete for the Lady Milne Trophy; they finished second to England. On 4 and 5 December, Donal Garvey, Micheál Ó Briain, Tom Hanlon, Hugh McGann, Niall Tóibín and Pat Walshe, with non-playing captain Gráinne Barton, defeated Wales in the CBAI's first Camrose match in more than forty-seven years.

Back in the championships it had helped to launch in 1937, the CBAI went on to win the Camrose five times: in 2000, and then four years in a row from 2005 to 2008.[16] Northern Ireland and Wales have yet to win. CBAI women's teams have finished second in the Lady Milne, but under-twenty-fives in the Junior Camrose, and under-twenties in the Peggy Bayer Trophy, have yet to make an impact.

Scotland and Wales decided not to continue the friendly matches with the CBAI. In England, reservations were expressed because of the cost involved. However, EBU council member Mr Mason pointed out that the Corn Cairdis was unique insofar as it brought club and county members into contact with international bridge. His argument prevailed, and the annual contest continues, with county, club and official teams from either side participating.

Ina McMenamin, Ireland's most popular player, in 1943

May McNulty partnering Sonya Britton, early 1960s

Paddy Paul Donovan, holding the Kelburne Cup, with (L to R): Des Purcell, Jack Kelly, Jimmy Bastow, 1952

Ruth Giddings – a class apart, with more national championship victories and more international appearances than any other Irish player, male or female

E. O. (Eddie) Barry, 1943. He and three of his children played for Ireland.

Kelburne Cup match, early 1950s. Players (L to R): T. D. Cooper, D. Egan, Dr Roche Kelly, Ina McMenamin. Standing (L to R): Harry Bridburg (head only), T. D. Purcell, Noel Peart, Jack O'Sullivan, unknown. Looking over Roche Kelly's shoulder: Marcus Shrage.

John Comyn, as the Student Prince, with soprano Louise Studley. John was the unanimous choice of the adjudicators when he won the John McCormack Cup at Dublin's Feis Ceoil in 1961.

The *Irish Bridge Journal*, March 1959. What an astute prediction! McHale and Pigot won more tournaments than any other Irish pair.

IRISH

Bridge

JOURNAL

Volume 1, No. 2.   MARCH-APRIL, 1959   Price 1/6.

THE COMING PAIR

J. P. MacHale and Peter Pigot—second National Pairs Championship; second in Panel Test, 1959.

IT'S A DATE!

NEWRY BRIDGE CLUB
CONGRESS
11th - 12th April
Ballymascanlon Hotel

♣

TRAMORE BRIDGE CLUB
CONGRESS
8th - 10th May

♣

SOUTH OF IRELAND
CONGRESS
6th - 14th June
Lake Hotel
Killarney

♣

European Championships, Dun Laoghaire, 1952. T. D. Purcell, left, and Dermot Egan v. Terence Reese (hand on chin) and Boris Schapiro (GB). Behind Reese, Ely Culbertson (USA). Behind him, looking towards camera: Noel Byrne (tournament director). Right of Culbertson: Kay Hyland, Mabel O'Kelly. Behind Egan: Edna Rayneau. To the rear, with diamond-design collar: Kay Byrne (Noel's wife). Scorer: Jackie Prost.

1954 European silver medallists (L to R): Eileen O'Sullivan, Nellie Faul (npc), Eileen O'Doherty, May McNulty, Ruth Giddings, Ina McMenamin, Alice Mahon.

Philip Quinn: E. O. Barry's partner, 1930s and 1940s, was bridge correspondent for the *Irish Times* and the *Irish Field*. His son, Maurice, is a leading player in Malahide Regional Club.

Kitty McCann (Tullamore) competed in national bridge tournaments. Her parents, G. S. and Mrs Smye, were founder members of Tullamore Bridge Club. She won the British Ladies Open Golf Championship in 1951.

1964 Polish visit. Seated (L to R): May and Denis Jackson, Mairéad O'Neill, Geraldine McConkey, Polish visitor, E. J. Boland, Polish visitor. Second row: (behind Mairéad O'Neill) Euphen Stephenson; (behind man in hat) Rita McLoughlin; (looking to right) Sonya Britton. Back row: (extreme left) G. F. Read; (centre) Barbara Seligman, (extreme right, head only) Elvina Spiro.

Rothman Kings, 1979 (L to R): D. Garvey, J. Comyn, M. O Briain, N. Tóibín, P. Walshe

Founders of the Irish Bridge Union, 1955. Seated: The Rt Hon G. B. Hanna, B. O'Kennedy, T. J. McAfee, Dr J. P. Brennan. Standing (L to R): P. Fitzgerald, C. N. Byrne, L. Bradley, N. H. Douglas, P. P. Donovan, W. Robb, Major G. Jackson, G. Sloane, E. Arnott, M. Dorgan, Ald. S. Bergin.

31

WHEN KINGS BEAT ACES

AND SMOKE GOT IN YOUR EYES

In March 1978, John Godden launched the magazine *Irish Bridge*. In order to promote it, he hit on the idea of bringing a team around the country to play matches against local clubs. Independent Newspapers sports journalist John Comyn, and P. C. Kiely (Mitchelstown), wrote for the magazine. Rothmans, the cigarette manufacturers, took advertising space.

Kiely was critical of Comyn's articles, which, he asserted, featured only Dublin-based players. In his view, Cork players were just as good. Comyn recognised a challenge. He also saw promotional potential, and approached Rothmans with the idea of forming a team, which would be called the Rothmans Kings, to challenge the Cork players. 'What beats Kings?' Paddy Kiely asked, replying, 'aces, of course.' Rothmans Kings versus Cork Aces! The idea appealed to the cigarette manufacturers: one of their brands was Rothmans King Size. Comyn and Godden could guarantee newspaper and magazine coverage.

The first Rothmans Kings – Comyn, Donal Garvey, Micheál Ó Briain and Pat Walshe – went to Fermoy, where they defeated Kiely, John Coman, and Denis and Anne Dillon. The contest was intended as a once-off match, but they talked about a return. Comyn, borrowing Godden's idea about touring the country with a team, went to Rothmans, and 'The Kings' went on the road again. Attired in shirts bearing the company's logo, they travelled to meet challenges all over the country. They played in regional and national championships as well as congresses. In 1979, they finished a close third in the Caransa international tournament in Amsterdam.

The end of the Kings came as a result of an organisational faux pas at the Dublin congress in the Royal Marine Hotel, Dun Laoghaire. Rothmans was the principal sponsor of the congress, and the Kings entered two teams for the main event. The organisers insisted that they play against each other in the first round. The implication was that if they met later in the competition, perhaps near the end, one team could throw the match in order to ensure victory for the other. To the players, this was insulting. The organisers refused to relent. To show their contempt, the two teams scored flat boards on every deal, resulting in a tied match. It was the end of the Rothmans Kings. If the organisers of a major congress had such a low opinion of their integrity, then they had had enough. The end may have come with some sense of relief. The schedule had been demanding: in their last year, they had played thirty-six times, in addition to the normal club, regional and other events in which the individual members participated.

During the time they were on the road, the Kings brought excitement to clubs around the country. Comyn chose top-class players: Niall Tóibín, Pat Walshe, Donal Garvey, Micheal Ó Briain, B. J. O'Brien, Brian Dolan and Joe Moran. Beating the Kings, or even losing narrowly to them, was a cause for pride and celebration. And, win or lose, celebrate they did. The greatest strain on the Kings resulted from the hospitality of their hosts. On any single occasion, it was just one night for the locals. But for the Kings, it was week after week – and sometimes the Saturday and Sunday nights of a weekend.

TOBACCO SPONSORSHIP

Tobacco companies supported bridge for a number of years, beginning with Messrs Murray Ltd and Craven 'A' sponsoring the visit of the French team in 1961. John Player & Sons lent their name to Malahide congress from 1965. In October 1968, a match was played in Belfast between an Irish selection and a W. D. & H. O. Wills team. The same company sponsored a national pairs competition in the CBAI jurisdiction during the 1979/80 season. Rothmans for five years, followed by Gallaghers, sponsored the printing of the CBAI annual programme. In addition, in the mid-1980s Gallaghers distributed sets of table covers bearing the Silk Cut logo to every member club in the country.

The days when smoking and bridge went together were to end, however – and not without pain. With fast-growing awareness of the health risks attached to smoking, a lobby grew, aimed at limiting the practice in the bridge room. Non-smokers, long-suffering and silent, became vociferous. The first recorded indication of discontent occurred at the AGM of Wexford Bridge Club in September 1972, when a Mr Burke offered the opinion that too many people smoked too much, leaving the atmosphere uncomfortable. However, no action was taken.

Some did take action, however. In Dublin, Mary Lawlor, who in 1973 had founded Ballyroan – for a long time the biggest club in the country – started Ireland's first non-smoking club, Marian, a few hundred metres down the road from its larger neighbour. Marian attracted a large membership from the start and continues to thrive. In Limerick, too, a non-smoking club was formed.

The thrust of the non-smoking lobby was to force the CBAI to take action to curtail the habit during competition. At the 1987 AGM, Pat Breslin (Waterford) proposed 'that all smoking, cigarettes, cigars and pipes be severely restricted at all national competitions from 1 September 1987'. The proposal was passed, 41–24. The move had limited success: a year later, Breslin was informed that the restrictions did not apply to congresses. At the AGM held on 25 June 1994, motions from Dublin South, North Munster and South-eastern regions aimed at prohibiting smoking at CBAI competitions were defeated. The association was not yet ready for a total ban. However, the executive, sensitive to growing unease about smoking among the membership, at its meeting on 3 September, banned smoking in the playing area for the first hour and a half of every session of the association's competitions.

In 1995, a proposal before the CBAI management committee aimed to ban smoking completely from all events organised by the association. The vote ended in a tie, but the chairman, Paul Hanratty, exercised his casting vote, not – according to tradition – for the status quo, but in favour of the proposal. Hanratty was vilified by the smoking lobby. Notwithstanding the fact that his region, Dublin South, had consistently backed moves to reduce smoking, he was not popular in certain clubs in the capital following his action. Had he known what was soon to come, he might have spared himself the trouble: the Department of Health soon imposed a statutory ban on smoking. It seemed a long time since the halcyon days of Rothmans and Silk Cut.

JOE MORAN'S CONTRIBUTION

For many years Joe Moran has been listed among Ireland's 100 richest people.[1] A television programme in January 2008 ranked him 17th among the country's highest earners of the previous year. Whatever the accuracy of such classifications, Moran is a force in the business world. To bridge he has rendered inestimable service. As a player he had potential. A good reader of cards and of opponents, he attained the rank of national master, contested trials and was selected for Irish seniors' teams at European and World championships; but he never took the steps which might have led him to the top. Bridge was recreation; other activities were more important.

A number of key developments, including the appointment of a full-time general secretary to the CBAI and the building of a national bridge headquarters, might not have occurred without his involvement. Had he not agreed to head the organising team for the 1991 European championships, they might not have taken place in Ireland. He played a role in the process that led to the CBAI's return to the home-international championships, and in the mid-1980s he steered the CRAM committee – the group that brought the organisation into the technological age. For many years, he headed the IBU's international selection and finance committees. Without his input, the Europe v. USA contest for the Warren Buffett Cup might not have been inaugurated in 2006.

THE 1991 EUROPEAN CHAMPIONSHIPS

Tom and Marie Gleeson were astute in inveigling Moran into organising the European championships in 1991. Fund-raising,[2] negotiations with European Bridge League president José Damiani, and finally the forced switch from Dublin to Killarney, all required his leadership. The championships were allocated to Ireland five years in advance, with space provisionally reserved at the Royal Dublin Society complex in Ballsbridge. Damiani, who customarily inspected proposed venues for European events, came to Dublin in August 1989, accompanied by EBL executive members Grattan Endicott (England) and Dirk Schroder (Germany). Unfortunately, Moran had overlooked the fact that their visit would coincide with the opening day of the Dublin Horse Show. On that morning, the perfume that wafted from the stables around the RDS was one that was unfamiliar to the sensitive nostrils of the visiting Parisian. What the visitors walked on was not a red carpet. The RDS was ruled out. Humorous in retrospect, it was not funny then. Joe MacHale brought the party to the sports hall at Belfield. It too was deemed unsuitable. No other venue in the capital city was both capable of accommodating the event and willing to do so. Ireland's hosting of the 1991 European bridge championships hung in the balance.

In the moment of crisis, Joe Moran turned to his native Kerry. It proved to be a perspicacious move. The championships in Killarney are remembered as one of the most successful European competitions, yet it was a touch of luck that they were held there at all. They might not have been, were it not for the co-operation of two hoteliers, the late Maurice O'Donoghue, owner of the Gleneagles Hotel, and Michael Rosney, currently the proprietor of Killeen House Hotel and who, at the time, was manager of the Great Southern. Both saw the potential gain for Killarney. Rosney had plans for a convention centre – then but an architect's drawing – at the Great Southern. Moran accepted his word that the building would be completed in time. O'Donoghue's marketing organisation, 'Destination Killarney', secured accommodation – a crucial step, as the Irish Open golf championship was scheduled for Killarney at the same time.

It had been the practice that the host country bore the entire expense of running European events. Denis Jackson, when he was a member of the EBL executive, insisted that no championship should be allocated unless the host could meet the total cost of the event. Joe Moran refused to accept that arrangement.

'This is your championship,' he told an EBL executive meeting. 'You are paying for it!'

An agreement was reached: Ireland would provide the venue, transport for participants within the country, and hospitality. The EBL would deliver equipment and technical staff. Moran was adamant that, as far as was feasible, the manpower would be Irish. Billy Mullins (Tralee) and Derek Stokes were nominated to the team of tournament directors.[3] Under the agreement, the cost, totalling a quarter of a million Irish punts, was divided equally between the two parties. Moran even negotiated a 50 percent share of the Generali Insurance sponsorship money, which amounted to £55,000 (c. €68,000). A percentage of hotel charges further added to the receipts. The balance sheet, when it was over, showed a profit close to £40,000 (almost €50,000) for the Irish Bridge Union.

A record twenty-six countries took part, some of them for the last time in international bridge. The map of Europe was changing even as play proceeded in Killarney. On 25 June, Croatia and Slovenia declared independence: Yugoslavian competitors would return to a different country. The Soviet Union would break up in December. In January 1993, Czechoslovakia would cease to exist and divide into separate states, the Czech Republic and Slovakia. Great Britain won the open championship, with Sweden second and Poland third. Fourth place was important too, as the first four qualified for the Bermuda Bowl in Yokohama. Indeed, it was fourth-placed Iceland that went on to win the world championship in Japan.[4] In the seventeen-nation women's competition, Austria, Germany and the Netherlands took the medals, with Great Britain coming fourth. The women's pairs (a contest which has since been discontinued), which had a record one hundred participating pairs, including twenty-two Irish partnerships, was won by Danielle Avon and Ginette Chevalley (France). Veterans Eileen O'Doherty and Anne Quinn were the only Irish pair to reach the twenty-eight-pairs final. The only disappointing aspect of the Killarney championships was the performance of the Irish teams, which finished fifteenth in the open and eleventh in the women's event.

APPOINTMENT OF A GENERAL SECRETARY

Towards the end of the 1980s, it became clear that a change in the management of Irish bridge was necessary. Joe Moran discussed the matter with Marie Gleeson. Such was Gleeson's control that it would have been impossible to bring about change without her assent. Moran was persuasive. 'Soon I'll be gone and you'll be gone,' he argued, during a private meeting. 'Let's leave something after us.'

Marie's decision not to stand for re-election, following her husband's death in April 1991, cleared the way for the appointment of a paid employee. Voluntary workers of her calibre were scarce and the volume of work had steadily increased. In 1975, when she took office, membership had stood at 14,500. By 1991, it had doubled to 29,000, and there were signs that the growth would continue.[5] From the mid-1980s, records had been kept for every individual member. An honorary public-relations officer-cum-press secretary had been appointed in 1988.[6] There was certainly enough work to occupy a full-time official.

However, budgeting for a salary and renting an office was a daunting undertaking. It was assumed that the office would be in Dublin – where rents were highest – although regarding the advanced state of communications technology, there was no compelling reason why this should necessarily have been the case. CBAI management would scarcely have been as resolute in pursuing the matter had Joe Moran not taken the lead. He convinced the association that the step was necessary. A simple calculation showed that a relatively modest increase in affiliation fees would suffice to meet the additional expense. He was assigned the task of finding the right person and a base from which to work.

There was uncertainty concerning the precise nature of the appointment. In Brighton in June 1987, EBL president José Damiani had advised Moran that Irish bridge needed a public-relations officer. Consultation with management consultants MSL resulted in the same recommendation. The CBAI executive, at its meeting on 25 April 1992, decided to appoint a professional PRO on a two-year contract. At the end of two years – by which time it was expected that office space would be acquired – a full-time general secretary would be appointed. However, the advertisement in both the *Irish Independent* and the *Irish Times* less than three weeks later invited applications for the position of a National PRO/Fundraiser. The addition of the word 'fundraiser' to the specification seems to have been Moran's own decision – arrived at following a discussion with Marie Gleeson. There is no record of a debate having been held on that aspect of the job at any meeting of the association.

Between the time the job was advertised and the date of interviews, Moran had another change of mind. He doubted the wisdom of having a full-time public-relations officer working alongside elected voluntary officials. He came to the view that the CBAI needed a general secretary or chief executive, whose job specification would encompass the whole range of the association's administrative, developmental and promotional activities, and that this position should be filled immediately, and not, as decided by the executive on 25 April, after two years. So applicants found that they were being interviewed not for the job which had been advertised, but for a more all-embracing position. Among the applicants, Moran saw only one name: Paul Porteous. Others had reservations, but Moran got his way.[7] Porteous was popular and easy-going, and related well to people – key attributes, in Moran's view, for the task ahead. Paul Porteous became the first full-time official in Irish bridge, in September 1992.

HEADQUARTERS

Initially, Porteous worked from his home, but from the date of his appointment, acquiring office space became more urgent. Moran again played a crucial role. For some years, he had led a group[8] in the Rathfarnham–Templeogue area, which sought a site for a bridge centre. His aim now was to acquire premises which could accommodate such a centre as well as a headquarters for Irish bridge. There was at least one aborted effort[9] before the site at Templeogue House became available. Moran formed a new, more select, committee, which, with the objective of building a community bridge centre, obtained a ninety-nine-year lease to a site from South Dublin County Council. When built, space could be leased by the community centre to the CBAI for its headquarters. The project at Templeogue was comprised of two separate and distinct entities, each funded from different sources. The community bridge centre was financed entirely by local players – the members of the five clubs which now play there. The cost of the CBAI headquarters was met by its country-wide membership. As a result of Moran's clever combining of the two projects, the CBAI got its headquarters for the bargain price of £125,000 (c. €156,000). The headquarters was officially opened during Peter Flynn's presidency in 1999.

33

TECHNOLOGY AND DEVELOPMENTS IN THE 1980s

Voluntary organisations are often slow to embrace technological developments. Fortunately, individuals with an interest in progress take initiatives which force themselves on such organisations. During the early 1980s, Brian Lawlor and Joe Murray, aware of the potential of the computer for tournament directors, wrote scoring programmes.[1] Suddenly, the director's task was transformed.

Neither Lawlor nor Murray was the first in Ireland to write a scoring programme. That achievement belongs to Donal Collins, a priest and science teacher in St Peter's College, Wexford. During the 1970s, Collins worked on a project with his students and produced a programme which he used to score competitions in Wexford Bridge Club and at Wexford Bridge Congress. (Collins, unfortunately, will be remembered less for his pioneering work in computer scoring than for being one of a number of priests named in the Ferns Report and convicted of sexual abuse.)

Scoring by computer quickly became commonplace, but twenty years would elapse before the next big leap forward. 'Bridgemate' was introduced at the final of the IBU inter-club pairs championship in May 2004. In this system, players enter scores on terminals placed on the tables. The results are updated instantly and there is no delay at the end of the session before the winners are known. Fearghal O'Boyle's experience of using Bridgemate when directing competitions for the European Bridge League facilitated its introduction to Ireland. In fact, the initial practice runs occured in Fearghal's own club in Sligo. Bridgemate is now used at all national events, and some clubs have invested in the device.

The computer, of course, made possible the development of the dealing machine, a Swedish invention which was first used in Ireland during the European championships in 1991. But it was in the storing and

201

processing of information that the computer had perhaps most to offer. Until the mid-1980s, the national governing bodies had no record of their overall membership. The CBAI had a total figure, based on an outdated affiliation system, but it was not possible to say exactly how many individual members there were, or *who* they were. The CRAM (Computerisation, Registration, Affiliation and Master-points) committee, headed by Joe Moran, was established in 1983, during Des Scully's presidency, and was given the task of overseeing the development of a data-processing system. When CRAM began its work, CBAI affiliations stood at 22,246. Four years later, in June 1988, when the committee disbanded, there were 26,459 – an increase of 14 percent. Heretofore, the only records available referred to registered players and those who voluntarily registered master-points. Now there was to be an account for every individual member of the association. Much of the initial work was carried out by Pat Walshe and Peter Pigot, with Joe Murray later taking over.

During that period, it became apparent that some regions had become too big to be administered efficiently by voluntary officers. In Dublin, where, in 1986, membership went over 5,000, there was rapid growth. Marie Cummins, who had become regional secretary in 1977, was virtually a full-time worker and was no longer young. When she retired, her successor would have a daunting task. South Midlands topped 4,000 members in 1985. That region was fortunate in having a succession of efficient secretaries during the period of rapid growth: Jim Brearly (Enniscorthy), 1980–83; Tony White (Newbridge), 1983–86; and Peter Flynn (Tramore), 1986–89. Membership peaked at 4,427 in 1986. The region covered a huge geographical area – from north County Kildare to the coasts of Wexford and Waterford. Both regions submitted proposals to divide to the AGM of 1989. In the first boundary revision since 1948, the two regions became four: Dublin North and Dublin South (with the natural and convenient boundary being the River Liffey); South Midlands, consisting of Counties Kildare, Laois, Carlow and Kilkenny; and South East, which was comprised of Counties Wexford and Waterford.

With the introduction of computerisation, the timing for a change in the affiliation and registration systems seemed opportune. From 1932 to 1986, a dual affiliation-cum-registration system had been in operation. A special general meeting was convened on 6 September 1986 in Athlone to consider a resolution, tabled by eight prominent members of the executive,[2] aimed at replacing the old system with a single affiliation fee of £2 per member.

On the Saturday morning before the meeting, the finance committee, headed by honorary treasurer Michael Lynch, had discussed the proposal and the consequences of its adoption. Lynch suggested that it would be simpler to charge all clubs an affiliation fee of £1.50 per member, regardless of the number of clubs of which they were members. Pat Breslin (Waterford) supported the executive members' resolution and reminded the delegates of the expectation that the single-affiliation pilot scheme which had been in operation in South Midlands during the previous year would be adopted by the rest of the country. Maurice O'Connor (Eastern region) put forward what proved to be a compelling argument: Lynch's proposal would be easier to implement. Vice President Joe Moran pointed out that the function of the finance committee, of which he was a member, was to make recommendations for the financing of the association. If the resolution were to be adopted, there would be an overall shortfall in funds. Following advice on procedure from legal advisor Michael Buckley – a future chief state solicitor – the meeting adjourned to allow delegates to consider their options. When it resumed, Barry Hogsett informed the delegates that the signatories were withdrawing the resolution. This was as close as the association ever came to introducing a single-affiliation scheme.

GOVERNMENT AND BRIDGE

There have been two periods of concentrated effort to secure government support for the game, the first during the time leading up to the 1991 European championships, the second when the Irish Sports Council Bill was going through the Oireachtas in the late 1990s. However, government aid for bridge was first sought in 1976. Marie Gleeson researched the position in other countries and, backed up by facts about schemes in the Netherlands and Sweden,[1] on 19 November she applied, on behalf of the CBAI, for a grant, to the then parliamentary secretary to the Minister of Education, John Bruton, who was responsible for disbursing grants to sports bodies. Bruton replied on 3 December:

> I regret to inform you that Contract Bridge is not regarded as an activity which would qualify for assistance under my Department's scheme of grants to sport.
>
> As a general principle the scheme of grants applies only to those sports which contain a considerable element of physical activity.

Following a change of government, another application a year later met with no better result.[2]

In April 1987, Mrs Gleeson, with the 1991 European championships particularly in mind, wrote to Mary O'Rourke, Minister for Education, on the question of funding, and in March 1988 Joe Moran appealed to Frank Fahy, Minister of State with responsibility for sport. In view of Gleeson's and Moran's connections with the ruling Fianna Fáil Party, expectation was high that support for the championships would be forthcoming. Moran, accompanied by deputy Tom Kitt, met Fahy in May 1988 and a letter to Fahy, signed by Moran and Gleeson, followed on 27 May. A delegation from the Irish Bridge Union met Minister O'Rourke on 19 July

1988.[3] Prior to the meeting, Gleeson had received advice from the Netherlands Bridge Federation as to the approach which should be taken.[4] In addition, European Bridge League president José Damiani sent her details regarding the status of the French Bridge Federation vis-à-vis its government and information about support for bridge in nine mainland European countries.[5]

Marie Gleeson's memo relating to the meeting reveals that discussions took place on the subjects of a grant towards the cost of running the European championships and an annual grant towards financing international competition, as well as various developmental projects. Moran followed up with a letter to Fahy on 25 July. Nothing resulted. The only official support for the European championships was a grant of £5,000 from Bord Fáilte. Tom Burke, on becoming president of the CBAI in 1992, made a personal presentation to the then Minister for Sport, Liam Aylward – again with no positive outcome. Thereafter, the effort to secure government funding petered out.

When the Sports Council Bill was going through the Oireachtas in 1998/99, lobbying by bridge players resulted in questions being raised in the Dáil on the issue of bridge being recognised as a sport by: Trevor Sargent (Green), 7 October; Ivor Callely (Fianna Fáil), 13 October; Éamonn Gilmore (Labour), 21 October; and John J. McGuinness (Fianna Fáil), 1 December. For bridge players, it was important from the very title of the Bill that the game should be recognised by the government as a sport.

The Sports Council Bill was designed to cater for competitive sport and recreational sport, which were defined in Part 1, Section 2, as follows:

> 'Competitive sport' means all forms of physical activity which through organised participation aim at expressing or improving physical fitness and at obtaining improved results in competition at all levels.

> 'Recreational sport' means all forms of physical activity which, through casual or regular participation, aim at expressing or improving physical fitness and mental well-being and at forming social relationships.

Clearly the framers of the bill did not regard bridge as a 'competitive sport' or indeed as a 'recreational sport'.

Minister for Sport Jim McDaid, speaking at the second stage of the bill on 4 February 1999, said:

> The recognition of bridge as a sport was raised by many deputies. I am well aware of the level of interest and participation in bridge. There was a recognition of bridge in my party's manifesto. . . . My priority has been to prepare this legislation to provide a framework for the future execution of sports policy, including policy on sports bodies. The recognition of individual sports and recreational activities, including bridge, will be a matter for the Sports Council to consider in the context of its statutory remit. Given the level of interest that has been expressed in this issue, I will ask the Sports Council to examine it as a matter of priority upon its establishment.

The point which turned out to be the death knell of hopes that bridge would be included among grant-aided sports is that the Sports Council, not the minister, would decide which bodies would receive funding – as set down in Part 2, Section 7 (2) (a) and Section 8 (1) of the Bill. The Council was precluded from awarding a grant to bridge due to the definitions included in the bill.

The only Dáil deputy who saw a way by which bridge and other mind sports could be included was Pat Rabbitte (Labour). At the select committee stage, on 11 February, he proposed amendments to change the definitions to all forms of physical or mental activity, and to delete physical fitness and mental well-being and substitute physical or mental fitness and well-being. Unfortunately, Rabbitte was on the opposition benches. McDaid and his colleagues, despite the fact that recognition of bridge had been in their party's manifesto, refused to accept the amendments. The Irish Sports Council Act became law on 18 May 1999. As far as bridge is concerned, nothing has changed since John Bruton replied to Marie Gleeson's application in 1976.

A number of bodies covering activities which do not seem to be physically demanding receive grants towards employing development officers from the Department of Sport. They include such well-known organisations as Gael Linn, Comhaltas Ceoltóirí Éireann and the Irish Countrywomen's Association.[6] In July 2001, the president of the CBAI,[7] accompanied by the general secretary, Paul Porteous, met the chief executive of the Sports Council, John Treacy. Having made it clear that bridge would receive no funding from his office, Treacy explained that the non-sports bodies which received funding did so under arrangements which had been in place prior to the passing of the Irish Sports Council Act, and, therefore, would continue to do so. The CBAI never applied for a grant to employ a development officer. There was never a plan to create such a position. We can but speculate as to what the response might have been had such an application been submitted prior to the introduction of the Sports Council Bill.

Bridge, in fact, has benefitted from government funding in two ways – but not under sports-funding legislation or regulation. Under a local-government scheme by which community-based organisations may receive funding for capital projects, a number of bridge centres have received grants for building, extending or renovating properties.[8]

CBAI headquarters enjoyed the benefits of the FÁS Community employment scheme for a number of years. In 1994, Eric Pelly,[9] FÁS placement officer for Dublin 14, approached the honorary secretary of the CBAI's Dublin South Region, whose address, conveniently, was in Dublin 14. At a time of high unemployment, FÁS was actively encouraging community-based bodies to participate. Pelly was convincing, and Dublin South region employed an assistant. Pelly pushed further. Paul Porteous was working from his home – which was also situated in Dublin 14. The FÁS community-employment scheme was extended to CBAI headquarters. Until the community-employment scheme was partly phased out in 2003, CBAI headquarters was staffed largely by FÁS employees.

35

HIGH JINKS

Tom Hanlon, in the autobiographical *A Bridge Too Far?*, is revealing about the antics of junior players abroad. One is not surprised to read of boisterous behaviour where young, single people are concerned. Sometimes the actions of youth are misunderstood. During Hugh McGann's illness in the late 1980s he wore a hat while playing, to disguise the temporary effects of medical treatment. His young friends took to wearing hats also. Their seemingly flamboyant appearance was misunderstood by some of the more staid players. In fact, the gesture was one of solidarity for a friend who needed support at a difficult time.

Exuberance and ostentation in bridge are not confined to the young. Maisie Cooper used the phrase 'high jinks' to describe some of the antics she witnessed. Maisie took up bridge during the 1940s in an if-you-can't-beat-them-join-them frame of mind. When she married, she was enlisted at weekends to drive her husband and his friends to tournaments because, by the time the game was over, none of them would be in a condition to drive. Boredom while waiting drove her to learn how to play.

One incident might have ended in tragedy. John Coman was renowned for leaving for a competition at the last minute, with the inevitable result – a rush at great speed towards the destination. On one occasion, he was still behind the counter of his shop in Tipperary when the other members of his team, on the way to a competition, called to pick him up.

'Hold on while I have a quick bath,' said the most laid-back player in Munster. The delay resulted in even greater than usual speeding. Coman was in the first car, with two companions. Maisie and her husband followed close behind, but when they rounded a bend on a bog road, there was no sign of the lead vehicle on the long, straight stretch in front of them. They reversed – to find the other car on its roof in the bog, and the three occupants crawling out. Muscular men, they righted the vehicle and put it back on the road: car bodies were solidly constructed in those days. The party arrived just in time for the start of the competition.

Personal rivalries built up in Monaghan Bridge Club – as they did in other clubs. During the 1950s, local butcher Joe Corr and solicitor Matt Lardner would look for opportunities to score off each other, and not just at the bridge table. One day, a dog entered the butcher's shop and took a quantity of meat. Corr crossed the road to Lardner's office.

'If a dog entered my shop and took meat, would its owner be liable for the cost?' asked Corr.

'There is no doubt about it,' replied Lardner. 'The owner would be held liable.'

'Well, it was your dog!' said Corr.

'Fair enough,' said the solicitor. 'How much damage did he do?'

'Five shillings should settle it,' said the butcher.

Lardner handed over the amount. Corr thanked him and moved towards the door.

'Oh, Mr Corr,' said the solicitor. 'See my secretary on the way out. The consultancy fee is seven and six.'

Seamus Kelly was arrested while playing bridge. Kelly and Andy Butler, regular competitors on the tournament circuit, liked a drink. One day in Virginia, while sitting out a round of a regional cup competition, they went out on the street for a breath of air. Having imbibed both air and nicotine, Butler left Kelly on the footpath drawing the last dregs of his cigarette. In the bridge room, the next round started, but there was no sign of Kelly. Minutes elapsed, and still he did not appear. The room completed the first board of the round. Still no sign. The street, of course, had been searched. Someone in the hotel had the inspiration to phone the Garda barracks. 'I think we have him here,' said the officer on duty, in response to the description. 'He's in the cells.'

Kelly, it seems, feeling the effects of the pints he had consumed earlier, hadn't looked in the best of order. A passing garda, with the best of motives, enquired if he was all right. The surprised officer of the law was met with a torrent of abuse. The precise details of what followed are not recorded but it would appear that the garda, not appreciating Kelly's tirade, marched him off to the barracks. Following pleas by respected bridge-playing citizens, he was allowed to return and resume the game.

The eccentricities of Johnny McRoberts, one of the best-known figures in Northern Ireland, attracted some notoriety. A wealthy man, he lived in Crossgar, County Down, where he owned a mill and employed about a hundred workers. Reputedly tight-fisted with money, he distrusted the banking system. Local belief had it that he kept large amounts of cash at home and in his office at the mill. What a disaster, then, when the mill went on fire one night and flames threatened to engulf Johnny's office! Summoned to the scene, he dashed into the burning building, resisting all efforts to stop him. Anxious minutes elapsed before Johnny, his face blackened and spluttering from smoke inhalation, emerged triumphant, hands held aloft, clutching two fistfuls of master-point certificates.

In 1961, heavy snowfall brought Belfast to a standstill. No one ventured outdoors for four days. Bridge players, unable to get a game, were suffering from acute deprivation. On the fifth day, the adverse weather abated and, since it was Tuesday – and duplicate night at the Malone Club – three intrepid players, all living nearby, made their way there on foot. Duplicate was out, but if a fourth came they could play rubber. After half an hour of sitting in the cold and talking about deals past, they were about to give up when they heard an extraordinary din outside – a sound that was certainly unfamiliar to residents of the city.

Earlier that evening, Johnny McRoberts, sitting at home beside his fire, had also felt the need for a game of bridge. He set out in his car but had not gone far before it got stuck in a drift. He abandoned the vehicle. Johnny was resourceful. The sound the three players in Malone Club heard was that of Johnny's tractor, which he had driven the twenty miles from Crossgar!

McRoberts was a keen competitor. He played on Northern Ireland teams in the Camrose and won congress competitions as well as major championships. He was a frequent visitor to the Republic and, during the period of strained relations between North and South in the 1950s, continued to support Southern events.

P. C. (Paddy) Kiely (Mitchelstown) was renowned for his outrageous antics. In his youth, he had looked forward to a bright future in athletics. Tragedy struck when he contracted a debilitating condition which gradually worsened, eventually forcing him to use a wheelchair. His impaired mobility did not prevent him from wreaking havoc in hotels during bridge weekends. During a period of more refined living, it was customary, before retiring for the night, to leave shoes outside hotel bed-rooms, from where they would be taken by staff, cleaned, polished and returned before morning. Kiely, never one to retire early, once gathered all the shoes and tossed them through a window on to the roof of a mez-zanine – all of the shoes, that is, except those of John Coman, the very person least likely to be involved in behaviour of that kind. The roof of the mezzanine could not be reached easily and it required a deal of inge-nuity on the part of hotel staff, and a considerable amount of time the next morning, to recover and sort out the items of footwear. Kiely, of course, was the first down to reception complaining that his shoes were missing. The unsuspecting Coman could not understand, when he appeared in the lobby, why his fellow guests were glaring at him: he was the only one wearing shoes!

George Ryan, bridge correspondent for the *Irish Times* after Jack Kelly died in 1970, is one of the world's longest-serving bridge journalists. Possessed of a unique sense of humour, he has written four novels.[1] His place in the canon of Irish writing was recognised when the last of his novels, *No Time For Work*, was included in Des Kenny's *101 Irish Books You Should Read*. Ostensibly merely a funny book which might appeal to a cer-tain sense of humour, it is also a serious work, a portrayal of the chaotic life of an alcoholic.

George was a regular contributor to John Godden's magazine *Irish Bridge* in the late 1970s. A typical Ryan quotation on the front page of one issue referred to: 'The Dublin woman better known for her bad manners than for her skill at the table.' It caused a sensation. Readers throughout the country wondered who it was, while Ryan chuckled at the widespread speculation. Godden was grateful for the attention it attracted to the mag-azine. George recently revealed that the story had been merely a journal-ist's trick to attract attention and that he had not been referring to anyone in particular.

When national teams competed abroad, reports of players' behavior occasionally found their way on to the agenda of Irish Bridge Union council meetings. During the first World Olympiad in Turin in 1960, an

Italian newspaper published a story of two Irish players who always played with two bottles of whiskey – one each – under the table. When the matter came up at an IBU meeting, there was outrage at the libel visited on the two players concerned. The honorary secretary was instructed to write to the newspaper in question, demanding an apology and a retraction. It appears, however, that the two players involved, Dick Belton and Jack Kelly, did indeed play with a bottle of whiskey each under the table. Belton threatened to sue for libel on the basis that it was not an invariable practice and, moreover, that the practice improved his performance!

Deauville, a tourist town on the Normandy coast a few kilometres east of the D-Day landing beaches, proved an eventful spot for the Irish at the World Olympiad in 1968. There was industrial and student unrest across France, and the strikes, which affected French airports, railways and buses, necessitated that players take a variety of unusual routes to Deauville: where, at the end of the day's play, some of the Irish visitors gravitated towards the casinos. Bridge players, because of their knowledge of percentage plays, might entertain hopes of success at the black-jack table. At roulette, the chances of making a fortune are more remote – except when you have a system!

Dr John O'Sullivan, Ireland's non-playing captain, practised medical hypnosis. He and Desmond Deery devised a sinister but ingenious system for roulette. Deery placed the bets, while O'Sullivan tried to hypnotise the croupier. They returned from the French resort poorer than they had been when they arrived, but twice during the evening the croupiers were changed when they complained of drowsiness and headaches.

Gerry Read, who preferred the bar to the gambling tables, also had a system. He placed two bets every night on the number of his house. One evening, the number came up twice in succession and he won a substantial amount. When he cashed in his chips, he discovered that he had been left short. He returned to the table. The croupier remembered the bets, plus the fact that there had been two winners on the particular spin, Read and a Malaysian prince who had been at the far end of the table, but he was adamant that he had paid out the full amount.

Read tracked down his fellow winner and bluntly asked him: 'Are you the little bugger who took my winnings?' The gentleman did not understand English. In response to Read's harangue, he kept nodding his head, smiling and repeating: 'Yes, yes, yes.' The manager was called, and in order to head off further trouble, he paid Gerry the amount he claimed he was owed – on condition he did not return to the casino.

Deery and MacNeill took a break from bridge in the 1970s, the former to concentrate on his law practice, the latter for family reasons. In 1974, Deery decided he needed a break from his law practice and persuaded Conor O'Hara to accompany him to the world pairs championships in Gran Canaria. Midway through the qualifying rounds, they met the Americans Alvin Roth and Barbara Rappaport (later Mrs Haberman). The lady, according to Deery's account, 'Wore at least two rings on each finger, had a complexion that would have put Percy French's London lass in the shade, and fluttered eyelashes that would tickle anything within a nine-inch radius'. As declarer on the first deal, she failed to make a possible overtrick and incurred her partner's wrath. On the next board, Deery opened 1NT, 12–14, following which Ms Rappaport became declarer again, this time, in four hearts. Her tenth trick depended on finding the queen of diamonds, for which she could finesse either way. Three tricks from the end, Deery had already shown thirteen points. He could not have the remaining queen. While she was still trying to figure which way to play, Roth, who was dummy, asked Deery to confirm that his opening 1NT showed 12–14, thus alerting his partner to the obvious. A furious Deery told Roth what he thought of his remark. Roth's lame reply – 'You Limeys can't take a joke' – served only to intensify the Irishman's anger.

Deery, a man of considerable height, looked down at Roth. 'On the first hand, you insulted your partner,' he said, in his slow, clear, northern intonation. 'Now you are insulting me. I presume you intend to insult my partner on the third hand.' The presence of Conor O'Hara, an imposing figure and a useful man on the rugby field, was enough to draw forth an apology from Roth. Ms Rappaport fluttered her eyelashes and muttered 'My heroes', before finessing the wrong way. Later the pair were invited to an American party at which an incident involving a fire extinguisher culminated in Roth being covered with foam. Tobias Stone, Roth's usual partner, congratulated the Irish pair. 'The Irish are the only ones able to extinguish Al's fire twice in one week,' he said.

The Kay Lowther episode, at the 1977 European championships in Helsingor in Denmark, was reported by the non-playing captain, Eileen

O'Doherty, and duly discussed by the IBU council. Mrs Lowther's partnership with Maeve Curran from Warrenpoint was not always harmonious. When Lowther told Curran that she was fit to play only golf-club bridge, it was not intended as a compliment. However, the principal complaint before the IBU concerned an incident which occurred one evening when a coach, carrying the players back to their hotel from the playing venue, was unable to advance up the avenue because of cars were parked on both sides of the road. The players were asked if they wouldn't mind walking up the avenue. Mrs Lowther refused to leave the coach and insisted that the driver proceed right up to the door of the hotel. When the driver convinced her of the impossibility of the task, she ordered him to take her back to the playing venue, from where she would get a taxi.

The Irish Bridge Union appointed a subcommittee to investigate the incident and to report back with recommendations. Des Deery headed the committee, which also consisted of Michael Lynch and Nell Foley. Lynch was unable to attend, so Deery and Foley met the parties involved and interviewed them at the Regent Bridge Club on 18 October 1977. Following a thorough investigation, Deery wrote a three-page report, which ended as follows: 'At this stage we all retired to the bar for a drink. We recommend that no further action be taken.' Following his Solomon-like closing of the incident, the Irish Bridge Union rewarded Deery by appointing him its legal advisor.

Prurient readers will wonder if there have been illicit romantic liaisons between bridge players or casual affairs when abroad. Of course there have, and my research has uncovered many of them, but you are not going to read about them in this book!

36

SORROW AND TRAGEDY

Those two imposters – sorrow and tragedy – are no strangers to the bridge-playing community. The premature death of Niall Tóibín in 2004, at the age of forty-four, served as a reminder that the lives of even the most talented among us are fragile. There has been no greater loss to the game, unless it is that of Paddy Walshe. One of the outstanding personalities in Irish bridge, Paddy, from Galway, was only forty-nine when cancer of the pancreas ended his life with stunning abruptness in February 1998. When he launched the *Irish Bridge Journal* in 1979, sceptics dismissed it, saying that it would not last. Thirty years later, it continues to thrive.

Paddy was one of Ireland's best bridge teachers. When the CBAI initiated its teacher-training programme in 1995, he was recruited as its chief instructor. Only excellent pedagogues were employed; among them, Paddy – that rare combination of expert player and expert teacher – was outstanding. Although he was part of the training programme for only three years, his influence remains. Sadly his wife, Nuala, herself a winner of the Kelburne, the inter-county and four inter-provincial titles, survived him by a mere two years. Their son David continues the family passion for bridge. Paddy's sister Una now edits the *Irish Bridge Journal*.

Tragedy also struck two well-known northern Camrose players. Johnny McRoberts was left emotionally scarred as a result of the death of his daughter following minor surgery. Jim O'Dempsey, a Belfast solicitor, during a visit to the seaside on 13 August 1971, saw two of his children getting into difficulties while bathing. Jim, in the course of rescuing them, lost his own life.

Perhaps the most heart-rending story centres on Harry Daly, a member of Dublin's Civil Service Club. Harry, a civil servant, and his wife,

Mary Agnes, like many young married couples in post-Emergency Dublin, had an accommodation problem. They rented rooms on Botanic Road, Glasnevin. Following the birth of a baby in February 1948, relations became strained between the tenants and their landlady, who started proceedings to have them removed. In order to pay some arrears of rent, Mrs Daly borrowed £3 10s from a priest. This money was in her purse when she visited the Church of the Seven Dolours, Glasnevin, to pray on 10 August.

Mrs Daly's account of what followed was that she caught an elderly lady, Mary Gibbons, 'fumbling' in two bags which Daly was carrying while both women were doing the stations of the cross. Daly grabbed the bags and from one of them pulled a hammer, which Gibbons managed to grasp. Daly pulled it from her and struck her on the head. A statement later taken from Mrs Gibbons in the Mater Hospital was at odds with Mrs Daly's version of the event. Gibbons claimed that 'someone had come up behind her and hit her'; she died from her injuries a week later. Mary Agnes Daly was charged with murder and was convicted. On 12 November, she was sentenced to death, with the date of execution set for 5 January 1949.

Leave to appeal was at first refused but eventually, at the end of January, following a stay of execution, the Supreme Court quashed both the conviction and the sentence. A deposition taken from Mrs Gibbons, in connection with original charges of wounding with intent to murder and causing grievous bodily harm, should not have been admitted in evidence in connection with the murder charge. However, the young couple's relief at the Supreme Court's ruling was brief. A retrial was ordered, and the accused was remanded in custody. The couple, separated through a tragic circumstance, and with their baby now a year old, had to live through three further months of agonising trauma. At the end of March, when an application for bail was heard, it was revealed that Mrs Daly, despite the fact that her conviction had been quashed, had spent eleven weeks in the condemned cell. The new trial, which opened on 25 April, lasted only four days, and at the end of it Mary Agnes Daly was again convicted of murder and sentenced to death on 18 May. The sentence was commuted to life imprisonment by President Seán T. O'Kelly on the advice of the government.

There was a disquieting element to the case. The purse which Mrs Daly had had in her possession in the church, and which contained the

£3 10s, had gone missing. Mrs Daly never accused Mrs Gibbons of either stealing or attempting to steal the purse. According to newspaper reports, the stealing of bags and purses in churches by women was a common offence in the city. A witness gave evidence of a scuffle between the two women. It is doubtful that Mary Agnes Daly would be convicted of murder if she were tried today.

The Civil Service club rallied round Harry Daly and supported him in his grief. He remained a popular member of the club until his death in 1961. Today, the club still plays an annual competition for the Harry Daly Cup.

John Morgan was active during the formative years of competitive bridge. He served in the British army during the First World War and was awarded the Military Medal. Armed with a commerce degree from UCD, he joined the staff of the comptroller and auditor general in 1923. He was a founding member of the Regent Club in 1925, as was the woman who subsequently became his wife, Frances Lee. In pursuing Frances, there was rivalry between John and his friend, work colleague and bridge partner, Charlie O'Neill. Morgan was elected honorary secretary of the CBAI in 1938, retaining the position until 1947. In 1949, he became president. A competent competitor, he played in a Camrose match with Charlie O'Neill against Wales in 1937. On the night of 15 August 1970, John Morgan was struck and killed by a car while crossing the road after leaving the Regent Bridge Club in Waterloo Road. It was a tragic end to the life of a good-natured man who had served bridge well. He was seventy-six years old.

Joe O'Donoghue (a native of Newcastle, County Down), Derek Stokes and Jimmy Powell (both Dublin-based) were three of Ireland's most prominent tournament directors in the latter part of the twentieth century. All three died within months of each other in 2001. The debonair O'Donoghue declined gradually, a victim of Alzheimer's disease.

The self-assured Stokes, a former international player, was laid low by a similar condition. The dapper, opera-loving Powell, a little man with a big, authoritative voice, was found dead in the apartment where he lived alone off Dublin's Meath Street, a short walk from the Civil Service Club; the members of this club were his second family.

Des Scully was the only senior official of the CBAI to have died in office. A three-time winner of the inter-county championship with Armagh, with George McCaw, Wilfie Robb and Greer Mackenzie, he also won the Kelburne with a County Meath team. A quiet man and an effective administrator, he was elected for a three-year term as chairman of the CBAI in June 1994. A year later, he was killed in a road accident.

Billy Kelso, one of Northern Ireland's most efficient and dedicated officials and, for seventeen years, joint honorary secretary of the Irish Bridge Union, died on 25 July 1995 while playing bridge at Kelvin-Malone Club in Belfast.

37

PLAYERS AND PLAYS

Bridge, like all competitive games, has its elite players: those who, through a combination of talent and hard work, raise themselves above the rest. Every era has produced a small number of such players. What makes a good player? Those who have been selected on Irish open teams for international championships have one thing in common: without exception, they started playing bridge when they were young – at college or earlier. Those who start later in life can achieve a great deal, but the young brain more easily absorbs – and retains – the complexities of the game. A few women players who made the Irish team took up the game in their thirties. But in the women's game too, a teenage or early-twenties start, in all but a few cases, has been the essential prelude to success.

Who were the best Irish players? In bridge at least, statistics are not quite the lies that Disraeli – according to Mark Twain – asserted they are. Major wins and international appearances point to the existence of some ability. You might win one national title with a bit of luck; if you win a second, you could be very lucky indeed; but further successes must indicate some skill. The opinions of contemporaries are important. Top-level players are reluctant to praise their rivals. Therefore, when admiration is expressed, it should be noted. For example, while statistics relating to Paddy Paul Donovan are not overly impressive, those who knew him nevertheless insist that he was an exceptional player. Finally, there is evidence from the table. Fortunately, writers have recorded brilliant plays right from the start of the competitive game.

There were good players among the pioneers of contract bridge. Eddie Barry and Philip Quinn, Harry Freehill and Harold Williams, and Harry Fine and David Rivlin emerged as the leading male pairs of the

1930s. Three husband-and-wife partnerships – David and Violet Pigot, Bill and Rosaleen O'Connell, and Joe and Mairéad O'Neill – won places on Camrose teams during the same period. Kathleen Lambert and Geraldine McConkey were the outstanding female pair. Bernard Williams was highly regarded. In this chapter, South has been made declarer in all deals, for the convenience of the reader.

B. L. (Bernard) Williams

Bidding in the 1930s was primitive by modern standards, but card play was of a high standard. The first report in an Irish newspaper of a deal from competitive bridge appeared in the *Irish Times* on 30 November 1932. It featured Bernard Williams.

Dealer East. Vulnerability not recorded.

North (H. Williams)
♠ A Q 3
♥ A 9 8 7
♦ A J 2
♣ 9 7 4

West (Mathieson)
♠ 9 8 5 2
♥ J 10
♦ 10 6 5 3
♣ J 10 2

East (Buller)
♠ K 10 4
♥ 6 5 4
♦ K 8 7
♣ K Q 8 5

South (B. L. Williams)
♠ J 7 6
♥ K Q 3 2
♦ Q 9 4
♣ A 6 5

West	North	East	South
-	-	1♣	Pass
1NT	Dbl	Redbl	Pass
2♣	Pass	Pass	2NT
Pass	3NT	All Pass	

220

Harold Williams described Buller's 1♣ light opening as a 'psychic bid, typical of his forceful play',[1] Mathieson's 1NT as 'pure bluff' and Buller's redouble as 'the bid of a master of psychology'. The psyches having been exposed, Barney got the ♣J lead, and held up. He won the club continuation and cashed four rounds of hearts before giving East two club tricks. This was the position with Buller on lead:

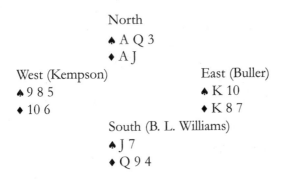

```
                    North
                    ♠ A Q 3
                    ♦ A J
West (Kempson)                    East (Buller)
♠ 9 8 5                           ♠ K 10
♦ 10 6                            ♦ K 8 7
                 South (B. L. Williams)
                    ♠ J 7
                    ♦ Q 9 4
```

Whatever he played, declarer had to make four of the last five tricks and his contract.

'Well done, sir!' the Colonel exclaimed. 'That hand was played as well as any I have ever seen.'

Three years spent in England (1936–39) almost certainly cost Bernard Williams places on Irish Camrose teams, but he was capped three times during the late 1940s.

Kathleen Lambert

Kathleen Lambert's principal legacy lies in the part she played in founding the CBAI and introducing duplicate. That she was a skilful player is demonstrated in Harry Freehill's 1949 publication, *The Squeeze at Bridge*. She won the Holmes Wilson Cup three times and partnered Geraldine McConkey in six Camrose matches. For more than sixty years, they remained the only Irish pair to be selected on a national team without having to compete in trials.

The 1911 census returns describe Mrs Lambert, aged thirty-five at the time, as a professional singer. For a number of years prior to her marriage to Septimus D. Lambert in 1906, Kathleen Barrett, as she was called then, was indeed a well-known soprano. Programmes and reports of concerts between 1900 and 1906 show her to have been an accomplished, busy and popular performer. Her nephew, a bank official named Oswald G. Giddings, married Ruth Wellwood from Cork, who, when she became Ruth Giddings, became Ireland's most renowned player. To her, the founder of the CBAI was just 'Aunt Kitty'.

GERALDINE MCCONKEY

Geraldine McConkey was to the forefront of Irish bridge, both as a player and an administrator, for five decades. She played in seven European championships, winning a bronze medal in 1952, and is one of only three women to have played on Irish open teams in European or world championships. A participant in six Camrose matches, her international career stretched from the inaugural Camrose contest in February 1937, to the European championships in Warsaw in 1966. She won twenty-seven national titles over thirty-years. Honorary secretary of the Dublin region for the first nine years of its existence, she became president of the CBAI in 1960; the following year, she became the first woman president of the Irish Bridge Union. She is commemorated by the Geraldine Trophy, which is awarded to the winners of the CBAI men's team championship. This is the only trophy in Irish bridge which bears a person's first name – a fact which perhaps says something about the affection in which she was held by her contemporaries.

Her play on the following deal bears testimony to her skill.

North
- ♠ KQ5
- ♥ A962
- ♦ J2
- ♣ A1053

West
- ♠ 3
- ♥ J854
- ♦ AQ4
- ♣ J9764

East
- ♠ AJ1094
- ♥ Q107
- ♦ 10875
- ♣ 8

South
- ♠ 8762
- ♥ K3
- ♦ K963
- ♣ KQ2

Mrs McConkey, South, declarer in 3NT, got the ♣6 lead. She won with the queen. A spade to the queen and ace was followed by the ♠J from East, which was allowed to win. Another spade put declarer in dummy. The ♦2 was covered by the seven and nine and the trick was won by West's queen. Next, a club was won by the king. The ♦3 was played, and West went up the ace to return another club, won by dummy's ten. Declarer had won four tricks, lost four and had to make the rest. This was the position with declarer to play from dummy:

North
- ♠ -
- ♥ A 9 6 2
- ♦ -
- ♣ A

West
- ♠ -
- ♥ J 8 5 4
- ♦ -
- ♣ J

East
- ♠ 9
- ♥ Q 10
- ♦ 10 8
- ♣ -

South
- ♠ 8
- ♥ K 3
- ♦ K 6
- ♣ -

McConkey played dummy's ♣A. East could do no better than discard the ♥10. Declarer's heart off the table brought the queen from East, with which she beat the king. McConkey cashed the ♦K and finessed the ♥9. That the defenders could have done better is irrelevant; what matters is that McConkey saw the squeeze possibility and executed it.

Geraldine McConkey was not always as sharp. A few years later, at the east of Ireland congress – an event which she helped to inaugurate – she and Ruth Giddings were defending against a slam. Ruth's opening lead was won by Geraldine's ace of the suit. For some time, she fumbled with her cards, shifting them from one hand to the other with a puzzled expression. Finally, with a shrug of resignation, she returned her partner's suit. Declarer won and claimed twelve tricks.

'Why didn't you cash your other ace?' asked Ruth.

Geraldine's reply will be received with empathy by players who are partial to the occasional glass of scotch: 'I couldn't find it.'[2]

H.G. (HARRY) FREEHILL

Harry Freehill, an outstanding all-rounder – player, director, administrator and author – had a central role in both home and international affairs during the 1930s. Active in the CBAI from its inception, he was one of its first tournament directors. He tirelessly travelled the country

Surviving CBAI founders, March 1958. Front: J. E. Hogan, F. T. Quin, Mrs Holmes Wilson, W. J. L. O'Connell (president CBAI), Mrs Hogarty, Geraldine McConkey. Second row: Dr B. Solomons, H. Hackett, Ina McMenamin, D. R. Pigot, J. P. Morgan, Lady Huggard, Miss Holmes Wilson. Back row: C. O'Neill, J. Monaghan, M. Collins, Dr F. McMenamin, Mairéad O'Neill, S. Woods.

Hugh Peacock (Kilcullen), international middleweight boxer, 1950s. A master craftsman who made shoes for Hollywood star Rita Hayworth, he has been the leading bridge mentor in County Kildare for many years.

CBAI'S first Camrose-winning squad, 2000: Front: R. Timlin, Kay Molly (president), N. Tóibín. Back: R. Boland, B. J. O'Brien, J. Clarson, G. Keaveney, R. Milne, M. Moran (NPC), C. Ó Dálaigh, H. McGann, T. Hanlon. Clarson and Ó Dálaigh did not get to play. When the team went ahead after the second match, the squad relied on the experience of Boland, Tóibín, Hanlon, McGann, Keaveney and Timlin to stay in front.

Camrose and Grand Slam winning team, 2005. Front: P. Ó Briain, T. Hanlon, P. Pigot, M. Ó Briain. Back: H. McGann, M. Moran, A. Mesbur, N. K .FitzGibbon, D. A. Jackson (NPC).

Fearghal O'Boyle (Sligo), European Bridge League tournament director, was a champion Irish step-dancer

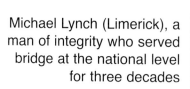

Michael Lynch (Limerick), a man of integrity who served bridge at the national level for three decades

Monty Rosenberg and Rex Anderson, Northern Ireland's most renowned pair, European team bronze medalists 1979

The family that plays together: the Prendergasts from Kilmacthomas: Tom, Anne (Heffernan), Hannah and Michael on right. Sean Reilly presents the cup, named after his father, Paddy 'Dasher' Reilly. Michael was a stalwart defender on the Waterford football team in the 1950s.

Maisie Cooper (Limerick) and Hilary Dowling Long (Sligo) in 2002

Peter Flynn (Tramore), an able administrator, at the opening of the national bridge headquarters in Templeogue in 1999

Australian expert Ron Klinger with pupils of Scoil Crónáin, Rathcoole, County Dublin, in September 2000. Bridge teacher Máire O'Keeffe and school principal Brenda nic Ginnea are in the back row on the right.

Jimmy Smyth of Ruan, County Clare, one of hurling's all-time greats and a bridge national master

Andrew H. Davidson, Master of the Rotunda Hospital, international player and donor of the Davidson Cup

Businessman Joe Moran, who made an immense contribution to the game

Novelist Mary Stanley, who competes in national championships and trials

George Ryan, author of four novels and bridge correspondent for the *Irish Times*

Nancy and Owen Rowe, who introduced intermediate grades to Ireland

Rebecca and Aileen O'Keeffe, the Rowes' grand-daughter and daughter respectively – the only mother-and-daughter partnership to play on an Irish team

encouraging groups to form branches, and he became the CBAI's second honorary secretary, succeeding Kathleen Lambert in 1935. He relinquished the position in 1938 to become the first vice-president, an office he held until 1942, when he did not go forward for re-election.[3] He missed no opportunity to promote the game. For example, in January 1938 he and Joseph O'Neill broadcast a series of talks on bridge on Radio Éireann.

That he was one of the leading players of the period is evident from his participation in seven Camrose matches between 1937 and 1939, all in partnership with Harold Williams. His last major success was in the Wigoder Cup in the 1940/41 season, also with Williams. He competed in the national panel test in January 1942, but following the AGM in September of that year, he disappears from the records. By September 1943, Williams was partnering his namesake, B. L. (Barney) Williams, in competition. Freehill resigned from his bank position, and, with his American wife and their daughter, emigrated to the United States some time during the 1940s.

He gathered material for a book, *The Squeeze at Bridge*, published in London in 1949. A superb work on various types of squeeze play, it is an invaluable document because those who executed the plays are named and it shows that, whatever deficiencies may have existed in bidding techniques at the time, the standard of card play was high. The book features Irish-based players R. D. (Roddy) Carroll, C. H. (Harry) Day, George B. Hanna, Kathleen Lambert, Geraldine McConkey, John Morgan, Bill O'Connell and his son Barry, Joseph O'Neill, Tom Shanks and Freehill's regular partner, Harold Williams.

Freehill, in a letter to Harold Miles, secretary of the Northern Ireland Bridge Union, in June 1939, suggested a union between the NIBU and the CBAI for the purpose of international competition. Among his victories were the Holmes Wilson, Revington, Kelburne and Wigoder Cups.

Relatives of Freehill still live in Clontarf but they are not aware of the fate of their illustrious ancestor.[4]

JOSEPH & MAIRÉAD O'NEILL AND GERARD CROFTS

Joseph O'Neill and his wife, Mairéad, made outstanding contributions to the game. Mairéad's involvement in bridge lasted from the 1920s to the

1980s. She was born Margaret O'Callaghan in 1893 near Charleville, County Cork, and in 1918 married Gerard Crofts, a participant in the 1916 Rising. The Crofts played in the Regent from its founding in 1925. That republicans such as them fitted easily into the bridge fraternity demonstrates what an all-embracing activity the game was, even at that turbulent time in the nation's history. Together, the Crofts actively promoted the budding CBAI. Mairéad's role tends to overshadow that of her first husband, but in November 1933 their visit to Tullamore was instrumental in setting up the first branch of the association in the midlands. Gerard Crofts died in November 1934, in his forty-fifth year. A leading tenor of the day, he recorded for Beltona Records and was a frequent broadcaster on Radio Éireann.

Mairéad had built up a successful partnership with Joseph O'Neill and, following Gerard's death, they became one of the country's leading pairs, winning eight national titles between 1933 and 1939. She was still Mrs Crofts when they played in the Camrose match against Northern Ireland in April 1937; when they won the Spiro Cup for the second time a year later, they were Mr & Mrs O'Neill. Both served on the CBAI executive. She was elected to the newly created position of assistant secretary of the CBAI in 1940 and remained in the office for eight years. In 1942, she became honorary treasurer as well. Joseph was president in 1947/48. Much of what we know about the Duplicate Bridge Control Board, the body which initiated the home international championship in 1937, and its short-lived successor, the Duplicate Bridge Board of the UK and Éire, comes from correspondence left by Joseph and saved for posterity by Mairéad.[5]

Joseph O'Neill was music critic for the *Irish Independent* and secretary of the Leinster School of Music, where Mairéad was a director. He was almost certainly responsible for *Irish Contract Bridge News*, a magazine launched in November 1937, and from 1948 to 1950 he and Noel Byrne published *The Irish Bridge Annual*. Joseph was the *Irish Independent*'s first special bridge correspondent, a position he took up in the late 1930s and held until just before his death in 1953. He also contributed to *Social & Personal* magazine. It is believed that O'Neill's broadcast of the Ireland v. Scotland match on the night of 2 March 1937 was the first radio coverage of a bridge match on this side of the Atlantic. Thereafter, he regularly broadcast home international matches. Mairéad was alo a journalist. Following Joe's death, she took over his position as bridge correspondent for the *Irish Independent*. She also covered the game for the *Irish Press* well into the 1980s, and contributed to *Model Housekeeping* magazine.

Mairéad O'Neill holds a singular honour in the annals of Irish bridge: she is the only person to have been made a life honorary member of the CBAI. Joseph O'Neill died in 1953. Mairéad passed away in 1987, aged ninety-four.

WILLIAM J. L. (SNAPPY) O'CONNELL

The O'Connell family from Cork produced four internationals: Bill and Rosaleen, and their sons Barry and Michael. The parents played twice in the 1937 Camrose. In 1946, Barry partnered his father in the first three post-war matches. Barry and Michael played for Ireland in the 1950s. Bill O'Connell occasionally displayed an irascible temperament, hence the nickname 'Snappy'. He was proud of his sons. They were good, of course, but their father often irritated other players by making comparisons between his boys and the rest. However well a hand was bid, declared or defended, his boys, in Snappy's opinion, would have done better. At the 1963 Killarney congress, Des Deery partnered Scottish player George Jesner, with Michael O'Connell and Gordon Holmes the other half of the team, in the Loch Léin trophy. Snappy, kibitzing at Jesner's table, frequently, to the annoyance of the players, pointed out how much better his boys would have done. Jesner excused himself and left the table. Not renowned for buying rounds, to everyone's surprise he returned with a tray full of drinks. When he accidentally spilled a pint over Snappy, suspicions were aroused. The session concluded with one spectator less.

The elder O'Connell occupies a proud position in the annals of Irish bridge. It was he who first broke the Dublin players' monopoly of the national championships when he won the individual title in 1936 and again in 1937. With Jack Murphy, he also won the Revington Cup in 1937. Those victories were important, proving that the Dublin-based players were not as invincible as they may have previously appeared. O'Connell had a reputation, beyond the jurisdiction of the CBAI, for his knowledge of the laws and frequently officiated at competitions. In 1947, he directed the Wales v. Northern Ireland Camrose match.

Apart from Erina Holmes Wilson, who retained the presidency of the CBAI for the first three years of its existence, W. J. L. O'Connell remains the only person to have been elected president for a second term. Having become Cork's first holder of the office in 1940, he was elected again in 1957.

T. D. (DES) PURCELL

Evidence suggests that T. D. Purcell, E. O. Barry, May McNulty and Ina McMenamin were the four best players of the 1940s. Des Purcell's name first appears as a big winner during the 1939/40 season, when he won the Wigoder Cup, the original CBAI teams trophy, partnering his brother, Gerry, with Frank McMenamin and Ina Hickey completing the quartet. McMenamin later married Ina but Purcell formed a bridge partnership with her to become one of the most successful pairs of the decade. He was the outstanding male player of the period: his total of twenty-three national championship wins was not surpassed until the late 1960s, when Joe MacHale overtook him.

Purcell's play on the following deal contributed handsomely to his team winning the CBAI men's teams championship of 1962/63.

Dealer East. N-S Vulnerable

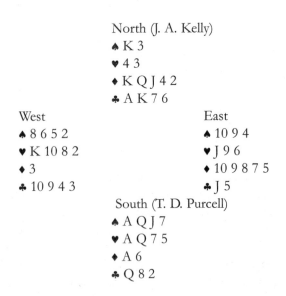

North (J. A. Kelly)
♠ K 3
♥ 4 3
♦ K Q J 4 2
♣ A K 7 6

West
♠ 8 6 5 2
♥ K 10 8 2
♦ 3
♣ 10 9 4 3

East
♠ 10 9 4
♥ J 9 6
♦ 10 9 8 7 5
♣ J 5

South (T. D. Purcell)
♠ A Q J 7
♥ A Q 7 5
♦ A 6
♣ Q 8 2

W	N	E	S
-	-	-	1♥
Pass	2♦	Pass	3NT
Pass	4NT	Pass	5♠
Pass	7NT	Pass	Pass
Pass			

Purcell won the spade lead, cashed two more tricks in the suit, discarding one of dummy's hearts, then wisely stopped. Timing was crucial. A fourth spade at this stage would have embarrassed dummy as there was no good discard. Purcell turned his attention to diamonds, taking four rounds, followed by the ace of clubs and a club to the queen in hand.

This was the ending:

```
                     North
                     ♠ -
                     ♥ 4
                     ♦ 4
                     ♣ K 7
      West                          East
      ♠ -                           ♠ -
      ♥ K 10                        ♥ J 9 6
      ♦ -                           ♦ 10
      ♣ 10 9                        ♣ -
                     South
                     ♠ A
                     ♥ A Q
                     ♦ -
                     ♣ 8
```

When Purcell played the ace of spades, West had no option but to throw a heart, hoping declarer might guess the suit incorrectly. Purcell at this point had a perfect picture of his opponents' cards. He knew West had two clubs and East a diamond. Therefore he discarded dummy's small club, forcing East to keep the diamond and, like West, to throw a heart. When he played his club to dummy's king, East had to throw another heart. So, knowing that each opponent had one heart each, he played a heart to the ace and dropped the king.

E. O. (EDDIE) BARRY

Eddie Barry, who remained at the top of bridge in Ireland for four decades, was the epitome of the ethical and gracious player. Few, then or subsequently, managed to reach his standard of decorum at the table. In Barry's obituary in the *Irish Times*, published in December 1969, Jack Kelly referred to 'his demeanour at the table, his graciousness to opponents and above all his meticulously ethical tempo of bidding and play'. He had 'judgement, flair and table presence in abundance'. With fifteen 'caps', he was the leading CBAI Camrose player during the pre-1951 era. His career as a bank official took him to several parts of the country. Wherever he went, he helped raise the standard of the game. He spent many years in Cork, where his circle included John Coakley and the O'Connell family. He and Michael O'Connell took the game seriously. Although living close to each other and playing bridge together regularly, they continuously exchanged letters about problems of bidding and play. Three of Eddie's children – his son Pat and his daughters Anne Dillon and Gráinne Barton – played for Ireland.

PERSONALITIES OF THE 1940S

May McNulty and Anrew Davidson were, arguably, more successful than Hickey and Purcell. McNulty's career is covered later, as is that of Ina McMenamin (née Hickey). Flora McLoone and Noel Peart, too, got their names on major trophies during the 1940s, as did Jack and Eileen O'Sullivan. All four mixed pairs played on CBAI Camrose teams.

A number of prominent 1940s players had connections in public life or had eminent personal careers. Eileen O'Sullivan, mentioned in previous chapters, who later won European medals, was a native of Derry and sister to Paddy McGilligan, who was Minister for Industry and Commerce from 1924 to 1932 and Minister for Finance in the inter-party government of 1948–51. She was technically sound. According to Ruth Giddings, she 'never let the side down'. Teammates felt comfortable when she was at the other table.

During the 1949/50 season, Claire Lyne partnered her husband in a Camrose match against Wales. She was a sister of future Taoiseach Seán Lemass. Active away from the table too, she served on the CBAI executive. Cleo Roy, who was honorary secretary of the CBAI from 1949 to

1951, was non-playing captain of Ireland's first women's teams in the European championships, and later played on Irish teams as Mrs Fellowes, was born Cleo Geldof. She was an aunt of the rock star and campaigner Bob Geldof.

Andrew H. Davidson, an eminent gynaecologist, was Master of the Rotunda Hospital from 1933 to 1940. He had succeeded another well-known player, Bethel Solomons, in the post. Freed from his arduous responsibilities at the hospital, during the 1940s Davisdon saw his bridge career take off. He won fourteen national championships, seven of them with May McNulty. Success continued into the 1950s. Between 1954 and 1958, Davidson, Gerry Read, Jack O'Sullivan and Joe MacHale, representing Fitzwilliam Tennis Club, dominated the inter-club championship, winning three times and losing one final. Davidson played in three Camrose matches with McNulty and represented Ireland in a European and world championship. His name is commemorated by the Davidson Cup.

MAY MCNULTY

'The best Irish woman player of all time' is how Ruth Giddings described May McNulty. 'I was terrified of her,' she added. A woman capable of terrifying Ruth must indeed have been forbidding – an image quite at odds with that of the young girl whose ambition was to be an opera singer. May McNulty left no recording of her voice, nor does her name appear in RTÉ's archives – although family members believe that she sang on radio.[6] Those who remember her speak of a deep timbre, which she projected well, and which suggests she was a contralto.

There is a signed photograph which May sent to her mother from Milan, a portrait of a young woman in her early twenties. She spent some time in Italy studying singing. The renowned Irish soprano Margaret Burke Sheridan was in Milan throughout the 1920s, when she was prima donna at Teatro Alla Scala, Italy's premier opera house. Sheridan's presence in Milan may have played a part in the decision by the young Dublin singer to go there. At some point, McNulty abandoned the idea of a professional singing career. Later, she confided to friends that her failure to fulfil her musical ambition was a disappointment to her. Instead, she was destined to become the best Irish woman bridge player of her era. Apart from that sojourn in Italy and occasional trips abroad, mostly to bridge championships, she spent her entire life at 15 Warrington Place, Dublin, from her birth in November 1900 until her death in June 1966. May McNulty was a smoker; she died of cancer.

She was in her late thirties before making her mark as a player, when, during the 1937/38 season, she won the Jackson Cup with a Mrs Fitzgerald, the first of thirty-three championship victories over a twenty-two-year period. Ruth Giddings is the only woman to have won more.

In the early 1940s, her partnership with Dr Andrew Davidson began. They became the leading mixed pair of the decade, winning eight major titles, including the Kelburne Cup four years in a row, from 1944 to 1947 – a feat that is still unmatched. The other half in different years consisted of alternating pairings from the trio of Noel Peart, Flora McLoone and P. Powell. McNulty and Davidson played together on three Camrose teams.

Her dislike of travelling deprived her of even more international honours, according to Ruth, who thinks she could have been ever-present on the Irish women's team had she so wished. Her record is still impressive: seven European championships, which brought her three medals – a silver in Montreux in 1954 and two bronze, in Dublin in 1952 and Torquay in 1961. She also participated in CBAI v. NIBU matches for the Colonel Walshe Cup. It is worth keeping in mind that places on Camrose and Colonel Walshe Cup teams were won against male opposition. Few women were as successful as McNulty against male adversaries.

The Giddings–McNulty partnership was one of the greatest in Irish bridge. The two women competed together for only ten years or so, coming to prominence in 1951 when they won the Davidson, the first of fourteen Irish championships they secured as a pair. The same year saw them appear on Camrose teams against Wales and Scotland (the last two matches before the CBAI withdrew from the competition). They remain the only pair to have won the Davidson Cup four times. Remarkably, they never played together in the Jackson Cup, although they each won it five times with other partners.

By 1961, the last year they played together for Ireland, May, according to Ruth, was losing interest in the game. May could have been on the team in Beirut in 1962 when Ireland's women won another bronze medal but didn't wish to travel abroad any more. It is possible that her health was deteriorating at that stage. She died four years later.

McNulty played with others, including Harry Day – who had owned

25 Waterloo Road before the Regent moved there in 1953 – with Ina McMenamin and Geraldine McConkey. She was honorary secretary of the Regent during the 1940s, when the club was in Harcourt Street, and was a member of the CBAI executive.

Ironically, few records of her performances have survived compared to those for other leading players. This deal was played against Belgium in McNulty's last European championships, in Torquay in 1961:

Dealer South. East-West Vulnerable.

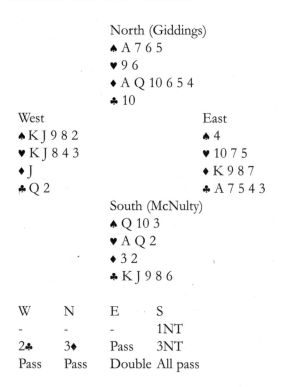

North (Giddings)
♠ A 7 6 5
♥ 9 6
♦ A Q 10 6 5 4
♣ 10

West
♠ K J 9 8 2
♥ K J 8 4 3
♦ J
♣ Q 2

East
♠ 4
♥ 10 7 5
♦ K 9 8 7
♣ A 7 5 4 3

South (McNulty)
♠ Q 10 3
♥ A Q 2
♦ 3 2
♣ K J 9 8 6

W	N	E	S
-	-	-	1NT
2♣	3♦	Pass	3NT
Pass	Pass	Double	All pass

The ♠9 lead was won by declarer's ten. A diamond picked up the jack and when McNulty covered with the queen, East allowed it to win. That was a mistake. Had East taken the king and switched to a heart, she would have defeated the contract. McNulty proceeded to punish the Belgian defender for her lapse. She played the ace of diamonds. West threw a heart. The ♣10 ran to West's queen. West had little option but to continue a club, which East won with the ace and played a heart. McNulty went up the ace and played out her club winners. These were the last four cards:

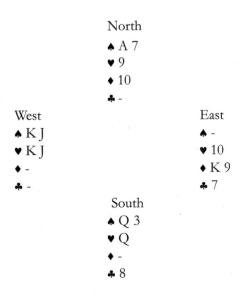

North
♠ A 7
♥ 9
♦ 10
♣ -

West
♠ K J
♥ K J
♦ -
♣ -

East
♠ -
♥ 10
♦ K 9
♣ 7

South
♠ Q 3
♥ Q
♦ -
♣ 8

Declarer played the club and West, with no winning option, threw the jack of hearts. McNulty played her heart and forced her opponent to lead away from the ♠KJ.

The evidence that has been gathered, along with opinions of contemporaries, points to May McNulty being an exceptional player. Only Ruth Giddings's own record stands in the way of accepting Ruth's assessment: that May McNulty was indeed the greatest Irish woman player.

INA MCMENAMIN

Ina Egan, born in 1898, was a strikingly attractive woman possessed of a vivacious personality and a competitive instinct. This instinct brought her success in such diverse activities as swimming, ballroom dancing and golf; but it was at bridge that she excelled. She married twice. Her first husband, James Hickey, of the well-known family of fabric specialists in North Earl Street, Dublin, died from Parkinson's disease, leaving Ina with two children.[7] Mrs Hickey's usual bridge partner was Dr Frank McMenamin. Together, they won the Wigoder, Holmes Wilson, Kelburne and Davidson Cups, as well as the inter-club championship. Ina was

CBAI individual champion in 1941. They made their international debut in March 1939 when the Irish Free State defeated Scotland in a Camrose match at the Royal Marine Hotel, Dun Laoghaire. In the course of time, romance blossomed between these two attractive and personable people, and in 1945 Ina Hickey became Mrs McMenamin. Their home, on the corner of Clyde Road, became popular in Dublin bridge circles.

'The Doc', as he was affectionately known, although a competent player, was not as good as Ina, but she found a partner of the highest calibre in Des Purcell, with whom she won numerous competitions, including the Moylan and Spiro Cups, and seven further Camrose caps. With thirty national titles to her name, she is one of the most prolific winners of Irish competitions. Ten European championships, including one on an open team, yielded a silver and two bronze medals. She remains the only woman to have captained an Irish open team – in 1948 – and she was the first female non-playing captain of a CBAI Camrose team – against Scotland in 1947. Her ten Camrose appearances, as a player, constitute an Irish women's record that is unlikely to be broken. When she played her last match, in 1948, only Eddie Barry, with eleven caps at that point, had more. Ina's last major trophy was the Egan Cup in 1966 – the trophy she herself had donated in memory of her brother.

Ina was a member of the organising committee for the Dublin European championships in 1967 – an appointment which would have required the approval of Denis Jackson, the Machiavellian chief organiser of the event. She arranged the concluding banquet, held on the evening of 16 September. Six days later, Frank McMenamin died, a victim of throat cancer.

Press reports of Ina McMenamin's performance at the table give the impression that she was a bold bidder and an imaginative player. In the celebrated Camrose match against England in Stockport in November 1946 she employed both of these qualities in what could be regarded as the key deal of the hundred-board match.

Dealer North. North–South Vulnerable

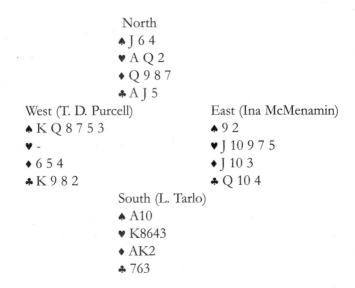

North
♠ J 6 4
♥ A Q 2
♦ Q 9 8 7
♣ A J 5

West (T. D. Purcell)
♠ K Q 8 7 5 3
♥ -
♦ 6 5 4
♣ K 9 8 2

East (Ina McMenamin)
♠ 9 2
♥ J 10 9 7 5
♦ J 10 3
♣ Q 10 4

South (L. Tarlo)
♠ A10
♥ K8643
♦ AK2
♣ 763

The auctions are not documented but it appears that North opened the bidding 1NT, following which South forced to game. Whatever the respective auctions, South became declarer at both tables. In one room, Ina McMenamin, East, doubled when 4♥ came round to her. The English South, Louis Tarlo, redoubled. Ina's double was speculative, based on her trump holding and, looking at her own meagre high-card strength, not unreasonably assuming that her partner had some honour cards which might convert into tricks. Tarlo's redouble was also speculative but the match was close. Each side was keen to assert superiority. Some minor spot cards were not recorded so the blanks have been filled in, but the relevant cards are as they were dealt.

Against 4♥ redoubled, Des Purcell led the ♠K. Declarer won, found the bad trump break at trick two, won in dummy and played a spade to the ten and West's queen. Purcell played another spade to neutralise dummy's jack, which McMenamin ruffed, over-ruffed by Tarlo, who next played his two top diamonds. On the second diamond, Ina McMenamin played the jack, a standard false card intended to give declarer a losing option. Tarlo, then one of England's best young players and a future European champion, fell for it and finessed the nine of diamonds into McMenamin's ten. He went two down: 1,000 points to Ireland. Bobby

Bastow, at the other table, made 4♥. A further 620, and a gain of 1,620 on the board. The winning margin in the match was 1,200.

Following the game, Ewart Kempson, editor of *Bridge* magazine, who had played in the match, in a BBC radio broadcast referred to Ina as 'Ireland's most distinguished player: charming, vivacious, popular'. Kempson was not the only Englishman she impressed. Reese and Schapiro invited her to play on their team at the Harrowgate congress in 1948.

When Ina McMenamin died suddenly in January 1974, George Ryan devoted his entire column in the *Irish Times* to recording some of the tributes to her. Her former teammate Jimmy Bastow left us with the best insight into her personality. 'Experts,' he wrote, 'particularly if they are women, are not very popular because of the envy generated through their coming out on top so often. Ina, however, was an exception: she was the best-liked player, male or female, to have represented Ireland in the past thirty years.' She still has no rival in that regard.

MOREEN MCCARTHY

Moreen McCarthy, the driving personality behind the game in Wexford for many years and president of both the CBAI and the IBU, was probably the best woman player from outside Dublin. During the 1950s, such was the talent in the capital that it was a major feat for a provincial player to get a place on an Irish team. Mrs McCarthy played in four European championships and three Camrose matches. She won the Davidson, Kelburne, Holmes Wilson and Moylan Cups, all of which are open to both men and women.

When she stood down as secretary of Wexford Bridge Club in October 1950, it was to become involved, along with her husband, Eugene – the proprietor of White's Hotel – in helping Dr Tom Walsh to prepare for the first Wexford Opera Festival, which opened the following year and became one of the World's leading opera festivals.

In September 1968, in the twilight of her career, she made a fine defensive play in a competition in Kilkenny. Her partner was Eddie Barry.

Dealer East. North–South Vulnerable

```
                        North
                        ♠ K102
                        ♥ 86
                        ♦ J93
                        ♣ AQ1053
        West (Barry)                    East (McCarthy)
        ♠ AQ84                          ♠ J97
        ♥ J942                          ♥ 1073
        ♦ 854                           ♦ Q10
        ♣ 87                            ♣ KJ962
                        South
                        ♠ 653
                        ♥ AKQ5
                        ♦ AK762
                        ♣ 4
```

West	North	East	South
-	-	-	1♦
Pass	2♣	Pass	3NT
All Pass			

Barry led the ♥2 to the 8, 10 and King. Declarer played the ace of diamonds and McCarthy dropped the queen! Next, a diamond to the nine was taken, to declarer's surprise, by McCarthy's 10. She returned a heart. Declarer won and played off the diamonds before playing a spade to the 10 and East's Jack. East played her last heart taken by declarer, who finessed a club. On winning the club, McCarthy played a spade. Barry won and he had a winning heart – the setting trick. Declarer could have succeeded by cashing the third heart after the diamonds and playing a spade to the King. However, that failure cannot detract from McCarthy's play at trick two, which confounded her opponent and led to declarer's defeat.

RUTH GIDDINGS

During one of many conversations I had with her, Ruth Giddings described herself as a 'freak'. She certainly was, and remains, an extraordinary person. She was born Ruth Wellwood on 3 September 1911 in Cork. On leaving school, she worked at the Bank of Ireland, where she met O. G. (Oswald) Giddings, her future husband. Bridge entered her life relatively late – in her mid-thirties – when she began to play bridge at Rathfarnham Golf Club. In 1947, her name first appeared among championship winners when she won the Holmes Wilson Cup with Dermot Egan, Rita McNally and Lily McDonagh. More than sixty years later, she is still winning in Dublin's Civil Service and Regent Clubs. In her ninety-fifth year, she won the president's prize in the Civil Service, and in her ninety-sixth the same prize in the Regent.

Giddings's fifty-four Irish major titles and twenty-eight appearances on the national team, including nineteen European championships,[8] from which she took two silver and three bronze medals, place her in a category apart. In addition, she won countless regional, congress and other competitions. The CBAI's secession from the home-international championships deprived Ruth of the opportunity to develop an even more illustrious career. The winners of the McMenamin Bowl in 1950 – the inaugural year of the competition – were chosen to play for the Lady Milne Trophy. Ruth's team finished second. Her team won the following year, but by then the CBAI had taken its fateful decision not to compete. The neighbouring islands were deprived of interesting clashes. Between 1950 and 1967, Great Britain won eight European women's titles, while Ireland was in the medals four times. During the same period, England won the Lady Milne Trophy on all but three occasions: Scotland won twice and Wales once. The Republic, with Giddings and her partner as its anchor pair, would have provided stern opposition to the English.

When, in 2005, Ruth was presented with a silver salver marking her attainment of grandmaster status, the honour was at least twenty years overdue. It had been more than two decades since she had regularly contested national competitions. However, during the twelve years before master-points were introduced, she won seventeen championships, finished second and third time and time again. From the introduction of master-points in 1958, she was the leading master-point holder, male or female, year after year.

Giddings retired from international competition in 1981. Her husband Oswald was ill and she did not go back to competing in trials afterwards. Only rarely did she take part in Irish championships after that. Her last major win was the McMenamin Bowl in 1987. Many people think that she could still make the Irish women's team – at the age of ninety-seven! I put the question to her: would she and Barbara Seligman get their places on the Irish women's team today? Her dismissive gesture told me that I had asked a silly question. Age has not dimmed her confidence.

In partnership with Barbara, she won twenty Irish titles. Her fourteen major wins with May McNulty were achieved over a shorter period, between 1951 and 1961. Her remaining national victories were shared with thirteen other players, including Harry Elliott, a member of the Dublin Jewish Social and Literary Club, with whom she won the Spiro Cup four times.

When you are in an impossible contract, the secret is to be composed, look confident and play smoothly. Ruth Giddings did all these things at the Olympiad in Valkenburg, the Netherlands, in 1980:

Dealer East. North–South non-vulnerable.

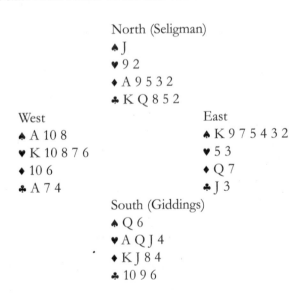

```
                 North (Seligman)
                 ♠ J
                 ♥ 9 2
                 ♦ A 9 5 3 2
                 ♣ K Q 8 5 2
West                             East
♠ A 10 8                         ♠ K 9 7 5 4 3 2
♥ K 10 8 7 6                     ♥ 5 3
♦ 10 6                           ♦ Q 7
♣ A 7 4                          ♣ J 3
                 South (Giddings)
                 ♠ Q 6
                 ♥ A Q J 4
                 ♦ K J 8 4
                 ♣ 10 9 6
```

W	N	E	S
-	-	Pass	1NT
Pass	2NT	Pass	3NT
All Pass			

Opposite Ruth's weak no-trump opening, Barbara eschewed a minor fit and invited game in no-trump: nine tricks might be easier than a club or diamond game. The contract had little chance: the defenders could take eight tricks, seven spades and the ace of clubs. However, opponents are not always alert – and you had to be when playing against Ruth Giddings.

West led the ♥6: third- and fifth-highest leads were becoming popular in 1980. Non-vulnerable, at team scoring, an extra trick or two down would not cost much. So Ruth played small from both hands – an

Irish Records Held by Ruth Giddings

- Most Irish championships, male or female: 54
- Most major titles for a women's partnership: 20, with Barbara Seligman
- Most international caps, male or female, world, European and EU championships: 28
- Most European team championship appearances, male or female: 19
- Most European championship medals for an Irish player: 5
- Most World Team Olympiads (joint record with N. K. FitzGibbon): 6
- Most wins in a single major event, CBAI women's teams: McMenamin Bowls: 15
- Most wins in CBAI mixed pairs: Spiro Cup, 8
- Most wins in CBAI pairs championship: Davidson Cup, 7
- Most wins for a partnership in the Davidson Cup: 4, with May McNulty
- Most wins for a female partnership in a single event: 8, in McMenamin Bowl, with Barbara Seligman
- Greatest time-span for a woman between first and last Irish championship win: forty-five years

unusual way to rectify the count, according to one commentator.[9] The ♥6 won! West continued a heart. Ruth won with the queen and played a club towards dummy, and West played low. She cashed five diamond tricks. West kept three hearts and the two black aces. Giddings played a club. West had to win with her bare ace and was forced to lead a heart from the king into Ruth's remaining ace, jack. Nine tricks made. West, of course, had chances to defeat the contract but her failure did not detract from declarer's imaginative play at trick one.

Barbara Seligman

Barbara Seligman, Ruth Giddings's long-time partner, won twenty-eight national championships, a figure exceeded only by Giddings, McNulty and McMenamin in the women's game. Her twenty-three appearances on the national team in world, European and EU championships has been bettered only by Giddings – male players included. Following her international debut in 1962, when she won a European bronze medal, she retained her place on the Irish team for the next twenty years, an unparalleled achievement. She added a European silver in 1973. While most of Barbara's international caps were won with Ruth, she also played with Sonya Britton and, following Ruth's retirement from trials, with Maria Barry (in 1991) and Pauline Maguire (in 1992). She remained the youngest player to win a place on an Irish women's team until another twenty-one-year-old, Rebecca O'Keeffe, played in Killarney in 1991.

Barbara was, to an extent, overshadowed by Ruth, and she in turn outshone her husband. However, Don Seligman was one of the dominant team players of the 1970s. He won eighteen Irish titles and was capped in three European and three EU championships. Archival evidence shows him to have been a remarkably good card player. Her brother Ralph played on the Bahamas national team.

MacHale and Pigot

The March/April 1959 issue of the *Irish Bridge Journal*[10] carried a photograph on its cover of two young men under the heading, 'The Coming Pair'. What an astute prediction! The picture was of Joseph P. MacHale and Peter J. Pigot. MacHale was already a champion when, in October 1955, Pigot, then twenty, won the congress pairs in Dun Laoghaire with the experienced Major George Jackson. A newspaper report of the match suggested that young Pigot had 'all the potentialities to reach international class very soon'.[11] In fact, he would not make the Irish team for another ten years, but when he did, he and MacHale became fixtures on it. A similar prediction had been made with regard to MacHale in January 1947, when, in one of his first outings in competitive bridge, he reached the final of Dublin's Quin Cup.[12]

There may be debate as to who was Ireland's all-time best pair. There is no disputing the fact that MacHale and Pigot dominated Irish competitive bridge throughout the 1960s and early 1970s to a greater degree than any other partnership, before or since. When they formed teams with other outstanding pairs – Gerry Read and Marcus Shrage, Gordon Holmes and Michael O'Connell, Des Deery and Eoin MacNeill – they proved to be formidable lineups. With Holmes and O'Connell, they won the men's teams (the Geraldine Trophy) for four consecutive years, from 1964 to 1967, and with Deery and MacNeill for the next three. With Read and Shrage, they won five Kelburne Cups – and a sixth when Conor O'Hara played with Shrage. They took the Holmes Wilson five times: three times with Deery and MacNeill, twice with Holmes and O'Connell. The Egan Cup came their way five times – on each occasion with one of the pairs mentioned above at the other table. They won pairs titles too: the Revington and Moylan Cups and the master pairs. The Davidson Cup eluded them, although Pigot won it with Peter Fitzgerald in 1957. Their first major success together came in 1959: the IBU teams championship for the Egan Cup. From that year until 1976, with the exception of 1972, they won at least one major title every year, and twice (in 1964 and 1970) they won four. Their total of thirty-three national championships in partnership is six better than that of FitzGibbon and Mesbur, and well ahead of the rest.

If those figures are not sufficiently impressive, then consider the pair's appearances on national teams in European and world championships. Their first European championships together was Ostend in 1965. Peter did not compete in the following year's trials, when Joe got his place on the team with Des Deery. Then, from 1967 until 1980 inclusive, MacHale and Pigot were fixtures on the Irish team, taking part in ten European championships and three Olympiads during that period,[13] and they had to compete in trials every year. In the men's game, no other pair can boast a record coming anywhere close to that. MacHale represented

Ireland in fifteen European team championships, including twelve in a row, as well as in three World Olympiads. Pigot took part in eleven Europeans and three Olympiads. Their sole international medal was a bronze at the 1979 Europeans in Lauzanne. In January 1974, they took part in the *Sunday Times* invitational pairs in London. In later life, MacHale played in European Union and European seniors events in partnership with Alex Montwill.

At the Oslo European championships in 1969, against Denmark, Pigot held ♠ J 10 7 6 4 2 ♥ J ♦ 10 9 5 ♣ 9 6 5. MacHale opened the auction with 1NT (12 to 14). The next player passed. Pigot had an obvious response, 2♠, weak takeout. (Transfers were not yet commonly used.) Pigot found a much more creative bid – one of the most imaginative ever recorded. This was the full deal and the auction:

Dealer North. East-West Vulnerable

```
                  North (MacHale)
                  ♠ K 5 3
                  ♥ 6 4 3
                  ♦ Q J 7
                  ♣ K Q J 7
    West                          East
    ♠ A                           ♠ Q 9 8
    ♥ K Q 10 9 5                  ♥ A 8 7 2
    ♦ A K 6 4 3                   ♦ 8 2
    ♣ 10 3                        ♣ A 8 4 2
                  South (Pigot)
                  ♠ J 10 7 6 4 2
                  ♥ J
                  ♦ 10 9 5
                  ♣ 9 6 5
```

W	N	E	S
-	1NT	Pass	2NT!
Pass	Pass	Pass	

To Joe MacHale's opening 1NT, Pigot, South, responded 2NT, promising a flat eleven or twelve points. What could West do? The auction, so far, indicated that East had a worthless hand. West did what any reasonable player would do: he passed. 2NT went four down, for –200.

Pigot gleefully anticipated the Danish players' conversation as they compared scores.

'Did you bid the slam?'

'What slam?'

'You know the hand. You held stiff ace, king, queen, ten to five, ace, king to five, doubleton small. The hand opposite has . . . '

'Bid a slam! We didn't bid at all!'

Deery and MacNeill, at the other table, played in 4♥ and scored 680. Pigot's inventive 2NT yielded 10 imps for Ireland. West was Steen Möller, Denmark's greatest player. To this day, Möller looks back with admiration on Pigot's wonderful bid and concedes that he was caught out by a very clever player.[14]

Clashes between Ireland and Britain or Ireland and England generate a special excitement in any sporting context, and bridge is no exception. The Irish particularly relished the victory against their near neighbours at the Olympiad in Miami in 1972, when they excelled, winning by the astonishing margin of 20 to –2.

Having compared scores with his teammates, a well-satisfied Peter Pigot left the playing area. On the way out, he met British team member Jeremy Flint, who, with his partner, Jonathan Cansino, had sat out the match. Flint was about to join the rest of his team.

'How did it go, Peter?' asked Jeremy.

'Oh, 20, – 2,' replied Pigot.

'Oh! Tough luck, you chaps. Better luck next time,' consoled the most gracious of British players.

Peter did not enlighten him. Why deprive him of the surprise that was to come when he rejoined his teammates?

Following a brilliant academic career, at the end of which he obtained the highest marks ever attained in the final commerce degree examination, Joe MacHale became secretary-bursar of University College Dublin. The competitive instinct which had brought him to the top in his studies was transferred into sport, and he was a fierce and first-rate competitor in both tennis and squash, becoming Irish champion in both. He represented Ireland in the Davis Cup and competed at Wimbledon in 1948. Even when he joined the country's elite bridge players, he continued to perform competitively at Fitzwilliam Tennis Club.

Coming from a cricket-playing family, it was inevitable that Peter Pigot would become accomplished at that game. He was also a low-handicap golfer. Away from the sports field and the bridge table, he was an accomplished pianist, and a regular performer at the all-male Bohemian Club. But it was as a journalist that he was perhaps best known to most followers of bridge. He wrote a bridge column for the *Irish Press* during the early 1970s and for the *Irish Independent* from 1977 until his death in 1989. When Jack Kelly died suddenly in 1970, Peter took his place on *English Bridge* magazine, and continued to bring news of Irish bridge to a readership in Britain and further afield. Pigot had a publishing success in 1979 when his book *Lausanne 1979*, a match-by-match account of Ireland's bronze-medal performance at the European championships that was written with extraordinary speed, was among the country's best-selling books that year.

Perhaps Joe MacHale's greatest achievement was to regain a place on the Irish team in 1995, at the age of seventy-three, after a fourteen-year absence. Partnering the English-born Ronald Milne, he was the oldest competitor in the open championship in Portugal. In an interview for the daily bulletin in Villamoura, he confided that he had been spurred on to take part in the trials because, as he put it: 'They were trying to write me off.' Who 'they' were is not quite clear – presumably the other trials contenders, especially the newly emerging school, or perhaps the IBU selectors. In any case, Joe MacHale did not like being written off.

His double victory in the CBAI men's team championship for the Geraldine Trophy and the IBU's Egan Cup in 2004, at the age of eighty-two, was another extraordinary feat. He and Ruth Giddings remain the only octogenarians to have won major national championships.

As with most successful partnerships, Joe MacHale and Peter Pigot were also good friends. At the table, there were no angry words in their respective vocabularies. Trust in each other's judgement was a MacHale/Pigot hallmark. On rare occasions when the judgement of one was found wanting, the other accepted the situation without a hint of displeasure. If MacHale betrayed signs of irration, this was directed against himself – for not finding a correct call or for failing to see a winning line of play. Towards the end of his life, affected by the normal cognitive impairment that comes with age, MacHale would become frustrated with his own performance.

JOE MACHALE'S RECORDS

- Most national championships won by a male player: 49
- Longest span between first and last major win: 1953 to 2004, 51 years
- Oldest player to win a major championship: 82, when he won the Geraldine and Egan Cups in 2004
- Most wins in CBAI men's team championship: Geraldine Trophy, 10
- Most Irish championship wins by a partnership: 32, with Peter Pigot
- Won the Geraldine Trophy seven years in a row, with Peter Pigot (record shared with David Jackson and Adam Mesbur, each of whom won seven successive Holmes Wilson Cups)
- Most wins in the Holmes Wilson: 9 (shared with David Jackson and Adam Mesbur)
- Most male international caps: 18 (shared with Nick FitzGibbon)
- Most European team championships for an Irish male player: 15
- Oldest player on an Irish open team: aged 73 (at European championships in Villamoura, Portugal, 1995)

At a time when smoking was customary at the table, Joe frequently used his cigar to effect. Management of cigar smoke was as much a part of his strategy as his handling of the cards. The habit did not enhance his popularity. When he and Tom Gleeson met in competition, the boards were played in a thick cloud of smoke. MacHale eventually became convinced of the dangers to his health posed by smoking and abandoned the practice.

READ AND SHRAGE

Gerry Read and Marcus Shrage must be included on any shortlist of great Irish bridge partnerships. Winners of sixty Irish championships between them, including sixteen in partnership, they appeared together on seven Irish teams in European championships and in one Olympiad.

Contemporaries thought there was little to choose between them and MacHale and Pigot, with whom they shared many team successes. Read came to the fore in 1942 when he was a member of the first Regent Club team to win the inter-club championship. During the 1950s, he won a number of major events, including three further inter-club titles with Fitzwilliam. He remained at the top for thirty years, ending his playing career by winning three consecutive Kelburne Cups, from 1969 to 1971, with Shrage, MacHale and Pigot.

Marcus Shrage, a medical doctor, also enjoyed thirty years at the top. His first big win was the inter-club cup, with the Dublin Jewish Literary and Social Club team in 1948. His last major success was in 1977, when he won the Revington Cup with Laur Sheeran. Shrage made a habit of winning the Revington, which decorated his sideboard eight times in total. He won the trophy with six different partners, including Eddie Barry, in 1952, and Eddie's son Pat, in 1974. Marcus partnered a number of leading women players, and won national championships with Elvina Spiro and Pauline Maguire.

Read captained Irish open teams nine times, twice as playing captain. Shrage was NPC for two European open teams, and for a women's team at the 1976 Olympiad in Monte Carlo.

HOLMES AND O'CONNELL

Gordon Holmes (Limerick) and Michael O'Connell (Cork) also belong with the best Irish players. O'Connell was the younger son of internationals Bill and Rose, who represented the Irish Free State in the 1937 Camrose. Michael and his brother Barry represented Ireland in four European championships between 1955 and 1961. During the early 1960s, Michael formed a partnership with Holmes, and although they were selected only once on the national team, in Baden-Baden in 1963, they nevertheless established themselves as one of the leading pairs on the home tournament circuit.

The battle for supremacy during the 1960s was not just between MacHale/Pigot and Read/Shrage: Holmes and O'Connell were contenders too. Although they competed as a pair for only eight years, they had a phenomenal success rate during that time. From 1961 to 1968, they amassed fifteen national titles together – a strike rate of almost two championships a year. Talent attracts talent: Holmes, O'Connell,

248

MacHale and Pigot came together to win four consecutive CBAI men's team championship for the Geraldine Trophy, from 1964 to 1967. The Munster pair also won the Holmes Wilson four times, and they demonstrated their versatility by winning pairs championships as well: the Revington once, and the Moylan twice.

O'Connell had a long playing career. He gained his first international cap in 1951. (In those days, individuals rather than pairs were selected.) Thirty years later, he won the last of his twenty-four national championships, the Kelburne, with Denis Dillon, Denis McGrath and John McKeon – an all-Cork quartet. It was their second victory in the competition in three years.

There is a large repository of Michael O'Connell's exceptional plays. This deal is from the 1959 trials he contested with his brother:

Dealer South. East–West Vulnerable.

                    North
                    ♠ A J 8 6 3
                    ♥ A Q J 7 5
                    ♦ 10 8
                    ♣ Q

West   East
♠ 9   ♠ K 10 7 5 2
♥ K 10 9 3   ♥ 8 4 2
♦ Q J 9 4 3   ♦ 7 6
♣ K 5 3   ♣ J 8 4

                    South
                    ♠ Q 4
                    ♥ 6
                    ♦ A K 5 2
                    ♣ A 10 9 7 6 2

W	N	E	S
-	-	-	1♣
Pass	1♦	Pass	2♣
Pass	3♥	Pass	3NT
All Pass			

The ♦Q lead created a difficulty for declarer as it removed an entry to his hand. O'Connell held up. Continuing with the jack would have resulted in declarer's five becoming a threat card, so West switched to the ♠9, ducked to East's king. A diamond continuation was won by the ace. Declarer cashed the queen of spades as West discarded a club. Next, O'Connell finessed a heart and cashed the ace and jack of spades. West was forced to discard a diamond and a heart. The queen of clubs ran to West's king, who exited with the queen of diamonds. Declarer had six tricks: three spades, one heart and two diamonds. He needed three more, but communications between his own hand and dummy had been severed. This was the end position:

```
                    North
                    ♠ 8
                    ♥ AQ7
                    ♦ -
                    ♣ -
  West                            East
  ♠ -                             ♠ 10
  ♥ K10                           ♥ 8
  ♦ 9                             ♦ -
  ♣ 5                             ♣ J8
                    South
                    ♠ -
                    ♥ -
                    ♦ 5
                    ♣ A109
```

O'Connell cashed the ace of clubs, discarding dummy's spade, and gave West a diamond trick. West kindly provided an entry to dummy's winning hearts.

JACK KELLY

Jack Kelly seemed to be in his prime as the 1960s drew to a close. He was an accomplished golfer and was involved in Portmarnock, the north Dublin seaside links, where he was part of the organising team for the Canada Cup tournament in 1960.[15] He was deputy director of the office of the comptroller and auditor general in Dublin, where he was approaching the pinnacle of his career, being heir apparent to the director, Kevin Fowler.[16]

Kelly was a player of the top rank, with an impressive competitive record. Many of his twenty-two national victories were achieved with Dick Belton, but he had other partners and was part of a group that included Paddy Donovan, Des Purcell and Jimmy Bastow. He won twelve consecutive Camrose caps from 1949, including the CBAI's last match before the withdrawal in 1951 – a total surpassed during that era only by Eddie Barry and Donovan. In those matches, he first partnered Joe Harold, and later Belton, and played one with Des Houlihan (Birr). In addition, he represented Ireland in five European championships and in the first two World Olympiads: Turin in 1960, and New York in 1964.

Following the death of Phillip Quinn in 1958, Kelly became bridge columnist and reporter for the *Irish Times*. In that capacity, he was the first bridge correspondent to travel abroad and report directly from championships, sometimes filling the dual role of player and journalist. He also wrote a regular column for the English *Bridge* magazine. In it, he brought Irish bridge news to readers in the United Kingdom and further afield. Like many leading Irish players of the period, Kelly was slow to adopt new methods. His newspaper articles reflect his dislike of such innovations as weak twos and unusual no-trump. However, his expert analyses reveal a thorough grasp of the techniques of card-play.

In 1964, he was elected president of the worldwide International Bridge Press Association, the only Irish journalist to be accorded that honour, and four years later he was re-elected for a second four-year term. He was a popular press representative and established lasting friendships with colleagues. For example, when Per Jannersten, son of IBPA founder Eric Jannersten from Sweden, came to Ireland as a young English-language student, he stayed at Kelly's home.[17]

Kelly died suddenly on Easter Saturday morning, 28 March 1970, while engaged in one of his two favourite pastimes. He passed away on the golf course, as he was taking a break from the bridge table, during the West of Ireland congress in Galway.[18] He was fifty-four.

DEERY AND MACNEILL

The partnership between Des Deery and Eoin MacNeill was relatively short – eleven years, from 1968 to 1979. They suffered from what was then considered the disadvantage of living relatively far apart: Deery in Belfast, MacNeill in Dublin. Nevertheless, they combined to win five Moylan Cups in a seven-year period (including three in a row), five Geraldine Trophies (also including three in a row) and three successive Holmes Wilsons. They also won the Egan Cup twice and the Revington.

Although Deery played at home when he was growing up in Monaghan, he took up the game seriously at Queen's University in 1957, when he befriended Peter Halmos, a young Hungarian who had fled his native land following the failed 1956 rising. After eighteen months, the pair were selected to play for Northern Ireland in the Camrose. Halmos went on to qualify in medicine and became an eminent heart surgeon in the American mid-west.

Deery first met MacNeill when the latter was playing with his father in the Egan. Deery, still in his twenties, was surprised to find someone his own age who could play as well as him. This is a rare admission from a top-level player, but MacNeill was indeed technically superb and had an ideal temperament for bridge. A few months after their first meeting, they played in the trials, and they won their places on the Irish team for the 1968 Olympiad in Deauville. It was the start of one of the great partnerships. Deery had already played for Ireland with Enda Boland (Beirut, 1962), Eric Goldblatt (New York, 1964) and Joe MacHale (Warsaw, 1966).

From 1968 to 1973, when European championships were held every year, they had an unbroken run of six consecutive years on the Irish team, an achievement bettered only by MacHale and Pigot.[19] Their retirement from the international game following the Ostend Europeans in 1973 was a loss to Irish bridge. Many people's idea of the dream team – MacHale/Pigot, Deery/MacNeill and FitzGibbon/Mesbur – never materialised.

Deery, who practised as a solicitor in Belfast, represented Northern Ireland in the Camrose many times. He was the most frequent, and certainly the most successful, raider southwards across the border, carrying off a total of twenty-two CBAI and IBU championships, mostly with MacNeill. Deery won the Egan Cup with his Dublin partner too, but in the All-Ireland contest he teamed up most frequently with Northern

Ireland colleagues, and he won the prestigious trophy seven times. Deery has the distinction of being the youngest official of any of the Irish governing bodies: he was twenty-four when he took over the duties of joint honorary secretary of the Irish Bridge Union following the death of Norman H. Douglas in 1962.

Eoin MacNeill was an exceptionally good player. I write 'was' because he rarely competes nowadays, and never in national events. An occasional monthly Friday teams event in the Regent or the odd Chicago among friends are the limits of his recent participation. He won the Moylan Cup a total of nine times, eight times between 1973 and 1984 – five with Deery, three with David Scannell. Then, after a twelve-year rest from tournament bridge, he returned, and won it again with Scannell in 1996, proving that they were capable of beating the new generation of players.

Deery emigrated to the south of Spain shortly after winning his last Irish championship – the Shamrock Lodge trophy, with Rory Boland, in 1984. He played for Spain in the 1987 European championship in Brighton, partnering former British international Louis Tarlo. He now runs a bridge club in Marbella.

FitzGibbon and Mesbur

The MacHale/Pigot dominance was broken in the 1970s by Nick FitzGibbon and Adam Mesbur. FitzGibbon, the older of the two, had already made his mark before they formed a partnership. During the 1970/71 season, he stormed to national prominence, winning four major championships: the Shamrock Lodge trophy with Diana Woodhouse,[20] the Davidson Cup with Tom Healy,[21] and two team events, the Geraldine and Egan trophies, both with Risteard de Barra. It was the most impressive beginning to a bridge career recorded in Ireland – and he was still a youth, the thinness of his frame giving him the image of a frail schoolboy. At the table however, Nick FitzGibbon was anything but frail. He and de Barra retained their team titles the following year and played on the Irish team at the Olympiad in Miami.

FitzGibbon and Mesbur are among the few players who have won places on Irish open teams while still juniors. Before he went to Miami in 1972, FitzGibbon had played at the European junior championships in Delft, the Netherlands, partnering Rex Anderson. In 1974, Nick and Adam were partners on the team that won European junior silver medals in Copenhagen, and the following year they were on the Irish open team in Brighton. MacHale and Pigot, whose mantle they were about to inherit, were teammates, as was Nick's former junior partner, Rex Anderson, who partnered Pat Barry. Adam Mesbur was twenty-three; only John Burke, in 1948, and Niall Tóibín, in 1980, had been younger when they first played on Irish open teams.

FitzGibbon and Mesbur were phenomenally successful bridge players. Adam won seven consecutive Holmes Wilson Cups, the first in partnership with David Jackson, the other six with Nick. Just as MacHale and Pigot had favourite teammates, so too did Nick and Adam: David Jackson and Don Seligman, Pat Walshe and Niall Tóibín, or Walshe and Rory Boland.

At the table, the two men are extremely focused. They appear distant to many, and their failure at times to greet opponents is perceived as coldness. They are never discourteous, however.

In the opinion of many, they are Ireland's greatest pair. However, there were gaps in their appearances on Irish teams. Following their debut in 1975, they retained their places on the team in 1977 and 1979, missed 1981, then played in Wiesbaden in 1983. They participated in four consecutive Olympiads, from 1976 to 1988, before quietly retiring from international competition. Marriage and subsequent family commitments were more important to them than bridge. Despite the gaps in their international appearances, FitzGibbon shares the accolade of most-capped Irish male player with Joe MacHale. Counting world, European and European Union events, he has turned out for Ireland eighteen times – two better than Mesbur, with sixteen. Statistically, there is little between them and MacHale/Pigot.

FitzGibbon and Mesbur were enticed into making their first comeback for the Killarney Europeans in 1981. Eleven years would elapse before they played for Ireland again. In 1992, at the request of the Irish Bridge Union, they took on coaching roles – Nick with the open squad, Adam with the women – prior to selecting teams for the Olympiad in Salsomaggiore, Italy. They won national championships that year too, but only one, the Holmes Wilson, in partnership. After that, they retired from domestic competition as well, although Adam made occasional appearances with Rory Boland.

When they returned to win the trials in 2002 and followed up by taking the master pairs and Moylan Cup the following year, knowing heads nodded. Hanlon and McGann had, by then, become the top dogs, and John Carroll and Tommy Garvey were also marking their territory. Was the FitzGibbon/Mesbur comeback motivated by a desire to demonstrate who the real bosses were? Whatever the case, they made a point that did not go unnoticed.

There are numerous records of brilliant plays from this pair. Their defence against a Portuguese declarer at the European championships in Salsomaggiore in June 2002 must rank among the best-defended hands by an Irish partnership.

North
♠ J 6 2
♥ A Q 10
♦ K 10 8 5
♣ A K 4

West (Mesbur)
♠ 10 8 4
♥ 9 7 6 3
♦ A J 2
♣ 7 6 5

East (FitzGibbon)
♠ K Q
♥ K 4
♦ 9 7 3
♣ Q J 9 8 3 2

South
♠ A 9 7 5 3
♥ J 8 5 2
♦ Q 6 4
♣ 10

W	N	E	S
-	1NT	2♣	2♠
Pass	2NT	Pass	3♥
Pass	4♠	All Pass	

Adam led the ♣7, taken by the king. Declarer had a sure diamond loser: one can be thrown on the ace of clubs. He would lose one or two spades. However, if the heart finesse worked, he could afford to lose two trumps, so it seemed correct to test the hearts as soon as possible. At trick two, he played a spade to king and ace. This was followed by a heart to the ten. FitzGibbon held up! Next, a diamond to the queen; Mesbur held up! In declarer's mind, the king of hearts was on his left, the ace of diamonds on his right. He was in for a surprise when he played a heart to the queen and FitzGibbon's king. He got a shock when Nick played a diamond to Adam's ace. Mesbur played a heart; FitzGibbon ruffed with the queen of trumps. The defence had three tricks. With Adam's ♠108 sandwiched between the nine and the jack, the Irish pair had to get another trick.

Some of Nick's sweetest victories have been in partnership with his wife, Kathryn, including the CBAI mixed pairs and team events for the Spiro Cup and Coen Trophy, respectively.[22] In addition, the FitzGbbons won silver medals at the European Union mixed teams championship, in Ostend in 1989, with Gráinne Barton and Pat Walshe.

At a time in their lives when many players would have been thinking of giving up the top-level game, a new twist in the FitzGibbon–Mesbur saga came in the form of Team Ireland. The story of that team is told below. Enough for now to state that it brought Nick and Adam deserved recognition and respect on the world stage.

Maria and Pat Barry

Maria and Pat Barry hold a unique record: they are the only pair to have won the CBAI premier pairs championship, for the Davidson Cup, three years in succession, 1973–75. Those successes took them to the Moylan Cup contest, and in 1974 they interrupted the Deery/MacNeill supremacy in that competition.

Maria and Pat both played on the Irish junior team in the 1970 European junior championship in Dun Laoghaire. Maria Nolan, as she was then, partnered David Scannell; Pat was paired with Rex Anderson. Two years later, when Maria and Pat were a young married couple, the same four, as part of an Irish party touring Poland, defeated the Polish national junior team in Warsaw. Perhaps surprisingly, Maria and Pat never won the Spiro Cup together, even though they were clearly the best mixed pair of the 1970s. Maria, however, won it twice with other partners: Joe MacHale in 1973 and David Scannell in 1975.

Maria made her debut on the Irish women's team as Ruth Giddings's partner at the 1975 European championships in Brighton. That Ruth chose her (following Lily Maguire's sudden death before the last weekend of the trials) indicates how she was perceived by the established players.

Her defence on the following deal against Spain was simple, clever and effective.

Dealer North. North-South Vulnerable

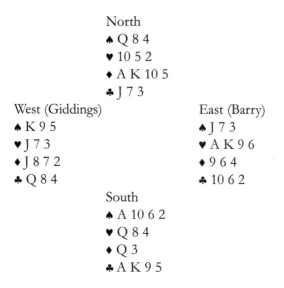

North
♠ Q 8 4
♥ 10 5 2
♦ A K 10 5
♣ J 7 3

West (Giddings)
♠ K 9 5
♥ J 7 3
♦ J 8 7 2
♣ Q 8 4

East (Barry)
♠ J 7 3
♥ A K 9 6
♦ 9 6 4
♣ 10 6 2

South
♠ A 10 6 2
♥ Q 8 4
♦ Q 3
♣ A K 9 5

Following a routine auction, South became declarer in 3NT. Giddings, with a difficult opening-lead, chose the ♦2. Declarer put in dummy's ten and when she played a spade to her ten and West's king she seemed to have nine tricks: three spades, four diamonds and two clubs. However, Giddings promptly switched to the ♥3. Maria Barry won with the ace! She returned the six. Put yourself in declarer's position. She 'knew' East did not have the king of hearts. Holding the ace and king, she would have won with the king, not the ace. So declarer played low and the defence took four heart tricks for one down. The Irish South made 3NT at the other table.

Maria Barry belongs to a rare group: Irish players who have won medals in international championships. She and Anne Montwill, together with Aileen and Rebecca O'Keeffe, won the women's silver medals at the European Union championships in Salsomaggiore in 1998.

Pat won his full international cap – also, incidentally, in Brighton in 1975 – when he paired up with his old junior partner, Rex Anderson. Pat has also played in a number of seniors internationals.

Risteard de Barra

During the 1989 trials, Risteard de Barra was dealt an unpromising ♠ 9 7 4 2 ♥ 8 6 3 ♦ J 5 ♣ J 9 7 5. His partner, Joe MacHale, was dealer and passed. His left-hand opponent, following a routine auction, became declarer in 3NT. Risteard would not have been criticised for playing a passive role in defence. He was rarely passive – and certainly not on this deal.

De Barra, a bilingual native of Kilmallock, County Limerick, was one of a number of talented players that came to the fore during the 1970s. His first partner in international competition was Nick FitzGibbon. De Barra and Rory Boland finished eleventh in the European pairs championship in 1989, the highest finish by an Irish pair in that event. He was a tricky opponent, as the following deal demonstrates:

Dealer West. North–South Vulnerable

North (Kelly)
♠ J 105
♥ 74
♦ AQ72
♣ AK82

West (MacHale)
♠ K63
♥ KJ92
♦ K93
♣ Q104

East (de Barra)
♠ 9742
♥ 863
♦ J5
♣ J975

South
♠ AQ8
♥ AQ105
♦ 10864
♣ 63

W	N	E	S
Pass	1♣	1♠	2NT
Pass	3NT	All Pass	

Joe MacHale, West, did not consider his flat, scattered twelve-points hand worth an opening bid. North, Pat Kelly, bid 1♣. De Barra, East, overcalled, 1♠. An outrageous bid, after which his opponents had a straightforward auction to game. From declarer's point of view, this was not a difficult contract. Two guaranteed tricks in each of the black suits, three diamonds if they break favourably – they do – and a reasonably competent player would end-play West to score two heart tricks. No danger of going down and, with a little bit of luck, perhaps an overtrick.

However, put yourself in declarer's position. West has passed, East has overcalled. The first effect of de Barra's intervention was to solve MacHale's opening lead problem. So a small spade was won by dummy's ten. The second effect was that declarer thought he knew where the missing high cards were – or at least some of them. At trick two he played a heart to the ten and jack. MacHale came back a club, won in dummy. Declarer played a diamond off the table, de Barra went up with his jack, which won. He played a spade to the queen and king. MacHale continued with his last spade. Declarer won and played a club. MacHale unblocked the queen and dummy's ace won. Next a heart to the queen and king. MacHale played the ten of clubs. De Barra overtook with the jack, cashed the nine of clubs and his last spade. The defence got two spades, two hearts, a diamond and two clubs for three down. De Barra's two-point hand won four tricks with his pair of jacks and his pair of nines.

The perpetrator of perhaps the most outrageous bid ever recorded still gets pleasure from the memory. His delight is heightened by the fact that declarer was Dublin-based, Iranian-born Rameen Sai, who was every bit as tricky an opponent as de Barra and frequently infuriated opponents with similar stratagems. De Barra, who had been on the receiving end of Sai's tactics, was constantly awake to opportunities to even the score. A talented player with strong opinions on many aspects of the game, de Barra served on the Camrose and Lady Milne selection committee from 2006 to 2008, although he remains in self-imposed exile from the bridge table.

Mr Monty

If one were to suggest that the term 'bidding system' was not in Monty Rosenberg's vocabulary, it would not be to slander him unduly. But he was a remarkably good player of cards. Monty learned the game by watching some of Northern Ireland's finest at Belfast's Jewish Institute – men like Davy Cohen, Sonny Diamond, Howard Schenker and Bertie

Vard, all Northern Ireland internationals. He soon followed in their footsteps: he was selected for Northern Ireland and went on to make a record
number of appearances in the Camrose competition, a total eventually
surpassed by Rex Anderson.

Monty partnered Marcus Shrage in the 1975 Irish trials.

Dealer South. Both Vulnerable

```
                      North
                      (Shrage)
                      ♠ Q98
                      ♥ KQJ10
                      ♦ A104
                      ♣ 853
      West                              East
      ♠ 1073                            ♠ 65
      ♥ 985432                          ♥ 6
      ♦ 93                              ♦ KJ72
      ♣ 94                              ♣ KJ10762
                      South
                      (Monty)
                      ♠ AKJ42
                      ♥ A7
                      ♦ Q865
                      ♣ AQ
```

W	N	E	
			2NT
Pass	3♣	Dbl	3♦
Pass	3♥	Pass	3♠
Pass	4NT	Pass	5♠
Pass	6NT	Pass	7NT
Pass	Pass	Pass	

Monty had to be a good player because of the way he bid. His partner's 3♣ was Stayman. No one but him would have replied 3♦. He was
known, at times, to conceal not just a five-card but even a six-card or
longer major suit. No case can be made for 7NT, a typical Monty
overbid.

The ♣9 lead was won with the queen. He had twelve tricks, one short. Monty cashed four rounds of hearts followed by four rounds of spades to reach this position:

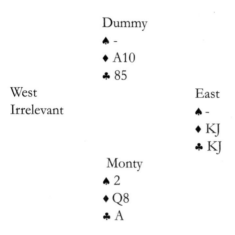

Dummy
♠ -
♦ A10
♣ 85

West
Irrelevant

East
♠ -
♦ KJ
♣ KJ

Monty
♠ 2
♦ Q8
♣ A

When he played the deuce of spades and threw the ten of diamonds from dummy, East was caught in a criss-cross squeeze. Monty's thirteenth trick would come from whichever suit East discarded. Vintage Monty: dreadful bidding, expert play.

Monty customarily spoke following an awards ceremony. He told the following story in the Shamrock Hotel, Athlone, in May 1987. Enda Glynn and Gay Keaveney had won the IBU club-pairs championship. Monty and his partner were runners-up.

'Last night after the second session, when I looked at the scores and saw that Father Glynn and Dr Keaveney were leading and I was only second, I felt I needed some help from above. So I went out to the lobby and telephoned.'

'"Celestial Mansions, can I help you?" answered an angelic voice.'

'"Hello, this is Mr Monty."'

'"Hello Mr Monty. How are you?"'

'"I'm quite well, thank you. I would like to speak to Mr Moses, please.'

'"Just a moment, Mr Monty, I'll see if Mr Moses is free."'

'She returned to the phone and said, "I'm sorry, Mr Monty, but Mr Moses is busy on another line. Can you call back later?"'

'So after half an hour I dialled the number again and the same young lady answered.

'"This is Mr Monty again. Is Mr Moses free yet?"

'"I'm very sorry, Mr Monty, but Mr Moses is still engaged."

'Another half-hour elapsed before I called again, and once more the same voice answered.

'"This is Mr Monty. I'm sorry for troubling you again."

'"No trouble at all, Mr Monty. You were looking for Mr Moses. I'm terribly sorry but I'm afraid he's still talking on the other phone. Could anybody else help you?"

'I thought for a moment, considering who the next-best might be.

'"If St Patrick is not too busy, perhaps I could speak to him."

'"St Patrick is not busy at all, Mr Monty. I can put you through straight away."

'"Hello! St Patrick speaking."

'"Hello St Patrick, this is Mr Monty."

'"Ah, Hello Mr Monty. How are you? How's the bridge game going down there?"

'"Well, that's what I wanted to talk about. I need a little help. But listen, St Patrick, I have to be honest. I really had hoped to talk to Mr Moses."

'"Ah, Mr Monty," St Patrick responded, "Mr Moses has been on the phone to Father Enda Glynn for the past hour."'

Monty frequently berated partners when dummy's cards were placed on the table, calling them complete idiots for putting him into such ridiculous contracts, or a snort would be followed by a phrase such as: 'A very arbitrary decision, partner.' They were ploys to upset defenders. Once at Ballina congress, he continuously reminded John Comyn that John was the world's worst bridge player. The more he repeated it, the more their opponents lost concentration.

On the same occasion, Monty alerted John's 2♣ response to his opening 1NT and explained to a confused female opponent that his partner had either a void or a singleton.

'Are you not playing Stayman?' she asked.

'If he has a singleton or void, two clubs is Stayman. Otherwise he passes or bids 3NT. If he has a five-card major, he bids two for weakness and three for game. This 4–4 major-fit nonsense is for beginners,' he replied.

For Monty, there was no such bid as an invitational 2NT. Furthermore, partners did not take him out of no-trump contracts without good reason. When asked about his system Monty would reply that he played bridge. During the 1930s, British players used to describe their bidding as 'original'; Monty was their true descendant.

ATR (REX) ANDERSON

Rex Anderson, the son of bridge-playing parents (parents and son featured on Ulster's interprovincial winning team in 1968), was Monty's favourite partner. By general consensus he is Northern Ireland's best player – with almost ninety Camrose 'caps' to prove the point. He represented Ireland eight times in World and European championships. His unshakable disposition at the table was the perfect foil for the enigmatic Monty. They won European team bronze medals in 1979. Anderson currently partners English-born David Greenwood who also has played for Northern Ireland and Ireland.

TÓIBÍN AND WALSHE

Niall Tóibín, a native of Enniscorthy, and Pat Walshe, who was born in Listowel, are some people's choice as Ireland's best pair. When considering their record, statistics do lie, as they won only a modest number of major titles and were selected on Irish national teams just three times. They played in international pairs championships too, proving their class by winning the EU pairs in Birmingham in 1981, when Tóibín brought off a double gold by taking the junior teams title as well.

Temperamentally, they were opposites. Walshe is hard on partners, intolerant of their shortcomings, sure of his own ability. Tóibín was the easiest of partners, a gentleman and a gentle man at and away from the table. They were highly regarded by their peers. The 2002 trials winners – FitzGibbon, Mesbur, Anderson and Greenwood – chose them in preference to Hanlon and McGann to complete the Irish team for the Europeans in Salsomaggiore.

Tóibín's work, from 1983 for the Agency for Personal Services Overseas and from 1993 with Trócaire, took him for long periods to various African countries. Those long absences deprived Ireland of the services of one of its greatest players and kept his personal tally of major victories relatively low.

There is a body of opinion, both at home and abroad, which regards Pat Walshe as Ireland's most outstanding individual player. His play against Adam Zmudzinski (Poland) at the Europeans in Killarney in 1991 is an example of his quick thinking. It was adjudged the best defensive play of the tournament.

Dealer North. Neither Vulnerable

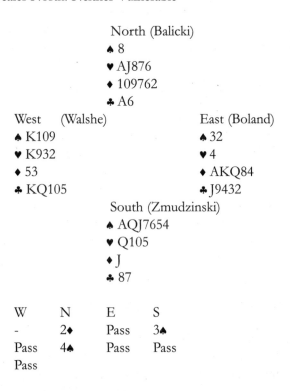

North (Balicki)
♠ 8
♥ AJ876
♦ 109762
♣ A6

West   (Walshe)
♠ K109
♥ K932
♦ 53
♣ KQ105

East (Boland)
♠ 32
♥ 4
♦ AKQ84
♣ J9432

South (Zmudzinski)
♠ AQJ7654
♥ Q105
♦ J
♣ 87

W	N	E	S
-	2♦	Pass	3♠
Pass	4♠	Pass	Pass
Pass			

Balicki's 2♦ opening bid showed two suits, either black or red. Zmudzinski's 3♠ was natural and invitational, 6 to 10 points. North thought he had enough for game. So he had – or at least so it seemed when dummy went down. Declarer would lose only a trump, a diamond and a club. Walshe led the K♣. Declarer won with the ace and finessed a trump. On winning with the ♠K, Walshe found the only play to defeat the contract, the ♥K. East, Rory Boland, had to get a heart ruff sooner or later in addition to the three natural losers.

Walshe has liberally given his time and expertise to advance the game, including coaching junior players many times. He processed affiliation and master-points data when the CBAI adopted computerised records in the mid-1980s. He has never sought reward. Widely regarded as Ireland's leading bridge theoretician, he is credited with introducing a number of innovations to the game. He has not always been popular with the game's establishment, however. Following an incident involving Padraig Ó Briain during the CBAI four-sessions pairs championship in December 1988, he was suspended from competition for a year when he refused to comply with an executive directive that he apologise, following an allegation made against his opponent. He seldom competes nowadays but victory in the Holmes Wilson Cup competition in February 2009 proved that he can still win.

That generosity which Niall Tóibín exhibited by devoting his life to serving those who needed aid was sometimes manifest when playing bridge. At the 1998 world championships in Lille, he and Teresa Rigney had a poor competition in the mixed pairs, an event in which they had realistic ambitions of at least reaching the final. Teresa, especially, went through a bad patch and was feeling dispirited. I was writing for a newspaper and a magazine at the time. Niall approached me, gave me a hand that his partner had played remarkably well, and asked me to report it. He wanted to draw attention to his partner's good play.

EILEEN O'DOHERTY AND ANNE QUINN

Eileen O'Doherty and Anne Quinn formed a regular partnership only late in life. Both had a string of victories and international appearances with other partners: Eileen with Alice Mahon (with whom she won a European silver medal in 1954), Anne mainly with Kay O'Sullivan and Doreen Cairnduff. Their first noteworthy wins together came in 1978 – the CBAI women's teams (McMenamin Bowl) and the IBU inter-club pairs. Also that year, they finished fifth in the world women's pairs championship in New Orleans. Gold medals in the women's pairs at the EEC (EU) championships in Birmingham 1981 confirmed their world-class status. In Killarney in 1991, in their twilight years, they became the first Irish pair to reach the final of the European women's pairs.

In their later years, they seemed to be the quintessential little old ladies. They did not consciously cultivate this image, but opponents who approached their table in that frame of mind soon rued their complacency. Rarely brilliant, they were consistently steady and gave nothing away, although the New Orleans championship records contain examples of dazzling play from both of them.

O'Doherty came to prominence in 1948 on a Kelburne Cup-winning team. In the course of one of the longest careers on record, she won nineteen Irish titles and was selected fifteen times for the national team. Her first European championship was Venice, 1951; her last, the pairs championship in Killarney forty years later.

Anne Quinn also won nineteen majors, including the McMenamin Bowl a remarkable ten times. She represented Ireland in fourteen team events and also in pairs. Male critics are reluctant to give credit to women unless they succeed against men: nine of O'Doherty's major wins and four of Quinn's were in competitions open to both sexes.

WHEN THE WEST AWOKE

Over the years, Dublin-based competitors have tended to monopolise national championships. Isolated pairs or individuals upset the trend from time to time – the O'Connells and E. O. Barry from Cork, northern raiders like Des Deery or Monty, and Moreen McCarthy (Wexford) in the women's game, for example – but otherwise Dublin players had the edge. That changed in the 1980s, with the emergence of a group of talented players in the west. Some of them were contemporaries at UCG. The western assault on national championships was spearheaded by Gay Keaveney and Paddy Walsh: they won the CBAI men's pairs (the Revington Cup) in 1980 and retained it for the next two years. Connacht, which had never previously troubled its rivals in the inter-provincial championship, took the title in 1982 and held it for four years. Where bridge was concerned, the west was well and truly awake.

New names from west of the Shannon appeared on the plinths of national trophies: Enda Glynn, Rory Timlin, Michael MacDonagh, Eddie Fitzgerald, Maurice Hession, Nuala Walsh, Seán and Anna Glynn (Loughrea) and Seán Gillen (Sligo). Sometimes Paddy Byrne (Letterkenny) joined his former college companions on championship-winning teams. First Paul Scannell, later Ray Brennan, and later still Donal MacAonghusa migrated to Galway. All three represented Ireland. Walsh and Fitzgerald were temporarily domiciled in Athlone and MacDonagh settled in Mullingar, but there was never any question as to where their allegiance lay when the inter-provincials came around.

Keaveney and Walsh were selected to play for Ireland at the European championships in Wiesbaden in 1983. For the next twenty-one years, only twice was the province without representation on the Irish team. When the CBAI returned to the home-international championships, Keaveney, Timlin and two of the new school, Ciarán Coyne and David Walsh, maintained the tradition of western players wearing the national shirt. In October 2008, Emer Joyce and Joan Kenny became the first western-based women to gain international caps – at the European championships in Pau, France, and at the World Mind-sports Games in Beijing.

To date, Gay Keaveny has won forty-six national championships (excluding inter-provincials) and is probably the person most likely to eventually overtake Ruth Giddings' total. Equally at home in pairs or team contests, he has shown that he is adaptable too: he has won his titles with eleven different partners (including nineteen with Enda Glynn). Only MacHale/Pigot, FitzGibbon/Mesbur and Giddings/Seligman have exceeded that number, in partnership. Glynn's calling as a Catholic priest has been an obstacle to his playing in trials; otherwise, the west might well have had another international player.

Rory Timlin claims a unique achievement. He has represented Connacht in the inter-provincial championship, without a break, for the past thirty-three years and is the only player to have been a member of every one of the province's twelve winning teams.

In 1983, Keaveney took the initiative to organise the first All-Ireland schools team championship. Some of Ireland's most renowned players, including Rebecca O'Keeffe, Tom Hanlon and Tommy Garvey, got their first taste of competition in the schools contest. Following Keaveney's lead, the late Gerry Joyce initiated a schools' pairs championship in Limerick in November 1991. Both competitions continue.

RORY BOLAND

Cork-born Rory Boland has won nineteen national titles, six Ireland 'caps' and six Camrose 'caps' but he has had long periods of absence from the table. A junior-team gold medal at the 1981 EEC championships in

267

Birmingham offered evidence of exceptional talent but his ambivalent approach to the game ensured he would never fully exploit it. Nevertheless he is regarded as one of Ireland's best players. In recent years he has confined his bridge to partnering his friend, PC Kiely, at County Cork congresses.

HANLON AND McGANN

Tom Hanlon grew up in Rochfortbridge, County Westmeath. He was introduced to the game by his mother, Annie, who bribed her somewhat wayward son to attend John Cunningham's bridge classes. When mother and son won the CBAI Intermediate B team championship (the Tierney Trophy) in 1984, with Kay Moore and Aileen Brett, he was not yet seventeen. Cunningham, a winner of many national championships and a close neighbour of Hanlon's, saw the talent and became mentor to the schoolboy. With three of the Cunningham children, Tom completed a team to represent Rochfortbridge in the Irish schools championship in 1984 and 1985.

John Cunningham played with his young protégé locally, regionally and nationally. Their partnership culminated in their winning the CBAI pairs championship (the Davidson Cup) in 1989 as well as being selected for Leinster and winning the inter-provincials in the same season. Together, master and pupil won the Moylan in 1990 and the Kelburne in 1993; in the latter year, with Eddie Fitzgerald and Michael MacDonagh as teammates, they brought the inter-county title and the Burke Cup to Westmeath. They won four more inter-provincial titles together but by the time they won the Davidson for the second time in 1997, the pupil had long since become the master.

In 1987, Hugh McGann was a medical student at UCC and not quite twenty when he won the Intermediate B pairs title (the Civil Service Cup), with Derek O'Gorman, who was to remain his regular partner for some time. Maternal encouragement was a factor in Hugh's case too. His mother, Jean, served as regional president in South Munster in 1996–97, a role which Annie Hanlon filled in the North Midlands region seven years later. Jean McGann was to become president of the CBAI in July 2007 but she died in March.

McGann won his first major championship in 1990, taking the master pairs title with O'Gorman. In 1993, he partnered Hanlon to win the

CBAI men's team championship (the Geraldine Trophy), their first major success together. The other half was O'Gorman and Terry Walsh. That was the begining of the winning partnership.

Tom made his international debut in 1986 in the European junior championships in Budapest with Heber O'Farrell, of the well-known Greystones family. Two years later, Hugh and Derek were on the team in Plovdiv, Bulgaria. After that, Hanlon and McGann were regulars on the Irish junior team but with different partners. It was Hugh who demon-strated the first sign of brilliance, and it was in Plovdiv where his play in a slam against Norway was judged to be the best by a declarer at the 1988 championship.

In 1993, Hanlon and McGann won the junior pairs silver medals at the European Union championships in Montechoro, Portugal. The Irish pair, leading going into the last session, had a big score – enough to win most competitions. However, the Italians, Alfredo Versace and Claudio Nunes, had an even better total and took the gold medal.

In 1994, Hanlon and McGann joined Rory Timlin and Paddy Walsh (Galway) to contest the Rosenblum Cup at the world championships in Albuquerque, New Mexico. They made a mark in the Rosenblum – but not entirely in the conventional way.

One hundred and eighty teams were divided into fifteen groups of twelve; each group played a round-robin, with the top four going forward to the next round, along with the four best losers. In that kind of format, world-class teams frequently fall at the preliminary stage. In Albuquerque, such a fate was facing the Americans, Deutsch/Rosenberg, Bates/Kasle, Martel/Stansby. They had a terrible start and it seemed as though even big scores in their last three matches would not be enough to see them through. The Irish had to beat a Netherlands team comprehensively in the last round to keep the Dutch out and let the Americans in. It seemed unlikely, but the Irish four not only knocked the Dutch out and got into the next round themselves, but the result allowed the Americans into a three-way play-off for the last qualifying place, which they won.

The drama did not end there. The next stage was another round-robin of eight teams, with four going forward to the knockout matches. Ireland's quartet got through to meet a Chinese team in the round of thir-ty-two. China finished in front, 173 imps to 169. But it was not over yet.

Timlin and Walsh claimed that failure to alert by a Chinese player, on a particular deal, deprived them of information, and as a consequence they misdefended. An appeals committee met in the early hours of the morning. Cathy Wei, the renowned Chinese-born player living in the United States, was called in to translate. The committee decided that the Irish players had indeed been damaged by the lack of information but the indemnity of two imps still left them short of victory. At that time, the world bridge authorities, like the rest of the western world, were endeavouring to woo China. Whatever the merits of the appeals committee's decision, there was an uncomfortable feeling that politics had played a part in it. (By an extraordinary quirk, the American team which had survived the preliminary stage as a result of the Irish beating the Dutch went on to win the championship.)

Thereafter, Hanlon and McGann were regulars on the Irish team. By 2001, they had established themselves as the undisputed number-one pair and as such were selected for the Europeans in Tenerife. Trials were held to select four to join them, but the resulting team performed poorly. When Hanlon and McGann were offered a place on the team the following year, they declined, preferring to take their chances in the trials, where they teamed up with Niall Tóibín and Pat Walshe. Their strategy backfired when Rex Anderson, David Greenwood, Nick FitzGibbon and Adam Mesbur beat them in the final. The winners, with the choice of selecting the third pair, opted for Tóibín and Walshe. The matter did not end there. Close to the date of the competition, Tóibín became ill and was forced to withdraw. The selectors went back to Hanlon and McGann but they declined the late invitation. John Carroll and Tommy Garvey were called up for their second full international caps.

The reputation of the Hanlon and McGann pairing was enhanced in 2001 when they were one of four pairs shortlisted for the International Bridge Press Association's Romex Award for best auction of the year. The deal is from the match against Turkey in the European championship.

Dealer West. East–West Vulnerable

```
                        North (Hanlon)
                        ♠ A 9 3
                        ♥ A K 10 5 4
                        ♦ 6
                        ♣ A J 10 8
   West                                   East
   ♠ K Q 10 7 4                           ♠ J 5 3
   ♥ J 8 3                                ♥ 6
   ♦ K Q 7 4                              ♦ A J 10 9 5 2
   ♣ 2                                    ♣ 7 6 4
                        South (McGann)
                        ♠ 8 6
                        ♥ Q 9 7 2
                        ♦ 8 3
                        ♣ K Q 9 5 3
```

W	N	E	S
1♠	2♥	2♠	3♣
Pass	3♠	Pass	4♥
Pass	6♣	All Pass	

The beauty of the auction is in its simplicity. There is no artificial bid. When Tom discovered the heart–club double fit, he simply gave his partner a choice of slams with his 6♣ bid. Hugh calculated that, for his bid, Tom couldn't possibly have two diamond losers and his own spade loser would be thrown on his partner's fifth heart. He correctly chose the minor slam. 6♣ cannot be defeated; 6♥ goes down on normal defence.

Tom Hanlon is one of Ireland's all-time best players. He excels under pressure. If your life depended on someone making a difficult contract, you would want Tom to be playing the hand. It is surprising, therefore, that he made the most costly error in the history of Irish bridge. On the last deal of the match against Poland in Tenerife in June 2005, his play in 4♠ cost Ireland a medal.

Board 28. Dealer West. North-South vulnerable

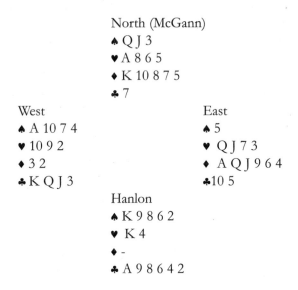

North (McGann)
♠ Q J 3
♥ A 8 6 5
♦ K 10 8 7 5
♣ 7

West
♠ A 10 7 4
♥ 10 9 2
♦ 3 2
♣ K Q J 3

East
♠ 5
♥ Q J 7 3
♦ A Q J 9 6 4
♣ 10 5

Hanlon
♠ K 9 8 6 2
♥ K 4
♦ -
♣ A 9 8 6 4 2

Stepinski, West, led the ♣K. Tom won and ruffed a club. It seems best to embark on a cross-ruff but he played the ♠Q. When West won and played another spade, the contract could not be made. Hanlon came back to hand with a heart and played another club. West switched to a diamond, won by East, who put declarer back in dummy with a heart. The only way back to hand now was by a ruff, which reduced his trumps to K9. When he gave up another club, the defence played another diamond, which he ruffed with the nine of trumps. West had two trumps left. Down two. Tom Hanlon was not the only world-class player who has made a costly error. The Italian Lorenzo Lauria lost a world title when he inadvertantly played a wrong card from dummy.

Solving the mystery of how great players make simple errors is best left to psychologists, but it is certainly the case that the pressures of playing in the final stages of a major championship are known only to those who have done so. Tom carried a heavy burden into the match. He was captain as well as player. His was the decision to sit out Carroll and Garvey, who had missed the previous round as well – and after they had been playing well. (In Tenerife, they were not competing as a national team, and there was no non-playing captain.)

Another factor was the environment in which the match ended. The table was beside the exit. Other players, as they finished, walked past, some talking loudly. When the door opened and closed, it squeaked. All four players, and a number of kibitzers, appealed to a director to try and restore quiet. The distraction was such that the director waived the normal time limit and allowed them to finish in their own time.[22] Tom Hanlon would not use those factors as excuses for what happened, however; they are recounted here to give the reader an accurate picture of the end of the match.

Two down vulnerable was –200. The Irish lost by one imp. One down, –100, would have taken Ireland into the medals. Furthermore, had the board been non-vulnerable, then two down, also –100, would have seen them through. There is such a thing as bad luck.

Hanlon and McGann are Ireland's most-travelled pair. Their skills and reputation have brought them to Japan, China, Dubai, Australia, the USA and many European countries. They were the first – and so far the only – Irish pair to participate in the million-dollar Cavendish invitational pairs in Las Vegas, where, in 2003, they led the field after two sessions. In 2008, they brought off a rare double at the Gold Coast congress in Australia, winning the pairs and team championships – and in the latter beating more than 400 rival teams.

The two men were among the twelve players selected for the European team to contest the inaugural Warren Buffett Cup against the United States in September 2006 at Templeogue. They retained their places for the second Warren Buffett Cup contest in Louisville, Kentucky, in September 2008, and made a significant contribution to the score as Europe emphatically reversed the defeat of two years previously.

CARROLL AND GARVEY

John Carroll and Tommy Garvey, still in their thirties, are somewhat in the shadows of their colleagues FitzGibbon and Mesbur and Hanlon and McGann, but time is on their side. Garvey, who lives in Britain, first tasted victory when playing for Terenure College in schools' competition. One of only six players to win places on Irish open teams while still a junior, he comes from a bridge-playing family. He and his father Donal played for Ireland in Montecatini, Italy, in 1996 – although not in partnership. His mother Lily is a bridge teacher. His brother, Donal junior, has won an Irish intermediate title. Tommy holds a unique record. He won national championships in three countries: Ireland, Scotland and England.

John Carroll's international debut was in Montecatini. His mother, Helen, and his wife, Anne Marie Horan, have both represented Ireland. Since taking his first national title during the 1995/96 season, he has won twenty-three major competitions, a success rate that has rarely been equalled.

TEAM IRELAND

Team Ireland, the most successful Irish side in international bridge, is the product of a number of factors. Coincidence is the first. It is fortunate that two outstanding players should arrive on the scene simultaneously, like playing together and have the ambition and commitment to work to achieve success. That three such pairs are around at the same time, in a small country, is remarkable.

The story of Team Ireland[23] began in June 2003 when Nick FitzGibbon, Adam Mesbur, Tom Hanlon, Hugh McGann, John Carroll and Tommy Garvey competed as a team at the European open championships in Menton on the south coast of France. Competitions in those championships are transnational: players from different nations come together in formidable squads, wealthy sponsors gather professional players into powerful teams, and there are more strong sides in contention than in contests for national teams. The Irish six reached the quarter-finals.

The achievement gave Tom Hanlon an idea. He was thirty-six and approaching his peak as a player. He noticed how seriously the Italians, who dominated European bridge, and the top American players took the game. He remembered how Iceland, a nation smaller than Ireland, with only a fraction of the number of bridge players, had won the world championship in 1991. The Netherlands, also a small nation, had been world champions too. If they could, why not Ireland? Hanlon understood the commitment, in terms of time, effort, money and personal sacrifice, that getting to the top demanded. He convinced the others that they should stay together as a team and aim for a top-six finish at the European championships in 2006, and thereby qualify for the world championships for the Bermuda Bowl, a feat which had never been achieved by an Irish team.

For the veterans Nick FitzGibbon and Adam Mesbur, who had all but given up international competition, the proposal gave their bridge careers a new lease on life. Now here were two pairs of younger players with the temerity to want to take on the world and the skill to match their ambitions. (If there had been a doubt about Carroll and Garvey – the least experienced pair – before Menton, it had been dispelled during that event.) Equally important, the six got on well together.

The objective required a plan, part one of which involved the players testing themselves in world-class competition. The European Bridge League introduced open championships in 2003. In order to accommodate the new event, the dates of championships for national teams were changed from odd-numbered to even-numbered years. Consequently, in 2004 there were two major fixtures on the calendar: the European teams event in Malmo and the World Olympiad in Istanbul. FitzGibbon, Mesbur, Hanlon and McGann won the Irish trials. Given the demands of their careers,[24] they opted to compete in Istanbul only;[25] they nominated Carroll and Garvey to complete the team.

In Istanbul, the Irish reached another quarter-final, and when their scores were compared with those of the other losing quarter-finallists, they were officially placed fifth. Following that achievement, their third consecutive major quarter-final – in the European open in Tenerife the next year – was an anticlimax: they wanted medals.

The next step was to recruit a non-playing captain. Niall Tóibín was to have been captain in Istanbul but his sudden death meant that they had to look elsewhere. David Jackson, a former bookmaker and statistician, and a team specialist as a player, was persuaded to take on the task. He had played for Ireland and had been a non-playing captain before.

Step three was potentially the most difficult. The Irish Bridge Union council runs trials to select teams for international championships. The format of the trials had been either pairs or teams of four, but entries from teams of six had never been accepted.[26] However, the IBU council accepted Jackson's arguments on behalf of his team. It departed from fifty years of established practice and accepted entries from teams of six in the trials.

Step four was to dominate the home international championship for the Camrose Trophy, or there was little hope of getting to the top in Europe. England had been virtually invincible in the Camrose, losing the trophy only occasionally to Scotland. To emphatically assert their authority over the English was a daring aspiration.

Trials for selection to the Camrose team are organised by the CBAI, the governing body for bridge in the Republic. Its trials convenor, Michael O'Connor, also headed the IBU selection committee, so there was some uniformity of thought between the two sets of selectors. In 2005, Carroll and Garvey did not compete in the Camrose trials. The other four did – and won – and were joined on the team by the Ó Briain brothers Pádraig and Micheál, Mark Moran and Peter Pigot. The squad won the CBAI's second home-international title.

Before Team Ireland left for the second European open championships in Tenerife in 2005, the CBAI selectors decided that, should the team reach the semi-finals, it would be chosen, without trials, for the following year's Camrose.[27] The decision was not revealed to anyone. In the event, the team failed to reach the semi-final by 1 imp. When the committee met subsequently, its members were unanimous in feeling that the team had proved itself sufficiently. Not to select them because they had failed to win a medal by such a small margin would be splitting hairs. The team, en bloc, with Jackson as captain, was selected to contest the 2006 home-international championship.

The uproar that followed was predictable. Various reasons underlay players' protests, but they all wanted trials. The selected team made an offer which diffused the situation: if the CBAI held trials, they would play the winners in a long match. That is what happened. Team Ireland went on to win the CBAI's third Camrose – its second in succession, and the first for the full Team Ireland.

Preparations for Warsaw included sessions with sports psychologist Betty Cody and weekly online practice matches against top-class worldwide opposition. In the Polish capital, having beaten Netherlands in the opening round, they lost the next four matches and found themselves, after two days' play, floundering in twenty-first place. They won their next eight matches and by the end of day five had moved up to fourth place. Among Ireland's victims had been Italy, who had annihilated most of their opponents as they moved inexorably towards their seventh successive European title. From then on, Ireland held on to a qualifying spot, and occupied fifth place with three matches remaining.

The Italians could have conceded the last three matches and still won the gold medals. Norway were in the silver-medal position, fifteen points ahead of Ireland. The Irish would meet the Norwegians in the

276

penultimate round. A top-six finish remained the aim, and while that looked likely at that stage, it was not a foregone conclusion. Iceland were only six points behind Ireland. Poland, who had averaged almost twenty-two points per match from their six previous games, were seventh, a further six points adrift.

For the last three matches, Jackson elected to play FitzGibbon and Mesbur, and Hanlon and McGann. From then on, it was not a question of ability; it was a question of keeping one's nerve. Carroll and Garvey had done their work; indeed, they had been the team's leading pair during the first week and had kept the Irish in contention when the other pairs had struggled. The captain's faith in FitzGibbon and Mesbur was justified when they played an error-free set against Russia, contributing handsomely to the 21–9 win.

The Norwegian match was crucial. The Scandanavians were capable of crushing any team, but Ireland's four outplayed them to win 17–13. With one round remaining, Ireland were tied with Netherlands in third place, six points behind Norway. Sweden and Poland were four and six points further back, respectively.

The last match was against Scotland. In the Camrose competition, the Scots had not posed a threat, but this time there was the added pressure of playing the final round of a European championship. The Scots had nothing to lose; the Irish had. After three boards, due to a combination of an over-ambitious Hanlon/McGann slam and results in other match-es, Ireland had dropped to sixth. In his book *Silver for Ireland*, Enda Murphy provides a superb description of Tom Hanlon's thoughts before he made the final bid on board eight. The bad result on board three was on his mind as he faced another tough decision. He called the moment just before he bid six on board eight his 'worst point of the whole tour-nament'. This time the slam made. Scotland stayed in game. Ireland moved up to fourth. On the next deal, FitzGibbon and Mesbur scored 500 from a penalty double. Ireland went into the silver-medal position by one point. Of course, the spectators watching the match in the Vu-graph Theatre and on the internet knew that, but the players did not. (Bridge is unique among games and sports in that the players do not know the score while they are playing.) The Irish quartet had to grind through the remain-ing eleven tension-filled deals in the dark. It helps when you have faith in your teammates at the other table.

By the end, they had increased their lead over Norway to four points, winning the silver. Not since 1973, when the Irish women won silver in Ostend, had Ireland achieved such a result.

PREPARING FOR SHANGHAI

It should be stated that it was Ireland which qualified for the 2007 Bermuda Bowl, not the players who had accomplished the feat in Warsaw, and the IBU council could have picked a different team. Of course, the question did not arise: Jackson and his men would go to China, and as a fancied team. However, qualifying for Shanghai posed a problem for the IBU, whose budgets are based on four-year cycles of participation in European and world events: there was no money to send the team to China.

BARON STORAGE'S GENEROUS SPONSORSHIP

The Ennis solicitor Desmond Houlihan is a long-time supporter of bridge in his native town and in Limerick. A good-standard player too, he has won national championships and has played for Ireland and the Republic at seniors level. He made a generous offer to the IBU. Baron Storage, a company with which he is associated, would match whatever sum the IBU raised for the Shanghai project – up to a maximum of €20,000 and the IBU launched its '100 club'. Supporters, asked to donate €100 each, responded generously, and the target was exceeded.

Team Ireland members had a quiet home season in 2006/07. Carroll and Hanlon won the Moylan Cup, the squad's only home victory before they went to China. However, as the year progressed, supporters felt uneasy. The team were not performing well in practice matches online and did not shine in big competitions abroad. They experienced a morale-cruching defeat in the Summer Nationals in Las Vegas, when they were knocked out in the first round. They played poorly.

Hanlon, in the autobiographical *A Bridge Too Far?*, highlights a truth about top-level performers in any activity: they can peak at certain times only. It was hoped that Team Ireland would be at the top of their game in China.

In the Bermuda Bowl qualifying rounds in Shanghai, the team failed badly. Following a disastrous opening day, they never got back into contention. During the second week, in the world trans-national championship, they found their form and once again reached the quarter-finals of a major world competition. It wasn't quite the expected Team Ireland, though. Hugh McGann, following the disappointment of the first week, went home and was replaced by Martin Jones, the non-playing captain of the English women's team.

At home once more, preparations began for their next objective: medals, or at least a place in the top six, at the European championships in Pau, France, and qualification for the Bermuda Bowl in São Paolo. In the meantime, they retained the home-international title and won a fourth successive Camrose Trophy for the CBAI.

In Pau, the entry of thirty-eight teams called for a new format to be created. The field was divided into two groups, with each playing a round-robin, and the top nine from each qualifying for a final – another round-robin. As previous runners-up, Team Ireland were expected to get through to the final rounds comfortably, but in fact they struggled from the start. When the qualifying rounds were over, they stood twelfth in the group. After Warsaw, they never achieved the same standard again. The team that competed in the first World Mind-sport Games in Beijing in October 2008, weakened by the absence of FitzGibbon[28] and Mesbur, finished eighth of seventeenth in their group, with four going forward to knockout matches. Nonetheless, Team Ireland is still the best Irish open side on record.

Dawn of the New Millennium

As the new millennium dawned, Team Ireland was not alone among Irish players who were in the spotlight. In November 2003, Hilary Dowling Long invited a number of players from abroad to take part in a tournament with Ireland's grandmasters at the Royal Dublin Society. Pat Walshe came out best among the sixteen world-class players who participated. The competition was repeated in April 2005 and Sabine Auken (Germany) was the winner.

Kay Downes, a former president of the CBAI and joint honorary secretary of the IBU, was awarded the European Bridge League Plaque in June 2003 for her service to the game.

In September 2005, at a European Bridge League seminar in Turin, during a session devoted to promotion of the game, B. J. O'Brien suggested a Europe v. United States bridge contest, similar to golf's Ryder Cup. Denis Robson, chairman of the English Bridge Union at the time, was present. When he returned to Manchester, Robson spoke to Paul Hackett, a professional bridge player, who liked the idea and determined to make it a reality. Ireland was due to host the Ryder Cup at the K Club in September 2006. What a wonderful occasion it would be if there could be a similar match in bridge during the same week at a location close to the Ryder Cup venue! As had previously occurred when major projects were planned, Joe Moran was asked to head an organising team.

Coincidentally, Robson was associated with the company that distributed admission tickets to the Ryder Cup. Moran's business acumen went into action. He would purchase tickets for the golf contest and offer them to corporate sponsors of the bridge competition. Hackett sold the idea to the leading players in Europe and America. It was the Americans who came up with the idea of naming the trophy after businessman

Warren Buffett. His name, it was thought, would enhance the contest and attract media attention.

The inaugural Europe v. USA competition took place at Templeogue from 3 to 6 September 2006. The format of the match was similar to that of the golf competition, with teams, pairs and individual contests. The scoring method was point-a-board. (The highest score on a board earns one point; a tied board gives half a point to each side.) Having trailed during the pairs and teams sections, the Americans gained the upper hand in the individual matches to become the first winners of the trophy.

Strangely, the European Bridge League, at whose seminar the idea was first mooted, was not involved in the contest. The European team was selected by Hackett. No official of the EBL was present at the occasion. José Damiani, president of the World Bridge Federation and a former president of the EBL, did attend.

B. J. O'Brien set a record during the 2005/06 season when he won five CBAI championships.[1] In addition, he took the inter-provincial title. Richard Boyd (Greystones) was a prizewinner in the youth section of the first World Mind-sports Games in Beijing in October 2008. Anna Onishuk and Karel de Raeymaeker have proved to be the outstanding Irish pair of the new millennium. Between 2001 and 2009, he has won seventeen, she sixteen, national championships, most of them in partnership. Onishuk, who represented the CBAI in the 2006 home-international championship (Lady Milne Trophy), comes from Moscow but has become an Irish citizen. De Raeymaeker was born in Belgium and grew up in Dublin.

Membership of – or, to be more accurate, affiliations to – the CBAI peaked at 35,377 in 1998. By 2008, the figure had dropped by almost 14 percent, to 30,439. The decline is disturbing, considering the association's commitments – including paying staff and maintaining a headquarters. During the previous ten years, 1988 to 1998, the association's membership had grown by 33.5 percent. There is an unknown number who enjoy the game privately but do not wish to be part of a nationally organised body. The potential for recruitment from that source is probably insignificant in the context of overall financing. The CBAI's affiliation system ensures that the optimum number of players is caught in the affiliation net.

Following a decision taken at the association's AGM in July 2008, management will explore the feasibility of changing to a single-membership system by 2012. Previous attempts to introduce single affiliation – in the mid-1980s and again in the early 1990s – were greeted with little enthusiasm. Michael O'Connor, the CBAI's current vice president, is a steadfast supporter of the present system. 'It has proved to be successful,' he argues, pointing to the large membership relative to population when compared with other countries. Furthermore, it is equitable: members contribute in proportion to the amount of bridge they play.[2] Besides, the collection method – the charge is on the club, not on the individual member – is easy to implement.

The same AGM decided on a new national structure. The executive was replaced by a governing body. Provisions were made for the appointment of county development officers. This would appear to be the first step towards setting up county committees. The idea of the county as a unit of the association was aired during the 1970s. An executive meeting on 26 March 1988 endorsed a recommendation, from a committee headed by former president Jackie Sheerin, that county committees be established. However, the response from regional committees, clubs and members was negative.

A significant breakthrough in advancing the game was to have bridge accepted on the transition-year programmes of more than eighty second-level schools in the Republic – something which could not have been achieved without the resources of CBAI behind it.

Bridge is a game for all people. At the table, the young and the old, the physically impaired and the athletic, compete on equal terms, with no quarter asked or given. It has been demonstrated that bridge, like a well-known beverage, is good for you.[3] Consultant psychiatrist Dr Marie O'Sullivan, when she was secretary of South Munster region during the late 1980s, drew on research to show that playing bridge alleviates, and indeed postpones, many of the effects of aging. It is not merely that the brain is kept active; more importantly, the social supports which the game provides greatly enhance a person's quality of life. The extraordinary camaraderie among the bridge-playing community was perhaps best expressed by the late John Cribben from Rathfarnham in Dublin, who might represent the great mass of anonymous players. Observing the crowds that thronged the church and the approaches outside as the remains of a member of his bridge club were being removed, he remarked: 'One thing about bridge – you get a great funeral.'

NOTES

CHAPTER 1: FROM THE EAST (P11–15)

1   Oscar Wilde, *Lady Windermere's Fan*, Act 1

2   Wilde could have borrowed the metaphor from whist or bridge-whist. However, in 1892 Henry Brabey published *A Short Précis of the Game* – of bridge – described by *The Official Encyclopedia of Bridge* as having made a major contribution to the technical development of the game. References to bridge by military and titled gentlemen before 1894 suggest that the game was already being played in Britain at that time.

3   First production, 22 February 1892 at St James' Theatre, London. Broadway première, Palmer's Theatre, 5 February 1893.

4   *The Walk of the Oysters*, Chapter 1, Rex Mackey, pub. W. H. Allen, London, 1964

5   *Bridge and How to Play It*, Archibald Dunn, 1899, 15th ed. 1909, pub. Geo. Routledge and Sons Ltd, London. Dunn wrote at least four other books on the game.

6   Mackey, op. cit.

7   *Summoned by Bells*, John Betjeman. John Murray, London, 1960, Betjeman's autobiographical poem.

8   *Damned to Fame*, James Knowlson, Bloomsbury, London, 1996. Beckett was at Portora from 1920 to 1923. He played bridge when he worked at the Irish Red Cross hospital in St Lô, in 1945 and 1946.

9   Maisie Cooper found that this attitude still prevailed in Castleisland in the late 1950s, when leading businessmen of the town approached her husband, the new bank manager, with a request to curb his wife's activities. Among her objectionable enterprises was her effort to get the women of the town to play bridge. Ref. interview with Maisie Cooper, 1997.

10   Letter to the author from Father Enda Burke, PP, Cloughjordan, Eimer and Eddie Burke's son, 29 August 2006

11   The articles were by 'Cut-Cavendish', author of *The Complete Bridge Player* and *How to Win at Bridge*. The name looks like a pseudonym, seemingly taken from the nineteenth century whist expert Henry James (not the novelist), who used the pen-name 'Cavendish'.

12   William Dalton wrote six bridge books during the first decade of the twentieth century. Later he wrote seven books on auction bridge.

13   *The Robertson Rule and other Bridge Axioms*, Edmund Robertson and A. Hyde-Wollaston, privately published, 1902.

14   *Pro Bono Publico* ('for the public good'). The letter was published on 9 January 1909.

15   Switzer's ads in the *Irish Times*, late autumn and winter, 1907 to 1909

16   Dunn, op. cit.

17   *Foster's Bridge*, Lawrence and Bullen, London, 1902

18   Record of CBAI competitions, 1932–35, kept by Fred Quin, now in the archives at CBAI headquarters

19   *Auction Bridge*, pub. Brown, Langham and Co., reviewed 8 May 1908 in the *Irish Times*. Its author is given as 'Vano Pennell': his first name was actually 'Vane'. See *Official Encyclopedia of Bridge*, bibliography.

20   *Complete Contract Bridge*, Harold Thorne, 1933, rewritten by Hubert Phillips. Pub. Eyre and Spottiswode, 1948.

21   *Royal Auction, Suggestions on the Game*, Katherine Emerson Seabury, pub. Grafton, 1912. *Royal Spades Auction Bridge*, Bascule, pub. Longmans Green, 1913.

22   Thorne, Phillips, op. cit.

23   Interview, Paul Hanratty, Alfie Hanratty's nephew, December 2005.

24   Interview with Mary Newport, John Joe Ryder's daughter, February 2007. When John Joe settled in Muff, County Donegal, an occasional bridge guest was Mrs Montgomery, mother of the renowned field-marshal.

25   John Joe Ryder's brother Tom, who lived in Dublin, partnered Tom Boden in a Camrose match against Scotland in 1946. Another brother, George, settled in Galway. The latter's wife, Maureen, was president of the CBAI in 1969. Their son Malcolm is among the best-known players in Galway.

26   Autobiographical notes included in *Dr Eamonn O'Sullivan, A Man Before His Time*, Weeshie Fogarty, Wolfhound Press, Dublin, 2007.

CHAPTER 2: THE *IRISH TIMES* BRIDGE COLUMN (P16–18)

1   The War of Independence, 1919 to 1921; the Civil War, 1922 to 1923

2   For example: *Up-to-date Auction Bridge*, J. W. F. Gillies, Routledge, London, reviewed 7 June 1924; *Modern Auction*, Ernest Berghold, Hutchinson, London, reviewed 6 February 1925; *Bridge for Beginners*, R. F. Foster, Lane, London, listed in new publications, 18 May 1928; *Aces and Kings*, Stanley Harris, Thornton Butterworth, London, reviewed 27 June 1930.

3   *Memoirs of an Italian Princess*, Dame Ethel Smyth. The Ex-Empress, Eugenie, recalled Pierpoint Morgan losing in a game in Rome and, having no money to pay up, being given a loan by the Duke of Sparta – the future king of Greece.

4   The Golf Hotel, Greystones, ran a series of advertisements offering bridge to its guests from the late 1920s through the 1930s.

5   The Reverend W. E. Woodhams-Denham, vicar of Chorley Woods, Herts, reported in the *Irish Times*, 16 December 1929.

6   Dr Stanton-Jones, Bishop of Sodor and Man, addressing a meeting in Oxford, the *Irish Times*, 18 November 1930.

7   The *Irish Times*, 24 May 1927.

8   The *Irish Times* and *Irish Independent*, 25 June 1927.

9   Dorothy Peart in conversation with the author, Hotel Westport, November 2005.

10   Two and six, or half a crown. Today's equivalent is roughly €0.15.

CHAPTER 3: THE FIRST BRIDGE CLUBS (P19–20)

1   The minutes of the Regent's AGM following the silver jubilee celebrations in 1950 recorded that 'on the occasion of the jubilee Miss McNulty paid a generous tribute to Mr F. T. Quin, the founder of the club'.

2   This account of the founding of The Regent was recounted to me by Gerry Murtagh, who carried out some research into the club.

3   Michael Brennan, telephone interview with author, September 2007. Also email to author, 14 August 2008. Brennan later spoke to Ita Shipsey, Kervick's daughter, who confirmed that the club was indeed founded in 1927.

CHAPTER 4: CONTRACT BRIDGE (P21–22)

1   Mackey, op. cit.

2   Alan Truscott, *The New York Times Bridge Book*, 2002.

3   Mackey, op. cit. The three friends were Frederick S. Allen, Francis M. Bacon III and Dudley L. Pickerman Jnr.

4   *Plafond* is French for 'ceiling'.

5   Mackey, op. cit.

6   Thorne, op. cit.

7   In the course of his research, Truscott had been in touch with Clayton's son, Tom, from Wimbledon, London.

8   *The Times of India*, 15 July 1914

9   *The Official Encyclopedia of Bridge*, sixth edition, refers to an article in *The Bridge World*, September 1931. Alan Truscott, who was executive editor of the encyclopedia, was responsible for the entry.

CHAPTER 5: ELY CULBERTSON AND THE BATTLE OF THE CENTURY (P23–28)

1   Although born in Romania, Culbertson was an America citizen by virtue of his birth being registered with the US consul. His father, of Scottish origin, was an American mining engineer working for the Russian government in the Caucasian oilfields. His mother was the daughter of a Cossack chief. *The Official Encyclopedia of Bridge*, sixth edition, 2001, American Contract Bridge League.

2   Ibid.

3   Born Josephine Murphy to Irish parents in New York in 1898, in 1919 she married James Dillon, who committed suicide shortly afterwards. She and Culbertson married in 1923. Ibid.

4   Mackey, op. cit.

5   Ibid.

6   *The Bridge World* is still published, and has a worldwide circulation.

7   Mackey, op. cit.

8   Ibid.
9   Ibid.
10   Ibid.
11   *Contract Bridge Blue Book*, Ely Culbertson, edited by Hubert Phillips, Faber and Faber, London, 1930.
12   For example: *Contract Bridge for All*, A. E. Manning Foster. Ernest Benn Ltd, London, November 1930; *Contract Bridge: Bidding Principles*, Colonel G. G. J. Walshe, De La Rue, London, 1932; *Strain's Contract Bridge*, William Strain, privately published, Belfast, 1932.
13   For example: *Where No Wind Comes*, Simon Dare, Hutchinson, London, 1931
14   *Irish Times*, 14 October 1930
15   *The Official Encyclopedia of Bridge*. As well as Courtenay and Work, the group included Sidney S. Lenz, P. Hal Sims and Wilbur C. Whitehead, all household names in American bridge circles.
16   Three-times Wimbledon champion between 1920 and 1930.
17   Winner of eleven major championships between 1914 and 1929.
18   World welterweight and middleweight boxing champion in the 1920s.
19   José Raúl Capablanca y Graupera, 1888-1942, Cuban world chess grandmaster.
20   Mackey, op. cit., and *The Official Encyclopedia of Bridge*
21   Mackey, op. cit., and *The Official Encyclopedia of Bridge*
22   Mackey, op. cit.
23   Ibid.
24   Culbertson's 4-5 NT convention bears no relationship to Blackwood's convention, which had appeared in 1931. Blackwood's was asking; Culbertson's was descriptive.
25   Mackey, op. cit.
26   Ibid.
27   *Contract Bridge Blue Book*, Ely Culbertson, ed. Phillips, Faber and Faber, London, 1930.

CHAPTER 6: THE CONTRACT BRIDGE ASSOCIATION OF IRELAND (P29–36)

1   Walton and John Cockford, who had collaborated with him, shared the Nobel Prize for physics in 1951.
2   It has not been established whether it was Lower or Upper Fitzwilliam Street.
3   The *Irish Times*, 26 February 1932. The committee members were not named, but at the general meeting on 19 September 1933 the following were elected to the committee: Mrs Bowles, Mrs H. Brown, Mrs Crofts, H. J. Freehill, Major French, Colonel Garrett, J. Maxwell Henry, J. E. Hogan, Mrs T. Kennedy, S. D. Lambert, Miss M. Leech, Mrs McMunn, Dr Kathleeen Murphy, Prof. Nolan, Joseph O'Neill, F. T. Quin, Frederick Sharpe, J. B. and Mrs Shortt, Dr Bethel Solomons, Dr L. Wigoder, B. L. Williams and H. Williams.

4   Erina Holmes Wilson's brother-in-law was Brigadier General Sir Samuel Wilson, Permanent Under-Secretary of State for the Colonies.

5   Joseph O'Neill, *The Irish Bridge Annual 1948.*

6   The *Irish Times, Irish Independent* and *Irish Press* all reported on the Culbertson-Lenz match. The *Irish Independent* published a large photo from the match on 1 January 1932.

7   *Lenz on Contract Bridge*, Allen and Unwin, London, 1928.

8   *The Irish Bridge Annual 1948.*

9   Jewish members included Lionel Wigoder, Bethel Solomon, Leonard Abrahamson, Mrs Sharpe and Joe Rubenstein.

10   Announced by de Valera on 16 March 1932 as part of his plan for government.

11   Reuters report picked up by the *Irish Independent*, 6 August 1932.

12   CBAI Record of Duplicate Bridge Competitions and Championships, 1932–35.

13   The *Irish Times*, 26 February 1932. Dr Lionel Wigoder was a grand-uncle of international bridge player Don Seligman (on Seligman's mother's side). Lionel's brother Zelig (known as George) had left Poland, bound for America, during the mass emigration of Jews from Eastern Europe in the 1880s. When the ship stopped at Queenstown (Cobh), he thought he had reached the New World, and disembarked. He went on to found the well-known Wigoder paint-and-wallpaper company in Dublin. (Author's conversation with Don Seligman, 31 May 2006.)

14   Interview, Ruth Giddings.

15   Harry and Miss Janet Jackson, participants in early CBAI competitions, had no family connection with later prominent bridge people of the same name. A Mrs Jackson also played in the 1930s but it is not known if she was related to the cup donor.

16   Details of competitions: CBAI Record of Competitions, 1932–35.

17   *Meath Chronicle*, 21 January 1938; *Kerry Champion*, 19 March 1938; Tralee team: Mr and Mrs Quinlan and Messrs Keating and Ryle.

18   Harold Williams was the *Irish Times'* first regular bridge correspondent. He first got the byline over the report on the Buller match, 30 November 1932. Although his name appeared irregularly afterwards, it is virtually certain that he continued as the correspondent for the remainder of the decade.

19   *Irish Independent*, 28 November 1932.

20   The *Irish Times*, 29 November 1932.

CHAPTER 7: THE CBAI SPREADS (P37–51)

1   The *Irish Times*, 21 May 1932.

2   Published by Healys, Dublin, 1932, reviewed in the *Irish Times*, 13 August 1932.

3   The *Irish Independent* of 21 December 1932 reported 1,500 people, and 250 tables. The *Irish Times* estimated the attendance at 1,300.

4   The *Irish Times*, 19 and 21 December 1932.

5   Among Limerick's founding members were: Larry and Mrs Byrne, Captain Campbell, Fred Conry, Dr Denis and Mrs Corboy, Lou Dondon, May and Maurice Gubbins, Mrs Mary Heffernan, J. Hurley-Byrne, Dr Charles McConnell and his daughter Doris McNamara, Cecil and Mrs Mercier, Charles and Mrs O'Malley, J. M. (Jack) and Eileen O'Sullivan, Mrs Roberts, Dr Hubert and Mary Roche-Kelly, Seamus and Dr Troy, Robert V. and Mrs Walker and F. W. Williams.

6   *Irish Times*, 26 November 1934.

7   Interview with Maisie Cooper, 1999.

8   1952 European championships, Dun Laoghaire. See Chapter 18.

9   *Irish Independent*, 27 January 1941. The tie was split according to the Gruenther method, named after Alfred Gruenther, the referee at the Culberson-Lenz match in New York 1931–32, and soon to play a major role as a US general during the war.

10   *Irish Independent*, 25 May 1938.

11   Vic Roughan, speaking at the Ennis v. Dublin match, January 1935. *Irish Independent*, 12 January 1935. Also *Connacht Tribune*, 12 January 1935 and 10 April 1937, and *Irish Independent*, 28 March 1938. Note: Williams is referred to in reports as both 'Fred' and 'Billy'. His full name was 'Frederick William Williams'.

12   Dublin team defeated by Ennis in January 1935: F. T. Quin, G. M. Linzell, A. G. Kibble and J. S. Quigley

13   July 1937, Ennis: V. Roughan, T. D. Cooper, W. F. O'Keeffe, P. Heffernan, lost to Belfast: G. B. Hanna, E. Goldblatt, B. Vard, J. R. McKee.

14   *Irish Bridge Journal*, 16.1, October 1994.

15   The *Irish Times*, 12 December 1934.

16   The *Irish Times*, 20 May 1935.

17   The *Kerry Champion*, 20 November 1937, reported: 'this is the third year that this championship has been played'. It was Mr Keating and Mrs Quinlan's second time to win it.

18   The committee of Kilkenny branch consisted of: W. F. McGarry (hon. sec.), G. N. Meares, (hon. treas.), Reverend J. O'Keeffe, P. Hannington, Mrs G. N. Drea, Mrs R. A. Duggan. *Irish Independent*, 14 November 1936.

19   The team was: Lambert, McConkey, David Rivlin, Harry Fine and the Pigots.

20   'Acol' was so named because it was created in a bridge club on the Acol Road in north London. The Acol club still exists today, but not in the same location.

21   The fourth member of the regular team, along with Marx, Simon and Harrison Grey, that used Acol in the early years, was Iain McLeod, who gave up bridge for politics and became Chancellor of the Exchequer.

22   R. J. McKee was Moyna Mackenzie's father. Moyna has been a leading Northern Ireland player for several decades. As Moyna Johnston, she was one of the few women who won places on Irish open teams (1981 European

championships).

23   *Clare Champion*, 6 December 1930. Quoted by Enda Glynn in *Ennistymon Bridge Club and Its Times*.

24   'Biographical Details', by O'Sullivan, in *Dr Eamonn O'Sullivan, A Man Before His Time*, Weeshie Fogarty, Wolfhound Press, Dublin, 2007.

25   More than a decade later the Department of Education refused to sanction the use of a room by Mountbellew Bridge Club, County Galway, in the local vocational school. Bridge did not 'come within the scope of the 1930 Vocational Education Act.' One VEC member, Mr Higgins NT, suggested that if the players spoke Irish while playing it could be regarded as a cultural activity (*Connacht Tribune*, 25 January 1947).

26   Now County Louth Golf Club.

27   The original letter is in the possession of Ray Norton, Castlebar, who kindly gave a copy to the author.

28   Dr d'Abreu's wife, Lucy, died in Scotland in 2007, aged 113, the oldest person in the UK or Ireland. Ref. Michael Brennan.

29   Louis Doolan died while conducting a beginners' class in the early 1970s.

30   J. H. Daly later turns up in Bagenaltown, Listowel and Tramore. Galway Bridge Club made a presentation to him in April 1941, following four years as the club's honorary secretary. *Irish Independent*, 3 May 1941. His daughter is Patsy Meehan, who has played on Irish women's and seniors' teams in European championships.

31   There are claims that the West of Ireland Congress dates from 1939. See Chapter 17.

32   Carlton's address when it won the club cup in 1936 was Lower Leeson Street. By 1940, it had moved to St Stephen's Green.

33   Dublin: Mairéad Crofts, Kathleen Lambert, Geraldine McConkey, H. G. Freehill and J. O'Neill. Belfast: Prof A. McKinnon, Norah McKee, G. B. Hanna, E. Goldblatt, B. Vard. *Irish Independent*, 2 November 1936.

34   The players invited to the Carlton tournament were: Mairéad Crofts, J. O'Neill, Kathleen Lambert, Geraldine McConkey, D. R. and Violet Pigot, Mrs Bowles, Mrs Colgan, J. M. and Eileen O'Sullivan, D. Murphy, T. O'Grady, J. P. Morgan, C. O'Neill, H. G. Freehill, H. Williams, D. Rivlin, H. Fine, H. G. Cowan and M. Freeman, the latter four from the Jewish Literary and Social Club. Erina Holmes Wilson and Mr Messervey could not avail of the invitation because Mrs Holmes Wilson was absent from town. Rivlin and Fine won, with the Pigots coming second.

35   *Meath Chronicle*, 2 April 1939. Kells teams: 'A': Miss Vance, Mrs Lynch, Mrs and Miss McCann; 'B': Mr and Mrs Brown, Miss McNally, Mrs Beatt.

36   *Irish Independent*, 22 April 1939.

CHAPTER 8: REGIONALISATION (P52–60)

1   Pat Ballantine, a garda officer, moved to Sligo, where he remained a promi-

nent player. His daughter is Mary Stephens (Donegal), who qualified as a CBAI bridge teacher in the mid-1990s. William Hourican's son Liam was a well-known face on RTÉ news programmes. Beaten finalists, Balbriggan: Messrs Gallen and Butler, Mr and Mrs Brown.

2   *Irish Independent*, 22 April 1939.

3   In 1937, the Southern zone provided nine finalists, and the Eastern seven, for the national pairs final. There is less certainty about the years 1934–36, but the pairs championship certainly started with branch qualifiers.

4   *Irish Independent*, 29 October 1938.

5   *Irish Independent*, 4 December 1937.

6   *Meath Chronicle*, 8 January 1938.

7   John Cunningham in conversation with the author, October 2007, and confirmed 19 September 2008.

8   George N. Jessop, auctioneer, general hardware merchant and coal importer. His company was Gaze & Jessop Ltd, Portlaoise. Their coal yard was in Roscrea.

9   *Irish Independent*, 10 August 1940.

10 *Irish Independent*, 19 August 1940.

11 The *Kerry Champion*, 11 December 1937, reported that Misses L. O'Sullivan and M. Healy, Tralee, were second in the Munster championship in Limerick.

12 *Irish Independent*, 18 January 1941.

13 The evidence for the date of the establishment of the Metropolitan Register is a pencilled entry on the first page of the CBAI's original record of competitions. The page contains a chronological order of events and lists of officers from 1932 to 1958, initially compiled probably by Hugh Hackett, a prominent Dublin player, whose signature is at the foot of the page. Since all other items of information on that page are demonstrably correct, there is no reason to question the entry concerning the Metropolitan Register.

14 Minutes, Wexford Bridge Club, October 1946.

15 *Irish Independent*, 17 July 1948. Also Joseph O'Neill, *Irish Bridge Annual 1948*.

16 The *Irish Times*, 9 August 1948.

17 The same J. H. Daly who had been a founding member of Galway Bridge Club and Galway Congress. In 1948, he was in Bagenalstown.

18 Minutes, Wexford Bridge Club, October 1948.

19 It is not clear whether a club in Limavaddy affiliated to the CBAI, but at least one player from there, Dr Joe Keohane, competed regularly in CBAI competitions.

20 The draw for the Kelburne was announced in the *Irish Times*, 7 May 1949: N. Munster v. Western; N. Midland v. S. Munster; S. Midland v. Dublin; Northern v. N. Eastern. Dublin was not yet a region as such.

CHAPTER 9: THE NORTHERN IRELAND BRIDGE UNION (P61–62)

1   The *Irish Times* and *Irish Independent*, 9 October 1934.

2   H. G. (Harry) Lindsay's son is Ian Lindsay, Northern Ireland grandmaster, Camrose player, and an effective and respected official.

3   The newspaper report gives the name as 'H. J. Miley' but this was almost certainly a typographical error. Whereas Harold J. Miles was an influential member of the NIBU during the late 1930s, the name Miley does not appear again.

CHAPTER 10: INTERNATIONAL AFFAIRS – THE 1930S (P63–76)

1   This should not be confused with a later body of the same name founded in 1939.

2   The representatives at the Belfast meeting were: G. Allen, G. B. Hanna (NIBU); D. Rivlin (CBAI); Dr McDonald, C. Ellis (Scottish Bridge Union); Colonel G. G. J. Walshe (London and Home Counties Contract Bridge Association); F. R. Chippingdale, B. Cohen (Yorkshire CBA); Captain Kempson (North Eastern CBA); and Hubert Phillips (National Bridge Association).

3   There were twenty-four delegates to the DBCB: English Bridge Union 12, Scottish Bridge Union 4, Welsh Bridge Union 3, CBAI 3, NIBU 2.

4   The thirty-two players, thought to be the best in the country, and selected to contest the trials, were: E. O. Barry, P. Quinn; Mrs Bowles, Mrs Colgan; H. G. Cowan, M. Freeman; T. D. Cooper, V. Roughan; Mairéad Crofts, J. O'Neill; B. Ebrill, F. T. Quin; J. Ingram, T. O'Grady; H. Fine, D. Rivlin; H. G. Freehill, H. Williams; A. G. Kibble, Mabel Spiro; Kathleen Lambert, Geraldine McConkey; Muriel Leech, May McNulty; J. P. Morgan, D. Murphy; W. J. L. and Rosaleen O'Connell; Jack and Eileen O'Sullivan; David and Violet Pigot. Substitutes: Erina Holmes Wilson, Mr McDermott, Mrs Fitzgerald, C. O'Neill. Holmes Wilson and McDermott deputised for Barry and Quinn when the latter became ill.

5   Harold Williams's report in the *Irish Times*, 23 January 1937.

6   The Tollemache Cup, donated in 1934, by Lord Tollemache, founding member of the National Bridge Association, the Pachebo, in 1935, by A. E. Whitelaw, who wrote under the pseudonym 'Pachebo.' The competitions continue today, with somewhat different formats, as important events on the English Bridge Union's calendar. Ref. *British Bridge Almanack*, ed. Peter Hasenson.

7   *Irish Independent*, 26 March 1938.

8   Previous correspondence is unclear as to whether Mobbs had invited anyone from Scotland. It seems, from Perry's report of 7 July, that Rowan had been invited.

CHAPTER 11: THE 1940S (P77–88)

1   What is known about the territorial division into regions, as well as extending the right to participate in CBAI competitions to associate members, in 1940,

is entirely due to reports in the *Irish Independent*.

2 *70 Years of the Gate Bridge Club*, privately published, 2007.

3 In Dr Paul Stern's Vienna system, hands of 18+ points were opened 1NT. 1♠, 1♥ or 1♦ promised a five-card suit and 11 to 17 points. 1♣ showed all other hands in the 11-to-17-points range.

4 Published by Brown and Nolan Ltd, Dublin, 1944; reviewed in the *Irish Times* on 27 January 1945.

5 Published Clonmore and Reynolds Ltd, Dublin, 1947.

6 Published Faber and Faber, London, 1949.

7 The team, representing the North-Eastern region, was completed by J. Gayer and W. Whitney.

8 *Official Encyclopedia of Bridge*, sixth edition.

9 *Kerry Champion*, 19 March 1938.

10 Among Burke's pupils at Nenagh Primary School was Michael O'Connor, the future president and vice-president of the CBAI.

11 Letter from Father Enda Burke, PP, Cloughjordan, to the author, 29 August 2006.

12 North Munster Journal Antiquarian, Vol XIX, article by Patrick Wallace, referred to by Father Enda Burke.

13 Tom Boden, with partner Tom Ryder, played in a Camrose match against Scotland, October 1946.

14 Boden was ahead of his time. Acol had, as yet, made little impact on Culbertson, which continued to be the system commonly in use.

15 Father Enda Burke, PP, Cloughjordan, thinks that Nenagh Bridge Club was functioning before his parents joined. However, the account here is that of Augusta Shouldice, who clearly remembered the events leading up to the club's formation when I spoke to her in December 2006. She attended the first meeting.

16 Interview with Augusta Shouldice and her son Michael, December 2006.

17 *Irish Independent*, 29 April 1940.

18 The *Irish Independent* of 14 May 1940 reported two unknown players, G. W. Ashton and T. D. Phelan, on Hickey's team. The *Irish Times* report of the same day includes the Purcells and is almost certainly the correct version.

19 *Irish Independent*, 18 May 1940.

20 *Irish Independent*, 6 May 1940.

21 Miss Spiller and Mrs Doughty (London) played with Mrs Cross and Mrs O'Malley in the team championship.

22 There are conflicting claims also as to when the first East of Ireland congress was held. Silver photo frames sponsored by Smyth's Pharmacy to celebrate the sixtieth anniversary in 2002 bear the caption '1942–2002'. *The Irish Bridge Annual 1948* gives 1943 as the year of the first one.

23 Geraldine McConkey's husband Robin was a bank official.

24 Autobiographical notes, Dr E. N. N. O'Sullivan, included in *Dr Eamonn O'Sullivan, A Man Before His Time*, Weeshie Fogarty, Wolfhound Press, Dublin, 2007.

25 According to O'Sullivan's autobiographical notes, thirty overseas visitors attended in 1946.

26 Participants in the Ireland v. Overseas match in Killarney, 1946: Ireland: Prof A. McKinnon, G. B. Hanna; W. J. L. and F. W. O'Connell; E. T. C. and P. V. M. Cotter; Colonel G. G. J. Walshe, Mairéad O'Neill; Eileen and Jack O'Sullivan; H. McCallum, Mrs Atkinson; Overseas: E. Mayer, S. M. Goldsmith; R. Niman, J. Tarlo; H. Franklin, S. Merklin; N. C. R. Frith, Mrs D. Hopewell; W. Ricardo, Mrs Morgan; Mrs T. G. Bonnyman, Miss McEachran; T. and Mrs Somers; C. Ellis, Mrs Davidson.

27 CBAI programme, 1941–42.

28 *The Irish Bridge Annual 1948.*

29 *Irish Independent,* 22 December 1942.

30 T. C. (Tom) O'Gorman died in September 2008, a few months short of his hundredth birthday.

31 Mrs H. Buckley, 8 Laurel Villas, Mardyke, Cork, took entries for the 1940–41 Revington. CBAI programme, 1940–41.

32 T. D. Cooper, Ennis, took entries for the 1941–42 Spiro. CBAI programme, 1941–42.

33 Willie Berrill, Drogheda, took entries for the 1943–44 Spiro. CBAI programme, 1943–44.

34 *Irish Independent,* 12 May 1942.

35 *Irish Independent,* 6 October 1942. Fourteen clubs took part but there were none from Munster or the west.

36 Norah McKee later married Larry Bradley and represented Ireland as Norah Bradley. Her daughter is Moyna Mackenzie.

37 Ref. Peadar Murnane, 2006.

CHAPTER 12: POST-WAR INTERNATIONAL ACTIVITIES (P89–92)

1 The *Irish Times,* 19 May 1947.

2 The period of the Second World War was referred to in the neutral Irish Free State as 'the Emergency'.

3 Joseph M. Stanley (Drogheda) was president of the CBAI in 1946/47, the first person from the north-east to hold the office. He directed the Wales v. Scotland Camrose match in June 1947. Stanley assisted in the birth of modern Ireland, and worked in numerous fields of endeavour for its development. He was a printer by trade, and type from his machines was used to print the 1916 Proclamation of the Irish Republic. During the Rising, he produced bulletins outlining the rebels' progress. He was an alderman of Drogheda Corporation and a member of Louth County Council. Disillusionment with the civil war and business interests influenced his withdrawal from public life from late 1923. In the 1920s, he opened cinemas in Drogheda and Dundalk, and later, one in Cavan. Up to the 1940s, Hollywood films showing in Ireland were distributed through Britain, so he set up a distribution company. From

1929 to 1935, he was a subeditor with the *Daily Mail* in London and, in the 1940s, went into the newspaper business himself when he bought the *Drogheda Argus and Advertiser*. Later, he added the *Monaghan Argus* to his portfolio. As a boy soprano, he was a contemporary of John McCormack in the pro-cathedral choir. He was a balladeer and composer, and the song 'The Shawl of Galway Grey', for which he wrote the music, is still occasionally heard. He had an affinity with the stage; his wife, Eileen, had been an Abbey actress, and her sister, Máire Ní Shiúlaigh, was one of the theatre's stars. In the late 1920s, he financed a troupe of actors, who travelled the country with caravans – and a steam engine to generate power. Joe Stanley died on 2 June 1950, age sixty.

4   Kathryn O'Keeffe (later FitzGibbon) played on an open and women's team in the European Union (EEC) championships. Moyna Johnston played on Irish open teams in a European and a European Union championship.

CHAPTER 13: BRIDGE AT THE TURN OF THE HALF-CENTURY (P93–95)

1   *The Irish Bridge Annual 1950*.

CHAPTER 14: CONFLICT (P96–98)

1   *Connacht Tribune*, 27 May 1950.
2   Ibid.
3   Minutes CBAI AGM, Warwick Hotel, Galway, 20 May 1950.
4   Harry Freehill had made a similar suggestion in 1939 but in private correspondence and informally, to Harold Miles, NIBU. See Chapter 10.
5   North Munster delegates and future presidents of the CBAI.
6   John Williams in *English Bridge*, April 1999.
7   *Irish Times*, 17 October 1950.

CHAPTER 15: THE IRISH BRIDGE UNION (P99–104)

1   Interview with Mrs Josephine Purcell, Des Purcell's widow, October 2006.
2   Purcell and Donovan, with Jack Kelly and Jimmy Bastow, won the Kelburne in 1951 and 1952.
3   The full team was: Donovan, Purcell, Marcus Shrage, Jack Kelly, Dermot Egan, Elvina Spiro and Ina McMenamin.
4   Dublin Jewish Literary and Social Club: 'A': D. Rivlin, H. Fine, H. Bridburg, H. Elliott, C. Gordon, L. Abrahamson; 'B': A. Bloom, J. Orman, A. Speirs, E. Seligman, D. Taylor, M. Freeman. Belfast Jewish Literary and Social Institute: 'A': D. Cohen, B. Vard, H. Diamond, C. Sampson, J. Samuels. 'B': A. Herbert, J. Hurwitz, H. Schenker, J. Steinberg, A. Morris, M. Rosenberg.
5   Colonel Walshe was president of the Northern Ireland Bridge Union but he lived in London.
6   Interview with Gerry Byrne, Noel Byrne's son, October 2006.
7   Neither the original proposals nor Brennan's modifications are recorded but

the minutes of 26 February record the step-by-step progress of the meeting.

8   *Irish Independent*, 19 March 1955.

9   Michael Lynch was of that opinion when I interviewed him, on 15 October 2005.

10   Minutes, CBAI executive, 2 April 1955.

11   The minutes of the inaugural meeting, in the handwriting of Norman Douglas, clearly date the meeting Friday 8 April. The *Irish Times* reported on the same day: 'delegates from the CBAI and NIBU met yesterday [7 April] and founded the Irish Bridge Union'. The *Irish Independent* also carried a report of the meeting on the eighth. Either a press release was issued and published prematurely or Douglas got the day and date wrong. The former scenario is more likely.

12   See Chapter 4.

13   Conversation with Noreen O'Grady, July 2005.

CHAPTER 16: UNLIKELY ALLIES (P105–106)

1   *British Bridge Almanac, 2004.*

2   Hanna was speaking in a debate on an inquest on a member of Saor Uladh – a breakaway group from the IRA – killed in a recent raid on an RUC barracks. The inquest had been held in secret in a farmhouse following intervention by Seán McBride. The farmhouse had been surrounded by Gardaí during the inquest. *Ireland in the 20th Century*, Tim Pat Coogan, Arrow Books, 2003.

3   'Why the Border must be'. Northern Ireland government publication, 1956. Hanna's contribution was entitled: 'Six Reasons for Ulster's Separation from Éire'.

4   Minutes, inaugural meeting of IBU, 8 April 1955.

5   Brennan had proposed McBride for the 1948 election.

6   The winning UCD team was J. Burke, M. Gallagher, B. Murnaghan and L. Paffrath.

CHAPTER 17: THE GOLDEN AGE OF IRISH WOMEN'S BRIDGE (P107–109)

1   Mollie O'Carroll and English-born Charlotte Fowler were on the team in 1961.

2   Sonya Britton and Barbara Seligman, the latter destined to become one of the all-time great women competitors, played in 1962.

3   There was one woman on the open team in 1954, Elvina Spiro.

4   Not all-women teams, but one or more women were on the teams referred to – the same goes for the other events listed.

5   Mr J. Curran was the fourth member of the team.

CHAPTER 18: THE 1950S – AN EVENTFUL DECADE (P110–122)

1   The *Irish Times* report on the McMenamin-winning team includes the name

Mrs D. Duffy. This was an error. It can be seen how a copywriter or typesetter might have taken part of Doreen Cairnduff's name; hence the error. Prost, Cairnduff, McNally and McDonagh played regularly as a team and won the McMenamin again in 1954.

2   The 1967 championship programme records Ireland finishing eighth of twelve in Dun Laoghaire in 1952. That was incorrect. Thirteen teams competed in 1952: Iceland was omitted from the 1967 list. The *Irish Times* of 29 September 1952 placed Ireland tenth.

3   The *Irish Times*, 19 May 1947.

4   Interview with R. Giddings, 2005.

5   The *Irish Times*, 11 January 1952.

6   Confirmed to the author by Joe MacHale, June 2002.

7   Ref. interview with Ruth Giddings, August 2006.

8   Ibid.

9   Aspinall loved animals. He set up an animal refuge at Howletts near Canterbury in 1958 and later opened a zoo at Port Lympne. Huge financial resources were required to keep them going.

10   *The Hustlers*, written by Douglas Thompson, was published by Sidgwick and Jackson in 2007.

11   Minutes, CBAI executive, 25 March 1954. Noel Byrne, John Lane and Michael Dorgan all expressed the view that the Dublin Metropolitan organisation had proved a failure.

12   The Belgian team was: E. (or F.) Bosmans, R. van Branchan, T. Jacobs, P. Pollack. Ref. *Irish Times* reports during congress week.

13   The Swedish team was: B. Nilsson, K. A. Hedberg, A. Gartner, A. Engereen. Ref. *Irish Times* reports during congress week.

14   Minutes, CBAI executive, 13 May 1955 – a report on IBU matters.

15   *Irish Independent*, 16 and 30 July 1955.

16   Minutes, CBAI executive, 11 February 1956.

17   The Bradleys separated around this time and understandably withdrew from the team. Ref. Moyna Mackenzie, Norah Bradley's daughter, in conversation with the author in Verona, June 2006.

18   Minutes, CBAI executive, 29 March 1958.

19   *Bridge Match in Dublin*, Ewart Kempson, pub. John Waddington, Leeds, January 1958.

20   The *Irish Times*, 17 December 1958.

CHAPTER 19: THE BEST OF THEM ALL? (P123–128)

1   Interview with E. O'Riordan, 6 April 2002.

2   Avril Doyle, MEP, is Dick Belton's daughter.

3   Conversations with 'Big Paddy' Walsh, early 1990s.

4   Interview with Wesley Burrowes, 30 January 2007.

5   Minutes, CBAI executive, 22 October 1953.

6 Harry Freehill had made the same suggestion, but informally, in 1939. See Chapter 5.
7 Minutes, CBAI executive, 10 September 1953.
8 Minutes, CBAI executive, 10 October 1953.
9 Minutes, CBAI executive, 14 December 1953.
10 Minutes, CBAI executive, 11 March 1954.
11 Fred Barry, a winner of CBAI mixed teams championship, Coen Trophy 2005, is Liam Barry's son.
12 Called the *Daily Tournament News*, the bulletin was edited by Herman Filarski, assisted by Alan Truscott.
13 The *Irish Times*, 6 August 1955.
14 Even though Jackson was not named as the director, it is a reasonable assumption that he was. He directed most of the major competitions at the time. Jackson brought the question up at an executive meeting. He did not mention another director being involved.
15 An Italian system, the name derived from the first names of its creators, Mario Franco and Michele Giovine. *The Official Encyclopedia of Bridge* describes it as 'probably the most unusual system ever played in serious international bridge'. Belonging to the strong-pass systems, a feature was that a player with 16 1/2 to 19 points in first or second seat passed. Partner balanced with five points or more. An opening bid of 2♣ showed three suits.
16 Interview with Ruth Giddings, July 2007.

CHAPTER 20: MASTER-POINTS (P129–132)

1 The American system dated from the mid-1930s. Ref. *The Official Encyclopedia of Bridge* and *The Mammoth Book of Bridge*, Mark Horton, Robinson Publishing, London, 1999.
2 Even though the names of the master-point holders were not published, it is probable that the one master was Ruth Giddings. On every list subsequently published, she was at the top.
3 Figures released to the newspapers gave the total as 560 but when the subtotals of the various grades were added, they came to 785.
4 Minutes, Galway Bridge Club AGM, 28 October 1958.
5 Minutes, Wexford Bridge Club AGM, October 1964.
6 The *Irish Times*, 14 May 1977.

CHAPTER 21: THE EXCITING 1960s (P133–145)

1 The teams: Visitors: H. Franklin, L. Tarlo, R. G. and Mrs Corwen. Home: L. F. Sheeran, D. Seale (North Midland), C. B. Higgins, C. Clune (North-western), P. J. Gallagher, C. Gilgunn (Western).
2 The Ghestem Convention: Over a one-level suit opening, the cue-bid of opener's suit shows the lowest and highest ranking of the other three suits – the extremes, 2NT the two lowest-ranking, 3♣ the two highest-ranking suits.

However over 1♣, 2♦ shows the majors. Five-card or longer suits, of course.

3   Poland has won world and European championships. Nowadays Polish players are invariably among the favourites for any event in which they take part.

4   Zbigniew Glowaty won Rás Tailteann in 1963. Poland won the teams classification also. *The Rás*, Tom Daly, The Collins Press, Cork, 2003.

5   North-eastern and Northern were the only regions not to play against the Poles.

6   The responses can be modified to suit any no-trump opening range.

7   Some months before Laur died, he gave the original typed manuscript of the convention to the author of this book. It consists of seven full A4 pages typed by its creator in October 1961. It is now in CBAI headquarters.

8   O'Riordan and Heidenfeldt finished sixth of eighteen pairs in the trials to select the team for the Olympiad in Deauville.

9   E. O'Riordan interview with author, May 2002. Helvic enables a partnership to find a fit when an opening 1NT is doubled for penalty. (a) Responder, with a five-card of longer suit, redoubles. Opener bids two clubs. Responder will pass or bid his own long suit. (b) Responder, with two touching four-card suits, bids the lower ranking. (c) Pass from responder forces opener to redouble. If responder is strong, that can be left in. Following opener's redouble, if responder bids a suit, it is the lower of two non-touching suits. With increasing use of strong no-trump, Helvic is less frequently employed.

10   Pigot indicated that the minutes of the EBL meeting recording the change from CBAI to IBU affiliation to the EBL were not available (presumably lost). Therefore he thought it prudent to raise the question at the EBL. Ref. Minutes, CBAI executive, 2 September 1961.

11   Dick Tierney was not a delegate to the next IBU meeting, 26 November 1961.

12   Jackson's skill can be read through the lines of minutes he wrote, especially for the meetings of the CBAI executive on 28 January 1959, 29 June 1968 and 10 June 1972.

13   IBU, 14 July 1963. Delegates who took the unamimous decision were: CBAI: Geraldine McConkey, Evelyn Arkins, D. R. Pigot, R. A. Dalton, T. Gleeson, R. A. Tierney, D. Jackson; NIBU: G. Sloane, H. Bell, H. D'Arcy, A. McKinnon, N. Percival-Price, D. Deery.

14   IBU, 30 July 1961. Delegates present: CBAI: McConkey, Pigot, Tierney, Jackson, Dalton, J. Honan, D. T. Waldron, E. McArdle; NIBU: D. A. Cohen, P. G. Fitzharris, W. S. Fyffe, H. A. Schenker, S. Blaney, J. H. O'Dempsey, N. H. Douglas.

15   IBU, November 1961

16   Delegates present: CBAI: Geraldine McConkey, D. R. Pigot, J. Honan, D. L. Stokes, R. A. Dalton, E. McArdle; NIBU: S. Blaney, W. S. Fyffe, H. S. Diamond and J. H. O'Dempsey.

17   Jack Kelly wrote conflicting reports, one stating that they were twenty-ninth, another that they were twenty-first. The *Irish Times*, 5 May 1962.

18   In 1962, three teams entered in each of the open and women's trials.

19   Catholic clergy differed in their attitude towards bridge. During the late
      1930s, while Fr Doris in Ardee actively promoted the game and Rev Prof
      Flanagan in Monaghan was the County's leading player, Rev Fenlon in
      Mountrath was warning the Brigidine Convent Past Pupils Union that
      'women gave too much time to playing bridge.' A generation later, Fr Jim
      Savage (Cork) and the Franciscan philosopher from Queen's University,
      Belfast, Theodore Crowley, were keen participants. Bishops too differed. In
      recent times Bishop Hegarty, when in Donegal, was a keen competitor. In
      Dublin, Archbishop McQuaid kept a tight rein on his priests, many of whom,
      including Father Crosbie (Celbridge), played a good competitive game. Once,
      at a diocesan meeting, the archbishop told an argumentive Crosbie that he
      'could not always be right'. The priest took the unintended cue. He became
      'B. Wright' in competition. Using that name, he and another priest of the
      archdiocese, Liam Shanahan (later canon), were the best of the Irish when
      they finished twenty-first in the pairs event at the first EEC (EU) champi-
      onships in the Hague, in 1973. Father Enda Glynn, in the Galway diocese,
      later used an alias, 'B. Clancy', when playing in tournaments which were like-
      ly to be reported in the newspapers.

CHAPTER 22: THE CONGRESS DECADE (P146–148)

1   There is no record of the first Butlin's congress in 1954, but on 10 August
     1955 the *Irish Times* printed an announcement for the second annual congress
     at the holiday resort, to be held from 2 to 4 September.

2   The tragedy in the Glen of Imaal occurred when an officer was demonstrat-
     ing a mine to a group of soldiers and it exploded. Many lost their lives; sev-
     eral others were severely maimed.

3   Conversation with Billy Mullins, July 2008.

CHAPTER 23: JUNIOR AND INTERMEDIATE GRADES (P149–148)

1   There is an estimate available for 1963 of about 5,250 affiliations.

2   The clubs in the first junior league were: Bankers, Civil Service, Engineers,
     Malahide, Regent, Trinity College and UCD.

3   Mrs D. Young was the daughter of Frances Morgan, founding member of
     the CBAI. Her husband, Derek Young, became president of The Regent.
     They emigrated to London.

4   The TCD team was: J. R. W. Orange, Miss L. O'Connor, Mr and Mrs P.
     Stocken.

5   Interview with Michael Lynch, October 2005

6   The only result of a Davidson-Barniville cup match that has been recorded
     is that of December 1964, when Trinity won the trophy. TCD teams: 'A': Dr
     R. J. Burwood, P. R. Gardiner, P. Stocken, Miss D. Wood (subsequently Mrs
     Stocken); 'B': R. Irvine Andrews, Miss J. Brodie, Miss T. O'Connor, J. R. W.

Orange. UCD: 'A': M. Buckley, D. A. Scannell, E. MacNeill, P. Reynolds; 'B': J. Fitzgerald, A. Lennox, N. Fitzpatrick, J. Loughnane, D. Melody, C. Ward.

7 *English Bridge*, March 1967; article by J. A. Kelly. Also Kelly's *Irish Times* column, 9 February 1967. Kelly's team was completed by Ted O'Boyle, Eoin MacNeill and Des Scannell.

CHAPTER 24: DENIS JACKSON (P154–164)

1 The author, who made the suggestion, was a member of the organising committee for the event.
2 Interview with Michael Lynch, October 2005.
3 Minutes, IBU council meeting, 31 March 1968.
4 Information, Florence McGillicuddy (a Dublin delegate in 1972), November 2006.
5 Interview with P. C. Kiely, November 2005.
6 Minutes, IBU council meeting, 25 March 1973 and 22 July 1973.
7 The laws were updated in 1975 but there is no indication that the use of bidding boxes was taken into account.
8 It is believed in some circles that the Multi Two-Diamond convention originated with John Grummitt. Reese and Flint are credited with its creation. Robert Sheehan, who had an input in developing the convention, (see *Official Encyclopedia of Bridge*) when asked by the author in Verona in 2006 if he was aware of any input by Grummitt, said he was not aware of any but that it was possible. Shirlie Browne remembered Reese's visits to Northern Ireland during the 1960s when he discussed bridge, including 'something like the Multi' with Grummitt.
9 The practice of the host country meeting the entire cost was in place until the 1991 championships in Killarney. See Chapter 32.
10 Interview with Joe Moran, 24 September 2008.
11 Interview with M. Lynch, October 2005.

CHAPTER 25: THE COMMUNIST AND BOURGEOIS GAME OF BRIDGE (P163–165)

1 Bray and Blackrock Colleges congresses. Connolly wrote articles on directing, cf. *Irish Bridge Journal*, Vols. 1, 2 and 3, January to June 1959.
2 Seán MacDiarmada (or McDermott), one of the seven signatories of the Proclamation of the Irish Republic in 1916, was executed following the Rising, as indeed was James Connolly, Roddy's father.
3 *Roddy Connolly and the Struggle for Socialism in Ireland*, Charlie Maguire, Cork University Press, 2008.
4 He won on transfers from the Clann na Poblachta candidate, the well-known writer Aodh de Blacam.
5 *Irish Bridge Journal*, Vol. 1, No. 3, June 1959.
6 *Roddy Connolly and the Struggle for Socialism in Ireland*, Charlie McGuire, Cork University Press, 2008.

7   Connolly also reported from Oslo, 1969, and Estoril, 1970.
8   The story was first told to me by Michael Lynch, later confirmed by Des Deery.
9   Letter from Deery to the author, 2005.
10   Minutes, IBU council meeting, 1 May 1966.
11   Minutes, IBU council meeting, 5 June 1966.
12   Minutes, CBAI executive, 6 November 1966. No copies of the Bulletin seem to have survived. Also, CBAI executive, 14 January 1967.

CHAPTER 26: THE BUENOS AIRES AFFAIR AND OTHER IRREGULARITIES (P166–170)

1   The *Irish Times*, 6 June 1965.
2   *Story of an Accusation*, Terence Reese, Heinemann, Simon and Schuster, 1966
3   The *Irish Times*, 3 December 1966.
4   *The Great Bridge Scandal*, Alan Truscott, Yarborough 1969.
5   The other accuser was B. Jay Becker, Hayden's partner. Becker's daily column ran in the *Irish Times* until his death, when his son, Steve, continued it.
6   Irish Bridge Union council meeting, 30 April 1967.
7   The *Irish Times*, 14 September 1967.
8   Rixi Markus was one of the world's all-time great women players. She won ten European championships, three for Austria before the war, seven for Great Britain afterwards.
9   The *Irish Times*, 9 June 1965.
10   *The New York Times Bridge Book*, p 169. St Martin's Press, New York, 2002.
11   *My Lady Love, My Dove* by Roald Dahl, in the short-story collection *Someone Like You* (Alfred A. Knopf, New York, 1953)
12   Interview with Eoin O'Riordan, May 2002.

CHAPTER 28: A PERIOD OF DISQUIET – THE 1970S (P176–179)

1   Minutes of IBU annual meeting, 24 August 1969.
2   Letter from Deery to the author, 25 January 2006.
3   Deery; op. cit.
4   IBU Annual Report, 1968–69, by Grummitt and Jackson.
5   Minutes of IBU council meeting, Athlone, 28 March 1976.

CHAPTER 29: THE GLEESON ERA (P180–183)

1   Story related by the late Lt. Col. Jim Power to the author, late 1990s, and also by John Cunningham, September 2006.
2   All references to meetings are from the minute book of North Midland region covering meetings from November 1948 to January 1970, given to the author by John Cunningham in September 2006.

CHAPTER 30: THE LONG ROAD BACK TO CAMROSE (P184–192)

1   Referred to in CBAI AGM minutes, 10 June 1962.

2   Minutes, CBAI AGM, 10 June 1962.

3   Viscount Camrose was, in fact, Welsh. He was born William Berry.

4   Minutes, CBAI AGM, 10 June 1962.

5   The minutes of the Dublin region meeting have been lost, but Jack Kelly reported on the meeting in the *Irish Times*, 29 June 1968.

6   Minutes, CBAI AGM, 29 June 1968.

7   Minutes, IBU Council, 4 August 1968.

8   Minutes, CBAI AGM, 26 June 1971.

9   Minutes, CBAI executive, 18 December 1971.

10   Minutes, CBAI AGM, 24 June 1978.

11   Minutes, CBAI special general meeting, 29 April 1979.

12   Ibid.

13   Minutes, CBAI AGM, 21 June 1980.

14   It is unlikely that opposition to an all-Ireland team in the Camrose was ever articulated within the CBAI. It was certainly not recorded in minutes of meetings. However the aim of having an all-Ireland team in the Camrose had, by the early 1990s, been abandoned.

15   Peter Stocken, email to author, 21 October 2008.

16   England has won the Camrose forty-six times, Scotland fifteen (including two ties with England) and the Republic of Ireland five. Northern Ireland and Wales have yet to win.

CHAPTER 32: JOE MORAN'S CONTRIBUTION (P196–200)

1   Moran's first enterprise was to take over a builder's provider. He expanded his portfolio to include interests in several countries.

2   £125,000 (€156,000) was raised over a five-year period.

3   Seventy-three Irish voluntary helpers from all over the country, North and South, worked at the championships.

4   In Yokohama, Iceland, Poland and Sweden won gold, silver and bronze respectively, demonstrating the strength of European bridge.

5   Membership of the CBAI or, more correctly, affiliations, reached an all-time high of 35,377 in 1998.

6   The author of this book was appointed PRO and Press Officer of the CBAI in 1989.

7   Michael Lynch stood down as treasurer of the CBAI in 1991 and at the AGM Paul Porteous defeated Noel Hickey (Limerick) in a ballot for the position. At the same meeting, Una Walsh defeated the author of this book and Jim Agnew (Dublin) in a ballot for the position of honorary secretary. In the latter ballot, the voting for the most part followed the old demarcation lines of country v. Dublin.

CHAPTER 33: TECHNOLOGY AND DEVELOPMENTS IN THE 1980S (P201–203)

1   Conversations with Brian Lawlor and Joe Murray, September and October 2008.

2   The resolution was signed by Pa O'Flaherty, Hugh Hone, Barry Hogsett, Tom Gleeson, Peter Flynn, Marie Cummins, Nell Foley and Marie O'Sullivan. Only three regions were not represented among the signatories: Western, North-western and North Munster.

CHAPTER 34: GOVERNMENT AND BRIDGE (P204–207)

1   Letter from N. J. Neelis, Netherlandse Bridge Bond, 11 November 1975, and document from Swedish Bridge Federation, undated but relating to the 1975–76 fiscal year.

2   Letter addressed to the Minister for Education, 13 November 1977. The Department of Sport was at that time a subsection of the Department of Education.

3   The delegation which met Minister O'Rourke on 19 July 1988 was Joe Moran, Marie and Tom Gleeson, Donal Garvey and the author.

4   Letter from Andre Boekhorst, Netherlandse Bridge Bond, 9 July 1988.

5   Letter from Jose Damiani, 7 July 1988, with attached document from French Ministry for Sport, dated 6 May 1988.

6   The list of grant-aided bodies, published in annual reports of the Department of Education's sports section, include Clarecare, Comhaltas Ceolteóirí Éireann, Connemara West, Cumann na bhFiann, Gael Linn, Irish Countrywomen's Association, Irish Wild Bird Conservancy, Killala Community Council, North Tipperary Community Services and Tallaght Welfare Society.

7   The president of the CBAI in July 2001 was the author of this book. Meeting Treacy was his first official action after taking office.

8   Among the bridge centres which have received capital grants are Malahide, Tramore and Waterford.

9   Eric Pelly's successes at the table include the CBAI novice pairs championship, J. J. Murphy Cup, in 1985.

CHAPTER 35: HIGH JINKS (P208–214)

1   George Ryan's four novels: *No Time for Work, No Time for Sex, Vexed at His Own Funeral* and *Time for a Smile.* Privately published.

CHAPTER 37: PLAYERS AND PLAYS (P219–279)

1   13 high-card points was the minimum value for an opening bid at the time.

2   Interview, Ruth Giddings, October 2006.

3   *Irish Independent,* 29 September 1942.

4   Mrs Shirlie Davies, niece, in telephone conversation, November 2006

5   Following Mairéad's death, her niece, Sheila Murphy, retained the correspondence and other documents.

6   Paul McNulty, nephew, interview June 2006.

7   Her daughter, Rhona, married Denis McCarthy, well-known steward of the Turf Club. His brother, Peter, married the renowned soprano, and voice teacher, Veronica Dunne.

8   Believed to be a European record. It has since been equalled by Nicola Smith (England).

9   Tony Priday in his newspaper column. Reese also reported the deal.

10 Not the current magazine of the same name, which started in 1979.

11 The *Irish Times*, 5 October 1955.

12 MacHale's partner in the 1947 Quin Cup was Pádraig O'Dowd, son of Dr P. J. O'Dowd – well-known player and NPC of Irish teams.

13 Until 1976, Europeans were held every year except during Olympiad years: 1960, 1964, 1968, 1972 and 1976. From 1977, they were held every second year during the odd-numbered years, until 2002, when the European Bridge League changed them to the even-numbered years.

14 Conversation with Steen Möller, Salsomaggiore, June 2002.

15 The Canada Cup at Portmarnock, 1960, was won by Arnold Palmer and Sam Snead (USA).

16 The Office of Comptroller and Auditor General has employed a number of prominent bridge players, including Charlie O'Neill and Johnny Morgan, both Camrose players; Kevin Fowler, Jack Kelly, Paddy Graham, the last of whom started the Fanagan League in Dublin South; and John O'Riordan, currently in the office, who has represented South County Dublin in the Burke.

17 Per Jannersten in conversation with the author, Pau, France, June 2008.

18 Eamonn O'Nolan, nephew of the comedian Jimmy O'Dea, was with Kelly when he died. O'Nolan, who plays bridge, related the account of Kelly's last moments to the author, in Westport, November 2005. Kelly's obituary is to be found in *The British Bridge Almanack*.

19 FitzGibbon and Mesbur also had a six-year unbroken run on the Irish team from 1975 to 1980. (This represented five appearances, as the Europeans were scheduled only every second year from 1975.)

20 Mrs Woodhouse, who was in the legal profession, went to live in England.

21 Tom Healy emigrated to Canada.

22 Kathryn died in February 2009 following a long illness.

23 Much of the story of Team Ireland has been told in two books by Enda Murphy: *Silver for Ireland* and *A Bridge Too Far?* Published privately in 2006 and 2007, respectively.

24 In 2007 Tom Hanlon became a professional card player. See *A Bridge Too Far?* Tom Hanlon with Enda Murphy.

25 Each event, Malmo and Istanbul, went on for fifteen days, thirty days in total, an impossible demand for most working people.

26   The CBAI advertised trials for teams of six in 1953. Only one team entered – a group of five – so no trials took place.

27   The committee that made that decision consisted of Michael O'Connor, Clare Pippet and the author of this book.

28   FitzGibbon's wife, Kathryn, had been ill for some months. FitzGibbon and Mesbur were replaced by Pádraig and Micheál Ó Briain.

CHAPTER 38: THE DAWN OF THE NEW MILLENNIUM (P280–282)

1   In 1970, Peter Pigot won five majors, which included CBAI and IBU events.

2   Michael O'Connor, email to author, 4 February 2009.

3   Probably the best-known slogan in Guinness advertising is 'Guinness Is Good For You'.

Appendix A: CBAI and IBU Championships Winners

Note: The year given is the year ending the season: e.g. 1966 refers to the 1965/66 season; some competitions were played between September and December of the earlier year.

CBAI Championships

Individual, Open

1933	Gertrude McMeekin
1934	J. O'Neill
1935	J. O'Neill
1936	W. J. L. O'Connell
1937	W. J. L. O'Connell
1938	Jacqueline Prost
1939	Muriel Leech
1940	N. Peart
1941	Ina Hickey
1942	(not found)
1943	B. McDonagh
1944	R. Sheehan
1945	Kathleen Kavanagh
1946	Molly Fox
1947	Babs Hooper

The championship was abandoned after 1947.

Individual, Davidson Challenge Cup
Qualifying through Major Competitions

1942	F. T. Quin
1943	C. O'Neill
1944	C. H. Day

The championship was contested three times only.

Once-off National Pairs Championships

This championship was held to compensate for wartime loss of opportunity for provincial players.

1942	Geraldine McConkey, Mrs McHugh (Dundalk)

Open Teams, Holmes Wilson Cup

This competition was called the 'President's Cup' in 1934/35.

1934	Mairéad Crofts, J. O'Neill, Kathleen Lambert, B. L. Williams, H. William
1935	Kathleen Bowles, Mrs Colgan, Muriel Leech, Mrs McMunn
1936	Mairéad Crofts, J. O'Neill, H. J. Freehill, H. Williams
1937	Kathleen Lambert, Geraldine McConkey, D. R. and Violet Pigot
1938	E. O. Barry, P. Quinn, H. Fine, D. Rivlin
1939	Kathleen Bowles, Mrs Colgan, Flora MacLoone, Mabel Spiro
1940	E. O. Barry, P. Quinn, H. Fine, D. Rivlin
1941	Ina Hickey, F. McMenamin, T. D. Purcell, B. L. Williams
1942	H. Fine, D. Rivlin, P. Quinn, Cleo Roy
1943	J. J. Bastow, W. R. Bastow, J. A. Kelly, Kathleen Lambert
1944	J. Boylan, B. McDonagh, C. H. Day, R. J. Sheehan
1945	A. H. Davidson May McNulty, Flora McLoone, Elvina Spiro
1946	Geraldine McConkey, D. R. Pigot, H. Williams, B. L. Williams
1947	D. Egan, Ruth Giddings, Rita McNally, Lilly McDonough
1948	H. Bridburg, H. Elliott, J. Harold, J. Ormond
1949	E. O. Barry, P. Quinn, P. P. Donovan, D. Rivlin
1950	C. H. Day, G. Jackson, Ruth Giddings, R. Sheehan
1951	E. O. Barry, P. Quinn, D. Egan, W. J. L. O'Connell
1952	R. A. Belton, T. D. Purcell, P. P. Donovan, J. A. Kelly
1953	P. P. Donovan, Moreen McCarthy, D. A. Houlihan (Birr), P. Purcell
1954	M. Cohen, Mrs Cohen, F. W. O'Connell, M. F. O'Connell
1955	A. H. Davidson, J. P. MacHale, J. M. O'Sullivan, G. F. Read
1956	Ruth Giddings, May McNulty, Marcus Shrage, Elvina Spiro
1957	Mrs S. Barry, J. Curran, Mrs K. Braund, Mrs A. Sandys
1958	Ruth Giddings, May McNulty, M. Shrage, Elvina Spiro
1959	Eileen O'Sullivan, P. J. Pigot, M. Shrage, Elvina Spiro
1960	J. A Kelly, M. Shrage, Eileen O'Sullivan, Elvina Spiro
1961	E. O Barry, G. A. Holmes, F. W. O'Connell, M. F. O'Connell
1962	R. A Belton, T. D. Purcell, G. F. Read, M. Shrage
1963	G. Holmes, M. F. O'Connell, J. P. MacHale, G. Jackson
1964	J. Coman, J. Fitzgerald, Babs Hooper, Clare Lyne
1965	C. Kelleher, W. O'Grady, W. N. O'Leary, R. A. Twomey
1966	E. O. Barry, F. W. O'Connell, P. C. Kiely, D. McGrath
1967	G. Holmes, M. F. O'Connell. J. P. MacHale, P. J. Pigot
1968	G. Holmes, M. F. O'Connell. J. P. MacHale, P. J. Pigot
1969	Doreen Cairnduff, Anne Quinn, Rita McQueen, Marie Preston
1970	J. J. Bailey, E. J. Boland, S. Reilly, V. Tomek
1971	Doreen Cairnduff, Anne Quinn, Rita McQueen, Marie Preston
1972	R. P. de Barra, S. Reilly, G. Ryan, D. Dillon, Anne Murphy
1973	Des Deery, Eoin MacNeill, J. P. MacHale, P. J. Pigot

1974	Des Deery, Eoin MacNeill, J. P. MacHale, P. J. Pigot
1975	Des Deery, Eoin MacNeill, J. P. MacHale, P. J. Pigot
1976	Risteard de Barra, Sean Reilly, David Jackson, Adam Mesbur, Harry Torney
1977	Nick FitzGibbon, Adam Mesbur, David Jackson, Don Seligman
1978	Nick FitzGibbon, Adam Mesbur, David Jackson, Don Seligman
1979	Nick FitzGibbon, Adam Mesbur, David Jackson, Don Seligman
1980	Nick FitzGibbon, Adam Mesbur, David Jackson, Don Seligman
1981	Nick FitzGibbon, Adam Mesbur, David Jackson, Pat Walshe
1982	Nick FitzGibbon, Adam Mesbur, David Jackson, Pat Walshe
1983	Aidan Cleary, Ena Cleary, D. A. Houlihan (Ennis), P. Quinn (Ennis)
1984	Rory Boland, Denis McGrath, Marie Coveney, Joan Crowley
1985	Hastings Campbell, Brian Senior, Sam Hall, Monty Rosenberg
1986	Nick FitzGibbon, Adam Mesbur, T.G.(Greer) Mackenzie, Pat Walshe
1987	Ray Brennan, Paul Scannell, Gay Keaveney, P.F.(Paddy) Walsh
1988	Paddy Byrne, Michael MacDonagh, Sean Gillen, Sean Glynn
1989	Rory Boland, Brian Senior, Joe MacHale, Peter Pigot
1990	Eddie Fitzgerald, Rory Timlin, Gay Keaveney, Paddy Walsh
1991	Ray Brennan, Rory Timlin, Gay Keaveney, Paddy Walsh
1992	Enda Glynn, Rory Timlin, Gay Keaveney, Michael McGloughlin
1993	Joe MacHale, Ranald Milne, W. F. Maclachlan, Don Seligman
1994	Maria Barry, P. J. Barry, T. R. Gibson, David Jackson
1995	Maria Barry, Pat Barry, Tom Gibson, David Jackson
1996	John Carroll, Tommy Garvey, Hilary Dowling Long, Rebecca O'Keeffe
1997	Alex Montwill, Ann Montwill, Aileen O'Keeffe, John H. O'Keeffe
1998	John Carroll, Tommy Garvey, Donal Garvey, Micheál Ó Briain
1999	Tom Hanlon, Hugh McGann, Gay Keaveney, Rory Timlin
2000	Donal Garvey, Micheál Ó Briain, Pádraig Ó Briain, Tomás Roche
2001	Manus Burke, Cearbhaill Ó Dálaigh, Ciarán Coyne, David Walsh
2002	Nick FitzGibbon, Adam Mesbur, Niall Tóibín, Pat Walshe
2003	Tom Hanlon, Hugh McGann, Pat McDevitt, Rory Timlin
2004	Adam Dunn, Gay Keaveney, Peter Goodman, Adrian Thomas
2005	Peter Clifford, Mary Lindopp, Karel de Raeymaeker, Anna Onishuk
2006	Peter Goodman, Adrian Thomas, Gay Keaveney, Les Steel
2007	Thomas MacCormac, B.J. O'Brien, Padraig Ó Briain, Peter Pigot
2008	Peter Goodman, Adrian Thomas, Gay Keaveney, Martin Jones
2009	D. Garvey, T. Garvey, A. Mesbur, P. Walshe

WOMEN'S TEAMS, MCMENAMIN BOWL

1950	Doreen Cairnduff, Jackie Prost, Lily McDonagh, Rita McNally
1951*	Ruth Giddings, Geraldine McConkey, Ina McMenamin, Eileen O'Sullivan Tied with: Charlotte Fowler, May McNulty, Alice Mahon, Eileen O'Doherty
1952	Ruth Giddings, Geraldine McConkey, Ina McMenamin, Eileen O'Sullivan

1953	Kay Byrne, Alice Mahon, Charlotte Fowler, May McNulty
1954	Doreen Carinduff, Jackie Prost, Lily McDonagh, Rita McNally
1955	Charlotte Fowler, Eileen O'Sullivan, Ruth Giddings, May McNulty
1956	Cleo Fellows, Eileen O'Sullivan, Kay O'Sullivan, Ann Quinn
1957	Mrs W. Dunne, Babs Hooper, Clare Lyne, Lily Maguire
1958	Alice Mahon, Eileen O'Doherty, Ina McMenamin, Molly O'Carroll
1959	Geraldine McConkey, Moreen McCarthy, Ruth Giddings, May McNulty
1960	Geraldine McConkey, Ina McMenamin, Eileen O'Sullivan, Elvina Spiro
1961	Ruth Giddings, May McNulty, Charlotte Fowler, Rita McQueen
1962	Geraldine McConkey, Ina McMenamin, Alice Mahon, Molly O'Carroll
1963	Geraldine McConkey, Ina McMenamin, Alice Mahon, Molly O'Carroll
1964	Kathleen Banks, Molly Jones, Kay O'Sullivan, Anne Quinn
1965	Sonya Britton, Lily Maguire, Ruth Giddings, Barbara Seligman,
1966	Alice Mahon, Eileen O'Sullivan, Ina McMenamin, Molly O'Carroll
1967	Sonya Britton, Lily Maguire, Ruth Giddings, Barbara Seligman
1968	Kathleen Banks, Kay O'Sullivan, Helen Daly, Sheila Kirwan
1969	Doreen Cairnduff, Anne Quinn, Cleo Fellows, Kay O'Sullivan,
1970	Sonya Britton, Lily Maguire, Ruth Giddings, Barbara Seligman,
1971	Doreen Cairnduff, Anne Quinn, Cleo Fellows, Eileen O'Doherty
1972	Doreen Cairnduff, Anne Quinn, Cleo Fellows, Eileen O'Doherty
1973	Doreen Cairnduff, Anne Quinn, Cleo Fellows, Eileen O'Doherty
1974	Maria Barry, Allie Pigot, Sonya Britton, Barbara Seligman
1975	Nell Arnold, Ruth Giddings, Amandita Nolan, Mary Trench
1976	Helen Boland, Mena O'Flaherty, Kay Downes, Marie Moran
1977	Maria Barry, Anne Quinn, Ruth Giddings, Barbara Seligman
1978	Kathleen Banks, Anne Quinn, Ruth Giddings, Barbara Seligman
1979	Kathleen Banks, Anne Quinn, Ruth Giddings, Barbara Seligman
1980	Bernie Gannon, Anne Johnson, Elva Gannon, Pauline Maguire
1981	Chris Doyle, Joan Ryan, Maureen Ryder, Maura O'Farrell
1982	Sonya Britton, Ruth Giddings, Eileen O'Doherty, Anne Quinn
1983	Valerie Hand, Mary Trench, Ann Montwill, Aileen O'Keeffe
1984	Helen Boland, Marie Moran, Peggy Shanahan, Agnes Costello
1985	Joan Crowley, Rosemary Ennis, Ruth Giddings, Barbara Seligman
1986	Gráinne Barton, Anne Dillon, Diane Senior, Teresa Rigney
1987	Kathryn FitzGibbon, Ruth Giddings, Elva Gannon, Pauline Maguire
1988	Anna Binley, Petra O'Neill, Una Hogan, Teresa Scanlon
1989	Valerie Hand, Anne Johnson, Ann Montwill, Aileen O'Keeffe
1990	Valerie Hand, Anne Johnson, Ann Montwill, Aileen O'Keeffe
1991	Nancy Coogan, Sheila O'Dwyer, Pat MacMahon, Pat Ryan
1992	Maria Barry, Ruth Giddings, Barbara Seligman, Gráinne Barton
1993	Maria Barry, Barbara Seligman, Gráinne Barton, Anne Dillon
1994	Anna Binley, Petra O'Neill, Pat MacMahon, Pat Ryan
1995	Maria Barry, Anne Johnson, Gráinne Barton, Anne Dillon
1996	Helen Carroll, Jill Kulchycky, Hilary Dowling Long, Rebecca O'Keeffe

1997	Helen Carroll, Jill Kulchycky, Hilary Dowling Long, Rebecca O'Keeffe
1998	Helen Carroll, Jill Kulchycky, Hilary Dowling Long, Rebecca O'Keeffe
1999	Pat MacMahon, Pat Ryan, Pat Meehan, Petra O'Neill
2000	Ena Cleary, Maureen Griffin, Marie Hanrahan, Bríd Kirby
2001	Gráinne Barton, Rosemary Ennis, Kathryn FitzGibbon, Barbara Seligman
2002	Ena Cleary, Mary Finn, Maureen Griffin, Bríd Kirby
2003	Grace Finegan, Clare Pippet, Heidi Lillis, Teresa Rigney
2004	Hilary Ferguson, Antoinette McGee, Bernie Rafferty, Liz Taaffe
2005	Grace Finegan, Miriam McConville, Aileen O'Keeffe, Mary Trench
2006	Ursula Devine, Sandra Newell, Mary Lindopp, Anna Onishuk,
2007	Carol-Ann Cummins, Maureen Pattinson, Pat McMahon, Pat Ryan
2008	Ciara Burns, Mary Finn, Ann Murphy, Anna Onishuk
2009	Joan Kenny, Emer Joyce, Jill Kulchycky, Teresa Rigney

* The tie for first place in 1951 was split for the purpose of awarding the prize but the two teams shared the championship. Records subsequently referred to 'joint holders'.

MEN'S TEAMS, GERALDINE TROPHY

1961	R. Belton, J. A . Kelly, G. F. Read, Dr M. Shrage
1962	E. MacNeill, P. MacNeill, E. A. McArdle, C. J. Sweeney
1963	J. A. Kelly, T. D. Purcell, G. F. Read and M. Shrage
1964	G. A. Holmes, M. F. O'Connell, J. P. MacHale, P. J. Pigot
1965	G. A. Holmes, M. F. O'Connell, J. P. MacHale, P. J. Pigot
1966	G. A. Holmes, M. F. O'Connell, J. P. MacHale, P. J. Pigot
1967	G. A. Holmes, M. F. O'Connell, J. P. MacHale, P. J. Pigot
1968	D. Deery, E. MacNeill, J. P. MacHale, P. J. Pigot
1969	D. Deery, E. MacNeill, J. P. MacHale, P. J. Pigot
1970	D. Deery, E. MacNeill, J. P. MacHale, P. J. Pigot
1971	A. T. R. Anderson, P. J. Barry, R. P. de Barra, N. K. FitzGibbon
1972	A. T. R. Anderson, P. J. Barry, R. P. de Barra, N. K. FitzGibbon
1973	D. Dillon, C. J. O'Hara, F. W. O'Connell, M. F. O'Connell,
1974	D. Dillon, S. Reilly, C. J. O'Hara, M. Shrage
1975	D. Deery, E. MacNeill, J. P. MacHale, P. J. Pigot
1976	N. K. FitzGibbon, A, Mesbur, D. A. Jackson, D. L. Seligman, R. Sai
1977	N. K. FitzGibbon, A, Mesbur, D. A. Jackson, D. L. Seligman, R. Sai
1978	D. Deery, E. MacNeill, J. P. MacHale, P. J. Pigot
1979	D. Garvey, P. Ó Briain, M. Ó Briain, P Walshe
1980	N. K. FitzGibbon, A, Mesbur, D. A. Jackson, D. L. Seligman
1981	N. K. FitzGibbon, A, Mesbur, D. A. Jackson, P. Walshe
1982	D. A. Jackson, P. F. Walsh, W. F. Maclachlan, D. L. Seligman
1983	R. Brennan, T. Walsh, E. M. Perrette, D. Ryan
1984	R. de Barra, D. A. Jackson, G. Keaveney, P. F. Walsh

1985	R. Boland, P. Walshe, N. FitzGibbon, A. Mesbur
1986	K. Barry, T. Gibson, D. A. Jackson, S. Sheehan
1987	H. Campbell, M. Rosenberg, B. Senior, P. Walshe
1988	T. R. Gibson, D. A. Jackson, M. F. McGloughlin, A. O'Sullivan
1989	D. Garvey, M. Ó Briain, G. Keaveney, P. F. Walsh
1990	D. Garvey, M. Ó Briain, G. Keaveney, P. F. Walsh
1991	N. Kennedy, D. A. Scannell, M. F. McGloughlin, A. O'Sullivan
1992	R. Boland, P. Walshe, N. FitzGibbon, A. Mesbur
1993	T. Hanlon, H. McGann, D. O'Gorman, T. Walsh
1994	E. Glynn, R. Timlin, G. Keaveney, P. F. Walsh
1995	R. Boland, P. Walshe, N. FitzGibbon, A. Mesbur
1996	P. Barry, D. A. Jackson, R. Timlin, P. F. Walsh
1997	E. J. Fitzgerald, M. MacDonagh, D. O'Gorman, T. Walsh
1998	T. Hanlon, H. McGann, N. Tóibín, P. Walshe
1999	T. Hanlon, H. McGann, J. Carroll, N. Toibin
2000	R. Boland, A. Mesbur, T. Hanlon, H. McGann
2001	J. Carroll, P. Ó Briain, M. MacDonagh, B. J. O'Brien
2002	E. Fitzgerald, E. Glynn, M. MacDonagh, R. Timlin
2003	P. Delaney, E. Galligan, T. MacCormac, P. Ó Briain
2004	M. McAuliffe, D. A. Scannell, J. P. MacHale, Alex Montwill
2005	H. Curran, M. MacDonagh, J. Heneghan, Terry Walsh
2006	J. Carroll, D. Walsh, T. Hanlon, G. Keaveney,
2007	K. de Raeymaeker, B. J. O'Brien, M. Ó Briain, P. Ó Briain
2008	C. Coyne, H. Curran, J. Heneghan, M. MacDonagh
2009	K. de Raeymaeker, T. Walsh, P. Goodman, T. MacCormac

TEAM CHAMPIONSHIP, KELBURNE CUP

1936	E. O. Barry, P. Quinn, A. G. Kibble, G. M. Linzell, Mabel Spiro
1937	Kathleen Lambert, Geraldine McConkey, D. R. and Violet Pigot
1938	Kathleen Lambert, Geraldine McConkey, D. R. and Violet Pigot
1939	H. G.Freehill, Harold Williams, Joseph and Mairéad O'Neill
1940	E. O. Barry, P. Quinn, H. Fine, D. Rivlin,
1941	Ina Hickey, F. McMenamin, G. M. Purcell, T. D. Purcell
1942	J. M. O'Sullivan, Eileen O'Sullivan, C. H. Day, May McNulty
1943	H. Fine, Mairéad O'Neill, Philip Quinn, Cleo Roy
1944	A. H. Davidson, May McNulty, N. Peart, P. Powell
1945	A. H. Davidson, May McNulty, Flora McLoone, P. Powell
1946	A. H. Davidson, May McNulty, Flora McLoone, N. Peart
1947	A.H.Davidson, May McNulty, Flora McLoone, N. Peart
1948	Geraldine McConkey, P. J. O'Dowd, Eileen O'Doherty, P. McKenna
1949	J. Gayer, W. Whitney, Charles and Mrs. Heron
1950	J. Gayer, W. Whitney, Charles and Mrs. Heron
1951	J. J. Bastow, J .A. Kelly, P. P. Donovan, T. D. Purcell

311

1952	J. J. Bastow, J .A. Kelly, P. P. Donovan, T. D. Purcell
1953	T. Brick, M. O'Brien, J. Kelly (Eniscorthy), S. Lynch,
1954	D. Egan G. Read, J. P. MacHale, J. O'Sullivan,
1955	J. J. Bastow, T. D. Purcell, R. Belton, J. A. Kelly
1956	Moreen McCarthy, H. Williams, Supt. J. Ryan, W. Kervick
1957	Mrs Branigan, A. Lund, Miss D. Kelly, Miss E. Kelly
1958	E. O. Barry, J. Coakley, F. W. O'Connell, M. F. O'Connell
1959	Moreen McCarthy, H. Williams, W. Kervick, E. J. O'Boyle
1960	Cleo Fellows, P. O'Dowd, K. Fowler, T. Murray
1961	Cleo Fellows, P. O'Dowd, K. Fowler, T. Murray
1962	E. O. Barry, J. K. Coakley, M. F. O'Connell, G. Holmes
1963	R. Belton, J. A. Kelly, T. D. Purcell, E. O'Boyle
1964	J. P. MacHale, P. Pigot, G. Read, M. Shrage
1965	J. P. MacHale, P. Pigot, G. Read, M. Shrage
1966	E. Boland, D. Seligman, Ruth Giddings, B. Seligman
1967	J. A. Kelly, E. J. O'Boyle, E. MacNeill, D. G. Scannell,
1968	P. Fitzgerald, D. Seligman, Ruth Giddings, B. Seligman
1969	J. P. MacHale, P. Pigot, G. Read, M. Shrage
1970	J. P. MacHale, P. Pigot, G. Read, M. Shrage
1971	J. P. MacHale, P. Pigot, G. Read, M. Shrage
1972	P. Barrett, P. J. Barry, S. Glynn, A. Kavanagh
1973	P. Barrett, P. J. Barry, S. Glynn, A. Kavanagh
1974	J. P. MacHale, P. J. Pigot, C. J. O'Hara, M. Shrage,
1975	P. Barrett, A. Kavanagh, Ruth Giddings, Geraldine Maguire,
1976	R. de Barra, S. Reilly, P. D. Fitzgerald, D. A. Jackson, H. Tormey
1977	Alex Montwill, Ann Montwill, Aileen O'Keeffe, John H. O'Keeffe
1978	Doreen Cairnduff, J. Godden, Nellie Cotter, Elizabeth Dowling
1979	D. Dillon, M. F. O'Connell, D. McGrath, J. McKeon
1980	J. Cunningham, T. Gleeson, Nuala Walsh, P. F. Walsh
1981	D. Dillon, M. F. O'Connell, D. McGrath, J. McKeon
1982	Sonya Britton N. Kennedy, Rosemary Ennis, N. Tóibín
1983	R. Boland, N. Kennedy, Rosemary Ennis, N. Tóibín
1984	E. Glynn, G. Keaveney, P. Scannell, R. Timlin, P. F. Walsh
1985	P. Byrne, Fr Sweeney, J. McIntyre, P. McLoone
1986	E. Glynn, G. Keaveney, P. Scannell, R. Timlin
1987	E. Balfe, D. Scully, P. Kelly (Kells), J. Ryder
1988	R. Fitzgerald, Valerie Hand, Alex Montwill, Ann Montwill
1989	Heidi Lillis, M. McGloughlin, G. Rafferty, T. Rigney
1990	Angela Hickey, Noel Hickey, B. Kirby, M. Hanrahan
1991	E. Glynn, G. Keaveney, R. Timlin, P. Scannell
1992	E. Glynn, G. Keaveney, R. Timlin, P. Scannell
1993	J. Cunningham, T. Hanlon, E. Fitzgerald, M. MacDonagh
1994	Anna Glynn, Sean Glynn, M. Hession, P. F. Walsh
1995	Gráinne Barton, N. Kennedy, N. Tóibín, P. Walshe
1996	E. Glynn, G. Keaveney, M. Hession, R. Timlin

1997	E. Glynn, G. Keaveney, P. Scannell, R. Timlin
1998	J. Connolly, P. Connolly, R. Masterson, S. Masterson
1999	R. Boland, T. Hanlon, J. Carroll. N. Tóibín
2000	E. Fitzgerald, E. Glynn M. Hession, G. Keaveney, R. Timlin
2001	Mark Burke, Pat Quinn, G. Connolly, P. Liston
2002	P. Delaney, E. Galligan, P. Kelly, D. Terry
2003	R. Boland, D. O'Gorman, Anne Dillon, Denis Dillon
2004	J. Carroll, P. Ó Briain, T. MacCormac, R. McMaugh
2005	Ger Connolly, Pat Liston, Bob Pattinson, Pat Quinn
2006	R. Milne, B. J. O'Brien, M. Moran, P. Pigot
2007	R. Milne, B. J. O'Brien, P. Pigot, T. Walsh
2008	K. de Raeymaeker, B. Sharkey, J. Heneghan, M. MacDonagh.

OPEN PAIRS, SHAMROCK LODGE TROPHY

1963	Babs Hooper, Clare Lyne
1964	Babs Hooper, Clare Lyne
1965	T. Gleeson, T. McCormack
1966	J. A. Kelly, E. J. O'Boyle
1967	J. A. Kelly, E. J. O'Boyle
1968	W. Cashen, D. T. Seale
1969	P. D. Fitzgerald, Ruth Giddings,
1970	P. J. Barry, D. A. Houlihan (Birr)
1971	N. K. FitzGibbon, Diana Woodhouse
1972	M. McGloughlin, A. Mesbur
1973	Anna Glynn, J. Wynne,
1974	N.K. FitzGibbon, A. Mesbur
1975	R. Kilduff, J. Wynne,
1976	T. Gibson M. McGloughlin,
1977	G. Keaveney, R. Timlin
1978	J. Cunningham, T. Gleeson,
1979	Eileen O'Doherty, Anne Quinn
1980	Chris Doyle, H. McDermott
1981	Anne Romaine, Pat Meehan
1982	P. J. Barry, B. Dolan
1983	P. F. Walsh, P. Walshe
1984	R. Boland, D. Deery
1985	Abandoned - fire in S'rock Lodge Hotel
1986	S. Dowling, Margaret Morgan
1987	R. Boland, G. Keaveney
1988	E. Fitzgerald, M. MacDonagh
1989	E. Fitzgerald, M. MacDonagh
1990	E. Fitzgerald, M. MacDonagh
1991	E. Fitzgerald, M. MacDonagh
1992	J. Cahill, M. McGloughlin

MIXED TEAMS, COEN TROPHY

1995	Kathryn and Nick FitzGibbon, Barbara and Don Seligman
1997	Hilary Dowling Long, John Carroll, Rebecca O'Keeffe, Tommy Garvey
1999	Carol Anne Cummins, John Noonan, Carmel Higgins, Joe MacHale
2001	Diane Greenwood, Eamonn Galligan, Iva Loncar, Dario Filjar
2003	Anne-Marie Horan, John Carroll, Anna Onishuk, Karel de Raeymaeker,
2004	Ena and Aidan Cleary, Jeannie Fitzgerald, Gordon Lessells
2005	Pauline Maguire, Fred Barry, Miriam McConville, Paul Porteous
2006	Heidi Lillis, Michael McGloughlin, Teresa Rigney, Gay Keaveney
2007	Anne-Marie Horan-Carroll, John Carroll, Anna Onishuk, Karel de Raeymaeker
2008	Ena and Aidan Cleary, Liz Taaffe, Michael MacDonagh
2009	Anne Dillon, C. Holland, Mary Finn, S. Ó Lubaigh

WOMEN'S PAIRS, JACKSON CUP

1932	Muriel Leech, Mrs McMunn
1933	Miss Kelly, Mrs Miley
1934	Mrs Holmes Wilson, Mrs Shortt
1935	Mrs Bowles, Mrs Colgan
1936	Mrs Bowles, Mrs Colgan
1937	Mrs Molly O'Donnell, Mrs Nan O'Mara
1938	Mrs Fitzgerald, May McNulty
1939	Kathleen Bowles, Mrs Colgan
1940	Kathleen Bowles, Mrs Colgan
1941	Flora McLoone, Frances Morgan
1942	Maureen Corboy, Mary Duggan
1943	Mrs Holmes Wilson, Mrs D. R. Pigot
1944	May McNulty, Mrs. Prost
1945	Kathleen Lambert, Mrs. Sierse
1946	Ina McMenamin, May McNulty
1947	M. Ní Thuama, R. O'Brien
1948	Alice Mahon, Eileen O'Doherty
1949	Charlotte Fowler, May McNulty
1950	Moreen McCarthy, Mrs. W.H.Milligan
1951	Babs Hooper, Rita McNally
1952	Babs Hooper, Rita McNally
1953	May McNulty, Eileen O'Sullivan
1954	Miss V. Dunne, Cleo Fellows
1955	Moreen McCarthy, Geraldine McConkey
1956	Babs Hooper, Frances Morgan
1957	Babs Hooper, Frances Morgan
1958	Geraldine McConkey, Ina McMenamin
1959	Mrs W. Dunne, Lily Maguire

1960	Kathleen Banks, Molly Jones
1961	Nellie Cotter, Miss V. Dunne
1962	Kay O'Sullivan, Anne Quinn
1963	Alice Mahon, Eileen O'Doherty
1964	Kay O'Sullivan, Anne Quinn
1965	Ina Byrne, Molly Jones
1966	Doreen Cairnduff, Anne Quinn
1967	Geraldine McConkey, Eileen O'Sullivan
1968	Doreen Cairnduff, Anne Quinn
1969	Ruth Giddings, Barnbara Seligman
1970	Ruth Giddings, Barbara Seligman
1971	Ruth Giddings, Barbara Seligman
1972	Miss J. Connolly, Miss M. Murphy
1973	Moreen McCarthy, Eileen O'Doherty
1974	Anne Hayden, Geraldine Rafferty
1975	Amandita Nolan, Mary Trench
1976	Amandita Nolan, Mary Trench
1977	Rita McQueen, Molly O'Carroll
1978	Doreen Cairnduff, Marie Preston
1979	Ruth Giddings, Barbara Seligman
1980	Nellie Cotter, Rita McQueen
1981	Una McLaughlin, Rita McQueen
1982	Chris Doyle, Kay Murphy
1983	Ann Montwill, Aileen O'Keeffe
1984	Ruth Giddings, Barbara Seligman
1985	Pat MacMahon, Pat Ryan
1986	Anne Montwill, Aileen O'Keeffe
1987	Grace Finegan, Heidi Lillis
1988	Joan Crowley, Rosemary Ennis
1989	Carmel Barnes, Eileen Hurley
1990	Maria Barry, Barbara Seligman
1991	Maria Barry, Barbara Seligman
1992	Carol McCarthy, Imelda McCarthy
1993	Margo English, Miriam McConville
1994	Helen Carroll. Mamie MacCormac
1995	Lily McRory, Maura Slattery
1996	Emer Joyce, Clare Pippet
1997	Hilary Dowling Long, Rebecca O'Keeffe
1998	Hilary Dowling Long, Rebecca O'Keeffe
1999	Kitty Long, Catherine Murphy
2000	Marie Hanrahan, Bríd Kirby
2001	Ena Cleary, Anna Glynn
2002	Patricia Kelly, Sandra Newell
2003	Hilary Dowling Long, Anne-Marie Horan

2004	Ena Cleary, Mary Finn
2005	Grace Finegan, Bríd Kemple
2006	Mary Lindopp Anna Onishuk,
2007	Hilary Dowling Long, A. M. Horan-Carroll
2008	Maureen Walsh, Mgt. Winters
2009	Ciara Burns, Mary Finn

MEN'S PAIRS, REVINGTON CUP

1936	H. G. Freehill, H. Williams
1937	J. F. Murphy, W. J. L. O'Connell
1938	H. Fine, D. Vard
1939	H. Fine, D. Vard
1940	N. L. Peart, T. D. Purcell
1941	N. L. Peart, T. D. Purcell
1942	A. H. Davidson and P. Powell
1943	H. Fine, J. Lynch
1944	J. W. Burke, T. P. Ryder
1945	N. L. Peart, T. D. Purcell
1946	J. W. Burke, T. P. Ryder
1947	H. Bridberg, H. S. Elliott
1948	R. Belton, J. A. Kelly
1949	P. P. Donovan, David Rivlin
1950	H. Bridberg and H. S. Elliott
1951	R. J. Sheehan, M. Shrage
1952	E. O. Barry, M. Shrage
1953	J. A. Kelly, T. D. Purcell
1954	T. Dunbar, M. McDevitt
1955	E. O. Barry, D. A. Houlihan
1956	G. F. Read, M. Shrage
1957	G. F. Read, M. Shrage
1958	J. J. Bastow, T. D. Purcell
1959	J. J. Bastow, T. D. Purcell
1960	D. A. Houlihan (Birr), L. Sheeran
1961	T. D. Purcell, M. Shrage
1962	J. P. MacHale, P. J. Pigot
1963	J. P. MacHale, P. J. Pigot
1964	A. Drewery, M. Lynch
1965	G. F. Read, M. Shrage
1966	G. Ryan, D. L. Stokes
1967	J. P. MacHale, P. J. Pigot
1968	R. Barry, D. Seligman
1969	D. Deery, E. McNeill
1970	C. Cunningham, H. Hartnett

1971	J. Coman, P. C. Kiely
1972	W. Cashen, D. T. Seale
1973	N. K. FitzGibbon, A. H. Johnson
1974	P. J. Barry, M. Shrage
1975	N. K. FitzGibbon, A. Mesbur
1976	M. McGloughlin, D. G. Scannell
1977	L. F. Sheeran, M. Shrage
1978	K. Murphy, D. Scully
1979	J. Hearn, P. MacNeill
1980	G. Keaveney, P. Walshe
1981	G. Keaveney, P. Walshe
1982	G. Keaveney, P. Walshe
1983	P. Kelly, R. Sai
1984	W. F. Maclachlan, D. L. Seligman,
1985	S. Burgess, S. O Lubaigh
1986	R. Boland, P. F. Walsh
1987	S. Gillen, M. MacDonagh
1988	E. MacNeill, D. G. Scannell
1989	M. Burke, G. Lessells
1990	G. Keaveney, R. Timlin
1991	J. Comyn, Andrew Cooke
1992	R. Boland, A. Mesbur
1993	Andrew Cooke, B. J. O'Brien
1994	E. Fitzgerald, M. MacDonagh
1995	P. J. O'Dea, Y. Yuan
1996	J. Carroll, T. Garvey
1997	J. Carroll, T. Garvey
1998	T. Hanlon, H. McGann
1999	T. Hanlon, H. McGann
2000	J. Carroll, T. Garvey
2001	B. Pattinson, L. Walsh
2002	M. McGloughlin, S. O Lubaigh
2003	C. Coyne, D. Walsh
2004	T. Hanlon, G. Keaveney
2005	D. MacAonghusa, R. Timlin
2006	T. Hanlon, G. Keaveney
2007	Liam McKay, John Phelan
2008	K.de Raeymaeker, T. Walsh
2009	R. Fitzgerald, J. McAndrew

MIXED PAIRS, SPIRO CUP

1937	Mairéad Crofts, Joseph O'Neill
1938	Mabel Spiro, David Rivlin
1939	Mairéad (Crofts) and Joseph O'Neill

1940	Mrs. H. J. Birmingham, D. J. Murphy
1941	Frances Morgan, G. M. Purcell
1942	Ina Hickey, Gerry Purcell
1943	Flora McLoone, Patrick Lynch
1944	Mairéad O'Neill, B. L. Williams
1945	Mrs P. J. Gallagher, John Morgan
1946	Ina Hickey, T. D. Purcell
1947	Miss F. Slaney, Hugh Hackett
1948	Flora McLoone, Noel Peart
1949	Flora McLoone, Noel Peart
1950	Supt Hughes and Mrs Hughes
1951	Ina McMenamin, Jimmy Bastow
1952	Frances Jennings, J. J. O'Grady
1953	Elvina Spiro, Marcus Shrage
1954	Ina McMenamin, T. D. Purcell
1955	Ina McMenamin, Michael O'Connell
1956	Ruth Giddings, Harry Elliott
1957	Ruth Giddings, Harry Elliott
1958	Doreen Cairnduff, Harry Bridburg
1959	Ina McMenamin, Gerry Read
1960	Ruth Giddings, Harry Elliott
1961	Ruth Giddings, Harry Elliott
1962	Mrs G. W. Browne, J. A. Kelly
1963	Ruth Giddings, Peter Pigot
1964	Barbara and Don Seligman
1965	Ruth Giddings, Peter Pigot
1966	Molly Jones, Eoin O'Riordan
1967	Mary Clare Riordan, Denis McGrath
1968	Allie and Peter Pigot
1969	Lily Maguire, Eoin O'Riordan
1970	Allie and Peter Pigot
1971	Eileen O'Doherty, George Ryan
1972	Nell Arnold, Jim Hearn
1973	Maria Barry, Joe McHale
1974	Ruth Giddings, Sean Sheehan
1975	Maria Barry, D. G. Scannell
1976	Kathleen O'Keane, P. C. Kiely
1977	Ruth Giddings, Arthur Kavanagh
1978	Sonya Britton, N. K. FitzGibbon
1979	Anne Quinn, Eoin MacNeill
1980	Rosemary Ennis, Pat Walshe
1981	Sonya Britton, Brian Dolan
1982	Pauline Maguire, Marcus Shrage
1983	Shirlie Browne, Paddy Kelly

1984	Joan Crowley, Rory Boland
1985	Clare Pippet, Laur Sheeran
1986	Heidi Lillis, M. F. McGloughlin
1987	Maureen Ryder, Malcolm Ryder
1988	Gráinne Barton, Pat Walshe
1989	Heidi Lillis, M. F. McGloughlin
1990	Diane Sloan, David Greenwood
1991	Elizabeth Dowling, Walter Maclachlan
1992	Kathryn and Nick FitzGibbon
1993	Bernie Lynch, D. A. Scannell
1994	Diane Sloan, David Greenwood
1995	Mary and Tomás Roche
1996	Teresa Rigney, Niall Tóibín
1997	Mary Trench, Paul Porteous
1998	Catherine Dowling Long, Eamonn Martin
1999	Miriam McConville, Rameen Sai
2000	Bernie Rafferty, James Heneghan
2001	Bernie Lynch, D. A. Scannell
2002	Anne Murphy, D. A. Scannell
2003	Hilary Dowling Long, Thomas MacCormac
2004	Anna Onishuk, Karel de Raeymaeker
2005	Mamie MacCormac, B. J. O'Brien
2006	A. Onishuk, K. de Raeymaeker
2007	Maureen and Bob Pattinson
2008	Hilary (Dowling Long) McDonagh, Thomas MacCormac
2009	Lucy and J. Phelan

PAIRS CHAMPIONSHIP, DAVIDSON CUP

There was some overlapping of seasons, resulting in two competitions being held in 1943.

1933	L. Abrahamson, Mrs Sharpe
1934	Johnny Morgan, C. O'Neill
1935	Kathleen Bowles, Mrs Colgan
1936	E. O. Barry, P. Quinn
1937	H. Fine, D. Rivlin
1938	B. E. Ebrill, F. Quin
1939	Denis and Maureen Corboy
1940	E. O. Barry, P. Quinn
1941	H. Fine, D. Rivlin,
1942	Ina Hickey, F. McMenamin
1943	J. Lynch, R. Sheehan
	Geraldine McConkey, D. R. Pigot

1944	C. H. Day, R. Sheehan
1945	F. W. O'Connell, W. J. L. O'Connell
1946	A. H. Davidson, May McNulty,
1947	P. Burke, M. J. Martin
1948	P. V. Carson, Moreen McCarthy,
1949	P. P. Donovan, D. Rivlin
1950	Ruth Giddings, May McNulty
1951	R. Belton, J. A. Kelly
1952	R. Belton, J. A. Kelly
1953	Mrs O. G. Giddings, May McNulty
1954	R. Belton, J. A. Kelly
1955	Moreen McCarthy, D. A. Houlihan
1956	Rita McLoughlin, Supt. S. Murphy,
1957	P. D. Fitzgerald, P. J. Pigot,
1958	P. Georgalas, Julius Orman,
1959	Ruth Giddings, May McNulty
1960	Ruth Giddings, May McNulty
1961	Geraldine McConkey, Ina McMenamin
1962	F. Fine, D. L. Stokes
1963	G. Holmes, M. F. O'Connell,
1964	Nellie Cotter, L. Shanahan
1965	Ruth Giddings, Barbara Seligman
1966	Geraldine McConkey, Eileen O'Sullivan
1967	Ruth Giddings, Barbara Seligman
1968	P. J. Barry, S. Reilly
1969	Ruth Giddings, Barbara Seligman
1970	R. P de Barra, D. Seligman
1971	N. K. FitzGibbon, T. Healy
1972	Nellie Cotter, L. Shanahan
1973	Maria and P. J. Barry
1974	Maria and P. J. Barry
1975	Maria and P. J. Barry
1976	N. K. FitzGibbon, A. Mesbur
1977	J. Cunningham, S. Gillen
1978	N. K. FitzGibbon, A. Johnson
1979	T. Gleeson, P. F. Walsh
1980	P. Ó Briain, S. Sheehan,
1981	D. Garvey, M. Ó Briain
1982	N. K. FitzGibbon, A. Mesbur
1983	N. Tóibín, P. Walshe
1984	P. Grant, S. Stack
1985	P. Ó Briain, S. Sheehan,
1986	P. Porteous, Mary Trench
1987	E. O'Riordan, S. Sheehan,

1988	B. Dolan, T. Walsh
1989	J. Cunningham, T. Hanlon
1990	Mark Burke, P. Liston
1991	D. A. Scannell, G. Murtagh
1992	M. Hession, P. F. Walsh,
1993	E. Glynn, G. Keaveney,
1994	J. Agnew, Bernie Gannon
1995	J. Comyn, B. J. O'Brien
1996	F. O'Farrell, S. O Lubaigh
1997	J. Cunningham, T. Hanlon
1998	Ena Cleary, G. Lessells
1999	P. Kelly (Portmarnock), D. Terry
2000	Heidi Lillis, M. McGloughlin
2001	K. de Raeymaeker, Anna Onishuk
2002	J. Carroll, T. Hanlon
2003	E. Glynn, G. Keaveney
2004	K. de Raeymaeker, Anna Onishuk
2005	K. de Raeymaeker, Anna Onishuk
2006	J. Comyn, S. Dowling
2007	Louise Mitchell, Diarmuid Reddan
2008	Carol Anne Cummins, John Noonan
2009	Carol Anne Cummins, John Noonan

Master Pairs

Referred to as 'Senior Pairs' initially. There were no master-pairs championships held in 1995, 1997, 1999 or 2001, when the IBU organised qualifying contests for the European pairs championships.

1976	Ina Byrne, Molly Jones
1977	Joe McHale, P. J. Pigot
1978	Eddie Fitzgerald, Rory Timlin
1979	Risteard de Barra, John Power
1980	Aileen and John H. O'Keeffe
1981	Niall Tóibín, Pat Walshe
1982	Niall Tóibín, Pat Walshe
1983	Nellie Cotter, Marie Preston
1984	Ray Brennan, Michael MacDonagh
1985	Ray Brennan, Michael MacDonagh
1986	Miriam McConville, Geraldine Rafferty
1987	Michael Coughlan, Terry Walsh
1988	John Comyn, Gay Keaveney
1989	Nick FitzGibbon, Adam Mesbur
1990	Hugh McGann, Derek O'Gorman

1991	Andrew Cooke, Miriam McConville
1992	A. Mesbur, P. Walshe
1993	Donal Garvey, Aileen O'Keeffe
1994	Robin Burns, Keith Singleton
1996	John Carroll, Tommy Garvey
1998	Mark Moran, Terry Walsh
2000	B. O'Farrell, F. O'Farrell
2002	Carol Anne Cummins, J. Noonan
2003	Nick FitzGibbon, Adam Mesbur
2004	B. J. O'Brien, Padraig Ó Briain
2005	John Carroll, Tom Hanlon
2006	John Carroll, Tom Hanlon
2007	Michael MacDonagh, B. J. O'Brien
2008	John Carroll, Tom Hanlon
2009	J. Carroll, A. Mesbur

LAMBERT CUP

Limited to players holding fewer than thirty national points. Initially called the secondary pairs championship.

1945	Mrs W. B. Butler, H. Prost
1946	J. Harold, S. Saline
1947	Rita McNally, J. O'Neill
1948	Mrs S. Fitzgerald, Miss A. O'Kelly
1949	Frances Jennings, Maura Jennings
1950	B. G. Kenny, J.D. O'Neill
1951	Anne Lenihan, Mrs. Sharpe
1952	T. Dunbar, P. McCallum
1953	J. Lane, S. O'Farrell
1954	J. Lynch, Frances Morgan
1955	C. N. Byrne, Mrs H. G. O'Neill
1956	P. J. O'Dowd, P. O'Dowd
1957	D. G. Jackson, J. P. Jackson
1958	W. Madden, T. O'Keeffe
1959	T. Gleeson, T. McCormack
1960	Una McLoughlin, Kay O'Sullivan
1961	Mr and Mrs M. Cohen
1962	J. Lane, J. Rubenstein
1963	Nellie Cotter, L. Shanahan
1964	Delia and Ross Carew
1965	Owen and Nancy Rowe
1966	D. Dillon, G. Ryan
1967	Mrs P. J. Mullins, Olivia Rowlette

1968	Una McLoughlin, Kay O'Sullivan
1969	John McElhinney, C. J. O'Hara
1970	C. Cunningham, H. Hartnett
1971	P. Greenan, T. J. O'Callaghan
1972	Mrs G. Browne, Jim Wynne
1973	R. J. Fitzgerald, W. F. Maclachlan
1974	J. Brearly, S. Lynch
1975	B. Mahon, T. O'Mahoney
1976	C. Griffin, M. O'Halloran
1977	C. McHugh, V. O'Brien
1978	Mrs K. Boland, Miss B. Murphy
1979	C. Foley, Nora Rhattigan
1980	Kathleen Byrne, P. Breslin
1981	Mrs E. Kehoe, Mrs M. Kilcullen
1982	Heidi Lillis, S. O Lubaigh
1983	N. Browne, Margaret Morgan
1984	P. Delaney, D. Smith
1985	Mark Burke, Noel Hickey
1986	J. Doherty, P. Hanratty
1987	Frances and James Sproule
1988	Anna Binley, Petra O'Neill
1989	M. Canning, J. Murphy
1990	F. O'Farrell, T. Sweeney
1991	Amy Cooke, Geraldine Nolan
1992	Cáit Flavin, May Hickey
1993	Brian and Margaret Madden
1994	Carmel Bell, K. Hayes
1995	Carol-Anne Cummins, J. Noonan
1996	C. Holland, K. Hayes
1997	Jean Kelly, K. McGarry
1998	Jean Kelly, Carmel Treacy
1999	C. Coyne, D. Walsh
2000	Kay Cussen, D. O'Sullivan
2001	Dario Filjar, Iva Loncar
2002	Margaret and Sean Cahill
2003	P. Kerins, Anne Moran
2004	G. McMahon, K. O'Neill
2005	L. Hyde, J. Whelehan
2006	P. Concannon, L. Hardy
2007	G. Hayes, D. Walsh
2008	M. Rudzinski, P. Seery

COOPER CUP

Teams championship limited to players with fewer than thirty national points.

2003   M. Carroll, Lynn Knight, R. Knight, O. Hyde
2004   F. Langford, E. Reville, G. McMahon, K. O'Neill
2005   C. Clarke, A. Timoney, B. Kenny, L. Hanratty
2006   E. Dodd, Pat Kilfeather, Marguerite Kilfeather, T. Woods
2007   E.Cosgrove, D.O'Brien, L.Murphy, M.Ryan
2008   Philina Dowd, Deirdre Reid, S. Newcomen, C. Tierney.

DUAIS AN UACHTARÁIN – THE PRESIDENT'S PRIZE

2005   Paddy Bonner, Michael V. Clarke
2006   Tony McDermott, Michael McLaughlin
2007   Thomas MacCormac, B. J. O'Brien
2008   Anne and Denis Dillon
2009   Mark Burke, P. Liston

INTERMEDIATE CHAMPIONSHIPS

INTERMEDIATE A TEAMS, BANKERS TROPHY

1968   S. Gallagher, J. O'Donnell, J. J. and Mrs Murphy
1969   J. Maguire, W. Lynch, Mrs H. Ryan, Mrs J. McDonald
1970   Nora Browner, Mrs K. Ó Briain, M. Ó Briain, P. Ó Briain
1971   J. Corcoran, S. Gilroy, Miss E. Gannon, Miss P. Maguire
1972   Mrs J. Brennan, Mrs J. Buckley, Mrs P. C. Dolan, Mrs J. McNamara
1972   J. Dooley, J. Kerins, Miss N. McMahon, Mrs K. Sheeran
1974   K. Barry, J. Nolan, D. O'Connor, P. Porteous
1975   Mrs P. Barry, Mrs F. Ronayne, Mrs K. Boland, Miss B. Murphy
1976   Mr and Mrs P. Kelly, Mr and Mrs J. Murray
1977   Mr and Mrs M.Hayes, Mr and Mrs E. S. O'Brien
1978   Agnes Costello, Mrs L. Tierney, S. O Lubaigh, Peggy Shanahan
1979   Mrs D. Barrett, Mrs S. Murphy, N. Harris, J. O'Mahoney
1980   B. Duffy, M.Quinn, M. and P. English
1981   S. Burgess, T. Walsh, J. G. Kennedy, E. Murphy
1982   H. Kelly, M. McDonald, Mrs A. Kavanagh, Katherine Lennon
1983   T. Burke, F. Murphy, J. Keane, T. Sheridan
1984   Pat MacMahon, Pat Ryan, D. Mulhall, K. O'Dea
1985   Marie Callanan, S. Dowling, Una Hogan, Teresa Scanlon
1986   C. Cullen, Frances Daly, Madge Kinahan, J. Walsh
1987   B. Curran, B. Lawlor, Margaret McIntyre, Gráinne McLoughlin

1988	B. Finan, L. Hanratty, C. Kelly, B. Kenny
1989	D. Barry, D. Bell, B. Kelly, J. Ryan
1990	M. Canning, A. McSweeney, B. Horgan, T. McGrath
1991	Mrs J. Coyle, Mrs C. Murphy, Mrs K. Long, T. Molamphy
1992	J. Kieran, B. Ruddy, A. and T. McGee
1993	Y. Bennett, B. Wardlaw, M. Larkin, P. Ryan
1994	Mgt. Gill, James O'Rourke, Hugh Peacocke, Fran Swift
1995	E. Caulfield, M. Kelly-Rogers, D. Doona, C. Higgins
1996	N. Doyle, D. Liddy, M. Griffin, A. Harte
1997	J. Dolan, F. McCurdy, G. Dunne, F. Kelly
1998	K. de Raeymaeker, F. O'Shea, G. Kelly, R. King
1999	K. Clarke, M. Flynn, S. Hagan, R. McNamara
2000	N. Dolan, D. Walsh, D. Dunne, J. Robinson
2001	Betty Duffy, B. Martin, Celestine Latham, R. Latham
2002	G. Hayes, D. Walsh, D. O'Brien, J. O'Flynn
2003	M. Clifford, Catherine Ward, Dolores Gilliland, J. Royds
2004	Pat Fitzgibbon, M. O'Shea, N. Fitzgibbon, T. Hardiman
2005	Cynthia Heffron, Harriet Sexton, D. Lynch, G. Simpson
2006	Eibhlín Counihan, Paula Tolan, Bríd Kavanagh, Gerry McKenna
2007	J. Cawley, V. McMahon, D. Durkin, M. Naughton
2008	Mgt. Lombard, Michelle Murray, J. Naughton, P. Tolan.

INTERMEDIATE A PAIRS, LAIRD TROPHY

This trophy replaced the Hagerty Trophy in 1992. Overlapping of seasons resulted in two results for 1968.

1968	J. O'Donnell, Miss E. Turner
1968	B. O'Keefe, P. Stephens
1969	C. Griffin, M. O'Halloran
1970	Mrs T. Cullen, C. J. Rafferty
1971	Mr and Mrs P. Ó Briain
1972	Mrs F. Dunne, Mrs P. Forde,
1973	Mrs E. Kehoe, Mrs M. Kilcullen
1974	B. Mahon, T. O'Mahony,
1975	P. Curran, B. McGonagle
1976	D. Ryan, S. Stack
1977	Patsy Meehan, Anne Romaine
1978	Mrs C. Moynihan, Mrs P. A. O'Connor
1979	H. Kelly, Mrs A. Kavanagh
1980	R. Kelly, J. O'Keeffe
1981	Mrs R. Butler, Mrs B. Reddy
1982	Mrs K. Cleary, Mrs C. Ross
1983	N. Browne, D. Mulhall
1984	Mamie MacCormac, Rita O'Donnell

1985	J. Gannon, J. O'Boyle
1986	Carol McCarthy, Imelda McCarthy
1987	Brendan and Helen Sheridan
1988	M. O'Connell, P. Walsh
1989	J. Mernagh, P. Murphy
1990	Seamus Buckley, Tom Egan
1991	Seamus Costello, Peter Howard
1992	Patsy Gibney, Annie Hanlon
1993	Peter Kerins, Ann Moran
1994	Ita Hoy, Mary Lindopp
1995	R. Knight, O. Hyde
1996	Donal O'Sullivan, Mary O'Sullivan
1997	M. Loughnane, T. McLoughlin
1998	C. McGoey, A. McGuckin
1999	L. Murphy, L. Ryan
2000	F. Kelly, B. Wallace
2001	R. Latham, S. Treanor
2002	Donal and Mary Morrissey
2003	A. Quinn, C. Quinn
2004	C. Fox, S. O'Rourke
2005	E. Kelleher, C. Slattery
2006	B. McCarthy, G. Mcsweeney
2007	J. Powell, S. Connor
2008	P. Geoghegan, M. O'Leary
2009	A. Doran O'Reilly, B. McShane

DIRECT ENTRY, NEW IRELAND TROPHY

1971	M. Ó Briain, P. Ó Briain
1972	J. Moran (Ballina), J. Rice
1973	Mrs K. Dowling, Mrs N. Gallagher
1974	D. O'Connor, P. Porteous
1975	M. Lavelle and N. Mattimoe
1976	no result, probably not contested
1977	B. Brennan, V. Brennan
1978	Miss A Flynn, J Walsh
1979	Padraig Breslin, Kathleen Byrne
1980	N. Harris, J. Walshe
1981	Mrs M. McInerney and Mrs A. Walsh
1982	C. Cullen, J. Walsh
1983	Gordon Lessells, Pat Liston
1984	F. Donaghy, G Murtagh
1985	D. Cahill, D. Terry
1986	M. O'Connell, Petra O'Neill

1987	no result, probably not contested
1988	Catherine Kelly and Bridie Kenny
1989	M. V. McDonnell and S. Kierans
1990	D. and S. Brilley
1991	Mrs M. Heffernan and Mrs E. O'Sullivan
1992	Y. Bennett, B. Wardlaw
1993	C. Costello, Ita Langan
1994	E. Madigan and M O'Mahony
1995	Mary Dolan and Phil McDonald
1996	M. Finn, C. Holland
1997	L.Gaynor, J. Riordan
1998	J. Dullea, J. Wallis
1999	L. Murphy, L. Ryan
2000	R. Conway, P. Waldron
2001	Gilda Pender, Noreen Pender
2002	K. Halpin, F. O'Donnell
2003	B. Coleman, C. Connolly
2004	A.Carr, M. Mooney
2005	M. Crawley, B. Shearman
2006	M. Dolan, J. F. Kilbane
2007	M. and T. Dalton
2008	Fionnuala Gill, M.O'Malley
2009	A. Sliney, C. Taylor

MIXED PAIRS, JIM FITZGERALD TROPHY

1969	Mrs E. Turner, J. O'Donnell
1970	Mrs T. Cullen, C. Rafferty
1971	Mrs J. Slattery, A. Bunyan
1972	Bernie Gannon, J. Agnew
1973	Kate Kelly, Michael Madden
1974	Miss E. Deasy, W. Deasy
1975	Mrs J. O'Connor, J. Madden
1976	Mr and Mrs J. Kelleher
1977	Miss K. Murphy, Dr K. Sehdev
1978	Rosemary Ennis, N. Tóibín
1979	Katherine Lennon, T. Tierney
1980	Mr and Mrs J. O'Keeffe
1981	Dr and Mrs F. Baradi
1982	Miss M. Atkinson, M. Kennefick
1983	Teresa Rigney, G. O'Gorman,
1984	No result, probably not contested
1985	Mrs H. Fox, J. Moore
1986	Evelyn Burke, S. Casey

1987	Mrs M. Moroney, B. Lawlor
1988	Not contested
1989	Not contested
1990	Not contested
1991	Not contested
1992	Imelda Mulcahy, Jim Sexton
1993	Hilary Dowling Long, John Carroll
1994	Mr and Mrs P. Gormley
1995	Mary Finn, J. Russell
1996	A. Timoney, A. Kelly
1997	Cathy Murphy, Steve Bearpark
1998	Mary O'Sullivan, Donal O'Sullivan
1999	Louise Mitchell, Claude Mitchell
2000	M. O'Gorman, P. Rochford
2001	Deirdre Reid, Christy Tierney
2002	D. Reid, F. Whelan
2003	M. Horgan, B. O'Neill
2004	K. Kelly, B. Murphy
2005	M. Timoney, J. Newman
2006	M. Dolan, J. F. Kilbane
2007	M. Kearns, J. Power
2008	M Reid, P. Cassidy
2009	M. and R. Wallace

INTERMEDIATE B (FORMERLY JUNIOR) TEAMS, TIERNEY TROPHY

1968	Teresa Breslin, J. Cunningham, Aidan and Ena Cleary
1969	N. K. FitzGibbon, T. Healy, A. Cole, D. Pearson
1970	J. Corcoran, J. Doherty, S. Gilroy, Pauline Maguire
1971	N. Byrne, P. Byrne, M. MacDonagh, P. Moynihan,
1972	Mrs S. Furlong, Mrs M. Moran, Mr and Mrs G. Hoolma
1973	J. Downing, H. McDermott, D. Garvey, M. Ryder
1974	P. Curran, H. Haverty, D. Killeen, C. Thornhill
1975	J. Daly, T. O'Donoghue, Mr and Mrs P. O'Toole
1976	Mr and Mrs P. Doyle, Mr and Mrs M. Heery
1977	Miss A. Burns, Emer Joyce, K. Ganderberger, B. J. O'Brien
1978	Una Hogan, Teresa Scanlon, Pat MacMahon, Pat Ryan
1979	B. Kernan, J. Short, D. Mulhall, Miss S. Shorten
1980	T. Crawley, Mrs M. Deighan, P. Marron, J. O'Rourke
1981	N. Browne, Margaret Morgan, Mr and Mrs R. Latham
1982	Mr and Mrs Kilroy, A. Gaffney, A. Stewart
1983	B. Conlon, V. McAneaney, B. Stewart, L. Whately
1984	L. Doyle, C. Johnston, H. O'Farrell, L. O'Toole
1985	Aileen Brett, Kay Moore, Annie Hanlon, T. Hanlon

1986	Mr and Mrs M. Burke, Mrs B. Murphy, Mrs M. O'Connor
1987	L. Costello M. McHugh, J. Kenny, D. O'Connell
1988	R. Agnew, K. de Raeymaeker, C. Dwyer, D. Nally
1989	L. Allen, L. Moran, S. Bearpark, F. Murphy
1990	L. Ahern, M. White, Mr and Mrs B Madden
1991	H. Jameson, G. Kelly, N. Minogue, A. Moran
1992	M. Flynn, M. O'Leary, K. Hayes, D. O'Brien
1993	J. Carroll, Hilary Dowling Long, P. Egan, T. Ryan
1994	J. Heneghan, J. Russell, J. O'Brien, F. O'Shea
1995	D. Byrne, A. MacHale, J. Dolan, J. McCurdy
1996	D. Garvey Junior, M. O'Brien, R. King, C. O'Driscoll
1997	Denis Sheehan, Donal Sheehan, M. Sheehan, J. Young
1998	Manus Burke, E. Gallagher, M. Maloney, C. Walsh
1999	Manus Burke, E. Gallagher, M. Maloney, R. Wyer
2000	N. Fitzgibbon, T. Hardiman, Pat FitzGibbon, J. Mulvihill
2001	Ann Fitzgerald, P. Kealy, J. Latham, Bettina Steffanini
2002	B. Brady, E. Muldoon, C. Leavey, T. Maguire
2003	T. Chambers, K. Nolan, B. Granville, M. Murray
2004	C. Cagney, F. McKittrick, R. Grogan, M. Lee
2005	M. Devereux, O. Dwyer, M. Harpur, J. Reville
2006	C. Clarke, T. Clarke, B. Guinan, J. O'Keeffe
2007	M. Hogan, R. de Jong, F. and M. O'Rourke
2008	Brigid Connolly, Rita Duff, Ann and Derek McDonnell

INTERMEDIATE B (FORMERLY JUNIOR) PAIRS, CIVIL SERVICE CUP

1968	C. and Mrs Rafferty
1969	P. Barry, P. Gearty
1970	Mrs Keane, Mrs Power
1971	A. Bunyan, P. Grant
1972	Mr and Mrs J. Rhatigan
1973	Mrs J. O'Dwyer, Mrs J. Wallace
1974	P. Curran, B. McGonagle
1975	D. Ryan, S. Stack
1976	Mr and Mrs P. Brennan
1977	S. Scallan, T. Tierney
1978	Pat MacMahon, Pat Ryan
1979	Mrs Comerford, Mrs Costelloe
1980	R. McDonald, D. Toibín
1981	Mr and Mrs R. Latham
1982	Mr and Mrs J. Aylward
1983	D. O'Farrell, H. Twomey
1984	P. Goff, N. Stewart
1985	N. Lennon, J. Malone

1986	Mrs M. Bray, Mrs M. Cleary
1987	H. McGann, D. O'Gorman
1988	D. Barry, D. Bell
1989	Mrs M. O'Connell, Mrs D. O'Meara
1990	B. Ryan, T. Ryan.
1991	G. Hayes, V. O'Brien
1992	J. O'Leary, M. O'Shea
1993	C. Holland, G. O'Regan
1994	E. and I. Meade
1995	J. and M. Power
1996	R. Langford, M. Walsh
1997	R. Langford, M. Walsh
1998	L. Hyde, J. Whelehan
1999	Gilda Pender, Noreen Pender
2000	J. Butler, M. O'Brien
2001	J. McLaughlin, S. McNutt
2002	J. McLaughlin, S. McNutt
2003	J. Doran, D. Maher
2004	J. J. Donlon, M. Gillen
2005	D. Fallon, M. Meggs
2006	J. Harkins, J. Kelly
2007	R. Pratt, P. Talbot
2008	F. Kelly, T. Banks
2009	G. Healy, I. Hoey

INTERMEDIATE B PAIRS – DIRECT ENTRY, KERVICK TROPHY

1972	J. C. and N. K. Bulger
1973	Helen Boland, Marie Moran
1974	Denis O'Connor, Paul Porteous
1975	A. Flynn, J. Walsh
1976	K. Luddy, T.Walsh
1977	A. Burns, Emer Joyce
1978	R. O'Brien, P. O'Shea
1979	Betty Fitzpatrick, Mrs A. Looney
1980	Richard McDonald. D. Tobin
1981	N. Cahill, M. Levins
1982	Mrs. P. Nolan, Mrs. N. Lott
1983	Brendan and Helen Sheridan
1984	Anne Hanratty, Michael Smyth
1985	M. Goulding, D. O'Driscoll
1986	Ger Cummins, T. Healy
1987	J. J. Cronin, N. Cronin
1988	C. Doyle, J. Doyle

1989	A. Barry, J. Doyle
1990	Danny Dillon, Tom Fitzgibbon
1991	A. Burnett, F. Chandler
1992	R. Dunn, A. Hogan
1993	Cian Holland, Geannie O'Regan
1994	K. Bannon, H. Collins
1995	B. and J. Houton
1996	T. Hargadon, Christy Tierney
1997	Nick Fitzgibbon Tom Hardiman,
1998	D. McElroy, J. Smith
1999	B. Martin, F. Radmall
2000	M. Fenton, E. Halpin
2001	A. Carlin, H. Hunt
2002	Bert McKay, Gerry McDonald
2003	C. Brennan, P. Purcell
2004	B. Coyne, E. Whittaker
2005	Maud Cremins, Lelia Warner
2006	K. and T. Mulcahy
2007	S. Carroll, D. Creagh
2008	L. and L. Curley
2009	M. Vaughan, I. Whittle

J. J. MURPHY CUP

Initially awarded to winners of CBAI Junior (Intermediate B) Mixed Pairs.

1969	Mr and Mrs C. Rafferty
1970	Mr and Mrs M. Carroll
1971	Mrs C. Fallon, J. O'Brien
1972	Mrs K. McGuinness, P. Holohan
1973	Sheila O'Dwyer, Dermot Downes
1974	Mrs V. O'Dea, Dan Brilly,
1975	Mr and Mrs L. Murdock
1976	Mr and Mrs W. M. Thompson
1977	Mr and Mrs Tom Sheridan
1978	Miss M. O'Connell, John G.Kennedy
1979	Mr and Mrs Ultan McCabe

NOVICE PAIRS (FROM 1980)

1980	S. Deegan, T. Griffin
1981	S. Dowling, E. Pelly
1982	L. O'Donnell, L. Power
1983	M. Durcan, F. Durkin
1984	Ms M. Livingstone, K.athleen Meade

1985	D. MacAonghusa, P. Williams
1986	D. Lynch, M. McEnery
1987	Mr and Mrs J.Doyle
1988	Donal Quinn, Matt Quinn
1989	S. Bell, T. McGrath
1990	Not contested
1991	M. and J. McDaid
1992	Joyce and Rodney Last
1993	G. and J. Moyles
1994	S. Coomey, M. O'Brien
1995	E. and K. Tiernan
1996	M. O'Kane, M. Tierney
1997	John Butler, Gerry Lawlor
1998	Joan and Kevin Mulligan
1999	L. Fitzpatrick, A. O'Sullivan
2000	J. Doran, D. Maher
2001	Fionnuala Gill, Michael O'Malley
2002	J. Kilbane, D. O'Keeffe
2003	M. Blake, R. M. Traynor
2004	E. Blennerhassett, B. Moore
2005	B. Cronin, P. Hogan
2006	K. and T. Mulcahy
2007	T. Reddy, J. Rogers
2008	Ann and Michael Mullen

NOVICE PAIRS, WATERFORD CRYSTAL TROPHY
(CBAI INTERMEDIATE CONGRESS)

1995	M. and N. Spillane
1996	M. Fitzgerald, P. O'Lomasney
1997	P. Brennan, A. Goodison
1998	H. Lynch, E. McCarthy
1999	M. and W. Murphy
2000	J. Doran, D. Maher
2001	C. Duggan, A. Walsh
2002	M. Blake, R. M. Traynor
2003	B. Burniston, F. Golden
2004	F. McGreevy, D. Speedy
2005	A. Duffy, P. Quigley
2006	M. and T. McCarthy
2007	O. Connachton, P. Kinsella
2008	M. Corcoran, M. Sweeney
2009	C. Fahy, P. Smyth

Irish Bridge Union Championships Winners

Teams: Egan Cup

1957	R. A. Belton, J. A. Kelly, G. F. Read, M. Shrage
1958	E. F. Agnew, T. J. McAfee, A. E. Anderson, J. McRobert
1959	J. P. MacHale, P. J. Pigot, G. F. Read, M. Shrage
1960	J. P. MacHale, P. J. Pigot, G. F. Read, M. Shrage
1961	E. O. Barry, G. A. Holmes, F. W. O'Connell, M. F. O'Connell
1962	Mrs Atkinson, D. A. Cohen, E. Goldblatt, M. Gabbey, A. McKinnon
1963	J. Bailey, E. Boland, W. McCann, S. O'Farrell
1964	J. P. MacHale, P. J. Pigot, F. W. O'Connell, M. F. O'Connell
1965	R. A. Corrrick, D. Deery, A. Lennon, K. Y. Singleton
1966	Alice Mahon, Molly O'Carroll, Ina McMenamin, Eileen O'Sullivan
1967	J. P. MacHale, P. J. Pigot, G. A. Holmes, M. F. O'Connell
1968	J. A. Kelly, E. J. O'Boyle, E. MacNeill, D. G. Scannell
1969	D. Deery, E. MacNeill, J. P. MacHale, P. J. Pigot
1970	D. A. Cohen, M. Rosenberg, D. Deery, K. Y. Singleton
1971	A. T. R. Anderson, P. J. Barry, R. P. De Barra, N. K. FitzGibbon
1972	A. T. R. Anderson, D. Deery, R. P. De Barra, N. K. FitzGibbon
1973	D. Deery, E. MacNeill, J. P. MacHale, M. Shrage
1974	P. J. Barry, Maria Barry, N. K. FitzGibbon, A. Mesbur
1975	N. K. FitzGibbon, A. Mesbur, M. McGloughlin, D. G. Scannell
1976	E. C. and Molly Andrew, Mrs M. McAleese, Mary Nimmons
1977	D. Deery, E. MacNeill, J. P. MacHale, M. Shrage, P. Kelly
1978	F. A. Boland, V. O Brien, Joan Crowley, Rosemary Ennis
1979	D. Garvey, P. Walshe, M. Ó Briain, P. Ó Briain
1980	A. T. R. Anderson, M. Rosenberg, D. Deery, H. Torney
1981	N. K. FitzGibbon, A. Mesbur, D. A. Jackson, P. Walshe
1982	N. K. FitzGibbon, A. Mesbur, N. Tóibín, P. Walshe
1983	Sonya Britton, Rosemary Ennis, N. Kennedy, N. Tóibín
1984	E. C. and Molly Andrew, H. Campbell, S. Hall, T. G. Mackenzie, K. Y. Singleton
1985	R. Boland, A. Mesbur, B. Dolan, P. Walshe, N. K. FitzGibbon, Kathryn O'Keeffe
1986	D. Garvey, M. Ó Briain, J. P. MacHale, P. Ó Briain
1987	E. Glynn, G. Keaveney, P. Scannell, R. Timlin
1988	G. Barton, P. Walshe, N. K. and Kathryn FitzGibbon
1989	P. Byrne, M. MacDonagh, S. Gillan, D. A. Houlihan (Ennis)
1990	P. Byrne, M. MacDonagh, E. Fitzgerald, S. Gillan
1991	R. Brennan, P. Scannell, G. Keaveney, R. Timlin
1992	R. J. Fitzgerald, Valerie Hand, Alex Montwill, J. H. O'Keeffe
1993	J. P. MacHale, R. Milne, W. F. Maclachlan, Alex Montwill

1994	A. T. R. Anderson, M. Rosenberg, D. K. Johnston, I. H. Lindsay
1995	Alex and Ann Montwill, Aileen and J. H. O'Keeffe
1996	R. Brennan, P. Scannell, E. Glynn, G. Keaveney
1997	R. Brennan, P. Scannell, E. Glynn, G. Keaveney
1998	R. Milne, P. Ó Briain, B. J. O'Brien, T. Roche
1999	A. T. R. Anderson, I. H. Lindsay, David and Diane Greenwood
2000	H. Campbell, T. G. Mackenzie, David Greenwood, I. H. Lindsay
2001	M. MacDonagh, M. Ó Briain, P. Ó Briain, T. Roche
2002	J. Heneghan, T. Walsh, M. MacDonagh, B. Pattinson
2003	R. Boland, N. Tóibín, Anne and D. Dillon
2004	J. P. MacHale, Alex Montwill, M. McAuliffe, D. A. Scannell
2005	P. Clifford, Mary Lindopp, K. De Raeymaeker, Anna Onishuk
2006	A. T. R. Anderson, David Greenwood, R. Burns, I. H. Lindsay
2007	A. T. R. Anderson, David Greenwood, R. Burns, I. H. Lindsay
2008	P. J. Barry, D. Jackson, B. J. O'Brien, T. Walsh

INTER-CLUB INTER-COUNTY CHAMPIONSHIP – BURKE CUP

The competition began as the CBAI Inter-Club championship, for the Club Cup.

1934	Herbert: Mairéad Crofts, J. O'Neill, Kathleen Lambert, B. L. Williams
1935	Mrs Roantree's Club, Bray: Mrs H. J. Bermingham, Mrs S. Harrison, Mrs Maxwell Henry, Mrs T. Kennedy
1936	Carlton, Mairéad Crofts, Kathleen Lambert, Muriel Leech, Geraldine McConkey
1937	Jewish Social Club: H. L. Cowan, B. Eppel, M. Freedman, H. Fine, D. Rivlin
1938	Roscommon: P. Ballantine, W. Hourican, J. and Mrs Hurley
1939	County Longford: P. A. Arkins, D. Coady, O. Boyle, R. Seagers
1940	Carlton: E. O. Barry, Philip Quinn, Ina Hickey, Geraldine McConkey, Frances Morgan
1941	Portmarnock GC: T. D. Purcell, G. M. Purcell, C. Casey, Dr F. McMenamin
1942	Regent: J. Lynch, R. Sheehan, N. Peart, G. F. Read
1943	Portmarnock GC.: Ina Hickey, T. D. Purcell, F. McMenamin, B. L. Williams
1944	Regent: P. P. Donovan, J. Lynch, P. J. and Mrs O. Dowd
1945	Regent: C. H. Day, R. Sheehan, J. Lynch, C. O'Neill
1946	Regent: D. Egan, May McNulty, Flora McLoone, P. J. O'Dowd
1947	York: C. H. Day, R. Sheehan, P. P. Donovan, K. Messervey
1948	Jewish Social Club: M. Freedman, J. Orman, P. Leon, M. Shrage
1949	Commercial Duplicate Br. Ass.: Kay Byrne, Babs Hooper, Miss K. Kavanagh, Miss F. Slaney
1950	Regent: Alice Mahon, Eileen O'Doherty, Philip Quinn, Cleo Roy
1951	Percy Place: C. H. Day, Mrs C. McGinley, Miss K. Kavanagh, Miss F. Slaney
1952	Regent: Ruth Giddings, May McNulty, J. Harold, Eileen O'Sullivan
1953	Jewish Social Club: H. Bridburg, J. Orman, M. Freedman, M. Shrage

1954   Fitzwilliam Tennis Club: A. H. Davidson, J. P. MacHale, G. F. Read, J. M. O'Sullivan

1955   Regent: Ruth Giddings, Lily Maguire, J. Harold, J. Lynch

In 1956, the last year under the CBAI, it became the Inter-County (Inter-Club) championship.

1956   Dublin: A. H. Davidson, J. P. MacHale, G. F. Read, J. M. O'Sullivan

The IBU took over the competition in 1957.

1957   Antrim: A. Lennon, Mrs D. Tempest, A. McKinnon, J. H. O'Dempsey
1958   Dublin: A. H. Davidson, J. P. MacHale, G. F. Read, J. M. O'Sullivan
1959   Dublin: P. D. Fitzgerald, Elvina Spiro, Geraldine McConkey, P. J. Pigot
1960   Wicklow: J. Bailey, E. Boland, W. McCann, S. O'Farrell
1961   Galway: P. J. Gallagher, C. J. Gilgunn, P. J. O'Donoghue, J. Wynne
1962   Carlow: Mrs Feore, Mrs Foley, D. and Mrs O'Leary
1963   Wicklow: J. Bailey, E. Boland, W. McCann, S. O'Farrell
1964   Tipperary: J. Coman, J. Fitzgerald, Mrs T. Cranley, Maura Kirby
1965   Dublin City: Miss V. Dunne, Molly Jones, W. Heidenfeldt, Miss M. Roantree
1966   Dublin City: Ruth Giddings, Barbara Seligman, Alice Mahon, Eileen O'Doherty

Since 1967, the Burke Cup has been awarded to the winners.

1967   Dublin City: Doreen Cairnduff, P. J. Pigot, Geraldine McConkey, Eileen O'Sullivan
1968   Armagh: G. McCaw, W. S. Robb, T. G. Mackenzie, D. Scully
1969   Armagh: G. McCaw, W. S. Robb, T. G. Mackenzie, D. Scully
1970   Dublin City: Henry and Rosalind Barron, Peter and Allie Pigot
1971   Armagh: G. McCaw, W. S. Robb, T. G. Mackenzie, D. Scully
1972   Antrim: A. E. Anderson, A. T. R. Anderson, D. A. Cohen, M. Rosenberg
1973   Derry: G. Clingan, E. Tierney, B. McShane, G. Ryan
1974   Dublin City: Henry and Rosalind Barron, Peter and Allie Pigot
1975   Cork: J. Coman, P. C. Kiely, D. Hanley, M. F. O'Connell
1976   Dublin City: R. De Barra, D. A. Jackson, S. Sheehan, Ruth Giddings, A. Kavanagh
1977   Galway: F. Barrett, Anna Glynn, R. Kilduff, J. Wynne
1978   Dublin City: D. A. Jackson, S. Sheehan, Barbara and D. Seligman
1979   Armagh City: Maeve Curran, Valerie Hamilton, D. K. Johnston, Antonina McNeice
1980   Westmeath: J. Cunningham, T. Gleeson, B. Mahon, Nuala and P. F. Walsh
1981   Dublin City: Alan Johnson, C. J. O'Hara, M. McGloughlin, S. O'Reilly

1982	Dublin City: R. Boland, B. Dolan, N. Tóibín, P. Walshe
1983	Dublin City: R. Boland, B. Dolan, N. Tóibín, P. Walshe
1984	Wicklow: S. O' Lubaigh, Anne Romaine, Clare Pippet, L. F. Sheeran
1985	Donegal: J. McIntyre, P. McLoone, P. and Mrs McLaughlin
1986	Down: J. Conlon, C. Richey, N. Cauwood, M. McFaul
1987	Limerick: Mark Burke, G. Lessells, P. Liston, Ena and A. Cleary
1988	Westmeath: C. Cunningham, J. Cunningham, T. Gleeson, J. Daly, B. Mahon
1989	County Dublin: Valerie Hand, Aileen O'Keeffe, Ann and Alex Montwill
1990	Antrim: Marjorie and W. M. Kelso, M. O'Kane, M. Rosenberg
1991	Galway: M. Hession, E. Glynn, Nuala and P. F. Walsh
1992	Galway: M. Hession, E. Glynn, Emer Joyce, P. F. Walsh
1993	Westmeath: J. Cunningham, T. Hanlon, E. Fitzgerald, M. MacDonagh
1994	Dun Laoghaire-Rathdown: Valerie and Damian Hand, Aileen and John H. O'Keeffe
1995	Galway: S. MacMathúna, Maura O'Farrell, Marlene and Michael O'Connor
1996	Dun Laoghaire-Rathdown: R. J. Fitzgerald, A. O'Sullivan, Ann and Alex Montwill
1997	Cork: Mary Finn, D. O'Gorman, K. Hayes, R. D. McGrath
1998	Derry: P. Bergin, J. McGonagle, P. C. Duffy, P. McDaid
1999	Derry: A. Alcock, I. K. Lindsay, R. Burns, A. Sharp
2000	Dun Laoghaire–Rathdown: R. J. Fitzgerald, A. O'Sullivan, Ann and Alex Montwill
2001	Limerick: Mark Burke, P. Quinn (Ennis) G. Connolly, P. Liston
2002	Clare: Ena and Aida Cleary , G. Lessells, D. A. Houlihan (Ennis)
2003	Limerick: N. Hickey, Gerri MacMahon, P. J. O'Dea, L. Walsh
2004	Limerick City: Ena and Aidan Cleary, G. Lessells, D. A. Houlihan (Ennis)
2005	Dublin South County: J. Comyn J. Moran, S. Dowling, B. J. O'Brien
2006	Dublin City: P. J. Barry, D. A. Jackson, R. Milne, D. A. Scannell
2007	Dublin City: R. J. Fitzgerald, Miriam McConville, Pauline Maguire, Mary Trench
2008	Dublin City: K. de Raeymaeker, Anna Onishuk, P. Ó Briain, B. J. O'Brien
2009	Dublin City: K. de Raeymaeker, Anna Onishuk, P. Ó Briain, B. J. O'Brien

ALL-IRELAND PAIRS, MOYLAN CUP

Originally awarded to the winners of the CBAI panel test (trials).

1943	C. H. Day, May McNulty
1944	Ina Hickey, T. D. Purcell
1945	J. Lynch, D. Rivlin
1946	F. W. O'Connell, W. J. L. O'Connell
1947	A. H. Davidson, May McNulty
1948	Flora McLoone, N. Peart
1949	J. Harold, J. Orman
1950	Eileen and J. M. O'Sullivan

1951	P. V. Carson, Moreen McCarthy
1952	E. O. Barry, D. A. Houlihan (Birr)
1953	Ina McMenamin, Eileen O'Sullivan
1954	Alice Mahon, Eileen O'Doherty
1955*	Ruth Giddings, May McNulty
1955*	F. W. O'Connell, M. F. O'Connell

In 1956, the IBU took over the competition. That year, it was awarded to the winners of the IBU trials.

1956	Norah and L. Bradley

In 1957 the all-Ireland pairs championship was first contested.

1957	F. W. O'Connell, M. F. O'Connell	1982	E. MacNeill, D. G. Scannell
1958	M. Rosenberg, H. Schenker	1983	P. Kelly, R. Sai
1959	J. P. Geoghegan, O. Rowe	1984	E. MacNeill, D. G. Scannell
1960	D. A. Cohen, E. Goldblatt	1985	N. K. FitzGibbon, A. Mesbur
1961	J. P. MacHale, P. J. Pigot	1986	E. MacNeill, D. G. Scannell
1962	G. A. Holmes, M. F. O'Connell	1987	N. K. FitzGibbon, A. Mesbur
1963	G. A. Holmes, M. F. O'Connell	1988	D. Garvey, M. Ó Briain
1964	J. P. MacHale, P. J. Pigot	1989	R. Brennan, R. Timlin
1965	Ruth Giddings, Barbara Seligman	1990	J. Cunningham, T. Hanlon
1966	G. F. Read, M. Shrage	1991	D. Garvey, M. Ó Briain
1967	G. F. Read, M. Shrage	1992	P. Ó Briain, T. Roche
1968	T. Gleeson, G. Ryan	1993	D. K. Johnston, I. H. Lindsay
1969	D. A. Cohen, M. Rosenberg	1994	T. Hanlon, H. McGann
1970	J. P. MacHale, P. J. Pigot	1995	Ann and Alex Montwill
1971	J. P. MacHale, P. J. Pigot	1996	T. Hanlon, H. McGann
1972	D. Deery, E. MacNeill	1997	E. MacNeill, D. G. Scannell
1973	Maria and P. J. Barry	1998	T. Hanlon, H. McGann
1974	D. Deery, E. MacNeill	1999	P. Ó Briain, T. Roche
1975	Ann Montwill, Aileen O'Keeffe	2000	J. Carroll, T. Hanlon
1976	D. Deery, E. MacNeill	2001	J. Carroll, M. Ó Briain
1977	D. Deery, E. MacNeill	2002	J. Heneghan, T. Walsh
1978	D. Deery, E. MacNeill	2003	N. K. FitzGibbon, A. Mesbur
1979	N. K. FitzGibbon, A. Mesbur	2004	J. Cunningham, Monica Harris
1980	P. Ó Briain, S. Sheehan	2005	P. Pigot, B. J. O'Brien
1981	Ann Montwill, Aileen O'Keeffe	2006	J. Carroll, T. Hanlon
		2007	J. Carroll, T. Hanlon
		2008	J. Heneghan, T. Walsh

* The CBAI 1955/56 annual programme credits the O'Connells with winning the Moylan Cup. However, on 10 January 1955 the *Irish Independent* reported that Giddings and McNulty had won. The *Independent* invariably reported correctly: Joe O'Neill was the correspondent. The O'Connells are given the benfit of the doubt. Two separate tests may have been held during the same season.

INTER-CLUB PAIRS

1975	N. K. FitzGibbon, A. Mesbur	1993	J. Cunningham, M. MacDonagh
1976	Elva Gannon, Pauline Maguire	1994	J. Cunningham, M. MacDonagh
1977	M. McGloughlin, S. Reilly	1995	E. Glynn, G. Keaveney
1978	Eileen O'Doherty, Anne Quinn	1996	E. Glynn, G. Keaveney
1979	P. Breslin, Kathleen Byrne	1997	E. Fitzgerald, Marie Gleeson
1980	B. Dolan, P. Walshe	1998	P. Howard, B. Sheridan
1981	B. Dolan, P. Walshe	1999	R. Milne, B. J. O'Brien
1982	Ena and Aidan Cleary	2000	D. Ellis, J. J. O'Doherty
1983	Diane Sloan, B. Senior	2001	D. Ellis, J. J. O'Doherty
1984	J. Cunningham, T. Gleeson	2002	K. de Raeymaeker, Anna Onishuk
1985	T. Bennett, I. H. Lindsay	2003	Sandra Newell, C. O'Driscoll
1986	B. Dolan, N. Tóibín	2004	J. Comyn, S. Dowling
1987	E. Glynn, G. Keaveney	2005	Grace Finegan, Petra O'Neill
1988	D. Johnston, I. H. Lindsay	2006	J. Comyn, S. Dowling
1989	Elizabeth Dowling, W. F. Maclachlan	2007	T. MacCormac, R. Milne
1990	D. Johnston, I. H. Lindsay	2008	P. Clifford, Anna Onishuk
1991	E. Glynn, G. Keaveney		
1992	Katherine Lennon, S. Scallen		

INTERMEDIATE 'A' WINNERS

1991	Celia and P. Claffey
1992	D. Kelly, S. Galligan
1993	M. O'Connor, J. Walsh
1994	S. Kennedy, C. Power
1995	T. Crowley, E. Murphy
1996	M. Ford, P. McCartan
1997	L. and T. McCarthy
1998	C. Coyne, D. Walsh
1999	Pat O'Reilly, Z. Rahman
2000	D. & L. O'Donovan
2001	A. Lyons, T. Rosney
2002	Anne O'Connell, Anne O'Rourke
2003	L. Carey, M. Sheehy

2004	Betty and E. Hardiman
2005	R. Landers, M. O'Brien
2006	A. Davey, M. Dolan
2007	T. Irving, M. O'Toole
2008	Catherine Horan, Mairéad Kearns

Intermediate 'B' Winners

1976	S. Scallan, T. Tierney	1993	F. Doorley. D. Naughton
1977	not known	1994	M. & R. Linehan
1978	W. Hunter, P. Murphy	1995	D. Curran, P. Johnston
1979	J. & Máire O'Keeffe	1996	M. Burns, Marian Davenport
1980	Ted and Mrs Keyes	1997	Brenda and F. Kelly
1981	D. McAughrey, R. Murray	1998	J. H. Murphy, P. Murphy
1982	J. J. Meade, S. O'Gorman	1999	M. Horgan, D. Walsh
1983	R. Donnolly, R. O'Neill	2000	N. Fitzgibbon, T. Hardiman
1984	not known	2001	D. & V. Smyth
1985	not known	2002	J. McLaughlin, S. McNutt
1986	F. Kellegher, G. Murtagh	2003	F. Brady, C. Moran
1987	Mr & Mrs P. Smyth	2004	R. Boyd, T. Hall
1988	S. Cairns, L. Hardy	2005	J. G. Doherty, M. Farran
1989	M. Doran, A. Kinsella	2006	S. Connor, M. Roche
1990	Mrs T. Molly, T. Rosney	2007	D. and F. Gill
1991	A. & B. Crowe	2008	Mary and S. Healy
1992	S. Howard, A. Kelly		

All-Time Rankings:
Number of CBAI and IBU Championships Won (Excluding Inter-Provincials)

Some 686 players have won CBAI or IBU major championships. Winners of all but one, the 1942 'individual', have been traced. Wigoder and Carroll Cup winners have been included up to the time they ceased to be national events. The Lambert Cup and the Cooper Cup are included. Winners of the inter-provincial championship, a representative event, have not been included. Records up to 31 March 2009.

Wins		Ranking
54	Ruth Giddings	1
49	J. P. MacHale	2
46	G. Keaveney	3
45	N. K. FitzGibbon	4
43	P. J. Pigot	5
38	A. Mesbur	6

36	M. Shrage	7
34	P. Walshe	8
33	May McNulty	9
30	Ina McMenamin [Hickey]	10
28	Barbara Seligman	11
27	T. Hanlon	12
27	Geraldine McConkey	
26	E. MacNeill	13
25	M. MacDonagh	14

WINS

24	D. A. Jackson, M. F. O'Connell, G. F. Read
23	J. Carroll, T .D. Purcell, R. Timlin, P. F. Walsh
22	D. Deery, E. Glynn, J. A. Kelly
20	Eileen O'Sullivan
19	P. J. Barry, R. Boland, P. Ó Briain, Eileen O'Doherty, Anne Quinn, Philip Quinn, N. Tóibín.
18	E. O. Barry, B. J. O'Brien
17	D. Seligman, K. de Raeymaeker
16	Maria Barry, M. McGloughlin, Aileen O'Keeffe
15	Cleo Fellows [Roy], H. Fine, E. J. Fitzgerald, G. A. Holmes, Alice Mahon, Flora McLoone, Anne Montwill, Anna Onishuk, D. Rivlin
14	R. A. Belton, Doreen Cairnduff, J. Cunningham, T. Walsh
13	M. Ó Briain, Elvina Spiro, D. Garvey
12	Ena Cleary, A. H. Davidson, C. H. Day, R. de Barra, P. P. Donovan, Babs Hooper, H. McGann, Alex Montwill, H. Williams
11	Hilary (Dowling Long) McDonagh, N. Peart, P. Scannell

THE FOLLOWING PLAYERS HAVE TEN WINS EACH:
A. T. R. Anderson, B. Dolan, H. Elliott, I. H. Lindsay, Moreen McCarthy, F. W. O'Connell, J. O'Neill, David.Scannell, R. J. Sheehan, J. M. O'Sullivan

THE FOLLOWING PLAYERS HAVE NINE WINS EACH:
Gráinne Barton, J. J. Bastow, R. Brennan, H. Bridburg, Sonya Britton, D. Dillon, T. Gleeson, J. Harold, J. Lynch, Molly O'Carroll, Mairéad O'Neill, Kay O'Sullivan, M. Rosenberg, B. L. Williams

THE FOLLOWING PLAYERS HAVE EIGHT WINS EACH:
Mark Burke, A. Cleary, Anne Dillon, Rosemary Ennis, T. Garvey, Kathleen Lambert, Heidi Lillis, T. MacCormac, R. Milne, J. Orman, S. Reilly, Des Scannell, S. Sheehan, Mary Trench

THE FOLLOWING PLAYERS HAVE SEVEN WINS EACH:
Kathleen Bowles, Mrs. Colgan, J. Comyn, Kathryn FitzGibbon, Charlotte Fowler, Valerie Hand, J. Heneghan, G. Lessells, W. F. Maclachlan, Lily Maguire, Miriam McConville, Frances Morgan, J. H. O'Keeffe, Rebecca O'Keeffe, D. R. Pigot

THE FOLLOWING PLAYERS HAVE SIX WINS EACH:
Kathleen Banks, E. J. Boland, Nellie Cotter, Carol-Anne Cummins, Mary Finn, R. J. Fitzgerald, David Greenwood, Diane Greenwood [Sloan, Senior], M. Hession, D. A. Houlihan (Birr), Mollie Jones, P. Liston, T. G. Mackenzie, Pauline Maguire, R. D. McGrath, F. McMenamin, Rita McNally, Rita McQueen, E. J. O'Boyle, W. J. L. O'Connell, P. J. O'Dowd, S. Ó Lubaigh, Jacqueline Prost, Teresa Rigney, T. Roche, G. Ryan

THE FOLLOWING PLAYERS HAVE FIVE WINS EACH:
Kay Byrne, Joan Crowley, S. Dowling, Grace Finegan, P. D. Fitzgerald, T. Gibson, S. Gillen, D. K. Johnson, N. Kennedy, Pat MacMahon, J. Noonan, D. O'Gorman, C. J. O'Hara, Petra O'Neill, Allie Pigot, Violet Pigot, G. M. Purcell, Pat Ryan, R. Sai, D. Scully, B. Senior (England), J. Wynne

THE FOLLOWING PLAYERS HAVE FOUR WINS EACH:
J. J. Bailey, R. Burns, C. N. Byrne, P. Byrne (Letterkenny), H. Campbell, Helen Carroll, D. A. Cohen, J. Coman, C. Coyne, D. Egan, M. Freedman, H. G. Freehill, P. Goodman (Wales), Anna Glynn, S. Glynn, Anne Marie Horan Carroll, D. A. Houlihan (Ennis), G. Jackson, Anne Johnson, A. Kavanagh, Kathleen Kavanagh, P. Kelly (Portmarnock), P. C. Kiely, Bríd Kirby, Jill Kulchycky, Muriel Leech, Mary Lindopp, Clare Lyne, P. O'Dowd, S. O'Farrell, C. O'Neill, A. O'Sullivan, R. Pattinson, Maureen Pattinson, P. Pigot, Clare Pippet, Marie Preston, P. Quinn (Ennis), L. F. Sheeran, D. Walsh.

THE FOLLOWING PLAYERS HAVE THREE WINS EACH:
P. Barrett, W. R. Bastow, Anna Binley, A. Bloom, J. W. Burke, P. Clifford, G. Connolly, Andrew Cooke, P. Delaney, Elizabeth Dowling, Chris Doyle, Vivienne Dunne, E. Galligan, Elva Gannon, P. Georgalas, H. Hackett, Marie Hanrahan, K. Hayes, N. Hickey, Erina Holmes Wilson, Emer Joyce, Gerri MacMahon, B. Mahon, W. McCann, G. McCaw, B. McDonagh, Lily McDonagh, Una McLoughlin, Anne Murphy, Sandra Newell, Amandita Nolan, E. O'Riordan, P. Porteous, P. Powell, F. T. Quin, Geraldine Rafferty, W. S. Robb, T. P. Ryder, L. Shanahan, K. Y. Singleton, Miss F. Slaney, Mabel Spiro, D. Terry, A. Thomas (Wales), H. Torney, Nuala Walshe.

99 PLAYERS HAVE EACH WON TWO CHAMPIONSHIPS:
A. E. Anderson, F. Andrew, Molly Andrew, Nell Arnold, H. Barron, Rosalind Barron, Mrs H. J. Birmingham, T .P. Boden, Helen Boland, P. Breslin, Mrs G. W. Browne, Margaret Browne [Morgan], J. G. Burke, Ciara Burns, Ina Byrne, Kathleen Byrne (Waterford), P. V. Carson, W. Cashen, J. Coakley, M. Cohen, Mrs M. Cohen, B. Comiskey, Maureen Corboy, H. L. Cowan, Colin Cunningham, Con Cunningham, H. Curran, T. Dunbar, Mrs W. Dunne, B. E. Ebrill, W. J. Ebrill, D. Ellis, D. Filjar (Croatia), F. Fine, J. Fitzgerald, Mrs S. Fitzgerald, K. Fowler, Bernie Gannon, J. Gayer, E. Goldblatt, S. Hall, H. Hartnett, J. Hearn, C. B. Heron, Mrs C. B. Heron, C. Holland, Frances Jennings, A. Johnson, P. Kelly (Kells), W. Kervick, A. G. Kibble, R.

Kilduff, J. Lane, A. Lennon, P. Leon, G. M. Linzell, Iva Loncar (Croatia), Bernie Lynch, S. Lynch, Mamie MacCormac, P. MacNeill, W. Malone, M. McAuliffe, T. McCormack, Mrs C. McGinley, J. McIntyre, P. McKenna, J. McKeon, A. McKinnon, P. McLoone, Mrs McMunn, F. McNamara, Patsy Meehan, Marie Moran, Mark Moran, J. P. Morgan, D. J. Murphy, T. Murray, V. O'Brien, P. J. O'Dea, J. J. O'Doherty, Fergal O'Farrell, Maura O'Farrell, S. O'Flynn, K. O'Neill, J. Phelan, P. Purcell, Bernie Rafferty, Anne Romaine, O. Rowe, J. Rubenstein, Maureen Ryder, S. Saline, D. T. Seale, D. L. Stokes, Liz Taaffe, D. Vard, L. Walsh, W. Whitney

334 PLAYERS HAVE WON ONE EACH:

L. Abrahamson, E. F. Agnew, J. R. Agnew, A. Alcock, P. A.Arkins, Mrs Atkinson, E. Balfe, P. Ballantine, Carmel Barnes, F. Barrett, F. Barry, K. Barry, Mrs S. Barry, Carmel Bell, P. Bergin, F. A. Boland, Mrs K. Boland, P. Bonner, J. Boylan, O. Boyle, Mrs Branigan, Mrs K. Braund, J. J. Brearley, T. Brick, Mrs H. Brown, N. Brown, Shirlie Browne, S. Burgess, Manus Burke, P. Burke, Mrs W. B. Butler, P. Byrne (Dublin), P. Caffrey, D. Cahill, J. Cahill, Margaret Cahill, Mary Cahill, S. Cahill, M. Canning, Delia Carew, Ross Carew, M. Carroll, C. Casey, N. Cauwood, C. Clarke, M. V. Clarke, G. Clingan, D. Coady, P. Concannon, J. Conlon, Miss J. Connolly, J. Connolly, P. Connolly, W. Considine, Nancy Coogan, Amy Cooke, Denis Corboy, R. A. Corrick, E. Cosgrove, Agnes Costello, M. P. Coughlan, Marie Coveney, Mrs Cranley, H. Cowan, Mr. T. Cranley, Mrs Cross, J. Curran, Maeve Curran, Kay Cussen, H. Daly, Helen Daly, J. Daly, Mrs H. Day, Ursula Devine, E. Dodd, Jim Doherty, Catherine Dowling-Long, Kay Downes, A. Drewery, P. C. Duffy, Mary Duggan, A. Dunn (Wales), K. Dunne, Margo English, B. Eppel, Mrs Feore, Hilary Ferguson, Jeannie Fitzgerald, Mrs Fitzgerald, Cáit Flavin, C. Foley, Mrs Foley (Carlow), F. W. Fowler, Molly Fox, M. Gabbey, P. J. Gallagher, Mrs P. J. Gallagher, J. M. Gargan, J. P. Geoghegan, C. J. Gilgunn, Marie Gleeson, J. Godden, P. Grant, P. Greenan, C. Griffin, Valerie Hamilton, D. Hand, D. Hanley, L. Hanratty, M. Hanratty, P. Hanratty, L. Hardy, Monica Harris, Mrs S. Harrison, Anne Hayden, G. Hayes, T. Healy, Mary Heery, W. Heidenfeldt, Constance Maxwell Henry, Angela Hickey, May Hickey, Carmel Higgins, C. P. Higgins, Una Hogan, W. Hourican, P. Howard, Supt. Hughes, Mrs Hughes, Eileen Hurley, J. Hurley, Mrs J. Hurley, L. Hyde, O. Hyde, D. G. Jackson, J. P. Jackson, Maura Jennings, M. Jones (England), Mrs E. Kehoe, C. Kelleher, Miss D. Kelly, Miss E. Kelly, Miss Kelly, J. Kelly (Eniscorthy), J. Kelly, John Kelly, Patricia Kelly, W. Kelso, Marjorie Kelso, Bríd Kemple, Mrs T. Kennedy, B. Kenny, B. G. Kenny, Joan Kenny, P. Kerins, Mrs M. Kilcullen, Marguerite Kilfeather, Pat Kilfeather, Maura Kirby, Sheila Kirwan, Lynn Knight, R. Knight, Freddie Langford, Anne Lenihan, Katherine Lennon, Kitty Long, A. Lund, M. Lynch, P. Lynch, D. MacAonghusa, S. MacMathuna, B. Madden, Margaret Madden, W. Madden, Geraldine Maguire, N. Malone, E. Martin, M. J. Martin, R. Masterson, S. Masterson, T. J. McAfee, Mary McAleese, E. A. McArdle, P. McCallum, J. McAndrew, Carol McCarthy, Imelda McCarthy, Mrs W. McCormick, P. McDaid, A. McDermott, H. McDermott, M. McDevitt, P. McDevitt (USA), M. McFaul, K. McGarry, Antoinette McGee, C. McGinley, J. McGonagle, J. McGowan, C. McHugh, J. C. McIlhenny, L. McKay, M. McLaughlin, P. McLaughlin, Mrs P. McLaughlin, Rita McLoughlin, R. H.

McLoughlin, R. McMaugh, Gertrude McMeekin, Antonina McNiece, J. McRobert, Lily McRory, B. McShane, K. Messervey, Mrs Miley, Mrs W. H. Milligan, Louise Mitchell, Anne Moran, J. Moran (Dublin), Mrs P. J. Mullins, Miss B. Murphy, Catherine Murphy, J. Murphy, J. F. Murphy, K. Murphy, Miss K. Murphy, L. Murphy, Miss M. Murphy, Supt S. Murphy, G. Murtagh, S. Newcomen, Mary Nimmons, Ms M. Ní Thuama, Geraldine Nolan, D. O'Brien, M. O'Brien, R. O'Brien, T. J. O'Callaghan, Marlene O'Connor, M. O'Connor, C. O'Dálaigh, J. H. O'Dempsey, Molly O'Donnell, P. J. O'Donoghue, Philina Dowd, Mrs P. J. O'Dowd, C. O'Driscoll, Sheila O'Dwyer, B. O'Farrell, Frank O'Farrell, Mena O'Flaherty, J. O'Flynn, J. J. O'Grady, T. OGrady, W. O'Grady, M. O'Halloran, M. O'Kane, Miss K. O'Keane, T. O'Keeffe, Miss A. O'Kelly, D. O'Leary, Mrs D. O'Leary, W. N. O'Leary, T. O'Mahoney, Nan O'Mara, Mrs H. G. O'Neill, Mrs J. D. O'Neill (Tullamore), D. O'Sullivan, E. M. Perrette, Lucy Phelan, J. H. Powell, J. Power, D. Reddan, Deirdre Reid, E. Reville, Mrs Revington, Nora Rhatigan, C. Richey, Mary Clare Riordan, S. Rivlin, Miss M. Roantree, Mary Roche, Nancy Rowe, Olivia Rowlette, M. Rudzinski (Poland), D. Ryan, Joan Ryan, Supt J. Ryan, M. Ryan, J. Ryder, M. Ryder, Mrs A. Sandys, S. Scallen, Teresa Scanlon, H. Schenker, R. Seagers, P. Seery, E. Seligman, Peggy Shanahan, B. Sharkey, A. Sharp, Mrs Sharp (Dublin), Mrs Sharpe (Athlone), B. Sheridan, Mrs Shortt, Mrs Siese, Maura Slattery, D. Smith, A. Speir, Frances Sproule, J. Sproule, S. Stack, L. Steel (Scotland), Mr Stewart, Mrs Stewart, C. J. Sweeney, Fr Sweeney, T. Sweeney, Mrs D. Tempest, C. Tierney, E. Tierney, A. Timoney, V. Tomek, J. Toohey, Carmel Treacy, R. A. Twomey, Deirdre Walsh, Maureen Walsh, J. Whelehan, Margaret Winters, Diana Woodhouse, T. Woods, Y. Yuan

Appendix B: Inter-provincial Championship Winners

1952 LEINSTER

A. Bloom, P. Purcell, T. Brick, J. Lynch, A. Butler, J. Lane, NPC P. Quinn, R. Belton, J. A. Kelly, D. Egan, T. D. Purcell, D. A. Houlihan, Moreen McCarthy, NPC Ina McMenamin

Elvina Spiro, May McNulty, Ruth Giddings, Eileen O'Sullivan, Mairéad O'Neill, J. Ennis, NPC J. P. Morgan

1953 ULSTER

Supt J. Ryan, Dr P. Deery, J. Kennedy, E. McCann, M. C. Lardner, Dr D. P. Cusack (all Monaghan); T. McCollum, N. Conaghan, T. Dunbar, F. McCarroll. (Derry)

1954 LEINSTER

Eileen O'Doherty, Alice Mahon, Elvina Spiro, Marcus Shrage, J. A. Kelly, R. Belton, W. Quirke, N. Malone, Kay Byrne, Frances Morgan, J. Lynch, Ina McMenamin, Eileen O'Sullivan, Geraldine McConkey, May McNulty, Ruth Giddings, Dr P. J. O'Dowd.

1955 LEINSTER

Ruth Giddings, May McNulty, Geraldine McConkey, Babs Hooper, D. Egan, G. F. Read, NPC T. P. Boden

BEAT CONNACHT

TEAMS V. MUNSTER AND CONNACHT NOT TRACED

1956 LEINSTER

D. A. Houlihan (Birr), Moreen McCarthy; G. Read, M. Shrage; P. Pigot, P. D. Fitzgerald

BEAT MUNSTER

Ina McMenamin, Elvina Spiro; N. Malone, S. O'Flynn; R. Wallace, P. Gaynor. NPC D. R. Pigot

BEAT ULSTER

TEAM THAT BEAT CONNACHT NOT TRACED

1957 LEINSTER

Maj. G. Jackson, J. Harold, O. Rowe, J. Geoghegan, Alice Mahon, Eileen O'Doherty; NPC J. A. Scannell

BEAT CONNACHT

TEAMS V. MUNSTER AND ULSTER NOT TRACED

1958 LEINSTER

G. F. Read, M. Shrage, A. H. Davidson, J. P. MacHale, P. Fellowes, J. F. Wallis

BEAT ULSTER

TEAMS V. CONNACHT AND MUNSTER NOT TRACED

344

1959   LEINSTER

J. F. Wallis, P. Fellowes, H. Bridburg, H. Elliott, J. P. MacHale, P. Pigot

Supt and Mrs Heron, R. Giddings, M. McNulty, G. F. Read, M. Shrage, NPC R. H. Watchorn

D. A. Houlihan (Birr), M. Shrage, T. D. Purcell, R. Belton, P. Donovan, F. Fine

1960   This event was held over one weekend, with all four teams competing at one venue for the first time, at Shamrock Lodge Hotel, Athlone.

LEINSTER

A. H. Davidson, P. D. Fitzgerald, W. Burrowes, D. L. Stokes, N. Malone, S. O'Flynn, D. A. Houlihan (Birr), L. Sheeran, R. Belton, J. A. Kelly, Moreen McCarthy, Elvina Spiro, J. P. MacHale, P. J. Pigot, G. Read, M. Shrage, Eileen O'Sullivan, Anne Quinn, NPC D. T. Waldron

1961   ULSTER

D. A. Cohen, G. E. McCaw; B. R. McKinley, S. Blaney; R. A. Corrick, T. Berry; B. Vard, D. Deery; A. McKinnon, N. Percival-Price; Ms M. G. Cole, L. Paffrath; A. E. Anderson, E. F. Agnew; J. McRobert, H. A. Schenker; Ms H. Dickie, Ms G. O. Barry, NPC G. L. M. Sloane

1962   LEINSTER

C. Sweeney, E. McArdle; P. MacNeill, E. MacNeill; Molly O'Carroll, Doreen Cairnduff; T. Gleeson, T. McCormack; D. A. Houlihan (Birr) L. F. Sheeran; D. and Mrs O'Leary; D. L. Stokes, F. Fine; P. D. Fitzgerald, D. Seligman; Anne Quinn, Ms Kay O'Sullivan

1963   MUNSTER

M. and Mrs Hurley; M. and Mrs Lynch; P. J. and Mrs Doherty; G. Holmes, M. F. O'Connell; Ms J. O'Sullivan, Ms H. Pollock; Mrs Wrixon, Mrs O'Keeffe (Cork); J. Coman, J. Fitzgerald; T. D. and Maisie Cooper; J. H. and Helen Daly (Listowel), NPC P. Dooley (Waterford)

1964   MUNSTER

R. A. Twomey, W. O'Leary; J. H. and Helen Daly; M. O'Sullivan, P. Rochford; M. and Mrs Lynch; Eileen Hanley, P. C. Kiely; Ms J. Kenny, Ms M. Costello; M. and Mrs Hurley; M. Gubbins, G. Fitzgerald; Ms J. Cadell, Ms R. Maguire; NPC W. McBratney

1965   LEINSTER

Geraldine McConkey, Eileen O'Sullivan; E. J. O'Boyle, T. D. Purcell; Sonya Britton, Molly O'Carroll; T. Gleeson, T. McCormack; J. P. MacHale, P. D. Fitzgerald; G. F. Read, M. Shrage; Ina McMenamin, Ruth Giddings; Doreen Cairnduff, Anne Quinn; Molly Jones, Ina Byrne; NPC Rita McLoughlin

1966   MUNSTER

Ms J. J. O'Sullivan, Ms P. Byrne; J. F. O'Sullivan, C. Kelleher; D. T. Seale, W. Cashen; T. D. and Maisie Cooper; K. Flynn, P. J. McMahon; Dr and Mrs H. O'Grady (Mallow); B. Stewart, D. Donovan (Nenagh); C. McCarthy, J.

Whyte (Skibbereen); Ms F. Deevy, J. D. Moore (Waterford); NPC J. H. Daly

1967 LEINSTER

Dr R. Belton, T. D. Purcell; L. F. Sheeran, D. A. Houlihan (Birr); R. de Barra, P. J. Barry; E. J. Boland, D. Seligman; W. Heidenfeldt, P. D. Fitzgerald; E. MacNeill, Barbara Seligman; Moreen McCarthy and Mimi Christopher; D. and Mrs McCarville, A. Walsh, S. Huet; NPC T. Gleeson

1968 ULSTER

Mary Nimmons and Mary McAleese; A. E. Anderson, A. T. R. Anderson; Mrs A. E. Anderson, Miss M. G. Cole; Réne McFarlane, R. A. Corrick; J. H. Grummitt, T. McCormack; H. J. Clark, Mrs R. Matthews; Prof. A. McKinnon, Dr J. O'Rawe; Mrs P. Hanna, Ms M. Moore. NPC E. A. Douglas

1969 LEINSTER

Moreen McCarthy, May Clare Riordan (Callan); T. Gleeson, T. McCormack; C. Griffin, M. O'Halloran (Tullamore); E. F. Smyth, H. Barniville; Ms P. Murphy, Ms J. Connolly; Mrs F. O'Sullivan, Mrs E. Walsh; L. and Mrs Murphy; Mrs J. Brennan, Mrs M. Gallagher; K. Peakin, F. Joyce. NPC Geraldine McConkey.

1970 ULSTER

D. A. Cohen, M. Rosenberg; A. McKinnon, Dr J. O'Rawe; Rev. E. Tierney, N. Kelly (Derry); R. A. Corrick, W. A. McCombe (Magherafelt/Ballymena); J. T. Nimmons, Mary McAleese; J. Nimmons, M. McAleese; P. G. and Mrs Fitzharris (Strabane). NPC S. Stewart (Downpatrick).

1971 ULSTER

D. Deery, A. T. R. Anderson; D. A. Cohen, M. Rosenberg; A. E. Anderson, H. F. Bell (Portrush); A. McKinnon, V. Russell; G. W. Clingan, D. B. McShane (Strabane); Rev. E. Tierney, N. Kelly (Derry); Mary Nimmons, Mary McAleese; E. C. and Molly Andrew; G. E. McCaw (Lurgan) W. J. Robb (Portadown)

1972 ULSTER

D. Deery, M. Rosenberg, D. A. Cohen, J. H. Grummitt, G. E. McCaw, W. J. Robb, J. T. and Mary Nimmons, M. and Mary McAleese, Rev. E. Tierney, G. W. Clingan, D. B. McShane, T. G. Mackenzie, J. Ryder; NPC G. Sloane

1973 ULSTER

D. Deery; M. Rosenberg; D. A. Cohen; J. H. Grummitt; A. E. and Mrs Anderson; J. T. and Mary Nimmons; E. C. and Molly Andrew; M. and Mary McAleese; Mrs P. G. Fitzharris; G. W. Clingan; D. B. McShane; Renée McFarlane; G. E. McCaw; R. A. Corrick; NPC J. M. O'Donoghue

1974 LEINSTER

J. P. MacHale, P. Pigot; J. Moran, J. V. Duffy; Paddi Scannell, Rita McQueen; H. D. Barron, M. Drum; H. K. and Mrs Ryan (Trim); M. Quinn, P. J. Conroy (Portlaoise); Comdt. W. McNicholas, Anne Lenihan (Athlone); Wm. and Mrs O'Keeffe, NPC P.MacNeill.

1975 LEINSTER

J. P. MacHale, P. Pigot; J. Nolan, K. Barry; Mrs B. Foley (Bagenalstown), Mrs D. Gilligan (Portlaoise); Ms N. Murphy, Sheila Kirwan; P. D. Fitzgerald, P. MacNeill; J. Comyn, J. MacMahon; C. Corry, Ms M. Roantree; D. Garvey, M. Ó Briain; Marie Gleeson, Nuala Walsh; NPC Conor Foley.

1976 LEINSTER

Eileen O'Doherty, Nell Arnold; Ruth Giddings, P. D. Fitzgerald; Rita McQueen, Paddi Scannell; T. Gleeson, P. F. Walsh; Nell Foley, Nora Rhatigan; H. D. and Rosalind Barron; C. Conroy, M. Toomey; J. Comyn, J. MacMahon; NPC Sonya Britton.

1977 LEINSTER

P. Porteous, D. O'Connor; W. Shanahan, J. Corcoran, T. Gleeson, P. F. Walsh; D. Garvey, M. Ó Briain; P. O'Farrell, L. Shanahan; Ann Romaine, Patsy Meehan; P. H. Torney, P. Walshe; T. Leahy, F. Stack (Drogheda); F. Meenan, N. Phelan (Kilkenny). NPC G. Deignan.

1978 ULSTER

Mary Nimmons, Miss M. G. Cole; J. A. Paul, K. L. Hawtin; Dr S. McCombe, I. H. Lindsay; M. Rosenberg, H. Campbell; P. McLoone, J. McIntyre; G. W. Clingan, Mrs P. G. Fitzharris; N. Percival-Price, K. Singleton; T. G. Mackenzie, Moyna Johnston; C. Richey, J. H. Grummitt (captain)

1979 LEINSTER

P. Porteous, K. Barry; T. Roche, M. Roche (Rosslare); T. Gleeson, P. F. Walsh; N. Tóibín, P. Walshe; Alex and Anne Montwill; Paul Kelly; Pat Kelly; Des and Mrs Scully; Kathleen Banks, Marie Preston; Eileen O'Doherty, Anne Quinn. NPC Conor Foley

1980 ULSTER

D. Deery; A Lennon; Mary Nimmons; M. Rosenberg; T. J. G. Bennett; I. H. Lindsay; E. C. and Molly Andrew; J. Paul; J. Hawtin; J. McIntyre; P. McLoone; R. A. Corrick; P. C. Duffy; Moyna Johnston; T. G. Mackenzie; N. Percival-Price; K. Y. Singleton; NPC H. J. Clark.

1981 LEINSTER

M. Shrage; A. Johnston; J. H. and Aileen O'Keeffe; T. Gleeson; J. Daly; Valerie Hand; Mrs J. Maguire; S. Sheehan; M. Trench; J. Lowry; W. Quinlan (Kilkenny); Doreen Cairnduff; B. J. O'Brien; J. Agnew; Bernie Gannon; J. MacMahon; Mona MacMahon; NPC D. L. Stokes.

1982 CONNACHT

P. F. Walsh; G. Keaveney; R. Timlin; E. Fitzgerald; J. Keaveney; J. Moran (Ballina); J. J. and Mrs Murphy (Longford); W. and Mrs O'Farrell (Longford); Fr Keane; F. Rhattigan (Castlereagh); Vincent and Mary Brennan; Ray Brennan; P. Scannell; Mrs M. O'Farrell; NPC Una Walsh

1983 CONNACHT

Vincent and Mary Brennan; Ray Brennan; P. Scannell; P. F. and Nuala Walsh; G. Keaveney; E. Glynn; R. Timlin; E. Fitzgerald; Seán and Anna Glynn; M. MacDonagh; M. Coughlan; Maureen Ryder; Maura O'Farrell.

1984 CONNACHT

Vincent and Mary Brennan; Ray Brennan; P. Scannell; P. F. and Nuala Walsh; G. Keaveney; E. Glynn; R. Timlin; E. Fitzgerald; M. MacDonagh; S. Glynn; M. Coughlan; Maura O'Farrell; F. and Mrs Davey (Charlestown); N. and Mrs Kilroy (Ballina); NPC Maureen Ryder.

1985 CONNACHT

P. F. and Nuala Walsh; G. Keaveney; E. Glynn; P. Quinn; Maura O'Farrell; H. Connolly; J. Connolly; P. Connolly; R. Masterson; S. Masterson; F. Kenny (Longford!); Seán and Anna Glynn; R. Brennan; P. Scannell; M. MacDonagh; R. Timlin; NPC V.Brennan.

1986 LEINSTER*

Gráinne Barton; P. Walshe; B. Dolan; D. Garvey; Kathryn and N. K. FitzGibbon; Lucinda Hanratty; L. Whately; Alex and Ann Montwill; Aileen and J. H. O'Keeffe; P. Ó Briain; B. J. O'Brien; T. Walsh; NPC J. Comyn

*No official record or report of team found. John Comyn listed the team members from memory twenty-two years later, in September 2008.

1987 ULSTER

M. O'Kane (captain)

1988 CONNACHT

R. Brennan; P. Scannell; M. MacDonagh; S. Gillen; Nuala Walsh; P. F. Walsh; Maureen Ryder; Malcolm Ryder; Collette Mulhern; M. O'Connor; E. Fitzgerald; R. Timlin; B. McHugh; Maura O'Farrell; Emer Joyce; J. Godden; E. Glynn; G. Keaveney; NPC V. Brennan.

1989 LEINSTER

Elva Gannon; Pauline Maguire; Ann Montwill; Aileen O'Keeffe; Eileen O'Doherty; Ann Quinn; Miriam McConville; Geraldine Rafferty; Katherine Lennon; J. McCormack; Bernie Gannon; J. R. Agnew; J. Cunningham; T. Hanlon; L. Shanahan; J. Fitzgibbon; NPC M. Lavelle

1990 CONNACHT

P. F. Walsh; M. Hession; G. Keaveney; E. Glynn; Maura O'Farrell; R. Timlin; E. Fitzgerald; Seán and Anna Glynn; Ray Brennan; P. Scannell; S. Gillen; M. MacDonagh; Michael and Marlene O'Connor

1991 LEINSTER

N. K. and K. FitzGibbon; D. Garvey; P. Ó Briain; J. Cunningham; T. Hanlon; M. Lavelle; T. Tierney; R. Fitzgerald; S. O'Lubaigh; Alex Montwill; W. F. Maclachlan; B. Sheridan; T. Leahy; NPC S. Dowling

1992 MUNSTER

D. A. Houlihan (Ennis – captain); C. McInerney; Ena Cleary; D. Reddan; R. Boland; P. Walshe; G. Lessells; A. Cleary; M. Burke; P. Liston; Bríd Kirby; Marie Hanrahan

1993 CONNACHT

R. Timlin and others

1994 LEINSTER

P. Ó Briain; T. Roche; T. Ryan; J. Clarson; Valerie Hand; Ann Montwill; Rita O'Donnell; Anne Hanratty; J. Cunningham; T. Hanlon; N. Kennedy; N. Tóibín; D. O'Keeffe; S. Udvari; NPC J. H. O'Keeffe

1995 LEINSTER

P. Barry; D. A. Jackson; J. Cunningham; T. Hanlon; T. Roche; P. Ó Briain; Alex and Ann Montwill; Aileen and J. H. O'Keeffe; J. Comyn; B. J. O'Brien; D. Scully; E. Balfe

1996 CONNACHT

P. F. Walsh; P. Scannell; G. Keaveney; E. Glynn; M. Hession; R. Timlin; S. MacMathúna; Maura O'Farrell; E. Feerick; Joan Kenny; R. Brennan; M. MacDonagh; Una Walsh; David Walsh.

1997 LEINSTER

J. Comyn; B. J. O'Brien; D. Garvey; M. Ó Briain; P. Walshe; Gráinne Barton; Maria and P. J. Barry; Rebecca O'Keeffe; Hilary Dowling Long; J. Carroll; T. Garvey

1998 LEINSTER

J. Comyn; B. J. O'Brien; D. Garvey; M. Ó Briain; P. Ó Briain; T. Roche; Alex and Ann Montwill; J. P. MacHale; Valerie Hand; J. Carroll; T. Garvey; NPC Alan O'Sullivan

1999 LEINSTER

J. Comyn; B. J. O'Brien; P. Ó Briain; T. Roche; T. Walsh; N. Tóibín; Alex and Ann Montwill; P. Pigot; D. MacAonghusa; J. Cunningham; T. Hanlon; NPC P. Hanratty

2000 LEINSTER

N. Tóibín; R. Boland; P. Pigot; T. Walsh; R. Milne; B. J. O'Brien; J. Comyn; M. Roche; Jill Kulchycky; Pauline Maguire; J. Heneghan; T. MacCormac.

2001 LEINSTER

P. Hanratty (captain); S. Dowling; Gráinne Barton; P. Walshe; Anne-Marie Horan; J. Carroll; B. J. O'Brien; R. Milne; P. Ó Briain; T. Roche; Jill Kulchycky; J. Comyn

2002 CONNACHT

R. Timlin (captain); E. Glynn; M. MacDonagh; D. MacAonghusa; D. Walsh;

C. Coyne; Manus Burke; E. Gallagher; Michael and Marlene O'Connor; S. MacMathúna; Maura O'Farrell.

2003 LEINSTER

T. Roche (captain); B. J. O'Brien; T. Hanlon. J. Carroll; P. Delaney; E. Galligan; Pat Kelly; D. Terry; Ann Montwill; Valerie Hand; Lily McRory; Aileen O'Keeffe

2004 CONNACHT

D. Walsh (captain); R. Timlin; Mary Trench; Manus Burke; C. Coyne; H. Curran; E. Gallagher; E. Fitzgerald; E. Glynn; J. Heneghan; D. MacAonghus; M. MacDonagh

2005 CONNACHT

D. Walsh (captain); C. Coyne; Manus Burke; E. Gallagher; E. Fitzgerald; Louise Mitchell; R. Timlin; E. Glynn; M. MacDonagh; P. Scannell; J. Heneghan; D. MacAonghusa; H. Curran.

2006 CONNACHT

D. Walsh (captain); C. Coyne; Manus Burke; E. Gallagher; E. Fitzgerald; Louise Mitchell; R. Timlin; E. Glynn; G. Keaveney; M. MacDonagh; P. Scannell; J. Heneghan; D. MacAonghusa; H.Curran.

2007 LEINSTER

Gilda Pender; Noreen Pender; Anna Onishuk; K. de Raeymaeker; J. Carroll; T. Garvey; T. Hanlon; A. Mesbur; R. Milne; B. J. O'Brien; M. Ó Briain; P. Ó Briain. NPC D.A.Jackson.

2008 LEINSTER

P. Barry; D. Jackson; R. Milne; B. J. O'Brien; Margo English; Miriam McConville; T. MacCormac; R. McMaugh; Jill Kulchycky; Teresa Rigney; M. Ó Briain; P. Ó Briain; P. Kelly; D. Terry; NPC M. Quinn

INTERMEDIATE INTER-PROVINCIAL

1995 LEINSTER

E. & M. Hayes, A. Kelly, E. Staunton

1996 CONNACHT

F. & M. Goodwin, J. MacDonald, M. Morrison, J. Fahy, J. Morgan

1997 CONNACHT

F. & M. Goodwin, F. Dolan, P. McDonald, J. MacDonald, M. Morrison,

1998 LEINSTER

F. Kelly, M. Keating, J. McCurdy, C. Tierney, G. Kelly, N. Minogue, R. King, C. O'Driscoll, A. Delaney, J. Timlin, B. McGuinne, P. Sparks, NPC A. Timoney

1999 LEINSTER

A. Breen, M. Hand, P. Reilly, P. Ward, M. Cox, S. Gleeson, L. Gaynor, J.

Riordan, J. McCuddden, S. McNamara, B. & F. Kelly, NPC A. Timoney

2000 CONNACHT

R. Conway, P. Waldron, D. & P. Townley, M. Burke, E. Gallagher, J. Fahy, J. Morgan, K. Coleman, M. & F. Goodwin, J. MacDonald, NPC B. Finan

2001 LEINSTER

A. Howard, P. Wills, M. Moran, I. Newell, J. Coyne, G. Franks, E. & R. O'Shea, N. Dolan, D. Walsh, D. Dunne, J. Robinson, NPC N. Madden

2002 LEINSTER

A. Howard, P. Wills, M. Moran, I. Newell, M. Moonan, S. Treanor, D. O'Connor, E. Scott, F. Gallagher, F. Carty, M. & T. Keyes, NPC R. McNamara

2003 MUNSTER

J. Fitzgerald, E. O'Neill, J. K. Ryan, S. McMorrow, N. Fitzgibbon, T. Hardiman, C. Connolly, B. Coleman, L. Hyde, J. Whelehan, E. Kelleher, B. Murphy, NPC N. Hickey

2004 ULSTER

D. & D. Brennan, J. McLaughlin, S. McNutt, R. Cochrane, F. Houston, A. & M. Levey, C. Doherty, M. McClenaghan, A. & P. Carr, NPC I. Lindsay

2005 LEINSTER

S. Horgan, E. O'Donovan, K. O'Shea, B. Walsh, M. Whelan, T. Hughes, D. Lynch, G. McDonald, B. McKay, M. O'Brien, C. O'Reilly, G. Simpson, NPC Rita McNamara

2006 ULSTER

D. & D. Brennan, E. MacNicholl, B. Sargeant, A. & J. Bergin, M. J. O'Sullivan, J. Clear, J. Bilberg, G. O'Donnell, M. McClenaghan, J. O'Sullivan, NPC I. Lindsay

2007 CONNACHT

A. Davey, E. Maloney, M. Donlon, P. Kenny, L. Duffy, R. Jennings, L. Faherty, H. Geraghty, E. O'Connor, G. Sheridan, A. Kelly, A. Kilcoyne, NPC D. Walsh

2008 LEINSTER

M. Delaney, M. Kane, B. Ronan, H. Williams, M. Lombard, M. Murray, P. Cassidy, L. Culligan, G. McKenna, D. O'Brien, J. Naughton, P. Tolan, NPC B. McKay

2009 LEINSTER

B. Coggins, F. OGallachóir, T. Irvine, M. Teehan, B. Eccles, C. Hawkins, M. Lombard, M. Murray, P. Geoghegan, M. O'Leary, A. Meagher, P. Stewart, NPC P. Tolan

Appendix C: Home-International Championships

Camrose Trophy

1937

First Match in the Championship

20 February 1937, Shelbourne Hotel, Dublin v. Scotland +3560

> Kathleen Lambert, Geraldine McConkey, Mrs Boles, Mrs Colgan, D. Rivlin, H. Fine, NPC J. Hogan

23–24 March, v. Northern Ireland +2280

> H. Williams, H. Freehill, J. O'Neill, Mairéad Crofts, Violet and D. R. Pigot, NPC F. T. Quin

24–25 July, Royal Marine Hotel, Dun Laoghaire, v. Wales +620

> E. O. Barry, P. Quinn, J. P. Morgan, C. O'Neill, Rosaleen and W. J. L. O'Connell, NPC F. T. Quin

15–16 October, v. England –2830

> Kathleen Lambert, Geraldine McConkey, E. O. Barry, P. Quinn, Rosaleen and W. J. L. O'Connell, NPC F. T. Quin

1938

19–20 February, Buchanan Club, Glasgow v. Scotland + 2,110

> Kathleen Lambert, Geraldine McConkey, H. G. Freehill, H. Williams, P. Quinn, D. Rivlin, NPC unknown

12–13 March, Royal Marine Hotel, Dun Laoghaire v. Northern Ireland +2,400

> Kathleen Lambert, Geraldine McConkey, H. G. Freehill, H. Williams, H. Fine, D. Rivlin, NPC D. R. Pigot

21–22 May, Cardiff v. Wales –1,330

> Kathleen Lambert, Geraldine McConkey, H. G. Freehill, H. Williams; Brian Ebrill, F. T. Quin, NPC D. R. Pigot

12–13 November, Royal Marine Hotel, Dun Laoghaire v. England –1,950

> Kathleen Lambert, Geraldine McConkey, H. G. Freehill, H. Williams; E. O. Barry, P. Quinn, NPC D. R. Pigot

1939

4 March, Royal Marine Hotel, Dun Laoghaire v. Scotland +1,490

> H. G. Freehill, H. Williams; E. O. Barry, P. Quinn; F. McMenamin, Ina Hickey, NPC D. R. Pigot

29–30 April, Belfast v Northern Ireland –3,730

E. O. Barry, P. Quinn; F. McMenamin, Ina Hickey; J. and P. Lynch, NPC D. R. Pigot

24–25 June, Dun Laoghaire v. Wales +50

E. O. Barry, P. Quinn; F. McMenamin, Ina Hickey; H. G. Freehill, H. Williams, NPC J. E. Hogan

Match v. England abandoned – Second World War started 1 September

1946

Camrose resumed after Second World War

2–3 March, Royal Marine Hotel, Dun Laoghaire v. Northern Ireland –2590

Ina McMenamin, T. D. Purcell, W. J. L. O'Connell, F. W. O'Connell, E. Boland, P. P. Donovan, NPC P. J. O'Dowd

30–31 March, Cardiff v. Wales, Wales won

Ina McMenamin, T. D. Purcell; B. L. Williams, H. Williams; C. H. Day, R. Sheehan. NPC C. N. Byrne

19–20 October, Central Hotel, Dublin v. Scotland +1050

Ina McMenamin, T. D. Purcell, W. J. L. O'Connell, F. W. O'Connell, T. P. Boden, T. Ryder, NPC P. J. O'Dowd

23–24 November, Stockport v. England +1200

Ina McMenamin, T. D. Purcell, W. J. L. O'Connell, F. W. O'Connell, J. J. Bastow, W. R. Bastow, NPC P. J. O'Dowd

1947

1–2 March 1947, Central Hotel, Dublin v. Wales +4330

J. J. Bastow, W. R. Bastow, A. H. Davidson, May McNulty, E. O. Barry, D. Egan. NPC P. J. O'Dowd

17–18 May, Central Hotel, Dublin v. England –1950

Ina McMenamin, T. D. Purcell, J. J. Bastow, W. R. Bastow, E. O. Barry, D. Egan, NPC P. J. O'Dowd

31 May–1 June, Glasgow v. Scotland –1610

P. P. Donovan, D. Rivlin, A. H. Davidson, May McNulty, B. L. Williams, H. Williams, NPC Ina McMenamin

12–13 September, Belfast v. Northern Ireland –1080

J. J. Bastow, W. R. Bastow, D. Egan, E. Barry, D. Rivlin, P. P. Donovan, NPC Dr P. J. O'Dowd

1948

31 JANUARY–1 FEBRUARY, ROSSES HOTEL, DUN LAOGHAIRE V. SCOTLAND +200

E. O. Barry, D. Egan, Flora McLoone, N. Peart, Ina McMenamin, T. D. Purcell, NPC J. O'Neill

28–29 FEBRUARY, QUEENS HOTEL, BIRMINGHAM V. ENGLAND –3480

E. O. Barry, D. Egan, B. L. and Harold Williams, J. Lynch, J. Harold, NPC J. ONeill

13–14 MARCH, ROSSES HOTEL, DUN LAOGHAIRE V. NORTHERN IRELAND –5340

Ina McMenamin, T. D. Purcell, B. L. and H. Williams, J. Rubenstein J. G. Burke, NPC J. ONeill

26–27 JUNE, CARDIFF V. WALES –2480

J. O'Neill (captain), J. G. Burke, May McNulty, A. H. Davidson, P. Burke, M. Martin, NPC unknown

1949

PRE-APRIL, NEWCASTLE V. NORTHERN IRELAND +1140

Eileen and J. M. O'Sullivan, J. Harold, J. A. Kelly, P. P. Donovan, P. Carson, NPC Geraldine McConkey

2–3 APRIL, EDINBURGH V. SCOTLAND –500

J. Harold, J. A. Kelly, D. Rivlin, P. P. Donovan, Eileen and J. M. O'Sullivan NPC P. J. O'Dowd

23–24 APRIL, COLLINS BARRACKS, CORK V. WALES +3480

D. Rivlin P. P. Donovan, Moreen McCarthy, Eileen O'Sullivan J. A. Kelly J. Harold, NPC Geraldine McConkey

21–22 MAY, DUBLIN V. ENGLAND –840

P. P. Donovan, J. Harold, J. A. Kelly, D. Rivlin, Eileen and J. M. O'Sullivan, NPC Geraldine McConkey

1949/50 IMPs SCORING INTRODUCED

3–4 DECEMBER 1949, DUN LAOGHAIRE V. SCOTLAND –40 IMPS

Moreen McCarthy, P. Carson, P. P. Donovan, D. Rivlin, R. A. Belton, J. A. Kelly, NPC D. Egan

28–29 JANUARY 1950, LONDON V. ENGLAND –62 IMPS

E. O. Barry, D. A. Houlihan, R. A. Belton, P. P. Donovan, J. A. Kelly, D. Rivlin, J. P. Morgan

25–26 FEBRUARY, DUNDALK V. NORTHERN IRELAND –32 IMPS

E. O. Barry, P. P. Donovan, J. Harold, J. Kelly, Eileen and J. M. O'Sullivan, NPC Ina McMenamin

29–30 APRIL, LLANDUDNO V. WALES +32 IMPS

Moreen McCarthy, Eileen O'Sullivan, Clare and D. Lyne, J. A. Kelly, D. A. Houlihan (Birr), NPC D. Egan

1950/51

18 NOVEMBER, V. ENGLAND 31

P. P. Donovan, P. Carson, J. A. Kelly, R. A. Belton, E. O. Barry, D. A. Houlihan (Birr), NPC D.Egan

JANUARY, V. NORTHERN IRELAND +29

P. P. Donovan, D. Egan, E. O. Barry, D. A. Houlihan (Birr), R. A. Belton, J. A. Kelly, J. J. Bastow

28–29 APRIL, V. WALES +50

R. A. Belton, J. A. Kelly, P. P. Donovan, D. Egan, Ruth Gidddings, May McNulty, NPC J. J. Bastow

19–20 MAY, GLASGOW, V. SCOTLAND +19

P. P. Donovan, D. Egan, R. A. Belton, J. A. Kelly, Ruth Giddings, May McNulty, NPC Cleo Roy

1998/99

4–6 DECEMBER, AWAY, V. WALES 48–12

T. Hanlon, H. McGann, N. Tóibín, P. Walshe, D. Garvey, M. Ó Briain, NPC Gráinne Barton

8–10 JANUARY, AWAY, V. NORTHERN IRELAND 27–33

T. Hanlon, H. McGann, D. Garvey, M. Ó Briain, J. Carroll, T. Garvey, NPC J. Comyn

5–7 FEBRUARY, ENNIS, V. ENGLAND 19–41

T. Hanlon, H. McGann, N. Tóibín, P. Walshe, J. Carroll, T. Garvey, NPC M. McGloughlin

26–28 MARCH, GLEN OF THE DOWNS V. SCOTLAND 25–35

N. Tóibín, P. Walshe, J. Carroll, T. Garvey, D. Garvey, M. Ó Briain, NPC Gráinne Barton

1999/2000 CBAI WON THE CAMROSE

3–5 DECEMBER, CAVAN V. NORTHERN IRELAND 53–37

T. Hanlon, H. McGann, G. Keaveney R. Timlin, B. J. O'Brien, R. Milne, NPC Mark Burke

7–9 JANUARY, DERBY V. ENGLAND, 58–30

T. Hanlon, H. McGann, G. Keaveney, R. Timlin, R. Boland, N. Tóibín, NPC Mark Moran

25–27 FEBRUARY, FENWICK V. SCOTLAND 53–37

> T. Hanlon, H. McGann, G. Keaveney, R. Timlin, R. Boland, N. Tóibín, NPC M. Moran

2–4 MARCH, DUNADRY INN, BELFAST V. WALES 54–34

> T. Hanlon, H. McGann, G. Keaveney, R. Timlin, R. Boland, N. Tóibín, NPC M. Moran

2000/2001

1–3 DECEMBER, CORK V. ENGLAND 36–51

> T. Hanlon, H. McGann, G. Keaveney, R. Timlin, R. Boland, N. Tóibín, NPC M. Moran

2–4 FEBRUARY, KNOCK V. SCOTLAND 43–47

> T. Hanlon, H. McGann, G. Keaveney, R. Timlin, R. Boland, N. Tóibín, NPC Grainne Barton

25–27 FEBRUARY, ABERPORT V. WALES 34–56

> G. Keaveney, R. Timlin, R. Boland, N. Tóibín, P. Ó Briain, T. Roche, NPC M. Moran

MAY, BELFAST V. NORTHERN IRELAND 47–43

> G. Keaveney (captain), R. Timlin, P. Ó Briain, T. Roche, M. MacDonagh, B. J. O'Brien

2001/2002

JANUARY, DUMFRIES V. SCOTLAND 53–47

> T. Hanlon, H. McGann, G. Keaveney, R. Timlin, N. Tóibín, P. Walshe, NPC M. Moran

KILKENNY V. WALES 36–54

> T. Hanlon, H. McGann, G. Keaveney, R. Timlin, N. Tóibín, P. Walshe, NPC Michael O'Connor

FEBRUARY, ROSSES POINT V. NORTHERN IRELAND 62–28

> T. Hanlon, H. McGann, G. Keaveney, R. Timlin, N. Tóibín, P. Walshe, NPC M. Moran

MARCH, NEWPORT WALES, V. ENGLAND 28–61

> T. Hanlon, H. McGann, G. Keaveney, R. Timlin, N. Tóibín, P. Walshe, NPC M. Moran

2002/2003

DECEMBER, WREXHAM V. WALES 41–47

> T. Hanlon, H. McGann, J. Carroll, T. Garvey, D. Garvey, M. Ó Briain, NPC M. Moran

JANUARY, ANTRIM V. NORTHERN IRELAND 39–51

> T. Hanlon, H. McGann, J. Carroll, T. Garvey, D. Garvey, M. Ó Briain, NPC R. Timlin

FEBRUARY, DROGHEDA V. ENGLAND 29–61

> J. Carroll, T. Garvey, D. Garvey, M. Ó Briain, T. MacCormac, P. Ó Briain, NPC R. Timlin

MARCH, PORTMARNOCK V. SCOTLAND 52–38

> T. Hanlon, H. McGann, J. Carroll, T. Garvey, T. MacCormac, P. Ó Briain, NPC M. Moran

2003/2004

DECEMBER, MANCHESTER V. ENGLAND 28–51.5

> D. Garvey, M. Ó Briain, C. Coyne, D. Walsh, G. Keaveney, R. Timlin, NPC T. Hanlon

JANUARY, DUMFRIES V. SCOTLAND 47–43

> D. Garvey, M. Ó Briain, C. Coyne, D. Walsh, N. K. FitzGibbon, A. Mesbur, NPC G. Keaveney

FEBRUARY, MULLINGAR V. WALES 49–41

> D. Garvey, M. Ó Briain, C. Coyne, D. Walsh, T. Hanlon, H. McGann, NPC G. Keaveney

CARRICK-ON-SHANNON V NORTHERN IRELAND, 58–32

> T. Hanlon, H. McGann, J. Carroll, T. Garvey, B. J. Ó Brien, T. Roche, NPC G. Keaveney

2005: NEW FORMAT: TWO WEEKENDS; TWO MATCHES EACH WEEKEND; CBAI WON

7–9 JANUARY, SCOTLAND V. SCOTLAND 30–28

> T. Hanlon, H. McGann, A. Mesbur, N. FitzGibbon, M. Ó Briain, P. Ó Briain. NPC D. A. Jackson

7–9 JANUARY, SCOTLAND V. WALES 43–17

> T. Hanlon, H. McGann, A. Mesbur, N. FitzGibbon, M. Ó Briain, P. Ó Briain, NPC D. A. Jackson

4–6 MARCH, KELLS, COUNTY ANTRIM V. NORTHERN IRELAND 32–28

COL. WALSHE TROPHY

> T. Hanlon, H. McGann, A. Mesbur, N. FitzGibbon, Mark Moran, Peter Pigot, NPC D. A. Jackson

4–6 MARCH, KELLS, COUNTY ANTRIM V. ENGLAND 38–22

FIRST COMPETITION FOR JOE MORAN TROPHY

> T. Hanlon, H. McGann, A. Mesbur, N. FitzGibbon, NPC D. A. Jackson

2006 Played Over Two Weekends; CBAI Won

6–8 January, Castleknock v. England and Wales

> T. Hanlon, H. McGann, A. Mesbur, N. FitzGibbon, J. Carroll, T. Garvey, NPC D. A. Jackson

3–5 March, Newport v. Northern Ireland and Scotland

> T. Hanlon, H. McGann, A. Mesbur, N. FitzGibbon, J. Carroll, T. Garvey, NPC D. A. Jackson

2007 Six Teams Competed, Two From CBAI, the Holders

In Oxford:

> 'A' Team: T. Hanlon, H. McGann, A. Mesbur, N. FitzGibbon, J. Carroll, T. Garvey, NPC D. A. Jackson

> 'B' Team: C. Coyne, D. Walsh, G. Keaveney, R. Timlin, M. Ó Briain, P. Ó Briain, NPC M. Moran

In Aberdeen

> 'A' Team: T. Hanlon, A. Mesbur, N. FitzGibbon, T. Garvey. NPC D. A. Jackson.

> David Jackson partnered Tommy Garvey when Tom Hanlon became ill and Éamonn Galligan stepped in as non-playing captain.

> 'B' Team: C. Coyne, D. Walsh, G. Keaveney, R. Timlin, M. Ó Briain, P. Ó Briain. NPC P. Quinn (Ennis).

2008 Two teams represented the CBAI, as host for the final weekend

In Belfast

> 'A' Team: T. Hanlon, H. McGann, J. Carroll, T. Garvey, A. Mesbur, NPC D. A. Jackson

> 'B' Team: M. Ó Briain, P. Ó Briain, M. Moran, P. Pigot, Jill Kulchycky, Teresa Rigney, NPC T. Walsh

In Castleknock

> 'A' Team: T. Hanlon, H. McGann, J. Carroll, T. Garvey. N. K. FitzGibbon, A. Mesbur, NPC D. A. Jackson

> 'B' Team: M. Ó Briain, P. Ó Briain, M. Moran, P. Pigot, Jill Kulchycky, Teresa Rigney, NPC T. Walsh

2009

In Cardiff:

> J. Carroll, T. Garvey, T. Hanlon, H. McGann, N. K. FitzGibbon, A. Mesbur, NPC D. A. Jackson.

In Oxford:

> J. Carroll, T. Garvey, A. Mesbur, P. Walshe, D. O'Gorman, T. Walsh, NPC D. Jackson.

Until 2005, a single match was played over a weekend, so counting the number of Camrose 'caps' was straightforward. When the format changed to a two-weekend competition, with each nation playing against two opponents each weekend, records depended on the accuracy of reports as to which players participated in the different matches. Counting 'caps' became more problematic when the format changed again in 2007 and an additional team –initially from the holders, thereafter from the nation hosting the final weekend – was added. From 2005, 'caps' have been counted one per weekend, as they are calculated in the Lady Milne Trophy.

NUMBER OF CAMROSE 'CAPS'

27	T. Hanlon		Eileen O'Sullivan
26	H. McGann		T. D. Purcell
16	T. Garvey	5	C. Coyne
15	E. O.Barry		May McNulty
	J. Carroll		W. J. L. O'Connell
	G. Keaveney		D. Walsh
	R. Timlin	4	J. J. Bastow
14	P. P. Donovan.		W. R. Bastow
13	N. Tóibín		D. A. Houlihan (Birr)
12	J. A. Kelly	3	A. H. Davidson
12	M. Ó Briain		Moreen McCarthy
11	A. Mesbur		M. Moran
	D. Rivlin		B. J. O'Brien
	H. Williams		F. W O'Connell.
10	Ina McMenamin (Hickey)		J. M. O'Sullivan
9	P. Ó Briain		P. Pigot
	N. FitzGibbon		B. L. Williams
	D. Garvey		T. Roche
8	D. Egan	2	J. G. Burke
	P. Quinn	.	P. Carson
	P. Walshe		H. Fine
7	H. Freehill		Ruth Giddings
6	R. Belton		Jill Kulchycky
	R. Boland		J. Lynch
	J. Harold		Rosaleen O'Connell
	Kathleen Lambert		J. O'Neill
	Geraldine McConkey		Teresa Rigney

THE FOLLOWING HAVE EACH PLAYED IN ONE CAMROSE MATCH:

T. Boden, E. J. Boland, Kathleen Boles, P. Burke, Mrs Colgan, Mairéad Crofts (O'Neill), C. H. Day, B. Ebrill, D. A. Jackson, P. Lynch, Claire Lyne, D. Lyne, T. MacCormac, M. MacDonagh, M. Martin, Flora McLoone, R. Milne, J. P. Morgan, D. O'Gorman, C. O'Neill, N. Peart, D. R. Pigot, Violet Pigot, F. T. Quin, J. Rubenstein, R. J. Sheehan. T. Walsh.

Fourteen women played in thirty Camrose matches between 1937 and 1951. In only five matches were there no women players. Since 1998, only two women have won places on Camrose teams.

SENIORS CAMROSE

2008 INAUGURAL YEAR

OXFORD

> E. Glynn, P. Scannell, D. A. Houlihan, G. Lessells, M. MacDonagh, B. Pattinson, NPC M .O'Connor

Appendix D: Home-international Championships

Lady Milne Trophy

CBAI Teams

May 1950, London

CBAI team: Jacqueline Prost (captain), Doreen Cairnduff, Rita McNally, Mrs G. J. Doyle.

June 1998, Cardiff

Grainne Barton, Rosemary Ennis, Maria Barry Anne Montwill, Aileen and Rebecca O'Keeffe, NPC Marie Cummins

June 1999, Belfast

Clare Pippet, Jill Kulchycky, Helen Carroll, Ita Hoy, Patricia Kelly, Catherine McCann, NPC T. Walsh

June 2000, Eastbourne

Helen Carroll, Jill Kulchycky, Pat MacMahon, Pat Ryan, Helen Holman, Carol McCarthy, NPC T. Walsh

June 2001, Malahide

Helen Carroll, Jill Kulchycky, Mamie MacCormac, Carol-Anne Cummins, Joan Crowley, Mary Finn , NPC Pauline Maguire

June 2002, Aberdeen

Helen Carroll, Jill Kulchycky, Hilary Dowling Long, Anne-Marie Horan, Patsy Meehan, Petra O'Neill, NPC P. Delaney

June 2003, Cardiff

Helen Carroll, Jill Kulchycky, Hilary Dowling Long, Anne-Marie Horan, Ena Cleary, Mary Finn, NPC P. Delaney

April 2004, Antrim

Helen Carroll, Jill Kulchycky, Hilary Dowling Long, Anne-Marie Horan, Emer Joyce, Joan Kenny, NPC T. MacCormac

April 2005, Manchester

Ena Cleary, Mary Finn, Heidi Lillis, Teresa Rigney, Nuala Lynch, Maureen Meade, NPC B.J.O'Brien

April 2006, Ballymena

Valerie Burke-Moran, Kathleen Vaughan, Grace Finegan, Petra O'Neill, Gilda Pender, Noreen Pender, NPC Valerie Hand

April 2007, Manchester

Ena Cleary, Jeannie Fitzgerald, Heidi Lillis, Teresa Rigney, Mary Lindopp,

Anna Onishuk, NPC G. Keaveney

APRIL 2008, SCOTLAND

Ena Cleary, Jeanie Fitzgerald, Carol-Anne Cummins, Maureen Pattinson., Grace Finegan, Petra O'Neill

INDIVIDUAL CAPS IN LADY MILNE

6:     Helen Carroll, Jill Kulchycky
4:     Ena Cleary
3:     Hilary Dowling Long, Mary Finn, Ann Marie Horan, Petra O'Neill
2:     Carol Anne Cummins, Grace Finegan, Jeanie Fitzgerald, Heidi Lillis, Teresa Rigney

THE FOLLOWING PLAYERS EACH HAVE ONE CAP:

Maria Barry, Gráinne Barton, Valerie Burke Moran, Doreen Cairnduff, Joan Crowley, Sheila Doyle, Rosemary Ennis, Helen Holman, Ita Hoy, Emer Joyce, Patricia Kelly, Joan Kenny, Mary Lindopp, Nuala Lynch, Mamie MacCormac, Catherine McCann, Carol McCarthy, Pat MacMahon, Rita McNally, Maureen Meade, Patsy Meehan, Ann Montwill, Aileen O'Keeffe, Rebecca O'Keeffe, Anna Onishuk, Maureen Pattinson, Gilda Pender, Noreen Pender, Clare Pippet, Jacki Prost, Pat Ryan, Kathleen Vaughan.

JUNIOR CAMROSE (UNDER 26) AND PEGGY BAYER TROPHY (UNDER 20)

1999

Junior: A. Barton, B. McKenzie, M. Clarson, T. MacCormac, Michelle and David Nolan, NPC H. Dowling Long

Under 20: E. Fox, N. Pierse, S. Gilmartin, F. McInerney, M. Delahunty, J. Martin, NPC R. King

2000, PORTCRAWL, WALES

Junior: B. McKenzie, T. MacCormac, A. Barton, D. Nolan, E. Fox, J. Martin. NPC H. Dowling Long

2001, EDINBURGH

Junior: A. Barton, D. Nolan, C. Heffron, F. O'Connor, T. Murphy, D. Kenneally, NPC H. Dowling Long

Under 20: S. Bavalia, J. Martin, E. Davis, P. Scannell, S. Gilmartin, F. McInerney, NPC R. King

2002, BIRMINGHAM

Junior: A. Barton, J. Latham, O. Walsh, R. Boyd, J. Martin, NPC H. Dowling Long

Under 20: S. Gilmartin, F. McInerney, E. Davis, C. Ó Muircheartaigh, Ho Ming Chan, P. Scannell, NPC H. Dowling Long

2003, BELFAST

> Junior: J. Martin, D. Nilan, S. Gilmartin, F. McInerney, H. Sexton, J. Latham, NPC T. MacCormac

> Under 20: E. Davis, C. Ó Muircheartaigh, P. Scannell, E. Ó Fiacháin, R. Boyd, M. Delahunty, NPC H. Dowling Long

2004, CORK

> Junior: E. Davis, E. Ó Fiacháin, S. Gilmartin, F. McInerney, O. Walsh, M. Delahunty, NPC H. Dowling Long

> Under 20: A. Considine, E. Liddy, P. Scannell, I. Hough, R. Boyd, M. McElroy, NPC B.J. O'Brien

2005, WALES

> Junior: E. Davis, E. Ó Fiacháin, S. Gilmartin, F. McInerney, J. Martin, R. McMaugh, NPC B. J. O'Brien

> Under 20: A. and B. Considine, I. Hough, L. Rooney, R. Boyd. P. Scannell, NPC J. Mullally

2006, EDINBURGH

> Junior: E. Davis, B. Sharkey, S. Gilmartin, F. McInerney, J. Martin, R. McMaugh, NPC T. MacCormac

> Under 20: R. Adams, M.O'Rourke, A. and B. Considine, I. Hough, L.Rooney, NPC J. Mullally

2007, BUNRATTY

> Junior: R. Boyd, E. Davis, J. Martin, D. Synnott, NPC P. English

> Under 20: R. Adams, M. O'Rourke, J. Cunningham, L. Devine, T. Hold, J. Quirke, NPC M. English

2008, MANCHESTER

> Junior: R. Boyd, E. Davis, J. Martin, D. Synnott, R. Adams, M.O'Rourke, NPC M. Brady.

> Under 20: E. O'Kane, B. Smyth, A. Woods, K. O'Connor, N. Doyle, H. Gormally, NPC K. Downes.

2009, BELFAST

> Junior: R. Boyd, B. Sharkey, K. O'Connor, D. Synnott, R. Adams, M. O'Rourke, NPC E. Counihan

> Under 20: N. Doyle H. Gormally, N. Gormally, B. Smyth, E. O'Kane, A. Woods, NPC W. Mevius

Appendix E: Irish Teams in World and European Championships

Irish Teams in World Open Team Championships

World Olympiad

1960 Turin

R. Belton, J. A. Kelly, W. Burrowes, D. L. Stokes, A. H. Davidson, P. D. Fitzgerald, NPC F. McMenamin

1964 New York

D. P. Deery, E. Goldblatt, J. A. Kelly, G. F. Read, F. Fine, D. L. Stokes, NPC E. J. Boland

1968 Deauville

R. de Barra, E. O'Riordan, D. P. Deery, E. MacNeill, G. F. Read, M. Shrage, NPC J. F. O'Sullivan

1972 Bal Harbour, Miami

R. de Barra, N. K. FitzGibbon, D. Deery, E. MacNeill, J. P. MacHale, P. J. Pigot, NPC G. F. Read

1976 Monte Carlo

P. Barrett, A. Kavanagh, N. K. FitzGibbon, A. Mesbur, J. P. MacHale, P. J. Pigot, NPC M. Rosenberg

1980 Valkenburg

N. K. FitzGibbon, A. Mesbur, J. P. MacHale, P. J. Pigot, N. Tóibín, P. Walshe, NPC D. A. Jackson

1984 Seattle

N. K. FitzGibbon, A. Mesbur, T. G. Mackenzie, P. Walshe, Alex Montwill, J. H. O'Keeffe, NPC J. Moran

1988 Venice

A. T. R. Anderson, M. Rosenberg, R. Boland, B. Senior, N. K. FitzGibbon, A. Mesbur, NPC J. P. MacHale

1992 Salsomaggiore

A. T. R. Anderson, David Greenwood, D. Garvey, M. Ó Briain, G. Keaveney, M. McGloughlin, NPC J. H. O'Keeffe

1996 Rhodes

R. Brennan, P. Scannell, T. Hanlon, H. McGann, G. Keaveney, R. Timlin, NPC N. Tóibín

2000 Maastricht

R. Boland, N. Toibín, T. Hanlon, H. McGann, G. Keaveney, R. Timlin, NPC H. Campbell

2004 ISTANBUL

> J. Carroll, T. Garvey, T. Hanlon, H. McGann, N. K. FitzGibbon, A, Mesbur, NPC G. Keaveney

WORLD CHAMPIONSHIP, BERMUDA BOWL – QUALIFYING THROUGH EUROPEAN CHAMPIONSHIP

2007 SHANGHAI

> J. Carroll, T. Garvey, T. Hanlon, H. McGann, N. K. FitzGibbon, A. Mesbur, NPC D. A. Jackson

WORLD MIND-SPORTS CHAMPIONSHIPS

2008 BEIJING

> J. Carroll, T. Garvey, T. Hanlon, H. McGann, M. Ó Briain, P. Ó Briain, NPC D. Coyne

IRISH TEAMS IN WOMEN'S WORLD CHAMPIONSHIPS

1960 TURIN

> Cleo Fellowes, Lily Maguire, Ruth Giddings, Elvina Spiro, Alice Mahon, Eileen O'Doherty, NPC Eleanor Faul

1964 NEW YORK

> Nellie Cotter, Lily Maguire, Ruth Giddings, Barbara Seligman, Sheila Kirwan, Beatrice Titterington, NPC Elvina Spiro

1968 DEAUVILLE

> Sonya Britton, Barbara Seligman, Ruth Giddings, Ina McMenamin, Alice Mahon, Eileen O'Doherty, NPC Eleanor Faul

1972 BAL HARBOUR, MIAMI

> Sonya Britton, Diana Woodhouse, Doreen Cairnduff, Ann Quinn, Ruth Giddings, Lily Maguire, NPC Eleanor Faul

1976 MONTE CARLO

> Sonya Britton, Mary Nimmons, Ruth Giddings, Lily Maguire, Ann Quinn, Barbara Seligman, NPC M. Shrage

1980 VALKENBURG

> Ruth Giddings, Barbara Seligman, Pauline Maguire, Mary Trench, Anne Montwill, Aileen O'Keeffe, NPC Sonya Britton

1984 SEATTLE

> Joan Crowley, Rosemary Ennis, Valerie Hamilton, Antonina McNeice, Anne Montwill, Aileen O'Keeffe, NPC Ruth Giddings

1988   VENICE

Gráinne Barton, Anne Dillon, Elizabeth Dowling, Marjorie Tormey, Anne Montwill, Aileen O'Keeffe, NPC P.Walshe

1992   SALSOMAGGIORE

Gráinne Barton, Anne Dillon, Pauline Maguire, Barbara Seligman, Anne Montwill, Aileen O'Keeffe, NPC R.Brennan

1996   RHODES

No team

2000   MAASTRICHT

Helen Carroll, Jill Kulchycky, Helen Holman, Carol McCarthy, Pat MacMahon, Pat Ryan, NPC T. Walsh

2004   ISTANBUL

Ena Cleary, Mary Finn, Hilary Dowling Long, Anne-Marie Horan, Bríd Kirby, Maureen Pattinson, NPC B. J. O'Brien

WORLD MIND-SPORTS CHAMPIONSHIPS, WOMEN'S BRIDGE TEAMS

2008   BEIJING

Helen Carroll, Jill Kulchycky, Ena Cleary, Jeannie Fitzgerald, Emer Joyce, Joan Kenny, NPC G. Keaveney

IRISH TEAMS IN EUROPEAN OPEN TEAM CHAMPIONSHIPS

1948   COPENHAGEN

Ina McMenamin (captain), Geraldine McConkey, P. Carson, D. Egan, J. G. Burke, N. Peart.

1949   PARIS

D. R. Pigot (captain), P. P. Donovan, F. Quin, E. Boland, J. Harold, F. McMenamin.

1950   BRIGHTON

E. O. Barry, J. A. Kelly; J. J. Bastow, T. D. Purcell; P. P. Donovan, J. M. O'Sullivan, NPC D. R. Pigot

1951   VENICE

J. M. O'Sullivan (captain), M. Shrage, A. H. Davidson, F. McMenamin, P. McKenna, M. F. O'Connell

1952   DUN LAOGHAIRE

E. O. Barry, D. Egan; R. A. Belton, J. A. Kelly; P. P. Donovan, T. D. Purcell, NPC J. J. Bastow

1953   HELSINKI

G. F. Read (captain), P. Purcell, J. P. MacHale, J. G. Burke, J. M. O'Sullivan

1954   MONTREUX

Elvina Spiro, J. Lynch; R. A. Belton; J. A. Kelly, G. F. Read, M. Shrage, NPC P. Fitzgerald

1955   AMSTERDAM

L. Bradley, M. Gabbey, G. F. Read, M. Shrage; F. W. O'Connell, M. F. O'Connell, NPC P. Fitzgerald

1956   STOCKHOLM

H. Bridburg, S. Murphy, S. Blaney, T. J. McAfee, D. Cohen, H. Schenker, NPC M. Shrage

1957   VIENNA

G. F. Read, M. Shrage, F. W. O'Connell, M. F. O'Connell; J. J. Bastow, T. D. Purcell, NPC D. A. Houlihan

1958   OSLO

G. F. Read (captain), M. Shrage, F. W. O'Connell, M. F. O'Connell, A. McKinnon, B. Vard.

1959   PALERMO

R. A. Belton, J. A. Kelly, J. J. Bastow, T. D. Purcell, P. P. Donovan, H. Fine, NPC G. F. Read

1961   TORQUAY

F. W. O'Connell, M. F. O'Connell, A. Lennon, J. O'Dempsey, H. Diamond, M. Rosenberg, NPC D. A. Houlihan (Birr)

1962   BEIRUT

J. P. MacHale, D. Seligman; D. L. Stokes, F. Fine; E. J. Boland; D. P. Deery, NPC G. A. Holmes

1963   BADEN-BADEN

J. Coman, J. Fitzgerald; G. F. Read, Dr M. Shrage; M. F. O'Connell; G. A. Holmes, NPC E. J. Boland

1965   OSTEND

J. P. MacHale, P. J. Pigot; J. A. Kelly; E. J. O Boyle; J. Fitzgerald, G. A. Holmes; NPC G. F. Read

1966   WARSAW

J. P. MacHale, Dr M. Shrage; D. P. Deery, E. Boland; G. F. Read, D. Seligman, NPC J. Fitzgerald

1967   DUBLIN

J. P. MacHale, P. J. Pigot, G. F. Read, Dr M. Shrage, D. Stokes, Dr F. Fine, NPC D. P. Deery

1969   OSLO

J. P. MacHale, P. J. Pigot, E. MacNeill, D. P. Deery, P. D. Fitzgerald, D. Seligman, NPC G. F. Read

1970 ESTORIL

J. P. MacHale, P. J. Pigot, E. MacNeill, D. P. Deery, R. F. Barry, S. Reilly, NPC M. Shrage

1971 ATHENS

J. P. MacHale, P. J. Pigot, E. MacNeill, D. P. Deery, E. Pigot, H. Robinson, NPC G. F. Read

1973 OSTEND

J. P. MacHale, P. J. Pigot; D. P. Deery, E. MacNeill; P. D. Fitzgerald, E. O'Riordan, NPC G. F. Read

1974 HERZLIA

J. P. MacHale, P. J. Pigot, P. Barrett, A. Kavanagh, C. Cunningham, H. Hartnett, NPC D. A. Cohen

1975 BRIGHTON

A. T. R. Anderson, P. J. Barry; J. P. MacHale, P. J. Pigot; N. K. FitzGibbon, A. Mesbur, NPC G. F. Read

1977 HELSINGOR

J. P. MacHale, P. J. Pigot, N. K. FitzGibbon, A. Mesbur, M. McGloughlin, S. Reilly, NPC P. D. Fitzgerald

1979 LAUSANNE

J. P. MacHale, P. J. Pigot, N. K. FitzGibbon, A. Mesbur, A. T. R. Anderson, Monty Rosenberg, NPC P. D. Fitzgerald

1981 BIRMINGHAM

J. P. MacHale, P. J. Pigot, P. Walshe, D. A. Jackson, T. G. Mackenzie, Moyna Johnston, NPC P. D. Fitzgerald

1983 WIESBADEN

N. K. FitzGibbon, A. Mesbur, P. Walshe, N. Tóibín, G. Keaveney, P. F. Walsh, NPC T. G. Mackenzie

1985 SALSOMAGGIORE

M. Rosenberg, R. Sai, H. Campbell, B. Senior, G. Keaveney, P. Walsh, NPC J. Moran

1987 BRIGHTON

M. Rosenberg, A. T. R. Anderson, R. Brennan, P. Scannell, B. J. O'Brien, T. Roche, NPC D. Garvey

1989 TURKU, FINLAND

G. Keaveney, P. F. Walsh, M. Rosenberg, A. T. R. Anderson, D. Garvey, M. Ó Briain, NPC R. Timlin

1991 KILLARNEY

N. K. FitzGibbon, A. Mesbur, P. Walshe, R. Boland, R. Brennan, P. Scannell, NPC P. F. Walsh

1993   MENTON, FRANCE

D. Garvey, M. Ó Briain, P. Ó Briain, T. Roche, A. T. R. Anderson, David Greenwood, NPC J. H. O'Keeffe

1995   VILLAMOURA

T. Hanlon, H. McGann; P. F. Walsh, R. Timlin; J. P. MacHale, R. Milne, NPC Alex Montwill

1997   MONTECATINI

T. Hanlon, H. McGann, D. Garvey, M. Ó Briain, J. Carroll, T. Garvey, NPC N. Tóibín

1999   MALTA

T. Hanlon, H. McGann; G. Keaveney, R. Timlin; R. Boland, N. Tóibín, NPC A. Mesbur

2001   TENERIFE

T. Hanlon, H. McGann, P. Ó Briain, T. Roche, B. J. O'Brien, M. MacDonagh, NPC G. Keaveney

2002   SALSOMAGGIORE

A. Mesbur, N. K. FitzGibbon, A. T. R. Anderson, David Greenwood, J. Carroll, T. Garvey, NPC G. Keaveney

2004   MALMO

G. Keaveney, R. Timlin, D. Coyne, D. MacAonghusa, P. Ó Briain, P. Pigot,, NPC M. O'Connor

2006   WARSAW

T. Hanlon, H. McGann; A. Mesbur, N. K. FitzGibbon: J. Carroll, T. Garvey, NPC D. A. Jackson

2008   PAU, FRANCE

T. Hanlon, H. McGann; A. Mesbur, N. FitzGibbon: J. Carroll, T. Garvey, NPC D. A. Jackson

IRISH WOMEN'S TEAMS IN EUROPEAN CHAMPIONSHIPS

1949   PARIS

Geradine McConkey, Elvina Spiro, Ina McMenamin, Moreen McCarthy, Eileen O'Sullivan, May McNulty, NPC Cleo Roy

1950   BRIGHTON

Geradine McConkey, Elvina Spiro, Ina McMenamin, Moreen McCarthy, Eileen O'Sullivan, Ruth Giddings, NPC Cleo Roy

1951   VENICE

Ina McMemamin (captain), Elvina Spiro, Eileen O'Doherty, Ruth Giddings, Eileen O'Sullivan, Alice Mahon

1952   DUBLIN
Ruth Giddings, May McNulty, Geraldine McConkey, Eileen O'Sullivan, Ina McMenamin, Elvina Spiro, NPC Moreen McCarthy

1953   HELSINKI
Not represented

1954   MONTREUX
Ruth Giddings, May McNulty, Ina McMenamin, Eileen O'Sullivan, Alice Mahon, Eileen O'Doherty, NPC Eleanor Faul

1955   AMSTERDAM
Norah Bradley, Babs Hooper, Ruth Giddings, May McNulty, Elvina Spiro, Moreen McCarthy, NPC A. McKinnon

1956   STOCKHOLM
Ina McMenamin, Elvina Spiro, Frances Jennings, Maura Jennings, Mary Clare Riordan, Eileen Hanley, NPC Eleanor Faul

1957   VIENNA
Geraldine McConkey, May McNulty, Moreen McCarthy, Eileen O'Doherty, Doreen Cairnduff, Alice Mahon, NPC Ina McMenamin

1958   OSLO
Eileen O'Doherty, Molly O'Carroll, Alice Mahon, Ann Quinn, Doreen Cairnduff, Eileen O'Sullivan, NPC Ina Byrne

1959   PALERMO
Geraldine McConkey, Ina McMenamin, Ruth Giddings, May McNulty, Ann Quinn, Eileen O'Sullivan, NPC D. G. Jackson

1961   TORQUAY
Elvina Spiro, Charlotte Fowler, Ruth Giddings, May McNulty, Molly O'Carroll, Doreen Cairnduff, NPC D. A. Cohen

1962   BEIRUT
Elvina Spiro, Ina McMenamin, Ruth Giddings, Eileen O'Sullivan; Barbara Seligman, Sonya Britton, NPC Mrs D. Cairnduff

1963   BADEN-BADEN
Alice Mahon, Eileen O'Doherty, Barbara Seligman, Ruth Giddings, Babs Hooper, Clare Lyne, NPC Ina McMenamin

1965   OSTEND
Ruth Giddings, Barbara Seligman, Cleo Fellows, Doreen Cairnduff, Ina McMenamin, Ann Quinn, NPC Mrs McConkey

1966   WARSAW
Ruth Giddings, Barbara Seligman, Eileen O'Sullivan, Geraldine McConkey, Molly Jones, Ina Byrne, NPC Molly O'Carroll

1967 DUBLIN

Ruth Giddings, Barbara Seligman, Moreen McCarthy, Mimi Christopher, Kathleen Banks, Molly Jones, NPC Eileen O'Sullivan

1969 OSLO

Ruth Giddings, Barbara Seligman, Kathleen Banks, Molly Jones, Sonya Britton, Mary Walsh, NPC Ina McMenamin

1970 ESTORIL

Ruth Giddings, Barbara Seligman, Kathleen Banks, Kay O'Sullivan, Ann Quinn, Doreen Cairnduff, NPC Sonya Britton

1971 ATHENS

Ruth Giddings, Barbara Seligman, Sonya Britton, Cleo Fellows, Nellie Cotter, Bernie Cullen, NPC Maureen Ryder

1973 OSTEND

Ruth Giddings, Lily Maguire, Olive Gray, Maeve Curran, Sonya Britton, Barbara Seligman, NPC Ann Quinn

1974 HERZLIA

Nell Arnold, Sonya Britton, Doreen Cairnduff, Rita McQueen, Ann Quinn, Barbara Seligman, NPC Kathleen Banks

1975 BRIGHTON

Maria Barry, Ruth Giddinga, Sonya Britton, Barbara Seligman, Anne Montwill, Aileen OKeeffe, NPC Ann Quinn

1977 HELSINGOR

Maeve Curran, Kay Lowther, Paddi Scannell, Rita McQueen, Kathleen Banks, Marie Preston, NPC Eileen O'Doherty

1979 LAUSANNE

Ruth Giddings, Barbara Seligman, Ann Quinn, Eileen O'Doherty; Maeve Curran, Valerie Hamilton, NPC Kathleen Banks

1981 BIRMINGHAM

Ruth Giddings, Barbara Seligman, Anne Montwill, Aileen O'Keeffe, Valerie Hamilton, Shirlie Browne, NPC Ann Quinn

1983 WIESBADEN

Aileen O'Keeffe, Ann Montwill, Elva Gannon, Pauine Maguire, Eileen O'Doherty, Ann Quinn, NPC Rita McQueen

1985 SALSOMAGGIORE

Rosalind Barron, Anne Hayden, Elva Gannon, Pauline Maguire, Elizabeth Dowling, Marjorie Tormey, NPC RuthGiddings

1987 BRIGHTON

Valerie Hand, Mary Trench, Joan Crowley, Rosemary Ennis, Maeve Curran, Valerie Hamilton, NPC Eoin MacNeill

1989   TURKU

Ann Quinn, Eileen O'Doherty, Elva Gannon, Pauline Maguire, Anne Montwill, Aileen O'Keeffe, NPC J. H. O'Keeffe

1991   KILLARNEY

Maria Barry, Barbara Seligman, Evelyn Bourke, Diane Sloan, Aileen O'Keeffe, Rebecca O'Keeffe, NPC Kay Downes

1993   MENTON, FRANCE

Gráinne Barton, Anne Dillon, Elva Gannon, Pauline Maguire, Elizabeth Dowling, Marjorie Tormey, NPC Clare Pippet

1995   VILLAMOURA

Elva Gannon, Pauline Maguire, Margo English, Mary Heery, Hilary Dowling Long, Rebecca O'Keeffe, NPC Anne Montwill

1997   MONTECATINI

Patsy Meehan, Petra ONeill, Valerie Hand, Anne Montwill, Aileen O'Keeffe, Rebecca O'Keeffe, NPC P. Ó Briain

1999   MALTA

Not represented

2001   TENERIFE

Not represented

2002   SALSOMAGGIORE

Pat MacMahon, Pat Ryan, Petra O'Neill, Patsy Meehan, Hilary Dowling Long, Anne-Marie Horan, NPC Mary Trench

2004   MALMO

Ena Cleary, Mary Finn, Bríd Kirby, Maureen Pattinson, Ciara Burns, Diane Greenwood, NPC S. Dowling

2006   WARSAW

Ena Cleary, Jeannie Fitzgerald, Hilary Dowling Long, Ann-Marie Horan, Dympna Friel, Diane Greenwood, NPC G. Keaveney

2008   PAU, FRANCE

Ena Cleary, Jeannie Fitzgerald, Helen Carroll, Jill Kulchycky, Emer Joyce, Joan Kenny, NPC G. Keaveney.

IRISH TEAMS IN EUROPEAN UNION (EEC) CHAMPIONSHIPS

1973   THE HAGUE

Open: D. L. Seligman (captain), C. J. O'Hara, P. D. Fitzgerald, E. O'Riordan, R. J. Fitzgerald, W. F. Maclachlan

Women: R. Giddings, L. Maguire, S. Britton, B. Seligman, M. Curran, Olive Gray, NPC Anne Quinn

Junior Team: P. F. Walsh, P. Barrett, M. and P. Ó Briain, D. Garvey, H. McDermott

1975   VITTEL, FRANCE

Open: N. K. FitzGibbon, A. Mesbur; M. McGloughlin, D. G. Scannell.

Women: Eileen O'Doherty (captain), Nell Arnold; Ann Montwill, Aileen O'Keeffe

Mixed: W. F. Maclachlan (captain), Rosalind Barron, R. J. Fitzgerald, Bernie Cullen

Junior: P. Porteous, D. O'Connor; C. McHugh, V. O'Brien

1977   OSTEND

Open: D. A. Jackson, D. L. Seligman, K. Y. Singleton, N. Percival-Price

Women: Maeve Curran, Kay Lowther; Paddy Scannell, Rita McQueen

1979   SALSOMAGGIORE

Open: R. J. Fitzgerald, W. F. Maclachlan; J. Furnival, S. Gillen, D. A. Jackson, D. L. Seligman

Women: R. Giddings, B. Seligman; G. Maguire, A. Pigot; E. O'Doherty, A. Quinn

1981   BIRMINGHAM

Open: D. A. Jackson, P. Walshe; Moyna Johnston, T. G. Mackenzie; N. Percival-Price, K. Y. Singleton

Women: R. Giddings, B. Seligman; S. Brown, V. Hamilton; J. Crowley, R. Ennis

Junior: N. Tóibín, R. Boland, R. Kelly, K. Cashen first

1983   OSTEND

Open: D. A. Jackson, R. P. de Barra, P. F. Walsh, G. Keaveney, NPC P. Walshe third

Women: E. O'Doherty, A. Quinn (captain), K. O'Keeffe, C. Doyle

Junior: R. Boland, R. Kelly, N. Tóibin, M. Roche

1985   BORDEAUX

Open: N. K. FitzGibbon, Kathryn O'Keeffe, Barbara and D. Seligman

Women: R. Barron, A. Hayden, E. Dowling, M. Tormey

Mixed: E. MacNeill, Rosemary Ennis; D. G. Scannell, Joan Crowley

Junior: M. Roche, P. McCreery, Ms L. Doyle, Ms C. Johnston

1987   VALKENBURG

Open: R. Brennan, P. Scannell, B. J. O'Brien, T. Roche

Women:V. Hand, M. Trench, J. Crowley, R. Ennis, E. O'Doherty, A. Quinn

Junior: T. Hanlon, M. Moran, J. Nolan, C. O'Mahony

1989 OSTEND

Open: G. Keaveney, P. F. Walsh, R. Boland, D. Dillon

Women: A. Montwill, A. O'Keeffe, E. O'Doherty, A. Quinn

Mixed Teams: N. K. and K. FitzGibbon, Gráinne Barton and P. Walshe second

Junior: T. Hanlon, J. Nolan, H. McGann, D. O'Gorman, D. Barry, D. Bell

1991 VOULIAGMENI, GREECE

Open: R. Boland, P. Walshe, R. Brennan, P. Scannell fifth

Women: M. Barry, B. Seligman, A. O'Keeffe, R. O'Keeffe sixth

1993 MONTECHORO, PORTUGAL

Open: R. Brennan, P. Scannell, P. Ó Briain, T. Roche second

Women: E. Gannon, P. Maguire; A. Montwill, A. O'Keeffe

Junior: T. Hanlon, H. McGann; T. Garvey, S. Udvari

1996 OSTEND

Open: D. Garvey, M. Ó Briain; R. Brennan, P. Scannell

Women: V. Hand, A. Montwill, A. Glynn, M. Trench

Mixed: G. Barton, P. Walshe, A. Dillon, N. Tóibín

Junior: Ciara Burns, Hilary Dowling Long; J. Carroll, T. Garvey

1998 SALSOMAGGIORE

Open: T. Hanlon, H. McGann, N. Toibín, P. Walshe

Women: A. and R. O'Keeffe, M. Barry. A. Montwill second

Mixed: G. Barton, A. and D. Dillon, R. Boland, N. Kennedy third

INTERNATIONAL CAPS – WORLD, EUROPEAN AND EUROPEAN UNION

W   World championship
E   European championship
EU   European Union or EEC championship

WOMEN'S NATIONAL TEAMS, WORLD, EUROPEAN AND EU CHAMPIONSHIPS

Ruth Giddings	[W 6, E 19, EU 3]	28
Barbara Seligman	[W 5, E 14, EU 4]	23
Eileen O'Doherty	[W 2, E 8, EU 5]	15
Aileen O'Keeffe	[W 4, E 6, EU 5]	15
Anne Montwill	[W 4, E 5, EU 5]	14
Anne Quinn	[W 2, E 8, EU 4]	14
Sonya Britton	[W 3, E 6, EU 1	10
Ina McMenamin	[W 1, E 9]	10

Elvina Spiro	[W 1, E 9]	10
Eileen O'Sullivan	[E 9]	9
Pauline Maguire	[W 2, E 5, EU 1]	8
Geraldine McConkey	[E 7]	7
May McNulty	[W 7]	7
Doreeen Cairnduff	[W 1, E 6]	7
Alice Mahon	[W 2, E 5]	7
Gráinne Barton	[W 2, E 1, EU 3]	6
Maeve Curran	[E 4, EU 2]	6
Elva Gannon	[E 5, EU 1]	6
Joan Crowley	[W 1, E 1, EU 3]	5
Anne Dillon	[W 2, E 1, EU 2]	5
Rosemary Ennis	[W 1, E 1, EU 3]	5
Valerie Hamilton	[W 1, E 3, EU 1]	5
Lily Maguire	[W 3, E 1, EU 1]	5
Kathleeen Banks	[E 4]	4
Maria Barry	[E 2, EU 2]	4
Ena Cleary	[W 1, E 3]	4
Elizabeth Dowling	[W 1, E 2, EU 1]	4
Valerie Hand	[E 2, EU 2]	4
Moreen McCarthy	[E 4]	4
Rebecca O'Keeffe	[E 3, EU 1]	4
Marjorie Tormey	[W 1, E 2, EU 1]	4
Mary Trench	[W 1, E 1, EU 2]	4
Rosalind Barron	[E 1, EU 2]	3
Hilary Dowling Long	[W 1, E 2]	3
Cleo (Roy) Fellows	[W 1, E 2]	3
Mary Finn	[W 1, E2]	3
Diane Greenwood	[E 3,]	3
Rita McQueen	[E 2, EU 1]	3
Nell Arnold	[E 1, EU 1]	2
Shirlie Brown	[E 1, EU 1]	2
Ciara Burns	[E 2]	2
Helen Carroll	[W 1, E 1]	2
Nellie Cotter	[W 1, E 1]	2
Bernie Cullen,	[E 1, EU 1]	2
Jeannie Fitzgerald	[E 2]	2
Kathryn (O'Keeffe) FitzGibbon		
	[EU 2]	2
Anne Hayden	[E 1, EU 1]	2
Babs Hooper	[E 2]	2
Anne-Marie Horan	[W 1, E 1]	2
Olive Gray	[E 1, EU 1]	2
Moyna (Johnston) Mackenzie		

	[E 1, EU 1]	2
Mollie Jones	[E 2]	2
Bríd Kirby	[W 1, E 1]	2
Jill Kulchycky	[W 1, E 1]	2
Kay Lowther	[E 1, EU 1]	2
Pat MacMahon	[W 1, E 1]	2
Geraldine Maguire	[W 1, EU 1]	2
Patsy Meeehan	[E 2]	2
Mollie O'Carroll	[E 2]	2
Petra O'Neill	[E 2]	2
Maureen Pattinson	[W 1, E 1]	2
Pat Ryan	[W 1, E 1]	2
Paddi Scannell,	[E 1, EU 1]	2

THE FOLLOWING HAVE BEEN CAPPED ONCE:

WORLD: Helen Holman, Sheila Kirwan, Carol McCarthy, Antonina McNeice, Mary Nimmons, Beatrice Titterington, Diana Woodhouse.

EUROPEAN: Norah Bradley, Evelyn Bourke, Ina Byrne, Mimi Christopher, Margo English, Charlotte Fowler, Dympna Friel, Eileen Hanley, Mary Heery, Frances Jennings, Maura Jennings,Emer Joyce, Joan Kenny, Kay Lowther, Clare Lyne, Flora McLoone, Kay O'Sullivan, Marie Preston, Mary Clare Riordan, Mary Walsh.

European Union: Chris Doyle, Anna Glynn, Allie Pigot, Mary Walsh.

NATIONAL OPEN TEAMS, EUROPEAN, EU AND WORLD CHAMPIONSHIPS

N. K. FitzGibbon	[W 7, E 8, EU 3]	18
J. P. MacHale	[W 3, E 15]	18
A. Mesbur	[W 6, E 8, EU 1]	17
P. J. Pigot	[W 3, E 11]	14
T. Hanlon	[W 5, E 6, EU 1]	12
H. McGann	[W 5, E 6, EU 1]	12
D. P. Deery	[W 3, E 7*]	10
G. Keaveney	[W 3, E 5, EU 2]	10
P. Walshe	[W 2, E 4, EU 4]	10
G. F. Read	[W 1, E 8]	9
M. Shrage	[W 1, E 8]	9
A. T. R. Anderson	[W 2, E 6]	8
J. Carroll	[W 3, E 4]	7
T. Garvey	[W 3, E 4]	7
J. A. Kelly	[W 2, E 5]	7
Eoin MacNeill	[W 2, E 4, EU 1]	7
R. Boland	[W 1, E 2, EU 3]	6
R. Brennan	[W 1, E 2, EU 3]	6
M. F. O'Connell	[E 6]	6

M. Rosenberg	[W 1, E 5]	6
P. Scannell	[W 1, E 2, EU 6]	6
D. Seligman	[E 3, EU 3]	6
N. Toibín	[W 2, E 2, EU 2]	6
P. F.Walsh	[E 4, EU 2]	6
F. Fine	[W 2, E 3]	5
D. Garvey	[W 1, E 3, EU 1]	5
D. A. Jackson	[E 1, EU 4]	5
M. Ó Briain	[W 1, E 3, EU 1]	5
T. Roche	[E 3, EU 2]	5
P. Ó Briain	[E 3, EU 2]	5
R. Timlin	[W 2, E 3	5
R. Belton	[W 1, EU3]	4
R. de Barra	[W 2, E 1, EU 1]	4
P. P. Donovan	[E 4]	4
F. W. O'Connell	[E 4]	4
T. D. Purcell	[E 4]	4
D. L. Stokes	[W 2, E 2]	4
E. J. Boland	[E 3]	3
J. J. Bastow	[E 3]	3
P. D. Fitzgerald	[W 1, E 2]	3
R. J. Fitzgerald	[EU 3]	3
David Greenwood	[W 1, E 2]	3
T. G. Mackenzie	[W 1, E 1, EU 1]	3
W. F. Maclachlan	[EU 3]	3
E. O'Riordan	[W 1, E 1, EU 1]	3
J. M. O'Sullivan	[E 3]	3
E. O. Barry	[E 2]	2
P. Barrett	[W 1, E 1]	2
A. H. Davidson	[W 1, E 1]	2
J. G. Burke	[E 2]	2
D. Egan	[E 2]	2
J. Fitzgerald	[E 2]	2
D. A. Houlihan (Birr)	[E 2]	2
G. A. Holmes	[E 2]	2
A. Kavanagh	[W 1, E 1]	2
M. McGloughlin	[W 1, E 1]	2
F. McMenamin	[E 2]	2
B. J. O'Brien	[E 2]	2
N. Percival Price	[EU 2]	2
S. Reilly	[W 2]	2
B. Senior	[W 1, E 1]	2
K. Y. Singleton	[EU 2]	2

THE FOLLOWING HAVE EACH PLAYED ONCE ON AN IRISH NATIONAL TEAM:

World: W. Burrowes, E. Goldblatt, A. Lennon, Alex Montwill, J. H. O'Keeffe

European: P. J. Barry, S. Blaney, L. Bradley, H. Bridburg, H. Campbell, P. Carson, D. A. Cohen, J. Coman, D. Coyne, C. Cunningham, H. Diamond, M. Gabbey, H. Hartnett, J. Harold, John Lynch, D. MacAonghusa, T. J. McAfee, M. MacDonagh, P. McKenna, A. McKinnon, R. Milne, S. Murphy, E. J. O'Boyle, J. H. O'Dempsey, N. Peart, D. R. Pigot, E. Pigot, P. Pigot, P. Purcell, F. T. Quin, H. Robinson, R. Sai, H. Schenker, B. Vard

European Union: D. Dillon, J. Furnival, S. Gillen, M. McGloughlin, C. J. O'Hara, D. G. Scannell

* Includes one for Spain.

Appendix F: European Junior Team Championship (David Pigot trophy)

1968 PRAGUE

R. Barry, D. Scannell, Noeleen Deignan, J. McElhinny, D. P. Deery, E. MacNeill, NPC E. J. Boland

1970 DUBLIN

A. T. R. Anderson, P. J. Barry, N. K. FitzGibbon, A. Johnson, Maria Nolan, D. G. Scannell, NPC E. J. Boland

1972 DELFT

A. T. R. Anderson, N. K. FitzGibbon, M. McGloughlin, D. G. Scannell, M. Ó Briain, P. Ó Briain, NPC E. J. Boland

1974 COPENHAGEN

N. K. FitzGibbon, A. Mesbur, M. McGloughlin, D. G. Scannell, S. McKeon, D. O'Donovan, NPC E. MacNeill and D. Deery

1976 LUND, SWEDEN

M. Lavelle, S. Gillen, P. Walshe, K. Luddy, D. Garvey, P. Ó Briain, NPC E. MacNeill

1978 STIRLING

B. Dolan, T. Roche, M. Ó Briain, P. Walshe, G. Keaveney, J. Wood, NPC M. McGloughlin

1980 TEL AVIV

R. Brennan, J. Wood, K. Cashen, M. Roche, B. Dolan, R. Kelly, NPC P. Porteous

1982 SALSOMAGGIORE

R. Boland, R. Kelly, Diane Sloane, D. Rosenberg, A. McCarthy, D. O'Farrell, NPC M. Rosenberg

1984 HASSELT, BELGIUM

N. Tóibín, R. Kelly, M. Roche, Miss T. Corcoran, P. McCreery, F. O'Boyle, NPC P. Walshe

1986 BUDAPEST

T. Hanlon, Heber O'Farrell, John Nolan, Colin O'Mahony, Mark Moran, Damien Carson, NPC P. Walshe

1988 PLOVDIV, BULGARIA

D. Barry, D. Bell, E. Bourke, D. MacAonghusa, H. McGann, D. O'Gorman, NPC B. Senior

1990 NEUMESTER, GERMANY

D. Barry, D. Bell, Evelyn Bourke, T. Hanlon, D. MacAonghusa, H. McGann, NPC G. Keaveney

379

1992 PARIS

T. Hanlon, D. Reddan, Fiona Conway, Gaye Cleary, D. Bell, H. McGann, NPC M. F. O'Connell

1994 ARNHEM, NETHERLANDS

Junior: D. O'Keeffe, Rebecca O'Keeffe, J. Clarson, T. Ryan, T. Garvey, S. Udvari, NPC P. Ó Briain

Schools: N. Pierse, P. O'Donoghue, D. Dillon, F. O'Connor, joint NPCs, F. Pierse, P. Rochford

1996 CARDIFF

Junior: J. Carroll, T. Garvey, C. Burns, H. Dowling Long, T. Ryan, S. Udvari, NPC, P. Ó Briain.

Schools: P. O'Donoghue, N. Pierse, F. O'Connor, S. O'Sullivan, E. Fox, E. Ryan, NPC P. Rochford

2000 ANTALYA

Junior: T. MacCormac, B. MacKenzie, S. Bavalia, J. Martin, A. Barton, D. Nolan, NPC, Hilary Dowling Long, coach Richard King

2002 TORQUAY

Schools: E. Davis, C. O'Muircheartaigh, H. M. Chan, P. Scannell Junior, A. Carrigan, A. Flynn, NPC Diane Sloan

2004 PRAGUE

Did not participate

2005 RICCIONNE, ITALY

Girls teams: Isobel Haugh, Lydia Rooney, Ruth Connolly, Riona Nichols, NPC Diane Greenwood, Coach David Greenwood

WORLD MIND SPORTS GAMES

2008 BEIJING

R. Boyd, E. Davis, B. Sharkey, E. Ó Fiacháin, D. Synnott, J. Martin

Appendix G: Irish Teams in World and European Seniors Championships

European

1999 Malta

P. Hanratty (captain), S. Dowling, Cáit Flavin, J. Godden, S. O Lubaigh.

2001 Tenerife

J. P. MacHale, A. Montwill, D. A. Jackson, P. Barry, T. G. Mackenzie, J. H. O'Keeffe, NPC Ann Montwill

2002 Salsomaggiore

J. P. MacHale, Alex Montwill, R. Fitzgerald, S. O Lubaigh, S. Dowling (sub – did not play)

2004 Malmo

Frances Burke, Carmel Higgins, Patsy Meehan, Rose O'Farrell, NPC A. Cleary

2006 Warsaw

J. Comyn, J. Moran, E. Glynn, P. Scannell, Desmond Houlihan, G. Lessells, NPC B. J. O'Brien

2008 Pau

J. Comyn, J. Moran, S. Dowling, J. Godden, D. Houlihan, G. Lessells, NPC M. O'Connor

World Olympiad

2004 Istanbul

J. Moran (captain), J. Comyn, A. Cleary, G. Lessells, S. Dowling, S. O'Lubaigh

World Mind Sports Games

2008 Beijing

R. Anderson, P. J. Barry, D. A. Jackson, P. McDevitt, NPC D. Garvey

Appendix H: Corn Cairdis

Annual Match: Republic of Ireland Teams v. England

1993	DUBLIN	186–169

Open: D. Garvey, M. Ó Briain, P. Ó Briain, T. Roche.

Women: Gráinne Barton, Anne Dillon, Elizabeth Dowling, Marjorie Tormey.

Junior: T. Hanlon, H. McGann, T. Garvey. S. Udvari

Officials: T. Burke, Clare Pippet, P. Flynn, P. Porteous

NPC: J. Moran

1994	MANCHESTER	309–403

Open: T. Hanlon, H. McGann, R. Timlin, P. F. Walsh.

Women: Anne Hanratty, Rita O'Donnell, Patricia Kelly, Catherine McCann.

Junior: J. Clarson, T. Ryan, D. O'Keeffe, Rebecca O'Keeffe

County: J. Cunningham, G. Keaveney, E. Fitzgerald, M. MacDonagh

Club: Yvonne Bennett, B. Wardlaw, M. Larkin, P. Ryan

NPC: G. Laird

1995	MULLINGAR	378–337

Open: R. Timlin, P. F. Walsh, J. P. MacHale, R. Milne

Women: Hilary Dowling Long, Rebecca O'Keeffe, Pat MacMahon, Pat Ryan

Junior: J. Carroll, T. Garvey, T. Ryan, S. Udvari

County: E. FitzGerald, M. MacDonagh, T. Hanlon, H. McGann

Club: Monica Harris, J. Cunningham, Ursula and J. Hearne

Officials: Clare Pippet, D. Scully, J. Moran, P. Porteous

NPC: Una Walsh

1996	BRADFORD	316–400

Open: R. Brennan, P. Scannell, G. Keaveney, R. Timlin

Women: Clare Pippet, Emer Joyce, Anna Glynn, Mary Trench

Junior: J. Carroll, T. Garvey, T. MacCormac, D. O'Keeffe

County: Marlene and M. O'Connor, Maura O'Farrell, S. MacMathuna

Club: P. Carr, T. O'Callaghan, P. Byrne, C. McLoone

Officials:	D. Dillon, J. Moran, P. Hanratty, P. Porteous	
NPC:	Una Walsh	

1997 GALWAY — 373–342

Open: Tom Hanlon, Hugh McGann, John Carroll, Tommy Garvey

Women: Aileen and Rebecca O'Keeffe, Ann Montwill, Valerie Hand

Junior: Matt Clarson, Hilary Dowling Long, Thomas MacCormac, Louise and Michelle Mitchell

County: Eddie Fitzgerald, Michael MacDonagh, Enda Glynn, Maurice Hession

Club: Marlene and Michael O'Connor, Maura O'Farrell, Seamus Mac Mathuna

Officials: Clare Pippet, Joe Moran, Seamus Dowling, Paul Porteous
NPC: Maisie Cooper

1998 SOLIHULL — 365–350

Open: T. Hanlon, H. McGann, N. Tóibín, P. Walshe

Women: Aileen and Rebecca O'Keeffe, Maria Barry, Anne Montwill

Junior: Matt Clarson, Thomas MacCormac, Richard King, Neville Pierse

County: Denis McGrath, Derek O'Gorman, Mary Finn, Karl Hayes

Club: Mark Burke, Gordon Lessells, Pat Liston, Bob Pattinson

Officials: Clare Pippet, Paul Hanratty, Pascal Buckley, Fergal O'Boyle
NPC: Marie Cummins

1999 ENNIS — 147–210

County: Desmond Houlihan, Paul Barrett, Pat Liston, Pat Quinn

Club: Noel Hickey, P. J. O'Dea, David Coyne, Liam Walsh

Officials: Clare Pippet, Joe Moran, Una Walsh, Michael O'Connor
NPC: Peter Flynn

2000 DERBY — 149–211

County: Joe Moran (captain), Petra O'Neill, Seamus Dowling, Martin Keane

Club: Betty and Dermot Cotter, Marian and Maurice Kennefick

Officials: Clare Pippet, John Cunningham, Michael O'Connor, Pascal Buckley

2001 CORK — 169–187

County: Joan Crowley, Mary Finn, Ger Cummins, Derek O'Gorman

Club: Betty and Dermot Cotter, Marian and Maurice Kennefick

Officials: Michael O'Connor (captain), Seamus Dowling, Clare Pippet, Joe Moran

2002 NORWICH 166–194

 County: Mark Burke, Pat Quinn, Brid Kirby, Ger Connolly

 Club: Seamus Cosello, Peter Howard, John Keane, Frank Murphy

 Officials: Seamus Dowling (captain), Martha Tuite, Michael O'Connor, Una Walsh

2003 DROGHEDA 168–192

 County: John Keane, Frank Murphy, Mary Wherity, Liam Shanahan

 Club: Clare Clarke, Bridie Murtagh, Maureen Walsh, Margaret Winters

 Officials: Seamus Dowling, Hilary Dowling Long, Joe Moran, John Cunningham, NPC Teresa McGrath

2004 MANCHESTER 173–187

 County: Noel Hickey, Gordon Lessells, Gerri McMahon, Donal O'Sullivan

 Club: Seamus Dowling, John Comyn, B. J. O'Brien, Tomas Roche

 Officials: Rita McNamara (captain), Paul Porteous, John Cunningham, Michael O'Connor

2005 DUBLIN 209–151

 County: Henry Barron, Tomás Roche, John Comyn, B. J. O'Brien

 Club: Helen Carroll, Jill Kulchycky, Paul Delaney, Seamus Dowling

 Officials: Joe Moran (captain), John Cunningham, Des Houlihan, Gordon Lessells

2006 HURSLEY, HAMPSHIRE 182–174

 County: John Comyn, Joe Moran, Seamus Dowling, Tomás Roche

 Club: Ciarán Coyne, David Walsh, Manus Burke, Henry Curran

 Officials: Paddy Carr (captain), Michael O'Connor, Kathleen Byrne, Katherine Lennon

2007 GALWAY

 County: Henry Curran, Maurice Hession, Enda Glynn, Paul Scannell

 Club: B. Finan, L. Hanratty, S. MacMathúna, Collette Mulhern

 Officials: M.O'Connor (captain), S. Dowling, D. A. Houlihan, G. Lessells

2008 NORWICH

 County: G. Cummins, T. McCarthy, Mary Finn, C. Holland

 Club: Margo and Paddy English, C. Higgins, M. Quinn

 Officials: M. O'Connor (captain), S. Dowling, D. A. Houlihan (Ennis), G. Lessells

Excluding Camrose and Lady Milne matches

1935   11–12 MAY, IMPERIAL HOTEL, BELFAST

CBAI: Mrs Boles, Mrs Colgan, Kathleen Lambert, Geraldine McConkey, D. R. and Violet Pigot, J. P. Morgan and C. O'Neill

NIBU: A. McKinnon, Mrs Sephens, G. B. Hanna, E. Goldblatt, J. Davis, T. Shanks, A. Fletcher, A. Frame

NIBU won. Score not recorded.

1936   21–22 MARCH, SHELBOURNE HOTEL, DUBLIN

CBAI: E. O. Barry, P. Quinn, D. Murphy, T. O'Grady, H. L. Curra.., H. Freeman, James and Constance Maxwell Henry

NIBU: G. B. Hanna, E. Goldblatt, J. Davis, Tom Shanks, A. Fletcher, A.Frame, H. G. Lindsay and H. J. Miles

Result not known.

From 1937 to 1939, the annual match was part of the Camrose series. See Camrose records for teams.

1943   20 MARCH, MERRION SQUARE, DUBLIN

CBAI: May McNulty, A. H. Davidson, E. O. Barry, P. Quinn, C. H. Day, P. Powell, Ina Hickey, F. McMenamin, NPC H. Williams

NIBU: A. McKinnon, Norah McKee, B. L. Llyod, E. Goldblatt, W. McCallum and B. Vard

NIBU won the hundred-boards match by 1,560 points.

1943   18–19 SEPTEMBER, GRAND CENTRAL HOTEL, BELFAST.

CBAI: J. Murphy, W. J. L. O'Connell, J. M. and Eileen O'Sullivan, N. Peart, G. Read

NIBU: A. McKinnon, A. J. Fletcher, G. B. Hanna, T. Shanks, E. Goldblatt, B. Vard, Norah McKee, NPC B. Llyod

NIBU won the hundred-board match by 1,310 points.

1944   11–12 NOVEMBER ROYAL, HIBERNIAN HOTEL – OVER ONE HUNDRED BOARDS

CBAI: Ina Hickey, T. D. Purcell; J. M. and Eileen O'Sullivan; E. O. Barry, P. Quinn. NPC J. P. Morgan

NIBU: A. McKinnon (captain), T. Shanks; E. Goldblatt, B. Vard, D. Cohen. L. Herbert; Norah McKee

NIBU won by 540 points

Colonel G. G. J. Walshe Cup

Colonel G. G. J. Walshe presented a cup in 1945, 'for annual competition between the champion teams of the CBAI and NIBU'. Matches were over one hundred boards.

1945 APRIL, BELFAST

CBAI: May McNulty, A. H. Davidson, N. Peart, P. Powell

NIBU: B. Vard, L. Herbert, D. A. Cohen, J. Samuels

NIBU: won

1946 23–24 MARCH, 84 HARCOURT STREET, DUBLIN

CBAI: May McNulty, A. H. Davidson, Flora McLoone, N. Peart

NIBU: B. Vard (captain), J. Samuels, L. Herbert, D. Cohen

CBAI won by 420 over a hundred boards

1947 JUNE; SEVENTY-TWO BOARDS PLAYED IN REGENT, DUBLIN; TWENTY-EIGHT IN BELFAST

CBAI: May McNulty, (captain), A. H. Davidson, Flora McLoone, Noel Peart

NIBU: E. Goldblatt (captain), B. Vard, H. Samuels, D. Cohen, L. Herbert

NIBU won by 4,500.

1948 1–2 MAY, DUBLIN

CBAI: May McNulty (captain) A. H. Davidson; Flora McLoone, N. Peart

NIBU: E. Goldblatt (captain) B. Vard, D. Cohen, L. Herbert, W. (or C.?) Gordon

NIBU won by 390 points

1949 26–27 MARCH, BALLYMASCANLON

CBAI: Dr P. J. O'Dowd, Geraldine McConkey, Eileen O'Doherty, P. McKenna

NIBU: E. Goldblatt, B. Vard, D. A. Cohen, D. Gordon + 860.

1950 APRIL, BALLYMACSCANLON

CBAI: Supt. and Mrs Heron; J. Gayer, W. J. Whitney

NIBU: G. B. Hanna, M. Gabbey; M. McLernon, Mrs J. M. Atkinson

NIBU won by thirty-six European match points (subsequently called imps)

CBAI: Misses Frances and Maura.Jennings, (Dundalk), Mrs L. Drew, J. M. Stanley; Mrs P. Connolly, Miss J. Tierney (Drogheda)

NIBU: R. Gardiner, G. W. Green; E. B. and Mrs Quigg; A. Herbert, J. Hurwitz (Belfast), NPC W. J. S. Robb

1950 JUNIOR OR 'B' INTERNATIONAL: VARD CUP

CBAI: George and Sheila Doyle; J. H. and Helen Daly +5 EMPs

NIBU: team not recorded. CBAI won after four extra boards.

Sonya Britton Trophy

CBAI scores first

1989	Newcastle		173–112

CBAI

Open:	D. Garvey, M. Ó Briain, G. Keaveney, P. F. Walsh
Women:	A. Montwill, A. O'Keeffe, A. Quinn, E. O'Doherty
Masters:	Heidi Lillis, M. McGloughlin, Gráinne Barton, Teresa Rigney
Inter A:	J. Ryan, Breda Kelly, D. Barry, Carmel Bell
Inter B:	S. Bearpark, F. Murphy, Leslie Allen, Linda Moran

NIBU

Open:	M. Rosenberg, B. Senior, T. G. Mackenzie, K. Y. Singleton, H. Campbell, R. Burns
Women:	Maeve Curren, Valerie Hamilton, Shirlie Brown, Mary Nimmons
Masters:	I. H. Lindsay, D. Johnston, A. Alcock, T. Bennett, A. Sharp, B. McDowell
Inter A:	B. Brannigan, E. Bryan, R. Hanley, A. Kelly, D. Leeman, S. McKay
Inter B:	J. Boyd, P. Burns, D. and M. Clarke, B. and R. O'Neill

1990	Dublin		133–149

CBAI

Open:	D. Garvey, M. Ó Briain, H. McGann, D. O'Gorman, P. J. Barry, D. Seligman, P. Walshe
Women:	Maria Barry, Barbara Seligman, Kathleen Byrne, Katherine Lennon, Kay Downes, Peggy Shanahan
Masters:	Carol McCarthy, Imelda McCarthy, F. O'Farrell (Greystones), T. Sweeney
Inter A:	S. Buckley, T. Egan, A. McGrath, M. McSweeney, A. McGrath, E. Gordon
Inter B:	L. Ahearn, M. White, B. Madden, Margaret Madden, NPC S. Dowling

NIBU

Open:	M. Rosenberg (captain) A. T. R. Anderson, T. G. Mackenzie, H. Campbell, R. Burns, K. Y. Singleton.
Women:	Valerie Hanilton, S. Henry, Rosario Heatherington, Clare Smith, Mary Nimmons
Masters:	T. Bennett, B. McDowell, I. H. Lindsay, D. K. Johnston
Inter A:	B. Brannigan, A. Kelly, R. Hanly, D. Leeman, P. McCloskey, P. O'Reilly

Inter B:	J. and Mrs Clarke, A. Mawhinney, S. McCaughan	

1991	NEWCASTLE	239–210

CBAI

Open: D. Garvey, M. Ó Briain; R. Brennan, P. Scannell

Women: Clare Pippet (captain), Emer Joyce, Gaye Cleary, Rebecca O'Keeffe

Masters: B. Dolan, T. Walsh, Jill, Kulchycky, Mary Toale

Inter A: S. Costello, Maureen Walsh, P. Howard, Bridie Murtagh

Inter B: Helen Jameson, Gerry Kelly, Ann Moran, Noel Minogue

NIBU

Open: M. Rosenberg, R. Burns, H. Campbell, T. G. MacKenzie, C. Richie, J. Conlon

Women: Shirlie Brown, Mary Nimmons, Maeve Curran, Valerie Hamilton, Rosario Heatherington, Clare Smith

Masters: A. Alcock, A. Sharp, Ed and Molly Andrew, David Greenwood, Diane Sloan

Inter A: Hilary Mawhinney, Sheila McCaughan, Freda McDonald, K. Ginn, J. Ferguson, Nuala Mooney, NPC T. Casey

Inter B: William Dukelow, Wilson Matthews, Collette Moorhead, Maire Parfitt, Jim and P. J. McAleer, NPC G. Fitzgerald

1992	MALAHIDE	149.5–130.5

CBAI

Open: D. Garvey, M. Ó Briain, G. Keaveney, M. McGloughlin.

Women: Gráinne Barton, Anne Dillon, Pauline Maguire, Barbara Seligman, Ann Montwill, Aileen O'Keeffe

Masters: P. Flynn, Nell Foley, M. Prendergast, J. Power

Inter A: Joan Kieran, B. Ruddy, Antoinette McGee, T. McGee

Inter B: Mary Flynn, M. O'Leary, K. Hayes, D. O'Brien, NPC T. Burke

NIBU

Open: A. T. R. Anderson, David Greenwood, H. Campbell, T. G. Mackenzie

Women: Helen Cole, M. Kelly, Maeve Curran, Valerie Hamilton, Norma Franklin, Sandie Millership

Masters: S. Hall, I. Hamilton, I. H. Lindsay, D. K. Johnston

Inter A: W. Dukelow, W. Matthews, K. Ginn, F. McDonald, K. and M. Roddy

Inter B: J. Boyd, G. O'Neill, J. Brown, A. Ferguson, G. and W. Roberts

1993 NEWCASTLE   232–215

CBAI

Open: P. J. Barry, D. Jackson, D. Garvey, M. Ó Briain

Women: Elizabeth Dowling, Marjorie Tormey, Elva Gannon, Pauline Maguire

Masters: P. Byrne, C. McLoone, P. Carr, T. O'Callaghan

Inter A: Y. Bennett, B. Wardlaw, M. Larkin, P. Ryan.

Inter B: J. Carroll, Hilary Dowling Long, P. Egan, T. Ryan

NIBU

Open: H. Campbell, T. G. Mackenzie, M. O'Kane, M. Rosenberg, I. H. Lindsay, D. K. Johnston, NPC David Greenwood

Women: Molly Andrew, Diane Sloan, Maeve Curran, Clare Smyth, Valerie Hamilton, Marjorie Kelso, NPC Mary Nimmons

Master: A. Alcock, A. Sharp, A. Kelly, J. Murchan, R. Plunkett, P. Tranmer, NPC S. G. McComb

Inter A: W. Dukelow, W. Matthews, Mr and Mrs Grimes, Beatarice Lowery, O. McKeague, NPC A. J. Casey

Inter B: M. Bloomer, N. Jack, A. Lundy, M. Steenson, J. McBride, T. Young, NPC G. Fitzgerald

1994 GREYSTONES   262–187

CBAI

Open: T. Hanlon, H. McGann, R. Timlin, P. F. Walsh

Women: V. Hand, A. Montwill, A. Hanratty, R. O'Donnell

Masters: E. Fitzgerald (captain), M. MacDonagh, J. Cunningham, L. Sheeran

Inter A: H. Peacocke, F. Swift, J. O'Rourke, Mgt. Gill

Inter B: J. Heneghan, F. O'Shea, J. O'Brien, J. Russell

NIBU

Open: R. Anderson, David Greenwood, R. Burns, K. Singleton

Women: M. Curran, C. Smyth, C. Burns, D. Sloan

Masters: D. Johnson, I. H. Lindsay, Tony Kelly, J. Murchan, M. Coffey, J. Lavery, NPC A. Hill

Inter A: Mgt. Boomer, Iris Orr, Doreen James, Renee Megahy, Beatrice Lowery, Olive McReagal, NPC Valerie Hamilton

Inter B: Roy Blair, John Nugent, Albert Carroll, Victoria Carroll, Anne Shannon, Elona Walmsley, NPC A. Hill

1995   Newcastle   256–276

CBAI

Open:	J. P. MacHale, R. Milne, R. Timlin, P. F. Walsh
Women:	M. English, M. Heery, E. Gannon, P. Maguire
Masters:	Denis McGrath, Tony McGrath, Donal Bell, Derek O'Gorman
Inter A:	Elaine Caulfield, Mary Kelly-Rogers, D. Doona, C. Higgins
Inter B:	Bríd Kemple, Aoife MacHale, Joe Dolan, John McCurdy
Officials:	Denis Dillon (captain),G. Laird, Kay Downes, J. J. Kiely, Joe Moran, Clare Pippet, Una Walsh, Marie Gleeson

NIBU

Open:	R. Burns, K. Y. Singleton, H. Campbell, David Greenwood, M. Coffey, J. Lavery.
Women:	Ciara Burns, Diane Sloan, Rosario Hetherington, Clare Smith, Norma Franklin, Sandie Millership
Inter A:	A. Burns, J. Taylor, G. Cunningham, R. Irvine, B. Lowry, O. McKeague
Inter B:	R. Cochrane, P. Pyper, E. McKey, J. Quinn, Elona Walmsley, A. Shannon
Officials:	G. Fitzgerald, D. Hannon, Valerie Hamilton, B. Hanley, M. O'Kane, M. Rosenberg

1996   Greystones   Tie: 354–354

CBAI

Open:	D. MacAonghusa, P. Pigot, J. Comyn, B. J. O'Brien
Women:	V. Hand, A. Montwill, C. Pippet, E. Joyce
Masters:	P. J. O'Dea, Yong Yuan, Ann Power, Ger Connolly
Inter A:	Maureen Griffin, Danny Liddy, Ann Harte, Danny Dillon
Inter B:	Donal Garvey Jnr. Conall O'Connor, Richard King, Colm O'Driscoll
Officials:	Maisie Cooper (captain), Una Walsh, Paul Hanratty, Joe Moran, Paul Porteous

NIBU

Open:	A. Kelly, J. Murchan, R. Plunkett, P. Tranmer
Women:	Ciara Burns, Diane Greenwood, Rosario Hetherington, Clare Smith, Valerie Hamilton, Marjorie Kelso
Masters:	M. Coffey, J. Lavery, W. Dukelow, M. O'Kane
Inter A:	R. Blair, J. Nugent, R. Cochrane, P. Pyper, C. and M. Grimes
Inter B:	D. Curran, D. Johnston, A. McKay, N. McGeehan, H. McKnight, G. Smyth

Officials: D. Hannon, Kay Murphy, G. Fitzgerald, M. Rosenberg

1997   NEWCASTLE   310–222

CBAI

Open: J. Carroll, T. Garvey, P. Ó Briain, T. Roche

Women: Patsy Meehan, Petra O'Neill, Hilary Dowling Long, Anne Marie Horan

Masters: Marie Hanrahan, Brid Kirby, Ann Power, Ger Connolly

Inter A: Hilary Moran, Joe Dolan, Grainne Dunne, Frances Kelly

Inter B: Denis, Michael and Donal Sheehan, John Young

Officials: Clare Pippet, Joe Moran, Kay Downes, Johnny Kiely, NPC Marie Cummins

NIBU

Open: R. Burns, K. Y. Singleton, R. Plunkett, P. Tranmer

Women: M. Curran, R. Heatherington, V. Hamilton, M. Kelso, N. Irwin, O. Cramp

Masters: M. Coffey, J. Ferguson, J. Lavery, A. Kelly, J. Murchan

Inter A: V. Trimble, D. and Mrs Curran, A. N. Other

Inter B: H. McKnight, G. Smyth, (?) O'Neill, A. Toner

Officials: G. Fitzgerald, D. Hannon, Margot McClure, Kay Murphy, M. O'Kane, M. Rosenberg, NPC I. H. Lindsay

1998   GREYSTONES   395–313

CBAI

Open: P. Pigot, D. MacAonghusa, P. Ó Briain, T. Roche

Women: Aileen and Rebecca O'Keeffe, Maria Barry, Ann Montwill

Masters: Peter Connolly, Sean and Raymond Masterson, James and Hugh Connolly

Inter A: Gerry Kelly, Richard King, Karl de Raeymaeker, Fergal O'Shea

Inter B: Denis Kennedy, Miriam Moloney, Manus Burke, Enda Gallagher

Officials: Peter Flynn (captain), Una Walsh, Clare Pippet, Joe Moran

NIBU

Inter A: Hilary McKnight, Grace Smyth

Inter B: Denise and Alan Anderson, Maeve Brennan, J. Steward, A. Hope, R. Houston

Officials: G. Fitzgerald, D. Hannon, Marjore Kelso, Sandie Millership, A. Hill

1999 NEWCASTLE 421–296

CBAI

Open:	Tom Hanlon, Hugh McGann, Niall Tóibín, Pat Walshe
Women:	Clare Pippet, Jill Kulchycky, Helen Carroll, Ita Hoy
Masters:	Mark Burke, Gordon Lessells, Aidan and Ena Cleary
Inter A:	Rita McNamara, Stasia Hagan, Mary Flynn, Keith Clarke
Inter B:	David Berber, Gerry Lawlor, Michael O'Brien, John Butler
Officials:	Joe Moran (captain), John Cunningham, Kay Downes, Pascal Buckley

NIBU

Open:	Ciara Burns, J. Murchan, W. Dukelow, M. O'Kane
Women:	Florence Boyd, Kay Murphy, Heather Hill, Sandie Millership
Masters:	M. Coffey, J. Lavery, J. Ferguson, I. Hamilton
Inter A:	H. McKnight, G. Smyth, B. Scott, P. McCartney, C. and M. Grimes
Inter B:	M. Brennan, R. Wilson, R. Cochrane, R. Houston, S. Greene, G. Stanley
Officials:	P. Dufton, Marjorie Kelso, A. Hill, J. Millership, D. Hannon, G. Fitzgerald

2000 MALAHIDE 750–683

CBAI

Open:	Tom Hanlon, Hugh McGann, Niall Tóibín, Rory Boland
Women:	Pat MacMahon, Pat Ryan, Helen Carroll, Jill Kulchycky
Masters:	Mark Burke, Michael O'Hehir, Pat Liston, Pat Quinn
Inter A:	Niamh Dolan, Detta Walsh, Donal Dunne, John Robinson
Inter B:	Tom Hardiman, Nicky and Pat Fitzgibbon, John Mulvihill
Officials:	Michael O'Connor (captain), Una Walsh, Clare Pippet, Joe Moran, Kay Downes, Johnny Kiely

NIBU

Open:	M. Coffey, J. Lavery, J. Ferguson, I. Hamilton
Women:	Florence Boyd, Kay Murphy, M. Kelly, Norma Franklin
Masters:	J. Conlon, C. Richey, I. H. Lindsey, R. Plunkett
Inter A:	C. and M. Grimes, E. Walmsley, A. Shannon
Inter B:	A. and D. Anderson, B. McCullagh, M. Taggerty
Officials:	J. Millership (captain), Sandie Millership, A. and Heather Hill

2001	BELFAST	790–639

CBAI

Open:	Gordon Lessels, Sean O'Lubaigh, Bob Pattinson, Liam Walsh
Women:	Helen Carroll, Jill Kulchycky, Grace Finegan, Clare Pippet
Masters:	Paul Barrett, Pat Quinn, Ger Connolly, Pat Liston
Inter A:	Celestine and Roger Latham, Betty Duffy, Brendan Martin
Inter B:	Jason Latham, Bettina Steffanini, Ann Fitzgerald, Paul Kealy
Officials:	Seamus Dowling (captain), Tomas Roche, Michael O'Connor, Una Walsh

NIBU

Open:	I. H. Lindsay, M. Rosenberg, V. Russell, K. Y. Singleton
Women:	Florence Boyd, Kay Murphy, Norma Franklin, M. Kelly
Masters:	J. Ferguson, I. Hamilton, J. Lavery, H. Kane
Inter A:	P. Johnson, P. Pyper, H. McKnight, G. Smyth
Inter B:	A. and D. Anderson, S. Mulholland, A. O'Reilly
Officials:	D. Franklin, C. Richey, A. and Heather Hill, J. and Sandie Millership

2002	DUNDALK	863–563

CBAI

Open:	Michael MacDonagh, B. J. O'Brien, John Carroll, Tommy Garvey
Women:	Helen Carroll, Jill Kulchycky, Hilary Dowling Long, Anne Marie Horan
Masters:	Paul Delaney, Eamonn Galligan, Pat Kelly, Dave Terry
Inter A:	Deirdre Walsh, George Hayes, David O'Brien, Jerry O'Flynn
Inter B:	Bridie Brady, Ellie Muldoon, Catherine Leavy, Teresa Maguire
Officials:	Olive Rose, Kay Downes, Mark Burke, Tomas Roche, Paul Porteous, NPC Teresa McGrath

NIBU

Open:	J. Ferguson, I. Hamilton, I. H. Lindsay, R. Plunkett
Women:	Florence Boyd, Kay Murphy, Rosario Heatherington, Clare Smith
Masters:	J. Conlon, C. Richey, R. Hill, D. McCaughey
InterA:	A. and D. Anderson, May Brennan, D. Lindsay
Inter B:	J. Cameron, B. Lomas, R. Carragher, L. McCloskey, G. Kay, R. Wilson
Officials:	M. Madden, A, Moyna, T. G. Mackenzie, Florence and M. O'Kane

2003	BELFAST	743–677

CBAI

Open: B. O'Brien, P. Pigot, Pat McCarthy, Cian Holland

Women: Helen Carroll, Jill Kulchycky, Emer Joyce, Joan Kenny

Masters: Maureen Griffin, Bob Pattinson, Brid Kirby, Maria Donegan

Inter A: John Royds, Dolores Gilland, Catherine Ward, M. Clifford

Inter B: Michelle Murray, Brenda Granville, Trudy Chambers, Lilian Fogarty

Officials: Rita McNamara (captain), Olive Rose, Seamus Dowling, Tomas Roche

NIBU

Open: J. Ferguson, I. Hamilton, R. Plunkett, P. Tranmer

Women: Florence Boyd, Kay Murphy, Hilary Ferguson, Sheila McCaughey, Ann Fitzpatrick, Mary Madden

Masters: A. Alcock, B. McDowell, R. Hill, D. McCaughey, J. Conlon, C. Richey

Inter A: May Brennan, D, Lindsay, E. McNicholl. B. Sergeant

Inter B: S. Barr, C. Byrne, D. and R. Cannell, G. Cairns, J. Morrow

Officials: B. Hanna, B. Scott, B. Lowry, R. Blair, J. and Sandie Millership

2004	MALAHIDE	727–702

CBAI

Open: B. J. O'Brien, Tomas Roche, Norbert van Woerkom, Willem Mevius

Women: Helen Carroll, Jill Kulchycky, Joan Kenny, Emer Joyce

Masters: John Keane, Peter Howard, Helen and Brendan Sheridan

Inter A: Tom Hardiman, Pat Fitzgibbon, Mick O'Shea, Billy McCarthy

Inter B: Freda McKittrick, Conor Cagney, Martina Lee, Ray Grogan

Officials: Michael O'Connor, Seamus Dowling, Gordon Lessells, Kay Downes, NPC Aileen Timoney

NIBU teams not known

2005	BELFAST	762–675

CBAI

Open: A. and E. Cleary; J. and L. Phelan

Women: H. Lillis, T. Rigney, N. Lynch, M. Meade

Masters: G. Connolly, B. Pattinson, M. Pattinson, B. Kirby

Inter A: Cynthia Heffron, Harriet Sexton, Denis Lynch, Geoff Simpson

Inter B Mgt. Devereux, Oona Dwyer, Michael Harpur, John Reville

Officials:	P. Carr (captain), M. O'Connor, S. Dowling, B. J. O'Brien	
NIBU		
Open:	R. Burns, I. H. Lindsay, R. Plunkett, P. Tranmer	
Women:	H. Cole, N. Irwin, D. Friel, Diane Greenwood	
Masters:	J. Ferguson, I. Hamilton, A. and Heather Hill	
Inter A:	A. Levey (captain) and M. Levey, E. McNicholl, B. Sergeant	
Inter B:	Ruth Connolly, Kerri Nash, B. Gallagher-Lyall, B. McMullan	
Officials:	R. Blair, B. Lowry, Florence Boyd, Sheila McCaughan	

2006   MALAHIDE   728–702

CBAI

Open:	B. Pattinson, D. Reddan, J. Phelan, Lucy Phelan
Women:	Valerie Burke-Moran, Kathleen Vaughan, Helen Carroll, Jill Kulchycky
Masters:	Kay Cussen, D. Liddy, D. Dillon, T. Fitzgibbon
Inter A:	Evie Counihan, Paula Tolan, Bríd Kavanagh, G. McKenna
Inter B:	Carmel Clarke, Tracy Clarke, B. Guinan, J. O'Keeffe
Officials:	Doreen McInerney (captain), P. Porteous, P. Carr, T. Roche, Brenda Kelly, F. Kelly
NIBU	
Open:	J. Ferguson, I. Hamilton, R. Plunkett, P. Tranmer
Women:	Heather Cole, Norma Irwin, Ann Fitzpatrick, Mary Madden
Masters:	S. Barr, C. Byrne, J. Conlon, C. Richey
Inter A:	A. and J. Bergin, E. McNicholl, B. Sargeant
Inter B:	S. Graham, J. Reid, P. and R. McComb
Officials:	R. Johnston (captain), W. Kerr, S. Jones, K. Ging

2007   ARMAGH   732–703

CBAI

Open:	Cian Holland, Pat Quinn, Micheál Ó Briain, Padraig Ó Briain
Women:	Ena Cleary, Jeannie Fitzgerald, Heidi Lillis, Teresa Rigney
Masters:	Louise Mitchell, Diarmuid Reddan, Bob and Maureen Pattinson
Inter A:	Liam Culligan, Mary Delaney, Anne Keane, Helen Williams
Inter B:	Maura Dolan, John Halpin, Ann and Paddy Whitty
Officials:	Michael O'Connor (captain), Paddy Carr, Seamus Dowling, Tomás Roche
NIBU	
Open:	A. T. R. Anderson, David Greenwood, R. Burns, I. H. Lindsay
Women:	Shirlie Brown, Roario Hetherington, Helen Cole, Norma Irwin,

Ann Fitzpatrick, Mary Madden

Masters:	Michael Coffey, John Lavery, Martin Devlin, Diane Greenwood
Inter A:	Danny and Deirdre Brennan, S. Graham, J. Reid, E. McNicholl, Bernie Sargeant
Inter B:	B. Clarke, G. Mulholland, M. McIlroy, M. Warnock, A. O'Gallagher, J. Redmond
Officials:	Alan Hill (captain), Heather Hill, Jeff and Sandie Millership

2008   MALAHIDE   749–685

CBAI

Open:	J. Heneghan, M. MacDonagh, Jill Kulchycky, Teresa Rigney
Women:	Ena Cleary, Jeannie Fitzgerald, Carol Ann Cummmins, Maureeen Pattinson
Masters:	Kathleen Byrne, Katherine Lennon, J. Doyle, J. Sexton
Inter A:	Mgt. Lombard, Michelle Murray, J. Naughton, P. Tolan
Inter B:	Brigid Connolly, Rita Duff, Ann and Derek McDonnell
Officials:	M. Hayes (captain), J. Fitzgerald, Mary Kelly-Rogers, Frances Kelly, G. Lessells, T. Roche

NIBU

Open:	N. Cauwood, M. McFaul, R. Plunkett, P. Tranmer
Women:	Helen Cole, Norma Irwin, Hilary Ferguson, Mary Madden
Masters:	G. Fitzgerald, P. Dynes, K. Ginn, D. Leeman
Inter A:	S. Barr, Christine Byrne, J. Crowch, K. Hinds
Inter B:	Katherine Johnston, Ros Young, F. McGreevy, A. Gallagher
Officials:	Ann Bergin, P. McDaid, G. McKeever, T. McKeever

Appendix J: Visiting Players

1932   NOVEMBER, ROYAL HIBERNIAN HOTEL, DAWSON ST, DUBLIN, CBAI V. ENGLISH SELECTION,

England: Col. W. Buller, Col. H. Mountifort Beasley, Captain G. Matheison, Alice Gordon Evers.

CBAI: Mrs H. J. Brown, Mrs W. McCormick; J. B. Short, Dr G. Tierney; B. L. Williams, H. Williams, Erina Holmes Wilson, Mrs Shortt, NPC H.G. Freehill

England won the hundred-board match by 6,490 points.

1934   15–16 DECEMBER, SHELBOURNE HOTEL, DUBLIN V. BRITISH BRIDGE LEAGUE SELECTION,

BBL: Captain R. Lederer, W. Rose, L. W. Dodds, W. Grew.

CBAI: H. Williams, H. G. Freehill, B. L. Williams, F. McMenamin, NPC J. E. Hogan

BBL won the hundred-board match by 4,300 points.

1937   INAUGURAL CBAI CONGRESS, ROYAL MARINE HOTEL, DUN LAOGHAIRE

England Team: J. C. Marx, S. J. Simon, M. Harrison Gray, H. Phillips, J. T. Reese, B. Cohen

1951   DECEMBER, SHELBOURNE HOTEL, DUBLIN V. LONDON

Dublin: P. P. Donovan, T. D. Purcell, M. Shrage, J. A. Kelly, D. Egan, Elvina Spiro, Ina McMenamin

London: Dr S. Lee, S. L. Booker, A. Meredith and L. D. Dodds

1954   APRIL, GALWAY, INTERNATIONAL AN TÓSTAL TOURNAMENT

Teams from Belgium, Italy, Netherlands, Sweden and Republic of Ireland competed.

First Belgium: E.(or F) Bosmans, R. Van Branchan, T. Jacobs, P. Pollack. on split tie from

Second Sweden: B. Nilsson, K. A. Hedberg, A. Gartner, A. Engereen.

Fourth CBAI: J. G. Burke, G. F. Read, Alice Mahon, Eileen O'Doherty, M. Shrage, Elvina Spiro.

1957   NOVEMBER, SHELBOURNE HOTEL, DUBLIN, INVITATIONAL MATCH V. TEAM OF EXPERTS,

Experts: E. Kempson, G. Fell (England) C. Goren, Helen Sobel (USA).

F. McMenamin's selection: F. McMenamin, J. J. Bastow, R. Belton, J. A. Kelly, Ina McMenamin, T. D. Purcell, G. F. Read, M. Shrage.

Visitors won the eighty-eight-board match by 3,840 points.

1958   MARCH, CBAI SILVER JUBILEE INVITATIONAL TOURNAMENT

First England: R.G. Corwen (captain), H. Franklin, L. Tarlo, S. Lee, G. Mathieson

Second Scotland: T. G. (captain) and Mrs Porteous, Mrs W. Davidson, D. Skinner

Third CBAI No. 1: G. F. Read (captain), M. Shrage, R .Belton, J. A. Kelly, F. W. and M. F O'Connell

Fourth CBAI No. 2: Geraldine McConkey (captain), Ina McMenamin, Ruth Giddings, May McNulty, Charlotte Fowler, Elvina Spiro

Fifth CBAI No. 3: T. D. Purcell (captain), J. J. Bastow, P. P. Donovan, P. Pigot, Cleo Fellowes, J. F. Wallis

Sixth Northern Ireland: G. L. Sloan (captain) A. McKinnon, D. A. Cohen, J. McRobert, R. D. Gardiner, W. H. Smyth, E. Goldblatt,

CBAI No. 4:. J. Orman (captain), H. Bridburg, H. Elliott, Babs Hooper, Mrs W. Dunne, Maj. G. Jackson

Eighth Wales: Dr J. S. (captain) and Mrs Spicket, S. Hoofman, E. Roberts, J. T. Jones, H. T. Thomas

1960   12–13 MARCH, ATHLONE

English visiting team: H. Franklin, L. Tarlo, Mr and Mrs R. G. Corwen

North Midland, Western and North Western Regions selection: D. T. Seale, L. F. Sheeran (Birr), C. B. Higgins, C. Clune (Sligo), C. Gilgunn, P. J. Gallagher (Galway)

Visitors won, score not recorded.

1961   FRENCH TOUR

France: R. Bacherich, R. Trezel, P. Ghestem, L. Malabat, R. Mantilla, Nadine Alexandre; NPC Baron R. de Nexon

12 MARCH, LIMERICK

Michael and Marjorie Lynch, Joseph and Mrs Honan, Moira Quaid. (probably a sixth player; only five names recorded). France won.

13–14 MARCH, ATHLONE

D. A. Houlihan, L. F. Sheeran (Birr), T. Gleeson, T. McCormack (Athlone), Maureen Ryder, Mrs N. Stewart (Galway). Irish won by twenty imps over sixty boards.

16–17 MARCH, DUN LAOGHAIRE

Ruth Giddings, May McNulty, Eileen O'Sullivan, Cleo Fellows, J. P. MacHale and P. Pigot

NPC D. R. Pigot. France won the hundred-boards match, score not recorded.

1964   FEBRUARY, POLISH TOUR

Poland: A. Wilkosz, C. Kuklewicz, M. Kasprzak, S. Lowinski (Krakow) J.

Klukowski, Z. Szurig (Warsaw), NPC S. Achmatowicz; manager, A. Wojtas; journalist, A. Rozecki

The Polish party arrived on 5 February 1964 and played matches (most of them forty-eight boards) against the following teams over the next eleven days. The Poles won all matches.

Eastern Region: E. J. Boland, J. J. Bailey, P. O'Dowd, Cleo and Peter Fellowes, Eileen O'Doherty, NPC K. M. Fowler –68 imps.

South Midland: D. C. and Mrs O'Leary (Carlow), C. I. Allison (Dungarvan), P. O'Reilly (Waterford), J .H. and Helen Daly (Tramore), NPC E. J. Boland –127

South Munster: J. O'Grady, H. O'Grady, W. O'Grady (Mallow), C. Kelleher, R. A. Twomey (Cork), G. Holmes (Limerick), J. Sugrue, P. Kiely (Mitchelstown), NPC M. F. O'Connell –73

North Munster: J. Coman, J. Fitzgerald, G. F. Holmes, M. F. O'Connell, Mrs M. Quaid, Mrs McMahon –21

Western Region: Dr T. Cunningham, Dr T. Waldron, Rev. Dr Mooney, L. Callow (Tuam), A. Kavanagh, P. Mee, (Galway), NPC R. A. Tierney –35

North Midland: Captain T. Gleeson, Captain T. McCormack, Mrs Madigan, Mrs Gaughan, Comdt J. and Mrs Power (Athlone), NPC M. Burke (Ferbane) –82

North Western: R. Dent, W. Glennon, Mr and Mrs O'Farrell, (Longford), Dr M. Martin, M. Kirby, C. B. Higgins, T. J. Hamilton (Sligo), NPC Dr Evelyn Arkins –35

Dublin 1: J. P. MacHale, P. J. Pigot, W. A. Burrowes, D. Seligman, G. B. Jackson, Charlotte Fowler, NPC Geraldine McConkey –45

Dublin 2: R. H. and Mrs Watchorn, Sonya Britton, May McNulty, Anne Quinn, Kay O'Sullivan, NPC Geraldine McConkey –34

Ireland Open Team: J. A. Kelly, G. F. Read, D. Deery, E. Goldblatt, F. Fine, D. L. Stokes, NPC E. J. Boland –93

Ireland Women's Team: Ruth Giddings, Barbara Seligman, Lily Maguire, Beatrice Titterington, Nellie Cotter, Sheila Kirwan, NPC Elvina Spiro –17

1965   FEBRUARY, ENGLISH–SWISS EXPERTS

E. Kempson, G. Fell, T. Priday, C. Rodrigues (England), J. Besse and D. Hakimi (Switzerland)

In Dun Laoghaire defeated E. Boland, J. J. Bailey, J. A. Kelly, G. F. Read, M. Shrage, J. P. MacHale, P. J. Pigot by 84 imps over forty-eight boards.

In Tipperary, played two matches against Boland, J. Fitzgerald, F. W. and M. F. O'Connell, E. O. Barry and G. A. Holmes with NPC John Coman, won by 16 imps over thirty-two-boards and by 41 imps over twenty-four.

1972 NOVEMBER, SWEDISH TEAM IN DUBLIN

Sweden: P. O. Sundelin, J. Lindqvist, S. O. Flodqvist, A. Morath.

Ireland: J. P. MacHale, P. J. Pigot, D. Deery, E. MacNeill, R. de Barra, N. K. FitzGibbon

1973 31 JANUARY–1 FEBRUARY, BURLINGTON HOTEL, DUBLIN

Precision club team: G. Belladonna, B. Garrozzo (Italy), J. Flint (England), O. Sharif (Egypt), C. C. and Cathy Wei (China)

v. A. T. R. Anderson, P. J. Barry, Maria Barry, D. G. Scannell, C. B. Higgins, J. McGown, NPC J. Coman. Visitors won 10–2 vp.

v. Ruth Giddings, Lily Maguire, Doreen Cairnduff, Anne Quinn, Sonya Brittton, Diana Woodhouse, NPC A. E. Anderson

Women won 9–3 vp.

v R. P. de Barra, N. K. FitzGibbon, J. P. MacHale, P. J. Pigot, D. Deery, E. MacNeill, NPC G. F. Read.

Visitors won 7–5.

1982 26–28 MARCH, SHELBOURNE HOTEL, DUBLIN, CBAI GOLDEN JUBILEE INTERNATIONAL TEAM COMPETITION

England: A. Priday, C. Rodrigue, I. Rose, R. Sheehan

Scotland: G. Cuthbertson. G. Hasse, V. Goldberg, B. Shenkin

Wales: Dr J. Butler, C. C. Smith, C. C. Heard, D. M. Powell

Sweden: S. O. Flodquist, J. Lindqvist, T. Gullberg, P. O. Sundelin

Switzerland: P. Bernasconi, J. Ortiz-Patino, P. Collaros, G. Fierz

President's IV: Rixi Markus, L. Tarlo, Eileen O'Doherty, Ann Quinn

Irish teams:

Jubilee Team: Ruth Giddings, Barbara Seligman, J. P. MacHale, P. J. Pigot

Northern Ireland: T. Bennett, B. McDowell, Maeve Curran, R. Johnson, M. T. G. Mackenzie

Connacht/Donegal: Vincent and Mary Brennan, G. Keaveney, P. F. Walsh, J. McIntyre, P. McLoone

Leinster: J. Agnew, Bernie Gannon, S. Burgess, J. Kennedy, J. Daly, Mrs P. O'Toole

Munster: Joan Crowley, Anne Dillon, D. Dillon, P. C. Kiely, D. McGrath, J. McKeon

Dublin: N. K. FitzGibbon, A. Mesbur, E. MacNeill, D. G. Scannell, N. Tóibín, P. Walshe

2003 GRAND MASTERS INVITATIONAL INDIVIDUAL TOURNAMENT, ROYAL DUBLIN SOCIETY

T. Hanlon, G. Keaveney, N. K. FitzGibbon, J. P. MacHale, A. Mesbur, P.

Walshe, J. Carroll, T. Garvey, P. Pigot, M. Ó Briain, Hilary Dowling-Long, Anne Marie Horan, J. Auken (Denmark), Sabine Auken, (Germany), Les Steel (Scotland), P. Jourdain (Wales)

2005   GRAND MASTERS INVITATIONAL INDIVIDUAL TOURNAMENT, ROYAL DUBLIN SOCIETY

T. Hanlon, G. Keaveney, N. K. FitzGibbon, A. Mesbur, J. Carroll, M. Ó Briain, J. Auken (Denmark), Sabine Auken, (Germany) Jason Hackett (England), P. Jourdain (Wales), Liz McGowan (Scotland), Zia Mahmood (Pakistan & USA)

2006   SEPTEMBER, WARREN BUFFETT CUP, TEMPLEOGUE, EUROPE V. USA

Europe: T. Hanlon, H. McGann (Ireland); N. Bocchi, G. Duboin (Italy); Jason & Justin Hackett (England); G. Helgemo, T. Helness (Norway); Sabine Auken, Daniela von Armin (Germany); Jan Jansma, Louk Verhees (Netherlands), NPC P. Hackett (England)

USA: R. Hamman, P. Soloway; Zia Mahmood, R. Welland, L. Cohen, D. Berkowicz; G. Hampson; F. Gitelman, S. Weinstein, R. Levins, Jill Levins, Jill Meyers, NPC Donna Compton

Appendix K: Trophies for National Championships

CBAI Competitions

Bankers Trophy

Presented by the Bankers Bridge Club. First contested in 1968. CBAI intermediate A teams championship.

Civil Service Cup

Presented by the Civil Service Bridge Club. First contested in 1968. CBAI intermediate B pairs championship.

Coen Trophy

Started as the Shamrock Lodge Trophy, the competition for which was discontinued after 1992. It was brought back into use for the CBAI mixed teams championship, introduced in 1995.

Cooper Cup

Introduced in 2002/03 to honour Maisie Cooper (Limerick), in recognition of almost seventy years' service to bridge. Team competition, entry currently limited to players holding fewer than thirty national master-points.

Davidson Cup

Donated by Dr Andrew H. Davidson, gynaecologist, master of the Rotunda Hospital, Irish champion and international player, originally for an individual championship in 1942, entry to which was confined to winners and high finishers in other events. Awarded to the winners of the CBAI pairs championship (qualification through regions) from 1945, although the competition had begun in 1936.

Duais an Uachtaráin (The President's Prize)

Intrduced by Aileen Timoney (Cavan) during her presidency of the CBAI, 2004/05. From 1991/92 (Claire Pippet's presidency), the President's Prize had been awarded along with the Spiro Cup. Before that, the Davidson was considered the President's Prize competition. In 1934 and 1935, the Holmes Wilson Cup was the President's Prize.

Jim Fitzgerald Trophy

Donated by the Fitzgerald Club in Jim Fitzgerald's native town, Tipperary, to honour his memory. CBAI intermediate mixed-pairs championship, first played for in 1968/69.

Geraldine Cup

CBAI men's pairs championship. It commemorates Geraldine McConkey. It is the only national trophy that bears a person's first name. First contested 1960/61.

Hagerty Trophy

Donated by John Hagerty, proprietor of J. P. Fashions, Clarendon Street, Dublin.

Mrs Hagerty attended Owen Rowe's bridge classes. Out of admiration of Rowe's efforts on behalf of intermediate players, Hagerty donated the trophy. First contested 1967/68. CBAI intermediate A pairs championship, qualification through the regions. The trophy has been replaced by the Laird Trophy.

HOLMES WILSON CUP

First contested in 1934, when it was referred to as the President's Cup, as it was donated by the CBAI's first president, Erina Holmes Wilson. Following her third term as president in 1935, it became known as the Holmes Wilson Cup. Awarded to the winners of the CBAI direct-entry teams championship.

JACKSON CUP

Donated by Harry Jackson and Miss Jackson, participants in early CBAI competitions. CBAI women's pairs championship. The competition dates to 1933. The Jackson Cup is first mentioned in 1935.

KELBURNE CUP

Donated by Sarah Bailey, proprietor of Phoenix Laundry. 'Kelburne' was the name of her house on the Howth Road in Clontarf. CBAI teams championship, qualifying through Regions. First contested in 1936, it was a knock-out competition for many years.

KERVICK TROPHY

Donated by William Kervick, bookmaker and prominent figure in Waterford Bridge Club. CBAI internmediate B direct-entry pairs championship.

LAIRD TROPHY

Donated by Graham Laird, Ballyshannon, County Donegal, CBAI president 1991/92. The trophy replaced the Hagerty Trophy for the CBAI intermediate A pairs, entry through regional qualification.

LAMBERT CUP

Donated by Kathleen Lambert, founder member of the CBAI, the cup was awarded from 1943–47 to the winners of the CBAI direct-entry individual championship – although the competition began in 1933. When the individual championship was discontinued after 1947, it was awarded to the winners of the secondary-pairs championship, which was first run in 1944. At present, it is open to players with fewer than thirty national master-points.

McMENAMIN BOWL

Donated by Dr Frank and Ina McMenamin. CBAI women's teams championship, first contested in 1950.

J. J. MURPHY CUP

Donated by John Murphy (Longford), CBAI president 1980–81, to the winners of CBAI Junior (Intermediate B) Mixed Pairs in 1970. The competition was discontinued after 1979. The following year it became the trophy for the CBAI novice pairs championship.

NEW IRELAND TROPHY

First awarded in 1970/71 for an inter-county intermediate pairs. It later beame the CBAI direct-entry intermediate pairs championship. Owen Rowe was responsible for procuring the trophy. His New Deal Club played at the New Ireland Assurance Company premises on South Frederick Street, Dublin.

REVINGTON CUP

CBAI Men's Pairs Championship. Mrs Revington was a prominent Dublin player in the early CBAI years. First contested in 1936.

SHAMROCK LODGE TROPHY

Sheila Coen, proprietor of the Shamrock Lodge Hotel, Athlone, donated the trophy in 1963 for the CBAI direct-entry open pairs championship which was discontinued after 1992. It became the Coen Trophy in 1995 when the CBAI mixed teams was introduced.

SPIRO CUP

CBAI Mixed Pairs Championship, first contested in 1936. Donated by Mabel Spiro. Her husband's family business was IMCO Cleaners and Dyers. Her brother in law, Harold, was married to the better-known player, Elvina Spiro. Mabel later married Victor Waddington, art gallery owner, and moved to London.

TIERNEY TROPHY

Donated by Dick Tierney (Galway) for the intermediate B – originally called junior – teams championship in 1968

WATERFORD CRYSTAL TROPHY

CBAI Novice pairs competition, played at the annual intermediate congress.

IRISH BRIDGE UNION COMPETITIONS

BURKE CUP

Donated by Eddie and Eimer Burke, Nenagh, in 1966, for the inter-county team championship. The competition started in 1934 as the inter-club championship.

EGAN CUP

Donated by Ina McMenamin in memory of her brother, Dermot Egan, who died in 1955. Awarded to the winners of the All-Ireland teams championship, confined to the winners of major team events on both sides of the border.

INTER–PROVINCIAL TROPHY

The inter-provincial championship began under the auspices of the CBAI in 1952. The trophy was introduced in 1954. The Irish Bridge Union took over the running of the competition in 1958.

MOYLAN CUP

Donated by Dr Patrick Moylan from Ennis in 1943, it was originally awarded to the winners of the CBAI panel test (trials). The IBU, on its formation, took it over. Awarded to the winners of the all-Ireland pairs championship since 1957.

COMPETITIONS WHICH WERE INITIALLY PLAYED AS NATIONAL CHAMPIONSHIPS BUT LATER BECAME REGIONAL EVENTS

CARROLL CUP

Donated by English-born Roddy Carroll who came to Dublin at the outbreak of Second World War. A team-of-four, knock-out duplicate rubber bridge championship, inaugurated during the 1942/43 season, it continued until 1958. Dublin region then took it over and it became a knock-out contest, qualifying for the IBU's inter-county championship. On the division of the region in 1989 it became the Dublin South City qualifier for the Burke Cup, but no longer a knock-out competition.

WIGODER CUP

The CBAI's first trophy, presented by Dr Lionel Wigoder at the association's inaugural meeting, 25 February 1932, for team competition. First contested in April of that year, it developed into a team-of-four league with entries divided into sections leading to knock-out play-off. Last played as a national championship during the 1961/62 season after which it became, first a competition jointly organised by Dublin and Eastern regions, later in alternate years by Dublin South and North. In 2000/01 it was handed over to the Regent Bridge Club, which continues the tradition of running an open competition for the cup on New Year's day.

APPENDIX L: CBAI ELECTED OFFICIALS

PRESIDENTS

1932	Erina Holmes Wilson	1971	Olivia Rowlette
1933	Erina Holmes Wilson	1972	J. A. Scannell
1934	Erina Holmes Wilson	1973	O. Meade
1935	Kathleen Lambert	1974	L. F. Sheeran
1936	Constance Maxwell Henry	1975	D. L.Madden
1937	J. E. Hogan	1976	M. Lynch
1938	D. Corboy	1977	Nell Foley
1939	Mrs H. Brown	1978	Una Walsh
1940	W. J. L. O'Connell	1979	D. L. Stokes
1941	H. Williams	1980	J. J. Murphy
1942	P. Moylan	1981	Sonya Britton
1943	F. T. Quin	1982	D. Scully
1944	T. P. Magnier	1983	P. McLoone
1945	D. R. Pigot	1984	J. Cunningham
1946	J. M. Stanley	1985	R. A. O'Leary
1947	J. O'Neill	1986	J. J. Kiely
1948	Dr Roche Kelly	1987	J. Sheerin
1949	J. P. Morgan	1988	B. Finan
1950	J. H. Daly	1989	Kay Downes
1951	W. J. McHugh	1990	Peg Murray
1952	Frank McMenamin	1991	Clare Pippet
1953	Stephen Bergin	1992	T. Burke
1954	Joseph P. Brennan	1993	G. Laird
1955	Eleanor Faul	1994	E. Fitzgerald
1956	D. A. Houlihan (Birr)	1995	D. Dillon
1957	W. J. L. O'Connell	1996	Maisie Cooper
1958	J. Honan	1997	Marie Cummins
1959	D. T. Waldron	1998	P. Flynn
1960	Geraldine McConkey	1999	Kay Molloy
1961	R. A.Tierney	2000	M. O'Connor
1962	Evelyn Arkins	2001	S. Dowling
1963	E. J. Boland	2002	Teresa McGrath
1964	A. G. Hunt	2003	Rita McNamara
1965	J. Ennis	2004	Aileen Timoney
1966	J. F. O'Sullivan	2005	P. Carr
1967	J. Coman	2006	Doreen McInerney
1968	Moreen McCarthy	2007	Phil Murphy
1969	Maureen Ryder	2008	M. Hayes
1970	O. Rowe		

PRESIDENT EMERITUS

2003   Joe Moran

VICE-PRESIDENTS

1938–42 H. G. Freehill
1942–48 J. E. Hogan
1954–56 D. A. Houlihan (Birr)
1956–65 D. R. Pigot
1965–72 R. Belton
1972–82 J. Coman
1982–03 J. Moran
2003–   M. O'Connor

In 1948 a chairman of the executive committee replaced the vice-president. The position of vice-president was restored in 1954.

CHAIRMAN

1988–91 P. McLoone
1991–94 P. Flynn
1994–95 D. Scully
1995–98 P. Hanratty
1998–01 J. Cunningham
1901–03 M. O'Connor
2003–06 Kay Molloy
2006–09 Aileen Timoney

The position was abolished by the 2008 AGM, with effect from 2009.

CBAI HONORARY SECRETARIES

1932–35   Kathleen Lambert
1935–38   H. G. Freehill
1938–47   J. P. Morgan
1947–49   P. J. O'Dowd
1949–51   Cleo Roy
1951–55   P. P. Donovan
1955–56   L. Barry
1956–72   D. G. Jackson
1972–75   R. F. Dalton
1975–91   Marie Gleeson
1991–02   Una Walsh

2002–07   Olive Rose
2007–   Emer Kee

ASSISTANT SECRETARIES

1940-48   Mairéad O'Neill
1948–49   Cleo Roy
Position not filled 1949–52
1953–54   Mr Haughey
Position discontinued after 1954

CBAI HONORARY TREASURERS

1932–36 Constance Maxwell Henry
1936–43 Geraldine McConkey
1943–47 Mairéad O'Neill
1947–51 W. B. Butler
1951–52 C. N. Byrne
(Mairéad O'Neill took over the duties when Byrne left Dublin for Carlow)
1952-56 E. O'Riordan
1956–64 A. G.Cullen
1964–67 A. Drewery
1967–76 M. Lynch
1976–77 C. Foley
1977–91 M. Lynch
1991–93 P. Porteous
1993–02 Clare Pippet
2002–05 Norma Madden
2005–   N. Burke

Appendix M: Irish Bridge Union Elected Officials

Irish Bridge Union Presidents

Fifty-five persons – forty men and fifteen women – have held the office of President, but of the first thirty-eight presidents only five were women. Since 1993 ten of the sixteen presidents elected have been women. In 1967 Dr R. Belton held the presidency for the duration of the European teams championships in Dublin, then in accordance with an agreement within the CBAI, he resigned to allow Dr John F. O'Sullivan take over the office for the remainder of the season. The year refers to the year of the election.

1955	Dr J. P. Brennan	1982	T. G. Mackenzie
1956	G. L. Sloane	1983	D. Scully
1957	D. A. Houlihan	1984	M. O'Kane
1958	Prof A. McKinnon	1985	P. McLoone
1959	J. Honan	1986	C. Richey
1960	D. A. Cohen	1987	J. Moran
1961	Geraldine McConkey	1988	I. Lindsay
1962	S. Blaney	1989	J. Sheerin
1963	R. A. Tierney	1990	G. Fitzgerald
1964	B. Vard	1991	J. Kiely
1965	E. J. Boland	1992	J. A. Hill
1966	A. E. Anderson	1993	Clare Pippet
1967	Dr R. Belton	1994	D. G. Hannon
	and Dr J. F. O'Sullivan	1995	G. Laird
1968	W. Robb	1996	Valerie Hamilton
1969	Moreen McCarthy	1997	Comdt E. J. Fitzgerald
1970	G. A. McCaw	1998	Marjorie Kelso
1971	Maureen Ryder	1999	Marie Cummins
1972	D. P. Deery	2000	Kay Murphy
1973	J. A. Scannell	2001	Kay Molloy
1974	G. W. Clingan	2002	J. Millership
1975	L. S. Sheeran	2003	S. Dowling
1976	Mary Nimmons	2004	Sandie Millership
1977	M. Lynch	2005	Rita McNamara
1978	M. Rosenberg	2006	Florence Boyd
1979	Una Walsh	2007	Paddy Carr
1980	P. C. Duffy	2008	Norma Irwin
1981	J. J. Murphy		

Joint Honorary Secretaries

NIBU

1955–62 Norman H. Douglas
1962–68 Desmond Deery
1968–78 John H. Grummitt
1978–95 W. M. (Billy) Kelso
1995– J. A. (Alan) Hill
2007– Tomás Roche

CBAI

1955–56 Paddy Paul Donovan
1956–72 Denis Jackson
1972–75 Lt Col. R. Dalton
1975–99 Marie Gleeson
1999–07 Kay Downes

Honorary Treasurers

From 1955 to 1958 the joint honorary secretaries were appointed joint honorary treasurers also. In 1959 Denis Jackson was elected sole honorary treasurer and the tradition of the joint honorary secretary from the CBAI taking on the duties of honorary treasurer has continued since then. The tradition of the CBAI honorary secretary automatically becoming joint honorary secretary of the IBU was broken in 1991 when Marie Gleeson was chosen by the CBAI executive to continue in the role despite the fact that she was no longer held national office in the CBAI.

Chairman

1990–91 Joe Moran

The position of Chairman of the IBU was created as an expedient to confer an official position on Joe Moran during the 1991 Killarney Euroean championships of which he was chief organiser. It was a once-off office.

Appendix N: Irish Bridge Publications

Books, Manuals, Pamphlets

Byrne, Noel and O'Neill, Joseph ed. *The Irish Bridge Annual*, 1948, privately published

The Irish Bridge Annual, 1949, privately published

The Irish Bridge Annual, 1950, privately published

Connolly, Roddy. *Aids to Beginners*, privately published, *c.* 1959

De Barra, Risteárd. *Improve Your Bridge Play*, privately published, 1970

– *Improve Your Bridge Bidding*, privately published, 1980

Dale, Thomas L. (pseudonym: Arfax): *Contract Bridge Calculator*, privately published, Dublin, 1937

Dowling, Seamus. *Bridge Teachers' Manual, Bidding 1*, CBAI, 2000

– *Bridge Teachers' Manual, Play 1*, CBAI, 2000

– *Bridge Teachers' Manuals, Bidding 2*, CBAI, 2002

Freehill, Harry. *The Squeeze at Bridge*, Faber & Faber, London, 1949

Glynn, Enda. *Ennistymon Bridge Club and Its Times*, privately published, 2007

Glynn, Sean. *A Guide to the Acol System of Bidding*, privately published, 1983

– *A Guide to Transfer Responses to Opening Bids of 1NT and 2NT*, privately published, 1987

– *A Guide to the Precision System of Bidding*, privately published, 1987

– *A Guide to Popular Bridge Conventions*, privately published, 1990

– *A Guide to Leads, Signals and Discards*, privately published, 1990

Hanlon, Tom *see* Murphy, Enda

Heron, Supt. Charles B.: *The Heron Club System of Contract Bridge*, Clonmore and Reynolds Ltd, Dublin, 1947

Hickey, Ina and Noel Peart. *Modern Contract Bridge, Bidding Made Easy*, Brown and Nolan Ltd, Dublin, 1944

Holmes Wilson, Erina. *Short Cuts to Contract Bridge*, Healys, Dublin 1932

Kelly, Hugh. *Contract Bridge, Back to the Basics*, privately published, Enniscorthy *c.* 1990

Kelly, Margaret. *The Bidding for the Game of Bridge*, privately published, 1997

MacDonald, Dick. *The Max Club, A Bidding System and Other Stories. c.* 1983

Mackey, Rex. *The Walk of the Oysters*. W.H. Allen, London, 1964

Mackinnon, Alan. *The Bridge of Alan Mackinnon*, Century, Belfast, 1976

McTear, J. *Abecedary of Nuhlo, The Improved Bridge*, 34 pages, privately published, Belfast, 1906

McTear, J. *The Improved Bridge, Synopsis of the Game*, 2 pages, privately published, Belfast, 1906

Mesbur, Adam. *Homegame Bridge on the Downhill*, Homegame International, Limerick, 1992

Murphy, Enda. *Silver for Ireland*, privately published, 2006

– *A Bridge Too Far?*, privately published 2007 – with Tom Hanlon

O'F., E. *Essentials of Sound Bridge*, 20 pages, Ponsonby, Dublin, 1906

O'Keeffe, Aileen and John H. *Home-game Bridge on the Nursery Slopes*, Homegame International, 1992

O'Neill, Joseph (*see* Byrne, Noel)

Peart, Noel. *Sixpence a Hundred*, privately published, 1943
    (*see* Hickey, Ina)

Pigot, Peter J. *Lausanne 1979.(Story of the Irish Bridge Team)*, privately published, 1979

Powell, James H. and Derek L. Stokes. *Tournament Direction for Bridge Clubs*, privately published, 1978

Revoke (a pseudonym). *The Grand Slam – A Modern Bridge Guyed*, 56 pages, Hodges, Figgis and Company, Dublin, 1906

Rowe, Owen. *First Class Play*, The Bridge Press, Dublin, 1983

– *First Class Bidding*, The Bridge Press, Dublin, 1984

(Although credited to Rowe these two publications were jointly written by his son John Rowe and his son-in-law, John H. O'Keeffe, from Owen Rowe's notes.)

Ryan, George. *The Bones of Bridge*, privately published, 1966

– *Some of the Flesh*, privately published, 1967

Ryan, John K. *Simple Explanation of the Rules of Bridge*, privately published, 2008

Stokes, Derek L. (*see* Powell, James H.)

Strain, William. *Strain's Contract Bridge*, privately published, Belfast, 1932

Walshe, Col. G. G. J. *Contract Bridge: Bidding Principles*, De La Rue, 1932

John Cotton's Finest Tobacco Hands, John Cotton Ltd, London, 1935

———. *Slams Made Simple – How to Use Cue Bids*, Methuen, 1938

———. *Let's Play Cab*, Methuen, 1945

———. *Count to Win at Bridge*, Benn, 1948

——— and F. Dudley Courtenay: *The Losing Trick Count*, Methuen, 1935

MAGAZINES & NEWSPAPERS

Irish Contract Bridge News, a magazine, approved organ of the CBAI, 1937

Irish Bridge Journal, 1959

CBAI Bulletin, ed. Roddy Connolly, CBAI, 1966

Irish Bridge, editor and publisher, John Godden, 1978

The Irish Bridge Journal, 1979, ed. Paddy Walsh; 1998, edited by Una Walsh

The Irish Bridge Player, 1994–98, a newspaper, edited and published by Joan O'Mara

CLUB ANNIVERSARY PUBLICATIONS

2004: *Blackrock College Bridge Club 60th Anniversary*

2006: *70 Years of the Gate Bridge Club*

2007: *Ennistymon Bridge Club and Its Times*, Enda Glynn, privately published, 2007

TAPES, CDs ETC.

O'Keeffe, Aileen and John H., *First Club Bidding, c.* 1989, an instruction tape later produced on CD.

Non-National Authors Who Resided in Ireland

Greenwood, David (England). *The Pairs Game*, Cassell-Faber, 1978
Peche, George (New Zealand). *Interventions at the Bridge Table*, privately published, 1986
Senior, Brian (England). His publications, totalling around fifty to date, are too numerous to list. Brian resided in and played for Northern Ireland and the Republic during the 1980s.